THE ANVIL'S PASSION

A memoir of mind and heart

Deacon Steven C. House, Ph.D.

SHP

Copyright © 2023 Steven C. House

All rights reserved. No part of this book. may be reproduced, distributed, or transmitted in any form or by any means, electronic or mechanical, including photocopying, recording or by any information storage and retrieval system without the permission in writing from the publisher.

Steven House Publishing (SHP)
71 Windwhisper Lane, Annapolis, Maryland, 21403
Shouse54@gmail.com

Printed in the US

This work is a memoir based upon the best recollection of events that occurred in the author's life. I have changed some names and situations, some events have been compressed, and some dialogue has been recreated.

For more information go to www.theanvilspassion.com

All the poems in the present work have been written by the author. Many were published in the book, By the Morning of Our Healing, copyright 2010 by Steven C. House, published by AuthorHouse.

Scripture passages are from the Revised Standard Version, Catholic Edition.

Cover design by Steven C. House with software from BookCreative.

Cover photo by iStock with permission.

Library of Congress Control Number: 2024901122.

ISBN 979-8-9897944-0-9 Paperback
ISBN 979-8-9897944-1-6 Hardback
ISBN 979-8-9897944-2-3 E Book

To my mother and father, whose struggles and love
were foundational, and to my wife, my companion,
with whom I built a home.

Contents

Introduction

I have been reminiscing lately. It happens when I am preoccupied with something and an old event or person from the past sneaks into the screening room of my mind, waves their hand and distracts me. A nudge from a forgotten trip, a conversation, or even old embarrassments can call out to me. However, these reminiscences occupy me more and more. It is like I am full of unconscious material written on notes that somebody keeps sliding under the door. I am getting desperate; they are all over the floor!

So, I am brought here, compelled to share with you several stories from my life. Now, I make no claims about anything extraordinary. Here, represented is one life among the billions. But I vouch for it as my life as I knew it. These pages hold my stories, my growth, my losses and my wins. As I find myself in a later decade, which feels short on time, let me paste words on these moments!

My life's journey has been a wonderful mixture of surprise, delight, and awe, edged by periods of uncertainty and anxiety. Like a crazy quilt, I have selected a variety of scenes to present. Some grand scenes will hold down the corners. Filling in the patchwork are smaller recollections. Indeed, it is a beautiful fabric that tells my story. Somehow, over morning after morning, that marvelous fabric of life brought me here. We can argue about who I am and certainly what factors and influences caused this or that part of me to flourish. I will take a stab at it. The facts are fairly clear, but I am less clear about how I emerged through it. I stand before you a retired psychologist, an ordained Catholic deacon, a married man with children, a Greek from Philly. These roles come with powerful social, intellectual, and emotional perspectives. I hope that telling the story can help to discern how these interesting ways of doing life came to be. You may hear a lot from Dr. House in these pages while the voice of Deacon Steve emerges as well. Of course, Stevie also pokes his head in the door!

This life has been thoroughly instructive. Along the way, my mind and heart have grown in understanding and sensitivity. The foundation of this growth is that I have loved and been loved. I count as good fortune the many instances of care and support I encountered. However, I must include the side classes of pain and suffering so important to my lessons. But really, it all comes down to the specific interactions in which I found myself. For instance, someone let me in the room where babies were born. Knowing my children has been my privilege and knowing theirs, an outright hoot! Beyond, with fractured bones, I have received the insult of the surgeon's scalpel. I have felt the slow ebb of health that comes in the tired cost of aches and pains. A sucker punch once victimized me. Happily, though, I also have received love letters. Seeking to fulfill my calling, I have wandered across state lines. The voyage has taken me down creeks and rivers and across a beautiful geography. I have lost my breath at the Milky Way and other incomprehensible realities. At other times, in sudden reaction, I have averted my eyes. Slowly, I learned to trust in the God of the universe. As a psychologist, I have been present to people who are suicidal, angry and falling apart. I have sat to interview those in jails, prisons and emergency rooms, and offered testimony in courtrooms. Speaking words of clarity, I have brought calm in the face of calamity. In my religious vocation, I have married people, baptized babies and buried the dead. I have opened each day willing to dance and to pray. But now, I need to report in!

Dear reader, my images, ideas and memories are fresh upon me and urging to be told. Let me speak with the assurance that most of the facts are true, the names sound right, and the ages, rounded off to the nearest decade. I have grown old and reminisce with a sense of joy at my successes and regret at my failures. Some days, I was even sure of the difference! I conclude I played the game and had some at bats. I made plays and got some outs. Will it read well? Don't know. Is it fantastic? Doubt it. I breathed in and out; I watched and took it in.

For certain, there are characters in these pages. Several of them played a trivial role, whose shoulders only brushed me. Others provided lifelong connections populating my soul and illuminating my identity. Taught by those around me, I learned many things, and only some of it was intentional. I imprinted those characters, good and bad, as my own character emerged.

Not a simple task, I might add. But as the poet in me reflects, my blood flows of these events and people of which I write.

Oh, the looks I received, the words I heard spoken, the hugs that wrapped me, the adventures I survived! I hope these pages reflect the splendor of the times that pushed and pulled the edges of my life. I can certainly say that I have seen changes in my life. My interior has held the explosive power of joy, the cold sense of sadness to the scary quake of anger. From that naïve and open eyed kid I scarcely remember, through those substantial first experiences of natural beauty, to those insights that took me below the surface of things, into the back room where the gears and belts and pulleys grinded out the processes of life. From a line of ants on the steps to the beautiful image of the Holy Spirit, I have been taken by this world. Starting with my grandparents and going through to my children, I will anchor my story to the places I have lived. These many places set the scene. Some places proved just temporary, easily torn down by the bulldozer of my indifference. I express my gratitude and awe for those important places that still stand. I have lived in small rooms and slept in rooms as large as the horizon. Let us take a trip to these places. Will you join me as I knock on some doors?

You will notice I am accompanied by the soundtrack of an anvil speaking its loud, sparking, syncopated words. On my journey, I have encountered a resonance, an echo, a transcendent whisper from God. This calling has emerged more clearly and distinctly over time. God has spoken to me through conversations, occurrences, and opportunities. My faith teaches me that the God of the universe has built all the good in my life, the opportunities, the places, and the situations. It is his hand that opened up the doors, offered the chair to sit, invited me to the table. God sent with purpose, I believe, the people I encountered The anvil thus rings out my formation in times of joy and trouble. Emphasizing a holy teaching, it serves me like a Greek chorus, slowly awakening me to God. It is right that I should give this mysterious power a presence here, for it has guided me my whole life.

I have included poems, many of which I wrote and later published under the title, "By the Morning of Our Healing". Let us start.

<u>Book Bones</u>

I have many stories
My bones are thick with the pain and joy of lives I've seen
My fingers and my shoes contain the echoes

Of smiles left behind by others
I move and my muscles squeeze
Words said in passion and in anger

1 From Far and Wide

Egg Harbor City Cemetery rested amid a stand of trees in a sloped field. Dark clouds waffled through the sky in large rivulets of gray. It could rain. The GPS on the phone found the place. Located northwest of Atlantic City, we drove several hours from the quaint New Jersey town of Cape May. We had ventured there for a week of relaxation in the sun and surf.

With the directions to his grave in hand, I was excited to fulfill my years-long wish to see my grandfather's grave. Like going on a voyage, I had my passport and camera ready. My brother sent me the directions. We just had to find it. While searching for his name, we became confused. Does row A start on this end or that end? It didn't matter. We found no House marker.

We stood in front of a patch of grass. Next to this unmarked grave sat a stone that bore the name of Watson. Looking at the dewy grass amid scattered stones, I felt surprised and dismayed. The ground, like my memory of my grandfather, stood empty. The gray sky felt appropriate.

We retraced our steps with growing dismay. A man in a Gator emerged down the road, emptying the trash cans lining the main thoroughfare of the cemetery. We flagged him down and asked if he could help us. Middle-aged, with an honest face, he said, "Sure. Looking for a grave?" I nodded my head yes. "I'm looking for Carl B. House. Supposed to be here." I shared. He walked the line with us, counting out the number of graves based on the letter from my brother.

He pulled out his phone. "Mary, this is Dave. I'm looking for a Carl B. House at the city cemetery. Yeah, thanks." A pause. He looked up at the sky. "Its gonna rain…yeah, that's right. Section A?" Another pause, while Mary searched an official database of deaths and burials. "Thanks." He turned to us, "Yep, this is the spot," pointing to the green earth before us that was my grandfather's eternal resting place. "Well, thank you so much. We were confused where it was. I appreciate your help." He nodded and walked back to his gator and to his duty. He turned. "There may be more information in town at the funeral home." He told us where we should go. We stood there for a few seconds. Frustration straddled my mind, racing through old photos and the heavy pressure of will that brought us here.

Unexpectedly, my long desire felt unfulfilled. My grandfather died in 1961. For years, I thought about visiting his grave. Just a kid at the funeral, I didn't remember much. My wife and I paused standing there, looking up at the many graves before us, all those souls. I sent off a quick but sad prayer and felt a tear. My *grandfather's grave* rested beneath our feet. Some 60 years ago, I stood here while prayers had gone up. I could now touch his bones! We were probably the first visitors in decades. A heavy feeling sat on my heart that I didn't encounter very often.

In my recollection, my grandfather counted as one of the good guys. Standing there brought back my youthful past and the joyful but heavy stuff of those years. My memory wrapped Connecticut in a fog. Lots of occasions stood out, but many still had sadly melted away. It felt like years of rain had washed clean the memory. "This is disappointing. I'm a little angry. There's no marker. There's no marker." I shrugged at my wife as we walked back to the car. "How come my father didn't honor his dad with a stone? Surely a military one, at least." I needed a marker to hold my meager memories.

In my head, a gong sounded, maybe more strident and piercing, like an anvil hit with a blacksmith's hammer. The resolution came fast, a slap against my skull. "He deserves a headstone. He's your grandfather." But not just that. A further, deeper mission materialized. An urge to find his story, our story, engulfed me. "I can't forget this bare place." I told my wife as we drove back. "This man represented more than an empty piece of ground. You know, I don't want my grandkids to repeat this embarrassment, to look for their grandfather's unmarked grave and scrape to remember me. I need to write what I know. And you know what, Rochelle? It feels now or never. Time is getting away." I felt a heavy need to pass on my story, not out of pride, God knows there were enough bad moments. But to complete the circle, the story.

I had many encounters with interesting people. Something had to be said about them. I had to honor and recognize them. My grandkids may not care much about the lives of a bunch of dead people, but it would be there for them if they cared to read it. If my father had given me such a book, I would still have it today.

"Yeah, you've talked about it." Her voice trailed off. We got into the car. The closing doors made that dumph kind of sound that tells you that you are inside. But I sat uneasily, my mind whirling.

We stopped at the funeral home the groundskeeper suggested we visit. After talking with the funeral director, we got good information about getting a stone. As we left, a light rain started, a gentle summer rain that smells dusty at first. The clouds felt my angst. What struck me, walking fast to the car, was how little I knew my grandfather. There were holes in my story. Driving away, I left with purpose.

A few weeks later, holding an old picture of my grandfather and me, I sat at the computer. I began an uphill walk through a vast geography of people and events, of storytelling and remembering.

As I begin, let me offer you, dear reader, the important context that occurred before I was born. A man and a woman met in Panama, where they began their life dance. There, two families collided, one propelled from Norwich, Connecticut and the other traveling from Andros, Greece. They crossed in that place and started for me, a consequential conversation.

My dad's family, and especially my paternal grandfather, grounded my early experience. Carl Browning House, served his country for 28 years, working as a Navy cook and chief steward aboard Navy ships and submarines. He spent time in Pearl Harbor in 1939. "Your grandfather served on the Nautilus submarine for a while as a cook," my father once told me. Of average height, my grandfather combed his dark wavy hair straight back. Unlike my thin father, he had a huskier build. I could see him hauling big pots of potatoes! Frankly, he was a kind of Popeye with an anchor tattoo on his arm. "Stevie, you want to take Blackey out with me? We can let him run. He likes that." Steady and direct, he showed little emotion. He was, for me, a gentle and giving presence. This fit his New England background, having grown up in Rhode Island. I knew little about his family. I believe his mother died when he was young. There was nothing shared about Charles, his father.

My father, Charles House, indirectly helped me fill in some spaces. He passed the story of his family down through a handwritten outline of his places of residence and his work history. It is a Rosetta stone of sorts. This and some genealogy detective work offered some glimpses of my history.

My father's family moved around from Groton and Norwich, Connecticut, San Diego, California and Panama because of my grandfather's military career. "Charles, our ride is here to the train station. Grab your bags. You packed plenty of socks?" "Yes, mother, don't worry." "Your sister is already waiting." She looked worried. "We can't miss the boat to Panama. Your father would be so disappointed." He was 6. Later, in Panama, as a young man, his family lived at an important submarine base called Coco Solo. Based on my father's history, he tended bar at several locations in Coco Solo, Panama, probably in his early twenties.

"Steve, in San Diego, I played sports, ran track, golf, baseball. All stopped when I got sick. Kept me from graduating!" At one point, he suffered from a tapeworm that just sounded horrendous. I could see a situation like that happening on a trip to Panama. Perhaps that explains why he found himself with his family in Panama as a young man. My father never said much about Panama or his bartending days.

I knew my father enlisted in the military during World War II and served in Panama. Surprisingly, he enlisted in the Army and not the Navy. "Dad, they offered me to fly in bombers and take pictures. It beats ships. Remember me getting sick on the boat going back home?" He served as a Tech IV in the Panama Canal Zone during the latter part of the war. Also, he played catcher and earned a golden glove for the Army in Panama. For the longest time, I thought my father went to Panama because he joined the Army. Rather, he worked in Panama before his enlistment.

My father's family manifested a quiet and persevering attitude. "Yes," he said to the interviewer. "I enjoy numbers, always have. Good with my hands, too. Metal fabrication? Not sure what you mean. But I'm willing to give it a try. There's a war going on." His early work was as a sheet metal worker. Of average height, he was thin with brownish receding hair, looking older than his age. He had a wisp of a moustache. Sheet metal opened up a career. He would later build helicopters. My brother Tony worked as a draftsman, and so would follow his father.

Given my dad's military family, I assume he knew routine and orders. Even though he later drank a lot, he fulfilled his responsibility and made it to work the next day. During the Vietnam War, we had several arguments. "Those protesters ought to be thrown in jail! That isn't right." "Dad, they are against the war. It's an unjust war." "What do you know about it, Steve? They're lazy hippies who hate this country." I voiced my generation's attitude and feelings about war. My father's position supporting the war came from family history and lived experience.

My psychological training started early being exposed to the neurotic side of life. Grandmom made many hypochondriacal complaints. A short woman with sweaters and hankies up her sleeves. I never saw her bare arms. "Doesn't it feel warm in here?" she would ask. She thought she had lots of medical issues. Passively, she hovered over my early life. I knew it felt wrong. Don't ask me. "Granny, I'm not warm." Maybe there were silences and looks after she spoke. "Don't be concerned," my mother would say, shaking her head. "It's a pity, Granny imagines all sorts of illnesses." My mother didn't tolerate her well.

An odd thing about my father's family concerned his sister, Barbara. My dad's older sister left early, got married, moved to Washington state and never contacted the family. I thought it was strange. She fled. We never knew her.

My grandparents didn't have family around save for Granny's brother George. I never met or heard about my father's grandparents or other relatives. I regret not having the presence to ask questions when I was young.

For my mother's family, I rely on a history put together by Artemis, her favorite cousin. My mother stayed with her family when she was young. I am proud to say that my mother's family were immigrants. My great-grandfather, Antonio Condos, was born in Andros, Greece and worked as a merchant marine on US ships. (Huh, another sailor!) "Mr. Antonio Condos," the official letter read, "in recognition of your maritime service to the United States of America during the Spanish-American War, we extend to you and your family the opportunity of United States citizenship." Seeking the promised land, Antonio said, "Yes!"

Great granddad only had one arm. He lost the other riding a bike in Philly when a car hit him while signaling to turn. The arm developed gangrene and had to be amputated. I remember him as a bear of a man with a remaining arm of steel. He had a bushy moustache and a quick laugh. His wife, Aneza, stood 5 foot 5 inches; a smiling, darkly complected Greek woman. She had a quick smile, intelligent eyes, a dark smock and apron.

Where one found food, she would be nearby preparing it. They spoke no English. My memory showed they were kind people, loved, and revered.

Antonio and Aneza had three daughters, Margaro, Francesca and Theodora. My grandmother, Theodora, or Yia Yia, as we called her, and her sister Margaro worked as maids in Athens to help with the cost of passage to the US. Francesca, the third sister, had poor health. They all came to Philadelphia in 1918. Upon entering the US with his family, Antonio, the entrepreneur, opened up a Greek coffee shop in Philadelphia. Margaro died at a young age in 1943. Aunt Francis, her sister, a joy filled person, friendly and kind, had a quick smile and always a hug. "Ah, Stavros, you are getting so big!"

My maternal grandfather, Steven Lousidis, another Stavros, came over from Andros, Greece as well. He met my grandmother through the intercession of her father. "Theodora, I love you so much. I never want to leave you. Let's get married?" Fairly quickly, they got pregnant with my mother. However, he became ill with leukemia, went back to Greece with his brother, and tragically died. I have one picture of him with my grandmother. Young and hopeful, their eyes say. People tell me I carry a strong family resemblance.

Yia Yia, was born in Greece in 1907. Unschooled when the family moved to the US, she worked at her dad's coffee shop. Later, working at a knitting mill in Reading, Pa., she met her second husband. Yia Yia stood upright with unusually short hair that conveyed a no-nonsense attitude. She was short, like her mother, but a formidable woman. With a scarf tucked into her neck collar held always with a pretty clasp, she wore lipstick and makeup. "Hi, Yia Yia," we would say, hugging her gently as she allowed us to kiss her tilted rouged cheek. "Oh, my darlings." Her hugs were tentative. On a visit, she could bark orders. "Ah, Anna, wonderful for you to be here. Make sure your boys take their shoes off. Come help us with dinner." She had a flair about her. "I am making baklava, to die for". I felt, however, a certain vulnerability. It almost felt like a performance. But below the appearance, she knew suffering with significant losses. Card playing and grand dinners filled her loud house. "Renee, get the card table out of the closet and set it up by the archway." "Yes, mom." "Joyce, get the cups that I like for the table." A fire plug of a person. She instilled fear in me at first and then pity as I got older. I saw in her a lack of authenticity, more air than substance. But I fear I judge her too harshly. She held a heart of sorrow.

My grandmother married her second husband, Walter Roski, in Philadelphia in 1933. He was Polish and the marriage probably reflected a break with tradition. But she was 25, a widow who could make her own decisions. They had two sons and two daughters. One son died at two and the other during his first year of life. One is not supposed to outlive your children. The other two girls were my two aunts, Renee and Joyce.

My mother, Anna Lousidis, was born in Reading, Pa. in 1927. She surprisingly lived with her aunt Margaro for several years when she was young. This suggests that my grandmother found it difficult to support a child after the death of her first husband. I wonder what impact this had on my mom's relationship with her mother? I wonder as well: how did Yia Yia's new husband react to the child who was not his? Maybe he rejected her, "I will be damned if I feed and clothe that child."

My mother only had an 8th grade education but showed responsibility and obedience. She was older than her half-sisters, Renee and Joyce, by several years. Unlike her loud and angry sister Renee, her sense of humor illuminated the room with an amiable smile and a dreamer's attitude. "Now, Renee, don't get so mad about it. You growl like a bear. Have patience, dear," my mom would say. She probably mothered Aunt Joyce, who would stay with us in Connecticut for a while. There is, however, a little more to the story.

In 1940, Roski, the second husband, went to Bogota, Columbia, to establish a textile mill there. He called for his family shortly after. He worked as a manager and my grandmother worked in the mill as she had in Philly. "Walter, I don't like working in the office. The workers say mean things about you." "Ah, don't worry, they are just jealous of my success." My mother would be 13. This would be about the time her schooling stopped. After several years in Bogota, my grandmother and children moved to the Panama Canal Zone, while Roski continued his work in Columbia.

My mother spoke sparsely about the time she spent in her teens in Bogota. She described it as a foreign and exotic place. "We had monkeys, a little one and a larger one called Bobo. One time, they went on a rampage and threw things off the table, broke dishes and tore down the window blinds." My eyes grew enormous, my mouth wide open. "My mother was so angry. There were also big iguanas that walked around the streets. Our doors were always open so they would come inside!" Bananas grew abundantly on trees. She worked long hours at a factory, rolling tobacco into cigars. In Panama, she volunteered as an aircraft spotter and witnessed the passing of the USS Missouri through the Panama Canal.

Years later, I found a red vinyl record in Spanish in our house. Looking at it one time in her presence, "Can I play it Mom? What's the name of it?" "No, give me that!" She abruptly put it away. Who knows what that record meant to her? Who knows what associations that Spanish record held?

Later in her life, in her 60s, while crossing a Philly street, a car hit her, much like her one-armed grandfather! I mention this because while high on painkillers, she spoke about her youth with great and unusual animation and clarity. "Steve," she said whimsically, "in Bogota, I would love to go to the wrestling matches." Picture a large airy building with a tall ceiling. Chairs are set up around the square, large, elevated wrestling ring with its canvas floor. The place grows alive with an aura of excitement and anticipation. Tobacco smoke fills the air. Men with hats and sweaty colored scarves around their necks sit expectedly around the ring. They exchange money in fists of bills. The thick air is hot and moist. "Oh, I would get dressed up, and I knew several of the Greek wrestlers who would call out my name. I would have married one if I wasn't so young!" The wrestlers, dressed in their colorful masks and shorts with ankle high shoes, each have a following who shout loudly when they appear. "Oh, there he is, El Toro," my mother would say, waving brightly to the wrestler. "El Toro!" As things get underway, the noise level increases. In the elite seats, with the mayor and the cheap politicians in their dark ill-fitting suits, sits the manager of the mill. He converses with the cigar makers and the banana merchants. Next to him sits his family and the beautiful teen woman who attracts the comments of the wrestlers and the other men alike. My mom describes herself almost as a prima donna and gets plenty of attention at these matches. She is a beautiful girl, and this garners the attention of men. Later, she told me with a sparkle in her eye, "One of those wrestlers could have been your father!" I imagined saying, "Hi dad" to a short and stocky, garrulous man with big arms and a hairy chest! As she described this, she looked off and smiled.

I only later discovered a significant development that would make up a dark milestone in the family's life. My mother's dreams were decimated by a tragic, sinister reality. An older man sexually assaulted her as a teenager in Bogota. My mother didn't speak about it, never spoke about it. As a result, she had a child. The family kept this a secret and quietly raised the child, Tonia, as my mother's sister. My grandmother apparently decided that no one would speak of this secret. Tonia did not know the truth. It only saw light much later and only under duress. I shiver at the pain and suffering my mother must have experienced. The repercussions psychologically and emotionally must have deeply reverberated. I have trouble writing about it. What swirling distrust and anger, sadness and withdrawal did she experience? What mental gymnastics to go through? My mother had to tread water amid deep and turbulent currents threatening to drown her. And how did she face her child, treating her as a sister, denying her mother's care? It must have pushed my mother's feelings underground even more. This burden invisibly altered her response to others judged, in terms of their level of threat. As I will share, my father and she fought over the years and undoubtably, her trauma contributed to these outbursts. This resulted in her depression, anger, and quiet suffering. It left her emotionally limited for her children. This is crazy making stuff! A loud, angry anvil gong sounds.

However difficult the reality, she persevered. It did not drown her. That speaks to the power of her spirit. Her dreams persisted. She married, had my brothers and me, and she endured. One crazy dream involved a vacant lot that existed by our house in Philly. She talked about buying it. Her idea was to put in a go-cart track and rent rides. She often spoke of her ship coming in. She would later open up a restaurant with little to no experience.

I think what remained for her from her youth was an elusive residue of hope, a vague memory of heaven. Things would be better just over the next ridge, a little beyond the horizon. Her ship was always about to come in. "Just you wait, Steve. Tomorrow, you'll see!"

Luckily, she could laugh and had a sense of humor that she passed on to her kids. For instance, at the end of rehab, while recuperating from the car hitting her, we spoke. "Mom, look, I set up a porta-potty in the dining room so you don't have to go upstairs all the time. I think we should bring your bed downstairs." Looking disparaging at the porta-potty and then at me, "I guess I will just stop going to the bathroom!" A pause. "I will be fine, Steve. I will manage, don't worry." "But Mom, how will you go to the grocery store? You can hardly walk." "Honey, I will be fine. I'll get a pair of roller skates." "Yeah, Mom, the car broke half of your body!" "Then I will only need one roller skate, Steve!"

Many years later, my brother offered that when young, he heard about a phone call. From South America, the perpetrator called and offered an apology for the trauma that had transpired. My grandmother refused to speak to the person.

My parents met at the end of World War II. They never shared much about their courtship. I can imagine my father living with his parents, searching for a life as a bartender or in the military, feeling middle age angst at 25. He meets this attractive woman, an American. "I have seen you walking by often. What's your name?" "Anna Lousidis," my mom shyly responded. "I'm Charlie, you American?" She smiles and nods her head. A little tense, his demeanor relaxes her. "What is a cute woman like you doing in this jungle?" "I'm walking home from work at the factory." "Can I walk you home?" He is 8 years older and perhaps seen as mature and protective.

My grandmother, however, approves. She liked Charlie, as she called him. Maybe her approval was to make up for the unprotected trauma suffered by her daughter. I have a posed picture of my parents standing behind their wedding cake in Panama. Unfortunately, there isn't much joy on their faces.

Strangely, after the war, my parents came back to the States separately. Yia Yia came back with Joyce, who was sick. My mother, leaving around the same time, brought Renee and three-year-old Tonia with her by a faster route. What this suggests is that my grandmother abandoned my mother. Grandmom took care of her outwardly sick daughter rather that the inwardly wounded one. My mom, who arrived home sooner to Pennsylvania, had to lie about the new child, Tonia, alone.

My father returned to Connecticut in 1948. He returned to his family when his or my grandfather's Panama service ended. I wonder if he visited my mother in Philly? Did she travel to Connecticut?

Here then, are my parent's families and the milieu into which I am born. They have endured storms of death, of war and of family. Accident and sickness play a role. For instance, my father's sickness cut short his education and perhaps brought him to Panama. My mother's favorite aunt dies young. My mother receives an emotional wound of trauma, affecting her inner life. Brokenness and woundedness have touched their lives. Secrets exist and silence prevails, having repercussions for my mother, her family, and beyond. They perpetrate a dark mean lie for the sake of social convenience and family pride, doubling the wound.

There are also bright signs of constancy and duty. My father carries on the legacy of his father's military life. They are all comfortable traveling the world. They have an ability to do hard, menial work.

My story has its beginnings with these complicated, struggling human beings. They will play out a difficult drama. My mother's trauma will inhibit her emotional expression and leave her with a general passivity and tentativeness. Her unavailability will affect my father's relationship with her. On the other hand, I recall a strong, active relationship with my father. Their emotions and aspirations will make up the lessons I will learn. Also, their shame, guilt, and pride will silently touch me. My early life will meander between the dance of their strengths and weaknesses.

And the anvil marks the movement of life with a slow cadence of deep percussions and bright sparks. It fears not the difficulties that we face, nor does it turn away. It invites the people it encounters to overcome and grow, to break through the shackles of hard circumstance and the mean schemes brought on by others.

To Those Passed
Do not forget the muffled voices
Links in the chain from then to now
What is due their names and faces?
But to brighten your light and love anew

2 Hartford

In 1948, my parents got back together. Lucky for me. In Hartford, Connecticut, in 1950, my life began. I'm sorry, but I have only one story about my birth. I started as a Yankee fan because my father bought me my first baseball cap, a Yankee's N and Y, white on blue.

When I was 3, probably my first actual memory also concerned baseball. I remember seeing my father round the bases charging for home in a baseball game. The sun glowed that day as I watched from a blanket. I recall many people around. The bright green of the field contrasted with the brown dirt of the baseline and around home plate. I didn't know the patterns, just the colors. The crowd cheered loudly and enthusiastically, grabbing my attention and frightening me a little. "Stevie, you father scored the winning run, that is great!" I stood up and clapped my hands like a baby seal, vaguely knowing why. A man waved on the white uniformed man running the bases in full stride. That was my dad. I am sure that there sounded a hit on the anvil, but my young ears didn't notice.

My first nine years, we moved around Connecticut, Pennsylvania and New Jersey. I have only small bits of memories like the above from early on. My father worked as a machinist for a while with Pratt and Whitney and then Piasecki, a helicopter company, over those early years. We lived in a couple of trailers; I have a tattered picture in my wallet of my father holding a young boy in his arms in front of a small trailer. This one caught fire.

These early years, I got exposed to the different families of my father and my mother. Like an abstract canvas, it took me a while to make out the shapes and give meaning to the colors! I am not sure why we moved every couple of years. Perhaps it occurred because my father grew up in a military family. Maybe my mom, restlessly, didn't like to stay away from her daughter.

In Connecticut, we visited my father's parents regularly. Except for my grandmother's brother George, there were few visitors, and the place had a quiet ambiance. They lived in a large house with a big porch and a second story. "Grandpa, how long have you had Blackey?" I asked. "Well, he has been around since we got back from Panama. Come here, boy. Yeah, he's a good old boy." "I think he sheds too much," said my grandma. "Aw, mom, he's good." I loved that friendly dog. My grandparents had rolling grounds behind their house for kids to run and roam. In one room hung a painting of a wooden masted war ship, sails full of wind, charging through the water full bore, waves splashing aside. That painting always struck a powerful chord in my heart. Several taps on hot metal speaks the anvil. It likes ships and the sea.

Let me note a couple of interesting experiences that stand out amid the haze. We had three small box turtles that were painted differently so we could identify them. The blue one got away, never to be seen again. "Mommy, Blue isn't in his box!" "Let's see. He couldn't have gotten far. He's a turtle. They don't move fast! Stevie, don't cry. It's only a turtle. You still have two more!"

A favorite memory I have is with my grandfather over a box of cereal. While visiting my grandparents' home in Norwich, Connecticut, I got up early. Sitting by the island counter with a few chairs, I wanted a bowl of cereal. My grandfather sat next to me. "Which would you like, son?" he asked. Looking expectedly at his little grandson. "That one!" He got out a bowl and poured cereal into it, then some milk. On the box on the counter, it advertised a toy that looked pretty cool. "I want that, grandpa." I said, pointing to the box. "Hmm." he said and looked at the toy in the picture. I took a bite of cereal. "I want it." Saying it again, I made sure he heard me. "Well," as he read the side of the box, "It says here, send away for it." This was unacceptable. I wanted it and I wanted it now. Grabbing the box, I shook it. "Grandpa, it's inside the box!"

"No, don't think so. You send for it in the mail," he said gently. "It's in the box," I insisted, looking inside the box expectantly, shaking it up and down. Without words, he opened up the cabinet and took out several bowls. He lined them up on the counter in front of me. "Let's pour this in these bowls. I'll show you, young man." He continued until nothing remained in the box. "See, Steve, it isn't in here." I looked at the empty box and the full bowls with dismay and disappointment. He made his point simply and dealt with his impetuous and willful grandson with great care. And the air around the anvil warmly resounds with the echo of metal on metal, tap, tap, and tap.

Before my brothers were born, my father found work with aviation genius, Igor Sikorsky, and thus began a long 5-year work stint. From the 40s, my father developed his skills as a machinist, a tool and die maker, a sheet metal worker, a lofts man. He took blue prints and magically made them real, building in real-life scale what the plan only imagined. He helped build the S58 helicopter and other interesting machines. The anvil, of course, likes that. It's revels in the making of machines.

I benefitted from being an only child. Giving me a good emotional foundation, I felt loved and accepted. At 4, I received from my grandparents a cowboy outfit. It included a cowboy hat, a tasseled shirt and pants and a large holster with two six-shooters. "Hey you little cowboy. Hun, get the camera. Stevie, look over here and smile." My mom said. I played out my imagination with my trusted steed tied up by the curb. This also goes along with my coonskin cap from my exposure to Davy Crockett.

In Bridgeport, during this steady period, my twin brothers were born, Nick and Tony. This must have been quite a new load on my parents. "Charlie, I am exhausted. They thought we would have two and sure enough. But my, am I tired and worn out!" "Dear, you made it through like a champ! Now the fun begins, huh?" laughing. "I can hold them with one hand! Can't tell them apart except for this mole on Nicky's wrist." My mom dressed them the same. Tony was born four minutes after Nicky. We were the only grandkids on my dad's side.

Now, my brothers brought the restless energy of youth. They chatted all the time, especially Tony. They laughed often and always played together. "Stevie, can we make you a mud pie? It's really good!" "Sure Tony, I need cherries on top!" "Here ya go!" I loved them but, frankly, they had invaded my life and worse; they out-numbered me! My mom was tired, I bet. "You boys wear me out. How do you find all the energy? You'll all need a nap this afternoon. I need a break!" Nicky had issues early on. Maybe he didn't make the same eye contact as Tony or progressed slower physically. He didn't walk as soon or talk at the same rate. He may have had autistic tendencies. It would follow him in his entire life.

I think I enjoyed myself as a child. At a store, "Aren't those twins so cute? They're dressed the same." "Yes," I would chime up. "They're my brothers, Nicky and Tony. Know how you can tell them apart? Nick has a mole on his hand, see?" Energetic, talkative and pleasant, I adapted well. My imagination was good, as was my memory. For instance, I got excited to see a World War II Catalina patrol plane on a lot by the road. "Dad, look a Catalina!" "You're right Steve. An old one from the war." My mom responded. Maybe I could have been a plane spotter like her. I also loved seeing new cars! I enjoyed the looks of cars. The shapes of the fins, the grill between the headlights, the side ornamentation, creating that unique look. I could identify a '56 from a '57 BelAir or a '63 and '64 Chevy Impala. The ugly Edsel was something to see. I always looked out for the Studebaker with the third eye between the headlights! "There goes a Cyclops," laughing.

There were several early car stories. At three years of age, we lived in a trailer park. My father drove to work one morning in his black Hudson and I followed him. I probably walked a kid's mile and a half before my mom caught up to me. "Stevie, never do this again," dragging me by the arm. "You could have gotten very hurt, young man," my mom scolded! Another story involved painting a neighbor's new car with paint that I believe did not coordinate with the style and color of the car. It got resolved and my parents had to pay for my artistry. I also sipped some turpentine that was in a beer can. That got my dad in trouble, as well.

The Hudson sat in the driveway for several years of my childhood. I have a picture of my father holding me in front of it. We owned it before my brothers were born. My parents then bought a red and white Chevy Belair station wagon. Twins will change your life, so they needed a bigger car. I sat on a chair, facing the big window opened to the car lot at the dealership when they bought it. A fire engine went screaming by while we waited. "Oh, my, a fire engine!" I was five.

Several other memories formed in Connecticut. Winter was long and hard, still white and silent. We wouldn't stay inside in winter, but get bundled up and take trips in the country. There were beautiful scenes overlooking houses, tree-lined roads and fields of white. "Oh, boys," my dreamy mother would say, "look at that big house with the porch. That could fit us all, I bet!" There would be horses in the enormous yards of several homes. "Mommy, I want a horse," my brother Tony would state. "Sorry Tony, we couldn't afford that! Where would we keep it?" "He could stay in our room!"

We lived in a small city house in Bridgeport. A significant difference from the great outward expanse seen on our trips. Those placid country houses on display had gentle whiffs of smoke coming from their chimneys. For me, their poignant beauty was painted in the gentle fields, insulated by the snow, between the tufts of trees. I drank it in. Maybe I also had a dreamer in me.

I had many joy-filled experiences in Connecticut. I affectionately remember a field by a library building. It had two large doors that you reached by going up steps guarded by two concrete lions. There is an old picture of me sitting on one lion by the front steps. Early on, my father established that our relationship would be based upon doing things together. For instance, he bought me a white Styrofoam airplane with a wingspan of more than a yard across! "Here, let's see if this thing can fly. Are you ready? Here it comes." "Wow, daddy look how high! Wow!" We also flew kites in that field and threw balls. I've always owned a baseball glove. My father saw to it. He had a catcher's mitt, big, round, thick, and worn. I know this field is important to me because I have visited it many times in my dreams, bringing peace and joy.

"Stevie," my father would say, "I want you to be an aeronautical engineer and attend MIT. You can build airplanes. What do you think of that?" "Wow, could I fly them too?" I imagine engineers were the doers and shakers of his world. He wanted his son to be one. And the air filled with percussive strikes on the anvil. It likes airplanes and strong relationships.

On a July 4th day, my brothers and I received little US flags my father brought home. "Kids, I got these at work. Here for all of you." "Thanks Daddy!" With flags in hand, we went out the front door, down the stone steps and onto the sidewalk. We ran, following each other, in procession, yelling at the top of our lungs, holding our flags high and waving. I felt exhilarated to fly flags and give voice to our naïve patriotism.

I had a lot of infectious energy as a young kid. In Fairfield, we lived on a hill. I used to ride my bike up and down the street, loving the experience of speed and wind. Well, I won't say much about the time I crashed into the stop sign because of a turning car.

Aunt Joyce stayed with us for a while in Connecticut. Kissing me, "Oh, Stevie, give me a hug, you handsome young man!" Coming once to school because I said I was being bullied, she wanted the principal to do something. For me, she was warm and loving.

We shared the large Fairfield house with another family, Joe and Sally Brigindi. They had 3 or 4 older children. This house had a big front staircase, a porch, and large grounds. We played a lot outside. My brothers were 3. My mom forced us into nap time in the afternoon (more for her sake than mine). Getting out of bed, I walked to the window. "This nap is stupid. Why can't I be outside?" as I watched the other kids through the curtains in the bedroom.

This house had a big apple tree in the front. "Mrs. House," said one of the older kids, "Steve fell out of the tree and hurt his arm bad." I painfully broke my right arm in third grade. The tree just called you to climb it and sometimes it was mean and kicked you out! My teacher heard about it and hoped that I broke my left arm so she could teach me to write right-handed. Unfortunately, I broke my right arm. I continued to be left-handed and right-brained!

A significant pastime I loved to share with my father, and Joe Brigindi was crabbing. They took me on many trips. Typically, we would start out early and take a drive to the boat. "Stevie, are you ready, little guy?" Joe would say. "The baskets and the bait are in the back. Charlie, we're ready to go!" Proudly the baskets came home filled with layers of green seaweed and crabs.

It was here that my father taught me how to crab in a traditional, manual manner, not using crab pots. "Now watch me. You tie a fish head on the end of a string with this weight." "Ew! That's ugly!" "Watch! Hold the string in your fingers. Lower it to the bottom, slowly move it up and down. You know when you got a bite. It gets tense and pulls." The crab would hold on if you brought it up slowly. "Hey, Charlie, look, your son got a nice one. Nice work, Stevie," Joe would say as my dad would get the long pole underneath the crab and voila! You got your crab. We threw back softshell crabs, females and pregnant crabs. We could tell by the underside pattern of the shell.

"Charlie, catch!" Joe threw him a crab with only one pincer. It landed on the bottom of the boat, all aggressive. I got pinched enough. However, at the close of the day, they ended up in the big pot of hot water. Our catch would cause a feast. We always had seafood on Friday. We would have fish, crabs, or lobster. One day, my father yelled, "Kids come here, quick!" There at the top of the steps, a big lobster wandered around with yellow bands around its huge claws. We all screamed when it moved its claws and scurried across the floor.

My dad taught me a lesson in crabbing I have kept with me my whole life. "Steve, you go steady. Watch the tension on the line. Feel the crab tugging at the fish head. Move slowly, keep looking, *pull the line up slowly*." This taught me to persevere.

I developed another skill as a kid. I could catch butterflies with my open fingers! Being punished one day, I sat inside looking out on a beautiful sunlit day. I noticed a beautiful Monarch butterfly fly on a milkweed bush in the front of our house. "Mom, can I go out and catch that butterfly out front? See it?" "What?" She thought I must have been crazy. But she said, "Yes, as long as you come right back in." I found a big mason like jar and went out. Following the butterfly as he skipped across several flowers, he rested on one, and I saw my chance. Slowly, I moved toward it. It opened its wings, then slowly shut them. I moved my fingers behind it and took it by the wings. It squirmed as they did, and its legs gyrated in the air. He went into the jar with a small twig of branch and leaf. I took it in to show my incredulous mother. She smiled. I looked at it for a while, then let it go. I had touched and held utter beauty! God smiled.

"What are you guys making?" his mom asked. "It's gonna be a flying ghost." "Did you ask your dad if you could use his tennis racket?" At that same house, next door, lived my buddy, Harold. We played a lot together. His basement was our official scary place for Halloween. "I'm gonna make some scary drawings. Look, mom, we made these bats out of wire." "Woah," said the mom. "I'm scared now." In the off season, he and I would play army.

Another experience of nature occurred here. Playing in the backyard with Harold, "Stevie, look, what is on your steps?" Getting closer, "Oh, my gosh, it's a line of black ants moving their stuff, carrying eggs, leaves and crumbs of stuff!" They went up a flight of steps in a fairly straight line. We watched for several minutes. They were an army on the march. My mom came out stepping on them, sweeping them away. "Steve, why didn't you stop these ants from entering the house?" angry and aghast. They were moving into her kitchen! Now, I could play army, but my budding pacifist world view dictated, I couldn't kill these peace-filled ants!

During this time, our family took several trips to Pennsylvania, where my mom's family lived. I bet this was to see Tonia. We would sleep in the back of the Chevy with the seat down, under a thick cocoon of blankets as they drove through the night. It was an adventure. The car stopped one time. I pretended to be asleep. As the front door opened, my mom said, "Be quiet.

I don't want to wake them." And then in another tone of voice, "Hi Aunt Francis. How are you? So glad we could meet." "Oh, dear Anna, how are you? Hello, Charlie. Let me see the children. My, they are getting big. The twins are so cute!" We would also go to the drive-in movies with the back seat down and blankets out. Us kids probably didn't see the end of many movies as we were asleep halfway in.

As I got older, however, family tension increased after my brothers were born. They needed lots of attention. Let me share a story wherein my mother had a significant emotional episode. My parents had argued about a visit to his parents. My father had gone to work, my brothers were sleeping. It was the dreaded nap time. I had been looking at books. My mother was in the bathroom. I think she was crying. I heard a loud cry and a noise as something dropped. Silence ensued then my mother said in a soft voice, calling for me, "Stevie, Stevie, I need your help." I opened the door with hesitation. She lay on the floor, her legs under her, one arm on the tub. Her tussled hair looked awry. "I can't get up," she said in a strained voice, holding her head. She thought she hurt her leg or her hip. She was too heavy for me. We sat there on the floor. She cried. "It will be ok, Mommy. Daddy will be home soon." I did the only thing I knew to do. "Can I get you a glass of water Mommy?" and I stayed with her. Against the stark white bathroom decor, I swore I saw anvil sparks flicking away.

My mom didn't seem happy and probably needed more than she emotionally received, or maybe her emotional control would unravel. It is hard to describe, but our mom wasn't very available to us. She had an exterior hard to penetrate. She lived like a wounded dreamer, faced with bursts of grief. I have seen many pictures of her where you can see the pain in her eyes. Later on, in a very candid moment, she told me, "Steve, I don't think I loved your father." That pierced me with sadness, but probably didn't surprise me.

Growing up, I knew one important family fact. My grandfathers were important to me because I had their names. "Steven and Carl." They were obviously important to others as well. This ties me to them in a deep and serious way.

I am not sure why we moved from Connecticut. My father had a decent job and my parents had friends. Maybe my mom needed more meaning or relief. Maybe she couldn't stay away from her daughter. It was in the evening. My father was reading the paper in his chair by the tall lamp. "Have you talked to them?" she asked. "I told you, I would talk with my boss. No, I haven't yet." "When? I can't do this much more." "Dear, this is a good job, the best I have had. I am moving up." My mom turned away in disgust, it seemed. My father told me once, "I could have been a manager of the Sikorsky plant had we stayed in Connecticut." I could feel the tension and felt the frustration.

Is my story about New England clam chowder or is it a Greek salad with feta, olives, cucumbers, lettuce and olive oil? Maybe it's both. We had a side dish of different languages, cultures and people. I speak English but hear Greek. I am connected to Greece, where my grandfather is buried. There is talk of Panama, where my parents met and married. The military offers a side dish whose aroma wafts in an out of the kitchen of my childhood. For instance, Aunt Joyce would say that I would look good in a uniform. As a kid, I loved the Silent Service, a show about submarines on Saturday mornings. My friends and I play army. The outdoors becomes the appetizer, filled with wonder. I know firsthand how to catch a crab or a butterfly. The water lapping the side of the boat leaves an imprint in my mind. My psychology develops as a sauce on all things. I learn people can dislike others. Tension between people is something I know. My brother is subtly different. The importance of family and the value of friendship are things I know. I love my brothers. Perhaps God is the cook, as I have an undeniable sense of God, an awareness of awe, tugging at me in the beautiful, natural world I love and admire.

Connecticut signified undoubtedly joy-filled moments with six-shooters and bikes. There are times of tranquility, smiling days tossing airplanes. I lived out joy and freedom, waving flags, being on the water or chasing butterflies. The dark side also floats in and out. In first grade, my role in the class play was as a genie in a green outfit. A classmate had a tiger costume with a tail. Playing with the tail, I accidentally pulled it off! "Please don't tell the teacher, please!" I pleaded.

My anxiety probably mirrored those around me. When frustrated, my mom would grab a belt, hold it in her hands, snap it loudly and threaten us with it. "When your father comes home, you boys are going to get it!" There were dark times, the lights too bright, the voices too piercing. Adults have the prerogative to choose how much they will attend to their children. When things threaten the adults, their attention is scarce. I lived with threatened adults.

I had a child's innocence, but a strong will. Enjoying people, I felt loved. I had a place. It got tougher when my brothers were born and the place got crowded. As time went on, my joy became tempered. Life became less lighthearted. I sat in rooms with others who were unhappy and distant. I felt the heritage of old trauma and rejection hanging in the air, though I was unaware. All of this joined to configure my developing sense of self, my parents, and my family. While certainly sensitive and anxious, I rested upon a firm foundation that would bode well for what lay ahead. I knew what care felt like. I could interact and bring smiles to others. Navigating the moving waters as best a kid could do, I wanted my father to be proud of me, for I brought the line up slowly.

<u>Family</u>

A concoction of people, sweet and sour
Chosen by God to be called
Brothers and sisters, mom and dad, uncles and grandma, aunts and yia yia
Cousins and nieces
Grandkids
Some, like a good suit, we love
Others, like a bad haircut, we love none the less, but forever are trying to comb out the frizz

3 Venice Park

I am not sure I want to admit it, but I lived in New Jersey for a while! Only in Jersey could the following happen. There had been sounds, creaks, and noises, but no one understood the signs. A small water leak developed from the ceiling. My brothers and I finished up school for the year and hadn't paid a lot of attention. Summer filled the air and our excitement grew. Outside the window, seagulls stood on the railing. You could see them skimming the water's surface and now and then, diving into the water to catch dinner. At low tide, they walked in the mud looking for things to eat. My mother had just folded clothes and laid the towels on the bed. A pile of socks, underwear and kid's clothes swished around in the washer. As the washer sound droned on, there came a slight, low-pitched sound. A whine developed, a stretching sound got slightly louder and then suddenly, a bomb burst hit the kitchen. A decibel-loud sound drowned out the washer. Glass broke and spilled on the floor. Pieces of broken porcelain echoed in the small apartment. My mother startled as the sudden and intense sound almost knocked her down. It shocked her mind awake. After several seconds, the slurry of sound became intermittent and less intense. Then it stopped.

She collected herself. "Oh, my God!" she said as she entered the kitchen. The scene before her amounted to a catastrophe. She saw a dark and gray smelly pile of silvery clam and mussel shells strewn on the table, the chairs, the range and over a large area of floor. A grayish dust cloud floated in the air. Above, splintered wood and broken plaster revealed a blue sky shining through a slit of a hole in the ceiling. The kitchen light slanted askew. One chair on the floor rested on its side. The seagull bomb squad had struck with significant force. We surrender, already!

The seagulls had for years used the roof for crashing shells. They had covered the adjoining roof of the apartment next door as well. The practice of generations of gulls had accumulated substantial weight on the roof. It would take a while to fix and clean up.

Let me start a little further back. The trip occurred around Thanksgiving 1959. We had been preparing for Thanksgiving in my fourth-grade class. We were making the typical turkeys and pilgrim hats, talking about our favorite desserts. Then, like in a dream, unsure how we got there, we were living in New Jersey on the outskirts of Atlantic City in a small island community called Venice Park. There had been no celebrations or going away parties or occasions of goodbye. We got in the car and drove to a new life. A loud and steady gong, says the anvil.

Two facts are a significant part of the picture. One is that my Aunt Renee lived in Atlantic City. So, we had moved closer to my mom's sister. Second, we were one hour from Philadelphia and, of course, closer to Tonia. It also took us away from my dad's family. Not sure if any of this mattered in the decision. I claim only to be a kid with not quite a decade under my belt!

Venice Park was a small island, somewhat like its namesake. A school, a church, a hotel and a store-apartment complex served the small community. We moved above Biondi's Store and Restaurant. To the back stretched a long dock with a gas pump at the end and a sign advertising marine gas. The broad river rendered a view of Atlantic City and a coal fired plant in the distance. Significantly for me, I saw and smelled water!

Water ways surrounded Venice Park coming from Absecon Bay and marsh land. Water lubricated my soul. I loved the wind off the water giving it that ocean smell. If I piloted that sailing ship in the painting in Connecticut, it would smell like this. Seagulls were plentiful and would rest on the pilings of the dock and sea wall. I often heard their cries as they flew above.

The apartments were accessible by the open wooden steps on the side of the building with a thin handrail. "Nicky, why are you walking on your hands and feet up the steps?" "These are scary!" he said. "Oh, you two scaredy cats!" At the top, a large patio area opened in front of the four apartments. We lived on the left.

The apartment fit us well. A long mirror on the wall made the room look bigger. We had a good view from the front room. A major street went from

Biondi's to the highway. The street connected with Absecon Boulevard and ran between Atlantic City and the rest of New Jersey.

My father had taken a job with a government facility in Pomona N.J. by the airport. They tested safety measures for commercial aircraft. "What were you doing when we came to see you, daddy?" "Today was special. We tested the use of foam on the runway. Sometimes a distressed plane has to land without landing gear." I went with my mom and took him his lunch that day. He worked by a long runway. A large radar tower stood where we dropped off his food among the pines. He had a hard hat and a badge. There were firetrucks with their lights on. He must have engaged in interesting work. I regret never asking much about it.

Atlantic City drew people as a resort town with a boardwalk, beaches, hotels and various attractions. Old folks flooded the town, strolling the boardwalk or riding on bicycle powered wicker chairs. These were plentiful and aggressive. Many places sold Salt Water Taffy, a wrapped, chewy, sticky roll of sweet. I loved to watch them draw it out on enormous machines with twisting, elongated arms. There were hotels with many floors and towers, and finely manicured gardens of bright flowers and evergreens.

Atlantic City had a long beach and various piers. For instance, a long pier called Steel Pier occupied a section of ocean front. It had many rooms, a ballroom, places to eat, benches to watch the water, rides, shops and, of course, the famous Diving Horse. A big car salesroom stood at the boardwalk end of the pier displaying Chevys. "Oh my, look, that is a Corvette Stingray!" I had no words for that. There would be an Impala, shining in its large presence, signifying success and wealth. Once they displayed a foreign car called a Honda. A small car, like a toy, it had a motorcycle engine underneath the open hood. Compared to the real American cars, this was obviously a joke, or at least an experiment that would likely fail.

We went to see the Diving Horse once. At the end of the pier, a large stand held 100 people. They faced a large circular and open area of water. The waves rolled in and darkened the many pillars. You could feel the excitement in the stands. "Please welcome our diving beauty, ladies and gentlemen. Keep your eyes on her as she mounts her brave steed. Watch as the pair prepare to dive into the tumultuous waves below!" A narrow and uncovered chute opened to the rolling water 10 feet beneath them. A pause increased the tension and then she took off down the ramp with the horse leaping outstretched. People held their breath as the pair descended and splashed loudly and fully into the water. Applause then erupted; breaths taken in again as the woman waved at the astonished crowd. She and the horse would swim over to a floating dock.

A distant cousin to the Steel Pier stood at the Million Dollar pier. It bragged about an amusement park on the water. This pier was my favorite. Out front were carnival attractions offering a chance to throw rings at objects or shoot at targets for a chance to win an enticing stuffed animal. During a stay with my Aunt Renee over the summer of 1964, I would go to the arcade in the front of Million Dollar Pier intent on winning a big, stuffed horse. Eventually, probably after $20 in loose change, I won it.

For me, the cages attracted me the most. These involved tall fenced boxes on hinges. While at rest, you opened up the door and stood inside. After the door closed and you were safely secured, you rocked back and forth inside to get it to move. After a while, if you timed your movements well, you could get it to go up and around in a full circle. I emerged from the cage, with arms raised, "I am the king. I am the king!" till my friend told me to shut up. Such were my successes. Chang, tad, chang says the anvil.

Back at home, I encountered an incredible thing. I would walk out of my way to pass it, going to school. A small pool of water stood in front of a house. Lined with grasses and rocks, it measured a foot deep. I could see brightly colored koi fish moving about the pool. It reflected the vision of another world down there. I felt just astonished at the presence of such a beautiful thing in the middle of the neighborhood. God's beauty could jump out at you.

A family lived in the apartment directly next to ours. Tommy, their son, and I became friends. His parents owned a bar in town. "Here you go boys, money for each of you. Tommy, you and Stevie stick together. I will meet you around 3 out front of the Steel Pier. Have fun, you two". The $5 he gave each of us seemed like an enormous amount of money and a sign of great generosity. They must have been very rich. Tommy also had an 8 mm projector (another sign of great wealth). We would watch the several "Woody the Woodpecker" movies that he owned. "And now for our show. Here he is, that cute and troublemaking woodpecker we all love." Once we had a water balloon fight in his apartment. His mom didn't like it. Maybe he needed more discipline!

Venice Park became an adventure because preceding from the gravel yard out back, stretched a long 30-foot dock. This runway represented the water's personal invitation to me. The dock became a window into the amazing world of the water. On the sides were a lower step, just the right height for getting into and out of the water. Sitting and watching, which I often did, would offer at least a crab swimming by or jelly fish gently opening and closing their way across. A small school of fish might suddenly dart by. Boaters would come by getting gas and show off their catch or bring it to Biondi's for sale.

One day while fishing off the dock, I had a wonderful bite. The thing tugged and ran hard. My excitement grew as the test between me and nature went on. "Tony and Nicky, come here. I got a big bite!" My enthusiasm shattered when it finally came to the surface and I realized it was an eel. These were evil creatures, snakes of the sea, ugly, slimy, twisting and turning demons. I swung it around, hoping it would get off the hook on its own. I had to stand on it to get it off. It twisted back into the dark ocean where it belonged, never to be caught again and, hopefully, to be eaten by a whale. "That was ugly!" Tony said.

Having a dock in your backyard served as a great playground for a kid. One day after a storm, a smaller piece of another dock came to rest by our dock. Fifteen by fifteen, well made, it floated because of large barrels under the wood joists. Us kids took it as a sign from God that he meant it to be ours. It became a great diving platform.

Now my mother worried about the water. During the summer, I went to the YMCA and took swimming lessons. They taught me what I needed to know, and I became one with the fishes afterward. My younger brothers were to stay away from the dock. She had a well-founded concern. While playing on the dock, Nicky fell in. He couldn't swim. Thrashing about and yelling, Tony grabbed him by the hair. "Nicky, pull yourself on the dock. Come on. I'm holding you." Eventually, Tony grabbed his torso and pulled him back onto the platform. Nicky was scared and spitting up due to swallowing some water. My hero brother Tony had saved his twin brother's life! My mother's fears were justified. But she forgot the courage of her other son. And the anvil sounds the power of love!

In nearby Atlantic City, with the ocean, came beaches! We would bring food and drinks, a blanket, towels, beach toys and there you have it, a good day. On beach days, we would go back and forth between the water, the beach, and the boardwalk. People crowded the beach on this day. Tony and I excitedly ran into the water. We came back to the blanket. "Where is your brother? Wasn't he with you?" Mom seriously questioned us, then looked frightened. Well, just like that, we couldn't find Nicky. Mom anxiously started searching for him. Our worst fear concerned him going into the water. The life guards searched. My mom spoke with a cop. After great fear and anxiety, late in the afternoon, the police brought him home. He had walked 5 miles on the boardwalk! When asked, he had little to say about it. He didn't seem upset or scared. It made my father angry.

Other lighter situations offset this scary moment. Mr. Biondi, who owned the store and the apartments, bought a lot of pizza sauce. Back by the sea wall, there were many 1-gallon cans of it. The stuff must be bad, we thought. Why else would you leave it out in the blistering sun all day? On the sea wall, there were silver metal spikes in the shape of stars that held it together with a pointed center spike. "Hey, I got an idea. What if we throw the can against the spike? Will pizza sauce come out?" Everybody thought that was a great idea. "Throw it Stevie!" They were heavy, I couldn't throw it far. But I got one pierced, and it made some noise. The next one was spectacular! The pizza sauce climbed 6 feet into the air, swishing around in a great arc. "Hey you kids, what are you doing? Stevie, I am going to tell your dad!"

As children, our mom would pray with us at night before bed. While baptized Greek Orthodox, my mom would let me go on a weekly basis to the community church. They had a children's group. One holiday, I took part in a festival program and sang America the Beautiful. It foretold of musical things to come. "Children, we have Bibles for all of you. Young man, you sang beautifully," said the pastor. I still have my Bible. My religious education came in fits and spurts. But as Augustine stated, "Our hearts are restless until they rest in thee." My heart was restless, and I felt open to God.

Another religious encounter occurred amazingly. I befriended a poor kid in my class. He didn't have many friends. His old clothes were often wrinkled and dirty. He seemed to be a gentle person, and we became friends. Living down the street from me, several times I visited his messy house. Well, Halloween awaited just around the corner and he invited me to go to a party at his church. "Greggy, my mom said I can go." Later, "Do you want to do the bag race with me?" "Sure." I spoke. Other kids and parents hung around. "How do you bite those apples when they're in the water?" "That's the fun of it, Steve." "Oh, boy, I'm not good at this." "Here, you go, have an apple anyway." I had found a little surprising gem in a pile of dirt; it seemed. The anvil rings its pleasure. Chang.

Now let me tell you about the Grand Mistake of 4th grade. My mother had heard that the elementary school at Venice Park was not very good. So, she sent me to a school in the city based on my aunt's address. I took a bus to get there. Well, a couple of weeks later, the school district realized my actual address and what school I should be attending. Going to the Venice Park school for the first time, my new 4th grade teacher asked, "Steve, tell us about yourself?" "Well, I just moved here a little while ago. My mom thought this school wasn't that good, so she sent me to another school." Smart, real smart Stevie! But to the contrary, this would be one of the best school experiences I had. The teacher for the combined 4th and 5th grade class was Miss Pigeon. She affected me powerfully. Well, my relationship with Miss Pigeon became special. Flowering in her class, I learned more than knowledge. We had lots of group projects in 5th grade. One time, Miss Pigeon asked me, "Can you take Susan into your group? She has trouble making friends." "Sure, Miss Pigeon. It'll be ok." We learned lessons about humility and giving from Miss Pigeon.

At one point, I won a spelling bee in her class. "Can I get the plant? My mom would like it, I think." It excited me to bring it home. But it didn't last long before it died. I guess you have to water it!

Over the years, I have gained old things that are impossible to discard. At the end of 5th grade, the school had a graduation. We all got these little geography books about the countries of the world. I still have that aged brown book, "The First Book Atlas", published in 1960. Inside the front cover, "Steven House, 1500 Riverside Drive, Venice Park, Atlantic City, New Jersey" in pencil. Gong, tad, di, tad. The anvil loves memories.

At school, there were disagreements about, of all things, baseball. Kids in the neighborhood were diehard Phillies fans. Stupidly, I said, "I like the Yankees. They're better than the Phillies. They got Yogi Berra and Mickey Mantle and Roger Maris!" "Why don't you go back to New York?" I lied, "It's better than here!" The kids spoke words and gave stares. Things were relieved when I impressed them by bringing a crystal radio to school. It looked like a rocket. On the playground, we clipped the wire to a line on a pole and could hear Philly baseball broadcasts through the earplug.

At a different level, I had a shining career in baseball in Venice Park. I played for two years. The community had a large Little League organization. My father wanted to see his son play and get enthusiastic about the game.

The first year, my team was the Yankees, and we did not do very well. My lanky frame wasn't so coordinated. I had a good arm but couldn't hit for crap.

Now let me share the bad news before the good. On one Saturday morning, I had almost been late for the game. I played on the Yankees in the outfield, probably right field. It could be boring and only occasionally exciting. But I came up to bat from time to time. This at bat was unusual. As I stood there, probably about to strike out, one kid in the bleachers shouts, "He peed his pants! He peed his pants!" There is a lot of noise at a ball field as parents often shout at their child players. But the crowd easily heard these comments. Being almost late, I skipped the bathroom at home. The game had been going on and I couldn't control it and wet my uniform. After my at bat, the coach asked, "Steve, do you want to go home?" "Yes, coach." I said and got my glove and left. I felt embarrassed for myself and for my dad.

The next year was different. This year my team was the Red Socks. We had a good season. We were playing a talented team for the "World Series", the end of the season tournament. I played left field on this team; my father and I had worked on catching and throwing, and I improved. My batting still needed work, but at least I could get the bat around. However, I caught the ball well and I could run. The time was late in the game, the 6th. Runners were at first and third. We were winning. One of their best hitters steps up to bat. This kid could hit the ball. I moved back a little. I get into my stance with hands on my thighs, feet apart, eyes attentive, waiting for the pitch. He hits one in the air, coming toward me. My glove is ready. I am running to catch it. All I hear is the thud of the ball in the glove. I still hear it. He's out, the inning is over. Cheers from our side. As I am running back to the dugout, this guy, who is their left fielder, comes to me, pushes me with a grunt, and says, "Jerk." I keep running. We win the game and the season is ours. We get trophies and ice cream. And so ends the banner game of my successful little League career! Tad, di, tad.

Let me share a delightful part of Venice Park. Here, we had several animals that thrilled us kids. A rabbit started us off. We kept it in a little fenced in area on the back patio and fed it carrots and lettuce. Next, we got a classic pet, a yellow, blue parakeet named "Twinkie". He had a contagious energy. "Can I let him out of his cage, mom?" "I guess it's ok. Keep track of him. Keep the front door shut." The bird would fly around the main room and land on your finger. "Twinkie, Twinkie, how are you? How are you?" Bobbing his head, "How are you, er, how are you? Love you. How are you?" Great peals of laughter. "I wanna hold him. Come here Twinkie," said Nick.

We all loved that bird. He loved to look at himself in the big mirror and talk to himself. He lightened the heaviness that appeared from time to time.

Around this time, I briefly entered the hospital with what seemed like a serious illness. The doctors suspected pneumonia. I felt exhausted and couldn't breathe well. Great anxiety and perceptual issues bothered me. I had nightmares. Falling asleep slowly, I watched as the swaying light behind the doorway seemed to get further away. Under the covers, eyes closed but awake, my psyche spun and felt off balance. The doctors were unsure about the diagnosis. They connected it to the bird. I used to clean out his cage. They said the bird had to go.

One last curious animal story here. During the winter, one evening, from over the water of the partially frozen river at low tide, we heard a cry of a large bird. As this went on for a while, my father investigated closer. He took a little sled with him and walked out on the frozen brackish water with a lantern toward the sound. I could see the light bobble around. "Mom, will Daddy be ok?" "He'll be alright. You kids get ready for bed. Don't worry about your father." It seemed like a baffling thing to do. We went to bed, and I didn't easily fall asleep. In the morning, we were all very excited to hear about the bird. There, on the back patio, in a box covered with chicken wire, shook a seagull with a broken wing. You could see blood where the bird had hacked at the box all night. "I am going to take the bird to a Natural Resources ranger, I know." I felt happy the bird lived, but was dismayed at the blood.

For my father and I, the tide came in on an old habit. Happily, we returned to our familiar activity of crabbing. There were many waterways and marshlands that were fed from the ocean. Our old interest was soon refreshed. We weren't as proficient as we were in Connecticut. "We're gonna get up early and take the boat out. Do a little crabbing, Steve?" "Yeah, great." I said with anticipation. There were herons standing in the shallows and seagulls flying overhead. "Steve, look, did you see it? A fish jumped out of the water." Those were peaceful times. Looking back, I am convinced that the good relationship I had with my father rested in part on our doing this together. We didn't so much as talk as do. I did not lose this lesson on my sons and I. Our boating around Venice Park ended when a dispute erupted over the ownership of the boat and motor.

Over the second summer, my father's parents moved to Venice Park. I enjoyed having them around. My father felt their presence as a positive. I surmise they wanted to be near their son and grandkids. "Hey kids, come on in," said our grandfather. "Just in time for a snack!" "How about a pbj for my best grandsons?" our grandma would say. We would take slow walks around the neighborhood with them. Granny would always take a dark sweater. It drove my mom nuts, however, because she did not like her. This must have caused my father pain. "That woman is such a complainer. Nothing suits her." She would tell us, "Now kids, don't drink the milk because you granny allows it to spoil. Your grandmother is not a good housekeeper. She doesn't keep the place clean, so don't touch things while you are there!" She thought the house smelled. We visited them and it seemed pleasant enough. But I felt the tension.

My grandfather and I had a special relationship. We capped it with a memorable boat trip. My grandfather sat first in the boat, with me in the middle and my father in the back managing the motor. We tooled around for several hours. My grandfather had been in the Navy, so he had a comfort with the water. His bunk on a real Navy ship measured bigger than this boat! But it left me with such a wonderful feeling. "Oh, look Steve, see that heron over there. See him? How long is his wingspan? Charlie, what do you think?" "Dad, I bet they are at least 4 feet. Beautiful bird!" With them, I celebrated. "Are we gonna do some crabbing, dad?" I asked. "No, just boating around." My grandfather nodded and smiled. My heart felt blessed and exhilarated to be with them. It seems like a dream to me now. I loved my father and my grandfather. There are negative parts of the story with my father. But this felt special, enchanted, and luminous. Sparks from the grateful anvil.

One day, dad told us that granddad fell and hit his head. I felt stunned. They admitted him to the VA hospital. He was maybe 68. My father took us to visit with our mom. As we approached the hospital, it felt like Fort Knox, a fortress on a hill. "Let me go up and see how he is doing. I'll come back to get you." Mom stayed with us in the car. He stayed a while. Slowly returning, he seemed affected by it. He told us, "It's best that you don't go in. He has bandages over his swollen face. I want you to remember him as he looked before the accident." He remained in the hospital for a little longer and then passed away. I felt numb, having little experience with death. At dinner, my father was quiet. A boat horn sounded from outside. He looked, turning to the window, and looked long for several seconds. The anvil's song resounds slow and deep, tears quenching the red-hot metal.

I don't remember much about the funeral. I assume there were military honors. We went to the gravesite for the burial. My parents were there, a few others, along with my grandmother. She wept. My father supported and attended to her. After my grandfather's death, my grandmother moved back to Connecticut. We never heard from her again, nor, it seems, did we try to communicate. This, I regret. Gong.

While I don't remember many birthdays, I also don't have any pictures of birthdays. I am sure they occurred. I remember one that occurred in Venice Park. It must have been my 10-year birthday. We had those little paper horns you blow in that toot. I also received a couple of great toys for my birthday. One, a ping-pong ball shooter, allowed me to annoy everybody. A second fed into my enjoyment of building things. It was an erector set with nuts and bolts, metal arms and frames, and a small motor. It had a metal box to keep them all in. I made everything in the manual that came with the set. Wow! I was in heaven!

As I mentioned, my Aunt Renee also lived in Atlantic City. We visited from time to time. She lived on the other side of town. Her husband worked as a firefighter, Al Emmons. They had 3 young kids my brother's age. We three and they three reached a critical level of hyperactivity. She could get emotional. "All of youse, up here, now. How many times have I told you no yelling? Sit on the couch and I will smack you if you make a sound." It could be tense visiting.

Her husband, Al, was a big Irish guy. He was Catholic, like my father, and had an outgoing personality. This contrasted with that of my fiery aunt. His sister became a Catholic nun. We met her twice. This was my first exposure to a religious sister.

During the second year in Venice Park, things deteriorated. More tension flared up between my dad and mom. My father stayed at the hotel once after drinking too much. Another evening, we got a babysitter; they got dressed up, and they went out. This didn't happen often. We went to bed optimistic. I spoke with Tony. "Don't they look nice, dressed up?" "Yeah, I like her dress. I'm gonna have good dreams tonight!" "Me too!" When they came home, however, they yelled at each other which dashed my hopes. Some jealous comment my father made and an accusation of disloyalty. They cursed at each other. I fell asleep tearfully.

I am not sure when it happened, but as things unraveled, my aunt pulled a knife on my father. She could be volatile but also my father drank and could get mouthy. It astonished me. I figured my father had been drinking and vigorously argued with my mom as her sister defended her.

Soon after this, with the hole in the roof temporarily patched, unlike the hole in my heat, our mom took us to Philly to stay with our grandmother. My father stayed in Atlantic City. In late summer, a hurricane hit the Jersey coast. My father stayed and endured it. He had a lot of tools that rusted because of being underwater. It seemed fitting that he should endure a hurricane. Maybe he displeased God. He took me to the movies shortly afterward. I forget the name of the movie. I was tearful and rubbing my eyes. "Are you ok?" he asked. "Yeah dad, I'm fine." "I understand, I understand." I think he did. The anvil sounds its understanding.

Before we left, I went fishing in the river with a friend and his father. I got a significant bite. However, the suddenness caught me off guard and the rod flew out of my hands, lost in the water. They later asked my dad to pay for it. This added insult to injury. I am convinced it was that hated eel!

And so ended our time in Venice Park. The place left me with wonderful and enchanted memories. I learned that water is special. It holds a mystical power. The ocean, so powerful and forbidding (my anxiety dreams are of an enormous wave overwhelming me) can also be a thing of beauty and communion. Seagulls provide a soundtrack to the ocean. But beware, they are unscrupulous! Being in a boat with my men represented the dream of love, belonging, and acceptance. It speaks of safety and peace. Atlantic City also carried that bittersweet relationship with my grandparents. While it ended with tension and loss, I still had that mighty sailing ship charging through the water, hanging on the wall of my mind!

<u>By Your Shore</u>

The ocean waves disturb me, tumultuous and moving
Their duty to stir up and loosen
My memories are waxed and oiled, the bottom is stirred and loosed on me
I am in an earlier time, the details of which were long forgotten
Their flavor had dulled, becoming weak
The stuff of that time had been put away, put under, hastily forgotten
And with it the pain of the moment, the hurts that accumulate when one must say goodbye to the sea
The water cleanses me so as it did then, a presence loving and stable that marked me deep and lasting
A first love, a grandfather, a friend next door willing to always playfully engage in being together
The mysterious sea, surprising and sudden, alive and deep
How I long now for you and realize how much I miss you

I ache with what you are to me
I face the task so hard when younger, of saying goodbye
I become unsettled in your air
Your birds and your shells push me inside and I cannot stop what I feel
I will not leave completely for I can't cut myself off
You are too deep within me
So, I will accept my stirrings that come from the waves and instigated by the call of the gulls
I am blown by your wind and the warm sand wherever I am
I have but to remember to return again for a piece of my home lies in the waves that stir by your shore

4 Howard Street

The gay, brightly dressed figure on the sidewalk cranked a musical organ. He stood on the corner and instantly, he captured my attention. Holding a music box on a stick, he cranked out a melodious song. The multicolored box displayed musical notes and joyous colors. A belt around his waist held up his dark pants; his flowery shirt had bright puffy sleeves that flowed. Under a black hat, he had a moustache. With his other hand, the man held the leash of a monkey who sat on his shoulder with a cup! Vested with sequin along the edge, the monkey's red hat had a long black tassel that flew around with his movements. The monkey jumped down from time to time and mingled with the growing crowd, holding out his cup, gathering up the change thrown at them. I witnessed a spectacle I had never seen before. I followed them down the block and onto the next street, hypnotized. The man smiled and said thank you to the people giving him money. The adults were just as taken by it. My mom had to come after me, breaking the spell and bring me back home!

The organ grinder reflected an enchanted experience. This was, however, rare. Beginning here was a difficult time! Monkeys were not a good sign!

The beginnings of conflict between my parents started in Atlantic City and brought us here to my grandmother's. The thought of moving never occurred to me. It was like I went to sleep in one bed and woke up in another. There was no chance to say goodbye. The good times by the ocean, the dock, the crabbing, the beach, the friends, the family, all changed in what seemed like an instant. I fear I developed regrets. The old faded away, and we entered a different time zone and a different planet.

The move showed a separation and not a planned move. We didn't wait for my father to find a new job. He stayed in New Jersey. My mother returned to her family. We didn't see my dad much and his name did not come up. Silence hung in the air. He became invisible. Maybe there were attempts at reconciliation and quiet discussions behind the scenes. On Howard Street, a life existed that didn't need my mother's other life. She joined her first family.

However, I felt lost with tangible grief. The perfect spell of wind and water broke, and the wind's resonance became out of tune. There were no more crabs to catch. The river faded away. A boat became unnecessary. I entered a period of dry exile. The anvil sparked.

My grandmother's house stood in the middle of a city of row homes. The block was a couple of streets down from Kensington Avenue and Front Street. This was so different from Venice Park. We weren't in Kansas anymore! Activity and motion filled Front Street. The elevated train called the "El", a silver bullet of a train, dominated the avenue. It regularly screeched and flew overhead, held up by large steel girders painted green. They looked like large spider legs. There were hoagie shops and grocery stores, barber shops and retail stores. A newspaper stand with newspapers and magazines from all places dominated the corner. The crowded street had people everywhere. They would double park their cars or trucks. People would be darting from side to side. Cars and trucks honked. The street moved and breathed.

From this hectic exterior, I retreated. Reading became my escape. I closed my life behind a wall of books. The neighborhood had a great public library. I would walk around the kid stacks in a daze and find gems of books. "Look, mom, I found a book about young space cadets. This one is about kids who live in a jungle with wild animals. I want to do that!" "Oh, Stevie!" Others were about classroom mischief and flying stories. On Howard Street, I entered World War I through the French Lafayette Escadrille. I flew those old planes in dogfights. The anvil sings its pleasure.

As a young boy, I was teased with a single volume of the Encyclopedia that my mother got perhaps from a traveling salesman. Rockets, maps, and exotic scenes populated the pages. We later got a set of Child craft books, orange covered volumes that brought the world to me, and spoke about things fantastic and distant. Those orange books enthralled me. They took me away, offered me hope.

With organ grinders on the loose, Philly had a unique character. I will always remember the corner grocery store that graced the neighborhood. It had wood chips on the floor and an enormous barrel with a plastic lid that contained the biggest pickles floating in it. The wide wooden planks would creek as you came in. A wood smell hit you at the door.

The street saw many sellers of items. A guy would come by during the summer shouting, "Iceberg Lettuce, Georgia Peaches, Fresh Strawberries!" His horse-drawn wagon contained bushels of veggies and fruit. The big brown horse had eye visors on. He told us, "Stay away from him, he gets ornery." My grandmother would go out and peruse his vegetables. An iceman in his horse-drawn wagon would visit regularly to offer us a large block of ice. An ice cream man came through in the afternoon. His white truck alerted us to all the marvelous treats he had inside his frozen bins. We weren't always allowed this great treat. But when we heard that truck, our hearts always jumped.

The Kent theater was just around the corner. With its tall marquee, the building represented a wonderful place of retreat and intrigue. My youngest aunt, Tonia, generously took us to the Saturday matinee. We watched western and science fiction movies at the theater, movies like, "Them" and "The Fly". My brothers would go from time to time. You could get in for a quarter. Add a bucket of popcorn and a drink and you were set! As the lights went down, another world took over.

The devil obviously had placed a small candy store in the neighborhood. It had a long glass display case of wonderful treats. The best thing about it, one could go in with an Indian head nickel and come out with candy. Whoa, that was a deal!

I had to walk down the block for sixth grade. Unfortunately, I recall several fights on the schoolyard over a disrespected girl or arrogant comments made. I never started them. My long arms defended me. But I enjoyed school. It felt like a retreat. It offered refuge and engaged me. I got decent grades. I had excellent reading skills. They would send me to another room, with a box of cards containing passages to read and questions to answer. Inquisitive, I showed good social skills and had friends. Once, I raced on a track and field day for my elementary school. In the city, there were tons of schools, so every small neighborhood had a school. My long legs allowed me to run fast. At this meet, I ran in several races and did pretty well, representing my school proudly.

We encountered little natural beauty in Philly. We often visited a concrete park with basketball courts not too far away. This became the testing site for a cheap rocket I got for my birthday. "Here, let's fill it with water, up to that line there. Now, we push this back and forth and put pressure on the water. Ready. I'm going to push the trigger. It should go really high. But we need to catch it. Ready?" Swoosh. Cape Canaveral, here we come!

Wooden tops also kept us entertained. We bought them at the grocery store. With some skill, the spinning top would crash on to another and thus knock it off its axis. Or you could crack the wood of the other top. We also played other games. We had balls, so we could play catch. Playing baseball didn't happen at all. There wasn't much green space. We didn't have bikes. But we entertained ourselves. However, Halloween was a tremendous time in Philly. There were millions of row homes to visit. We came home with grocery bags of candy piled high on the table! My future dentist thanked me.

In this neighborhood, a factory existed next store. They manufactured wood products. "Now Steve, take this bag and fill it with wood pieces. Go where I showed you. They'll let you in." The wood was for the furnace. I also took on the role of errand boy who, with a brief note from my grandmother, would retrieve items from the drugstore. My reward would be a quarter and I would go to the candy store to get candy. She gave me a quarter when teaching me to tie my shoes correctly. "Ok, let's try this again. Take this lace and make a little loop…" She had more patience with me than with my brothers. Not very expressive, the quarters were signs of her love. Chang.

The street grew quiet at night, save for the conversations of neighbors. They rolled out their aluminum chairs or sat on the marble stoops to talk, smoking cigarettes. The summer night air sat always heavy with heat and precipitation.

My grandmother had eclectic furniture. But, on tables and surfaces everywhere, there were doilies. By the window sat a black and white console TV with a rabbit ear antenna, and along the wall stood a long and low stereo record player cabinet. With doilies. My Aunt Tonia often fixed herself by the record cabinet, listening to Elvis or West Side Story.

The good-sized kitchen was probably the heart of the place. The ice box literally, a box with a top compartment used for the big translucent block of ice, stored the food. Later, they replaced it with an electric refrigerator. You got to the cellar via rickety death trap steps. The cellar contained the furnace. A coal bin by the front chute had dusty and black chunks of coal and wood about. "Yia Yia, I don't like that cellar. It's dark and smelly down there." I mention this because they would ask me to feed the red-hot furnace which I didn't like. I risked my life; the cellar was spooked!

The house had large windows, and let in lots of light. Going up the steep and creaky stairs, you faced an interesting, cold utility room. Inside stood a bed covered with boxes and clothing. A large, surprising picture of Mount Fuji in Japan dominated the wall. Like a fireplug in a desert, no one ever explained it. There were other bedrooms and a bathroom with a porcelain tub on feet grasping large glass balls. It felt like an old Victorian lady of a house.

Early on, lifting the lid of an opaque glass jar on the sink in the bathroom, I looked down, horrified to find a set of dentures staring up at me. I closed the lid quickly and vowed never to say anything about it for the rest of my life! I just broke my promise.

Now I have to say, this move brought us to the Mediterranean side of my life, our emotional, lively, loud Zorba the Greek heritage. On the living room wall in my grandmother's house were two black wooden masks, each the size of a large hand. One laughed, the other cried. These were good icons for the dichotomous emotions that I felt. Life could be carefree with my brothers, for instance. When they played cards at the house, laughter, frivolity and a lightness of spirit swept through the busy air. The family carried the pride of the Greeks. However, the other side of the Greek tragedy existed here as well. Uncomfortableness lurked in that house. Maybe the shadow of family secret and conflict sat under the veneer of lighthearted joy. Perhaps my mother's three sons awakened in Yia Yia the grief of her lost sons and lost husband. But this house centered on the family of sisters. The seating arrangement had few chairs for men. There was no room for my grief. No consolation existed there.

It must have been difficult for my grandmother to be accosted by three energetic kids. We were messy, loud, and obnoxious. But really, she wasn't very hospitable! She would lock my brothers and I in the back bedroom so she could get a little more peace in the morning. I read Gulliver's Travels with the door locked. I hardly cared as I read until late in the morning. My brothers played with their cars and trucks. "You can come out now. Be quiet!"

She would try to keep down our rowdy natures. "You boys, stop it right now. Put that blanket back on the bed and stop riding down the steps. You are making too much noise. I need some peace this morning, please!" Who knows what other commotion we created? How many balls got tossed around her living room? What of the snow tracked on her clean floors? How many doilies misplaced?

Contrary to my contrite sense of loss, that house saw a loud and energetic life! It could dance! There were always visitors. A celebrity of sorts named Pedro visited from time to time. He worked as a dressmaker and had probably rich and famous clients. Handsome and apparently rich, he came from Columbia, the old country. My brother later surmised that he was gay. Great laughter and commotion erupted when he visited. "Ah, Teddy, my dear, how have you been? You look wonderful. And where are your beautiful girls? How is Joyce?" he would ask. "I bet Renee is still a troublemaker! Dear, I can only stay a little while; I have business in New York." "Here, sit, please sit. Tonia, get Pedro something to drink. Are you hungry? I will make you a wonderful Greek dinner. Tell me how is business? Pedro, dear, you are so charming, handsome as always," she would say. "Teddy, you are beautiful and gracious, my sweet. It is so nice to see you. I love to catch up with you." There were other family friends and neighbors who visited. As well, my aunts were often around. Tonia lived there in her late teens when we moved in. The family of my grandmother's sister, Aunt Francis, would visit. My mother's close cousin, Aunt Artie, the daughter of Margaro, visited with her many kids. Other Greek relatives would occasionally come around.

A distraction for me, and a delight for Yia Yia were big meals. Like all Greeks I assumed, she cooked well and loved to feed people. Several neighbors would often come over and have dinner. The food was always plentiful. My mom, Aunt Joyce, and Aunt Tonia would be around and help. They would grace the dinner table with wine and Greek salad. Deviled eggs, meatballs, a green bean casserole and onion strings, or a dish of sliced baked potatoes in a white sauce appeared. Wonderful pastries of lemon squares or other pastries my grandmother made would await the end. I loved baklava with nuts. Kourabiethes satisfied my sweet tooth. They passed around small delicate glasses of wine or the Greek licorice tasting ouzo. Laughter and conversation would then get loud. We kids would be at a small table. "Oh, this is so tasty! She makes the best baklava, doesn't she?" "Where did you find these tomatoes? I have been looking for days." "These potatoes are just delicious! Smell the cheese." "Teddy, I love that pin, dear. How long have you had it?" "I bought it in Reading, years ago." Chatter and laughter usually prevailed. There would be talk about the family always, such as, "I spoke with Aunt Francis and she said Uncle Tom hurt his back last week". "Oh dear, what happened?" "Artie called and Paulie is going into kindergarten this year. Do you believe it?" "Tonia, are you dating anyone, dear?"

After the dinner, after dishes, the card ritual would start. Foursomes spontaneously organized and decks of cards were found in the drawer. The atmosphere changed. This activity occurred as a fun thing, yet it was serious. There were egos on the line. Small talk would abound, but also loud statements like, "There, I knew you had the Ace!" "Why didn't you play the 10 of hearts?" or, worst of all, "You reneged. You reneged, how awful!" My grandmother would be the queen of the table. She had a poker face and took delight in winning. This would go on for hours.

They often played Canasta, but pinochle was the favorite. We were all taught to play. In every drawer of the house, there sat a deck of cards or two. If a thief came in the night to rob the house, they would find only decks of cards where ever they looked. My grandmother played with a strong, competitive attitude. If you made a mistake, expect no mercy. She made me nervous. You didn't want to cross her. She was hard-nosed and used guilt very well. She yelled little, using her quiet voice to great effect. "Stevie, now didn't you see me play the 10? Show me your hand. You were supposed to play the jack! Pay attention." And looking sternly, "Now, watch what we are doing!" I half waited for her to pull out a gun and shoot holes in the ceiling! As the evening would close early for us kids, we would go around to everyone and either give them a kiss or shake hands. But the laughter and conversation would waft up the steps for a while after we went to bed. Sparks from the anvil illuminated the night.

I don't think that Joyce liked cards that much. She was younger than Aunt Renee and looked a little like Elizabeth Taylor. Usually, she wore a lot of makeup. She had a mole by the side of her mouth that added to her intrigue. Her hair was always nicely done. She had fashionable clothes. Aunt Joyce called me "honey" and "darling" often. She didn't have the confidence that Aunt Renee had, but she exhibited generosity and warmth. Joyce later married Uncle John, a friendly but quiet, bespectacled computer expert with a pen protector in his pocket.

Aunt Renee, who visited occasionally, had that volatile temperament. She reacted quickly, loudly and usually with a forceful presence. The tallest of the sisters and also the most physical, she always had a hug. She scared my brothers. I would later stay briefly with her and Uncle Al in Atlantic City.

Aunt Tonia was the youngest. In her late teens, when we moved in, her youth brought her energy. Often with her friends, she didn't stay around much. Maybe she worked. One time, we went down to the docks in Philly by the Delaware Bay. Tonia had met a Greek sailor on a merchant ship docked at the port. "Mom, can we go on that boat?" "Yes, we are gonna meet a friend of Tonia's." "Wow, it is big!" Painted a rusty white, we walked through the cargo ship's open doorways. They had a chain across some of them to keep you from falling into the water. I recall he might want to stay in America to be with her. She later married Uncle Don. She became my favorite aunt as time went on.

One kid thing we discovered in a box at the house was an old Lionel train set. We readily played with it and it became special. It had a large transformer with wires that ran to the tracks. The tracks made an oval pattern. The train had a black locomotive, a coal car behind it, a flat car with barrels, a boxcar, and a caboose. We set it up around Christmas time around the tree. It added to the wonderful occasion that gave warmth and joy to the place. This train eventually gave way to an HO set that had rockets that could shoot the box car and make it explode with a plastic thud.

Speaking of Christmas, my grandmother and my mother loved tinsel on Christmas trees. They used a copious amount. When they took down the tree, a trail of it went out the door. You could see it reflected across the street and down the block. Of course, they accumulated boxes of old ornaments. The house looked special during the holidays. The anvil smiles in sparks.

I have to admit my sin during Christmas. I knew where they hid the gifts! They hid toys in the closet in the middle room. I got them down a couple of times when the adults left the house. I looked surprised when we opened them up. But I already knew!

During this time, my religious faith grew. God was on my mind and I felt his presence in my life. I still had my Venice Park Bible. An old Greek crucifix adorned the wall. The transcendent had a place in my family and in myself. My mother prayed often with us at night. "Now I lay me down to sleep…" My grandmother had a faith tied up with her ethnic background. We were proudly Greek Orthodox. The Greek church, St. George, loomed large with marble steps and columns downtown on Spruce Street. We went usually at Easter and Christmas. Often, we would see several members of the Greek side of the family. The beautiful church had ornate icons behind which stood the almost hidden altar. The priests loved chanting and incense. Lasting a long time, the service comprised of standing, sitting and kneeling, guided by an annoying red light above the altar.

"Mom, Freddie from school, wants me to go to a program at his church. Can I go?" My mom said I could go. At the tall church, "Children, there is a beautiful story about a Good Samaritan in the Bible. This tells us Jesus wants us to help others." I enjoyed the program. However, my grandmother reacted unhappily. She pointed out that I was Greek Orthodox, baptized and confirmed. Open to God, I wanted to learn more. But for her, God spoke Greek. My only involvement with Sunday School at the Greek church occurred when my mother took me to enroll. I sat downstairs while she met with the priest. After a while, she came back, and we left. "Are we done, mom?" "Yes, there are only girls in that class. That won't work!" So much for learning Greek! Gong.

Around Easter, we endured a yearly ritual. For Lent, we fasted in a progressive manner. Each week, they would eliminate a new food group from our diet. It got tougher as it went. By the time Easter came around, we were starving, ready to die, having only bread and water that last week!

At my grandmother's, an odd experience occurred that perhaps contributed to my choice of psychology as a career. One day, my grandmother told me about the troubled daughter of a friend she knew. She said, "Steve, here, talk with Esther." And handed me the phone. The childish voice said, "Hi," then rattled off a list of experiences. "Today I helped my mommy make the bed, and I saw a bug on the floor and oh, I got scared and ran into the bathroom. Oh, my. I have a lot of homework to do, my books are so heavy! It is raining, I'm not scared of the thunder but it is so loud…" For several months, I engaged in a stream-of-consciousness conversation with Esther. I mostly listened and made conversation where I could. She had only a few friends, they told me. I guess I was one of them! Maybe here I began doing therapy!

Adding to my blossoming awareness, my brother Nicky's neurodivergent limitations became clearer to me. No one outwardly acknowledged his issues. They dressed him and Tony the same. Nick developed a "lazy eye" and needed a patch on his glasses. "Nicky, wear your glasses with the patch. I will not tell you again. Don't take them off" scolded Yia Yia! One time they put pepper on his tongue as punishment. He cried. For me, I felt pity for my special needs brother. I recognized that voice of criticism and judgment. Observing and listening to these unfiltered adults around me, I learned lessons about control and power as they revealed themselves unintentionally! Hot metal, usefully shaped and forged!

Really, my grandmother's generosity allowed us to stay with her. It lasted probably only a couple of years, but it still meant a big change for her. Did she enjoy having her eldest daughter around? Did she like us kids under foot? Probably not. I bet there were whispers, "those damn kids!"

At grandmom's house, a culture chattered away, gossiped and glibly conversed. A planet of predictable social interaction flowed with little care for its young dazed inhabitants. We were left to join the drama we barely understood. My brothers and I felt like outsiders, the wrong gender, the wrong age. We had intruded at a bad time. My grandmother's house embraced an inside life. My brother Tony told me he didn't enjoy living with grandma in Philly. It felt they barely tolerated us.

Philly offered me glimpses of a family, mainly of women, whose way of relationship differed from doing things with my father. There was a lot of talk. They directed little of it to us. The identity of this place, the mark of it, involved a meal's conversation and a card game's voice. My brothers and I felt estranged. We made up a late addendum. Our mom did not serve us well because she seamlessly joined her family and we lost her. She took her place in the conversation and it seemed she receded into the background. Perhaps this was her unobtrusive and passive personality. Maybe it repeated the action of years ago when she gave up her daughter. She gave us up, and we became the children of all the adults in the room and, really, sons of none. I felt unsettled and anxious. I felt the need for self-protection. My guard was up. We were foreigners in exile. I didn't quite unpack all my clothes. My silent, inner sense of reality, however, despaired. These were not really my people. My allegiances and interests rested elsewhere.

Another truth here: I had sailors on both sides and I missed contact with the water. Emotionally, these were land locked and dry times. My grandmother and mother spoke Greek when they didn't want us to know what they were saying. This experience taught me about the secretive lives of adults. We were castaways. It didn't fulfill my need for the open water.

For me, my emerging masculinity suffered. I felt I wasn't the preferred gender. As I learned the entire story much later, they probably did not trust masculinity and sought to control it. This really stood as a family of women with their judgments and their sensitivities. None of these women probably knew how to throw a ball. The identity of my Greek family said they were carefree, successful and blameless. Maybe this was a subtle way to denigrate my father, or maybe all men. As a child, my God-mother gave me a male doll of a Greek soldier. He had a red beret with a tassel. It represented a mannish doll. Coming from a different world, it spoke to my distant and foreign heritage. In a schizophrenic way, a part of me was a Greek from Philly. Yet I identified more with House, not Stavros! I got fed here, but felt out of balance and vulnerable. The integrity of my self felt at risk. But then, I was only a kid and what the hell did I know?

School, however, represented heaven. But first let me take you to purgatory. I sat on the floor in my white tee shirt and my blue gym shorts. There above my head lay the nemesis of my current life, the rope. I might as well hang myself with it! It dangled in my lap. The task required pulling yourself up by your arms and climbing the 30 feet to the ceiling, closer to heaven than to earth! This took place in the gym of mighty John Paul Jones Jr. High.

The ropes in the gym were there in groups of 8 in a row, dangling not completely to the ground but several inches off it. Fat chance of me ever accomplishing that Olympic feat! My hand wrapped around the thick and fibrous rope. I took a breath and pulled up. My arms were getting higher, but my body stayed on the floor. How many times did I begin up the rope with enthusiasm and confidence, only to be thwarted by my muscle memory that said, "No way, Jose!" The bat whiffed after the catcher caught the ball already, again. It gave me a bad complex about my scrawny chest and arms. No one would see me without a tee shirt.

We had to bring gym clothes for the weekly class. On other weeks we had health class where we saw pictures of our sexual parts, which always drew a comment from the back. They divided us, however, by sex in health class. I felt troubled by health class information. I worried about being skinny. My father had told us about the time that he had a tapeworm. I thought maybe I had one!

A change in me began around this time. Family life got lowered down the list of priorities. I had lost a strong relationship with my father. This caused me to withdraw from mom and her family. My 11-year-old understanding took a more oppositional stance. Outwardly, I cooperated and did what I was told. But I made a judgment deep and severe. I did not speak it, and I did not take any action. Nothing really changed, but I lost interest in their inside games. My heart hardened. My shame told me that some was my fault.

In my state of mind, frankly, I could have run away, although I had nowhere to go. Also, I couldn't leave my brothers. Maybe this was the same impulse that led me to follow my father's car as he left for work. My connection with my mother was not as strong. I guess I am sad to admit this, but she didn't feel as present. She loved us and we loved her, but she had a paralysis.

In school, I prospered. At lunch, at school, "Albert, are you ready for the math test?" "Did you study?" "Ah, yes, I did. For ten minutes!" I said. The lunch room was loud with talk. "I hate it when we have to climb the ropes. I can't do it." "It's torture," said Robert, "child abuse. Goes against the Geneva Convention." "What?" I shook my head. "How's your brother? You said he broke his glasses." "He's ok. But we don't like living with my grandmother. My dad's not around. It's boring." "You should come live at my house. My dad yells all the time!" "We used to go crabbing in Atlantic City. I really miss that." I admitted. "Beats Ma Jones and her math tests!" Robert added.

Over Jr. High, I matured and grew several inches in height. But as far as muscles go, no progress. While being tall and very skinny, I made up for it with running speed. I could move. An embarrassment, and this is a deep, dark secret, in Junior High, my probably erratic gyrations earned the nickname, "Wiggles". My manly proportions did not result in any female interest, however. So, I had to make up for my physical lack with humor and personality.

We had to take a language, so I signed up for Spanish class. Maybe I had long legs or maybe the class seats were small. Regardless, in Spanish class, I sat in the front and my feet hung out in the aisle. Next to me sat a black kid who had a similar problem. We became the class's comic duo.

There were plenty of opportunities to make sly remarks or utter a verbal grimace or complaint. The rest of the class, except for maybe a nerd or two, were very willing to be entertained. They voiced their pleasure commensurate with the degree of the joke. "I have the results of the writing assignment. Some of you need improvement," said the teacher. "Sammy, she's talking about you!" Laughter just warmed your heart. However, you shouldn't make fun of the teacher. I usually had a good rapport with my teachers. Miss Pigeon had taught me well. But the mishaps and failures of other students were open game. One time, while passing out papers, a student tripped and dropped papers that flew up in the air and landed on my friend's outspoken legs in the aisle. Everyone saw it. "That plane is having trouble on its approach!" "Whoa, where did that foot come from?" "Yeah, be careful, Godzilla is crashing down," narrated the event. Of course, our humor had an experimental quality. Like doing stand-up, we honed our timing and material, but we didn't always hit pay dirt. We tried often enough to get a rise, and we were successful. Except for my 8th grade Spanish teacher. Unimpressed, he wound up throwing an actual book at the class in frustration. Tad a tad.

On other occasions, a very embarrassing thing happened. Every teenage boy has gone through this experience. "Senior House, can you write the Spanish words that go with the table setting pictures, por favor?" However, my resistance focused on the thing that happened just prior to being asked. As my body often did, without my permission or agreement, I would become sexually aroused! Now, no sexual ruminations caused it. I was thinking about dinner plates! Why did my body do what it wanted suddenly and without permission? So, I did what a red-blooded American teen would do. "Ah…let me think…which ones again?" I fumbled for an invisible shield! I looked at the students sitting next to me and down on the floor, doing my best to make invisible what had become a colossal problem. "Por favor, here is the chalk." More sternly. I slowly got up and went to the board in such a fashion that no one saw the front of me. But as I wrote the words to the displayed items, my activation receded, but not so my embarrassment.

An important place at Jones was the large school auditorium that could hold all the classes. We had general assemblies during the school year where the principal would speak or there would be a program. At night, we had musical performances and plays. This location opened up my life as I happened upon a surefire way to succeed. I just stumbled into it, really. *I became a part of the drama club.* This resonated with me. My life contained acting, and this felt like a natural activity.

With about ten other students, we were the core characters in the English department plays. Our English teacher was Mrs. Ulrich, a wonderful, sensitive and supportive teacher. "Now, students, today, your job is to write free verse poetry centered on your favorite object. Take a breath and let your mind open!"

<u>It's lost</u>
So, wish you may

(And yell all you want)
It's lost
Kites don't listen to people
When the wind calls

One of the lasting effects of Mrs. Ulrich was being on the school paper staff and writing poetry. And this went on for most of my life. Thank you, Mrs. Ulrich! I proudly took my place on the staff of the "Jones Jr. Journal".

Many in my section took part in the drama club and the journal. We did several plays in 8th and 9th grade. I did fairly well at rehearsals. It came naturally to me to play a role and to be expressive. However, I didn't remember my lines well. In one play, we tried to solve a murder mystery, "Mr. Sullivan, do you have any clues as to the identity of the murderer of Mrs. Noble?" A pause while I tried to remember a clue. I had no clue! "Ah.." I was supposed to speak. "Mr. Sullivan, do you have any…" "Yes, I do…have a clue." Laughter from the audience. My anxiety is up. "I found some …rope in the closet and… a knife, a knife in the sink, which I think the killer used. My instinct tells me it was probably someone in the family. Someone in this very room!" My fellow actors are looking bewildered but trying to play along. It became improv! The teacher kneeled on the side, behind the curtain, frantically motioning us and trying to give us our lines to say. This play must have turned out ok, however. We found the killer, and we were all allowed to continue to the next production. But also, when we began the next play, as we entered the stage, people applauded and whistled. We were entertaining. Gongs to that.

One time I was upset because my father said he would come and watch the play. However, he didn't show up. For one play, I brought in several of his medals from the war. My role was as a general. I had a metal helmet that didn't fit very well. It kept sliding down on my face. I, of course, made the most of it and hammed it up. At the pinnacle of my career, I played Abraham Lincoln. At the end, I got shot in Ford's Theater. The last performance, I died and fell beyond the front edge of the curtain. As the curtain came down, I had to be dragged back behind it. Our drama troupe served as the comic relief for the school. Like Bob Hope, we entertained the troops!

Junior High taught me a great deal about social skills. If one could succeed at making friends, that spoke well of intellectual and emotional balance. Going down the hall, "Hey, Wiggles." "I told you Sammy not to call me that." "Hah!" Walking, "Alice, I swear to you, he's lying, I didn't say that." "I don't know. It was mean to say." Before class, "Did you ask your mom about coming over?" "She said ok!" "See ya after school on the playground." Making friendships with classmates stood as a test of one's communication and social maturation. I came into my own and grew in confidence and social competence. I felt a grounding of my person. For me, the three years at the school honed my social skills.

The culture of the school was an interesting blend of personalities, race, and gender. Our class had several Hispanic kids and several black kids. A couple of kids were Jewish. We had kids with Italian heritage, Polish, and, of course, Greek. It created an interesting soup for people. Flossy Drake, for one, had a colorful personality. We hung out a lot but never were really boyfriend and girlfriend. She would connect with me on Face book years later. I loved Alice Reyes, a top student in my class. "Alice, your handwriting is beautiful compared to mine." "Thanks, Steven." Smart and pretty, we had a special connection. She took part in the Journal staff and shared my section all three years. In 9th grade, the American Legion gave an award for the outstanding student of our class. It was a heavy bronze medallion. That year, she and I shared the honor. She would appear later in my life in a hard moment.

While school was the most important time of the day, things continued to happen at home. Aunt Tonia got married about this time. I have no recollection of the wedding. I am sorry about that! Her husband, Don de Paul, worked as a high school English teacher. Over the years, they traveled, which gave them fascinating stories about India and Greece.

Uncle Don and I had a good relationship. He showed interest in me. At their house one time, "Hey, before you go, I have something for you." Out came a metal framed amplifier with tubes, a cord and a big transformer. "Here, plug in this mic and attach the speaker wires here. It will amplify what you say!". He gave me a small black plastic mic attached to a round metal band that fit on your head. Quite 1943! This added to a long line of electronics I would dabble in. It included the train set transformer, the crystal radio, later, an electric guitar amp, a reel-to-reel tape recorder, turntables and speakers and eventually computers. As a teen, I bought a Heath kit radio receiver which required that you solder the many parts together. Much later, I put together a recording studio in my basement. My dad had his helicopters. I had my amateur degree in electronics! Tat, tat.

Later, Uncle Don wrote a book called "Caterfly" a book about discovery and development. That affected me and made real the idea of writing books. I saw Aunt Tonia as my favorite aunt. Later years, of course, would see the relationship change in significant ways.

I am proud to say, at one point, I worked for my uncle. His Italian parents had a bakery up north. Going with him, we walked through the neighborhood close to the bakery and knocked on doors. "Hi, I'm with the de Paul Bakery, and we are taking orders for donuts to be delivered on Sunday morning. Could we bring a dozen warm donuts to you? Let me show you what we have." We would deliver donuts the next morning. This went on for a summer. I don't recall if I got paid or just ate my profits!

Happily, we eventually left my grandmother's and moved down the block. I am not sure of the circumstances of the move, but our father soon moved in with us. That overjoyed me. This small row home had a large front window. It probably had served as a store. Having been burned before, I cautiously held my breath.

A significant item I put in the display window of our new home fascinated me. The small glass bulb was called a Crookes Radiometer. When the sun shone on it, the inner colored flags would rotate at increasing speed. I had to have one. The shiny front window served as a good place for it. Also, I displayed my plastic models and a cactus plant in the window. This continued my long running love of plants started by the long dead plant I won at the spelling bee.

One of my early religious experiences occurred here. Lying in my bed in the dark room, one night I woke up. I looked up and by the doorway stood a shadowy figure. I didn't see a face or much more that an outline of a figure. The figure raised his hands, and I felt energy being directed toward me. I wasn't sure the identity of the person, but I thought it could be God standing there. During this vague experience, I felt unsure whether a blessing or a curse had occurred. This vague event was really a blessing. My parents were together and would never again separate. My religious experience would support a continuing interest and faith in God. That moment in bed stayed with me.

After a while, my parents planned a move to a neighborhood further north. This left us excited and hopeful. But secretly, I expected the worst to happen. I learned to get through tough circumstances with a strong persistence and a quiet resolve. Probably God's grace helped. But catastrophe always loomed a possibility.

We moved in 8th grade. I remained at Jones and took the El back and forth. In 1964, I rode the train to junior high and passed over a Ford dealership. There were several of the new Mustangs only 30 feet below. I felt ecstatic!

I am glad I stayed at Jones. It supported and carried me at a tough time. Simply, the place saved my life. I would have suffocated without it. Those years were powerful for me. My confidence and skill in relationships increased. I learned to be in front of people with little anxiety. It was fun to make people laugh. I wrote poetry and expressed experiences and feelings in writing. I did not leave them to fester into worse fantasies or fears. I realized I had a powerful spirit. Here I came into my own. This time showed my tendency to think, my ability to feel, my comfort to perceive, and my gift to believe. Of course, I still didn't have any arm strength!

<u>Give rise to new beginnings!</u>

Give rise to new beginnings!
Let loose the chains of past mortality with its anchored being and cloistered experience
This day is like no other
This breath felt never before
Do not mistake me for another
You do not know me
But if you open your eyes, I shall greet you with a kiss as sweet as any you have tasted
I am the chariot that rides to a new day
I am the source where the river leaves the soil
For the first time, rise and greet the new day
I am the glimpse of tomorrow's sun

5 Dyre Street

My friend asked, "Woah, what is that?" "I don't know what you call it, but watch this!" I sat down on it. In a matter of seconds, like Evel Knievel, I was speeding down the long hill on Duffield Street, coming down from Wakeling street. Here before you stood the testing facility of the Philly Skateboard, an invention I swear, we developed on our street. Taking the front of an old dresser drawer, I nailed old roller skates to the underside. I took my speedy vehicle and at first, sat on it going downhill. It took balance for sure. However, I could get moving fairly fast. I just had to watch for cars! Only after more practice could I stand up on it. After a while, the entire neighborhood had them. I reacted with shock recently as I found out that several men friends thought they had invented the skateboard!

With great anticipation, we moved to the corner house at Dyre and Duffield Streets. This was the first time I knew when we were moving. The brick building had two stories with an attic. A roofed in porch and several wooden steps invited you to the front door. The street side wall, down the house, extended without windows till a dormer of sorts on the second floor bulged out. The small backyard had a tall holly tree. For one season, we remarkably had an owl in the holly tree.

The block of Dyre Street had maybe 10 other row houses on either side. There were plenty of kids. On our side of the street were the Serfasses, the Flaglers, and the Koenigs. On the other side of the street were the Congelosi family with their 5 or 6 kids. Across Duffield were several couples without kids. On the opposite corner were the Schmidts, an older, cranky German couple.

The first time my father took me to the house, we took the El from Kensington. Although he forgot the key, seeing it thrilled me. "Oh, dad, this place is great. There seem to be kids all over the place!" The excitement of a new neighborhood and a new beginning overwhelmed me. It was still Philadelphia, so close by stood many stores, an elementary school, and a church. The elevated train was nearby. The area percolated like Kensington. A big Penn Fruit grocery store fed the neighborhood, with its 20-foot tall, half-moon front window. At Pratt and Frankford were buses and trolleys extending to the northeast, and the last stop of the El. Like a river full of beavers, the block was always busy with people. Nearby was a grassy park with concrete basketball courts. These courts saw many furious basketball battles. It represented our NBA.

We moved to Dyre Street uneventfully. My parents didn't have a lot of stuff. The house was nicely painted. We were excited to be there. The place took us away from grandmom and the emotional heaviness of Howard Street. Sound the anvil!

Even though we moved into a new place, I continued to go to Jones Jr. High. Now an 8th grader, I had been going on 2 years on the staff of the Journal and in the drama club. I would say I felt pretty good about myself. What also continued were the Kensington friendships. Flossy Drake and several of the gang of friends came up to Dyre Street. We continued to visit my grandmother, especially on holidays. She eventually moved in with my Aunt Joyce and left Howard Street.

One of the earliest experiences I had at Dyre Street occurred in November 1963. A day after my birthday, leaving school and walking to the train, a tall guy walking by told me, "Did you hear Kennedy was shot in Dallas today? It's terrible!" I just looked at him and shook my head slightly. On the train, others were talking quietly about Texas. When I got home, my mother sat on the couch with the TV on, looking troubled. I felt suddenly unstable. Our class went down town one time to hear Kennedy speak. We didn't get very close but could hear him. The broadcasted scenes felt like a gut punch. The day became a very sad one. Oswald's blatant killing and the funeral scenes led to a loss of trust in the world. Coming from work, my father appeared saddened and said, "I don't know what this means, but we are in serious trouble." He now worked for Boeing in South Philly, a company that built flying machines. It fit him.

After the initial upheaval, however, things took on a rhythm at the house. There were plenty of kids to play with. My brothers went to a school down the street. Nicky did and said unusual things. He played with us all, but he stood out as a little out of step. Everyone accepted him and did not criticize or make fun of him, at least as far as I knew. He didn't have good eye hand coordination, but he tried. While my brothers had worn identical clothes, that now stopped.

Through Flossy Drake, I met a girl with whom I would have a two-year relationship. It isn't what you think, hearing that statement. Maybe we kissed once or twice. However, over the course of a couple of years, I sent Judy Wilder probably 50 letters. She lived in Florida but stayed in Philly with her grandmother for a part of the summer. I am not sure what energized the relationship. We shared the song "Wild Thing". She would sign her letters, "Love Judy, Wild Thing". The relationship by most standards was much less than "wild". I guess at that age, to be truthful, I was practicing how to be a boyfriend. But the letters were genuine. They comprised a sort of journal that included things that were happening, complaints, feelings, and experiences. We were more than pen pals. For two summers, we got together and would sit on her steps or walk around the neighborhood and talk. We were trying on a safe and innocent relationship.

At one point, my father managed a softball team through the Little Brown Jug, a bar he frequented. I would go with him sometimes and watch the games. One time, I was in trouble with my mom. However, she let me go with my father to the game. It was near where Judy stayed and so my father allowed me to visit her while the game went on. My father didn't go against my mom, but he bent the rules.

The relationship ended with Judy the second summer when I found out that she liked an older guy. I lost track of the letters. The last time I saw them, I tied them up in a bundle and safely kept in a box. Going off to college, the box unfortunately disappeared. I would love to read those letters or maybe not. The anvil respects lessons learned.

As I liked to build plastic models, I found a nice hobby store next to the bank. A yellow Mustang model caught my eye. I was called to a large plywood slot car track in the basement. Slot cars were small, motorized vehicles that ran on a grooved track. They were fast and primed to race. This track had about 8 separate lanes. It cost for time on the track. It wasn't quite Andretti level racing, but it was fun. The air in the basement smelled electric, burned rubber and old burned newspapers. It went with the random, sparking sound of the cars on the track.

This brought out, of course, all the questions about mechanics and speed. A good bit of allowance money went to buying time and spending it on cars. "Hey, kid, I like that dragster you have. It is boss looking!" It was my second-place car. This car moved respectably fast, not quite the track's fastest. I kept my stuff in a shoe box, identified with an electric, lighting arrow.

Another toy would engage my imagination. For my birthday, I received a plastic Stuka Dive Bomber with a small gas motor. They called it a line control airplane. You stood in the center of a circle and controlled how high or low the plane went. The gas engine started with a battery. It looked great. I hardly flew the plane, however, because I would get dizzy turning in circles. Maybe twice around and I felt the need to sit down. The sound and the feel of it excited me. I felt connected in a small and distant way to the flying machines I heard about as a kid.

The story of Dyre Street cannot be told without reference to the mighty invention of the pimple ball. The pimple ball is a rubberized ball made of two spheres fused together. These gems were readily available at the local grocery store. Because of our common genius, we played many kinds of pimple ball.

One variation was a five-on-five game of stickball. Our diamond was the street intersection. Stick ball, also called box ball, required a pimple ball and a broom handle for a bat. With a pitcher and a couple of basemen, you had a team for stick ball. After a while, a pimple ball would get ripped along the seam and become a half ball. Thus, we would have two halves. This afforded greater ball movement by the pitcher and made it perhaps harder to hit. But it didn't go as well in the air.

Wire ball involved hitting the wires above our heads. The game involved only two players and required accuracy and skill. Now, if the ball hit the wire and you did not catch the ball, it gave you a man on. A hit wire and a missed catch with bases loaded, of course, made it a grand slam. The harder you threw it, the further the ball would deviate from straight up and down.

Now step ball involved hitting the ball against the front steps while the other person tried to catch it. If you hit the corner of the step, the ball could really go a respectful distance. If you missed the outward corner and bounced on the top or against the back of the step, you got little distance and you were easily out.

Finally, on the enormous brick wall, we played wall ball and ass ball. Wall ball is self-explanatory. You got a little running start and threw the ball up against the wall as hard as you could. A variant, ass ball, did not make up our most genteel sport. Your opponent would line up with their head crouched down against the wall, hands and rear exposed. You had to use a full pimple ball. At 15 feet away, you hurled this rubberized rocket at your opponent and tried to hit their innocent body. The more you made contact, the more you would win. To win, you had to be accurate. It, of course, didn't help our love of neighbor! Sometimes tempers flared a little.

Ball
Wall ball
Box ball
Wire ball
Step ball
Ass ball
Half ball
Stick ball
These were my friends growing up
And I miss their
Conversation

A few months during the summer of 1964 would be a significant time for me. I stayed with my Aunt Renee in Atlantic City to help watch her kids. As I have mentioned, she had three children. Alfred, Mark and Vicky were probably under 9. They were a handful. This created a problem because their mom liked control and peace. My aunt yelled often and intensely. It made me feel uncomfortable. I felt she cared for me, but her volatility created stress. Uncle Al and Aunt Renee both worked and so I watched kids for periods of the day. Uncle Al had a weird schedule as a firefighter. Aunt Renee worked part time. There would be things to do and a schedule to follow. We would take walks with the dog. Dealing with the kids seemed like herding cats. They were not mean, but they did argue with each other. They listened to me.

I have spoken to you about my skinny chest. My aunt wanted to put meat on my bones, so she put wheat germ on everything I ate! She sprinkled wheat germ in soup, on eggs, in spaghetti sauce and on hamburgers. I came to hate it. It did not result in weight gain. I remained a tall, skinny chested kid.

One day, while cooking breakfast for the kids, "Oh my God, the stove is on fire! Afred, Mark, Vicky, we got to get out." I blamed the greasy stove. But I have to take a portion of blame; my cooking started it. Regardless, the kids got out safely and we called the fire department from a neighbor's phone. My aunt came home upset with me. She said, "You should have let the house burn down." I thought it ironic that a firefighter's house should catch on fire.

As background, in the summer of 1964, the Democratic National Convention took place in the Atlantic City Convention Center. The Miss America pageant occurred in Atlantic City for years, centered at the Convention Center. My uncle had the enviable job of driving Miss America contestants around town in a convertible as they did their wavy hand greeting to all they saw.

This day, I intersected with history. Taking the dog for a walk, I walked by an airfield called Bader Field. A plane landed when I walked close to the field. Several men came to the gate where I walked. Several people had gathered. One man told me clearly and tersely to "hold on to that dog, son". "Yes, sir," I replied. Suddenly, an entourage came to the gate from the plane. A moment later, the President of the United States, Lyndon B. Johnson, walked by! He shook my hand and several others and then hurried to a waiting car. Me and the dog were stunned!

The ultimate coup de grâce over the summer of '64 would happen next. My uncle had connections in town. Shortly before leaving to go back to Philly, Aunt Renee gave me an envelope and said, "You have really helped us out this summer. We want you to have this as our appreciation." I thought I came there to gain weight! I opened it up. Inside was a ticket to the Beatles Concert at the Convention Center. On their Hard Day's Night Tour, I was going to be there! More than surprised, I felt numb. Whatever difficulty the wheat germ had posed, whatever hardship corralling three energetic kids had proved, whatever anxiety the yelling had provoked, whatever trauma burning down the house had instilled, the ticket wiped all the injustice away. I would attend the Beatles concert and sit 10 rows back! A big gong!

The evening of the concert is burned into my memory. After being dropped off, I found my seat as the place filled. I sat near the center. The screaming started even before the performances began. The Righteous Brothers opened the show no less! Their music blew me away. They sang, "Unchained Melody" and it lifted me. They became my favorites on the spot.

After a pause, as the screaming continued, out they came, four figures in gray suits and long hair, smiling and waving to the crowd. The noise from the crowd almost drowned out the music. Paul appeared with his left-handed bass. John came out with his big Rickenbacker guitar. George took his place in the middle. Ringo got on his skins, and smiling broadly, twirled his stick between his fingers. The bass drum convinced me this wasn't a dream, but I saw the honest to God, real thing. The Beatles. They did their set to the screaming crowd. A Hard Day's Night. Can't Buy Me Love. And I Love Her. They talked in between songs, but you couldn't hear them. Their encore was the iconic "She Loves You". They waved, bowed, unplugged their guitars. And then they were gone. I had been in the presence of greatness; I felt out of my body. At 13, I witnessed greatness. The summer of '64. There is a song in that. Symbol crash. Sparks abound.

Going back to Philly and engaging in my ordinary existence felt like a task. My status was like a minor celebrity, for I was in the same room as the Beatles! I used my fame and supplied girls with Beatle magazines I bought at the newsstand. I even showed off my ticket.

Inspired by the Beatles, I had to learn to play the guitar. I clarified my vague aspirations. A musical career now seriously presented itself. My parents bought me a cheap guitar and gave me lessons at a local music store. This truly started a skill set that would bring me great joy over the course of my life. Fortuitously, I met Johnny Flagler, a kid down the block, who also had an interest in playing guitar. One night at his house, "Hey, Johnny. Let's write a song! Just like Lennon and McCartney! I got an idea. How about, let's call it, Angie? This boy loves this girl, but she doesn't care." I came up with the melody and we were in the music business! While I was attracted to the possibility of writing another "I Want to Hold your Hand", nobody told me that my fingers would hurt building up calluses from the strings! My musical interests expanded, and I started listening to the Beach Boys. We listened to the radio and the WIBG station, Top Forty. I fell for the Four Tops and that Motown Sound. Also, I got into Bob Dylan and Peter, Paul and Mary, Dave Von Ronk, John Prine, the Band. I enjoyed the story tellers with passionate voices. Great rhythms also grabbed my attention. My guitar work always had a more percussive and rhythmic quality. The acoustic suited me well.

Music invaded my life. Chuck Serfass asked me to go on a trip with his family. Chuck lived next door, a kid who was a day older and about 40 pounds heavier. We would go to his backyard and play a variation of football called, "I need the practice and you, Stevie, are a skinny kid, so let me tackle you to the ground." On the trip, we went to a park. Well, we drove in their station wagon with the back window that rolled down. It felt like old times. He and I sat in the back and sang, "Satisfaction" by the Rolling Stones for however long the trip took. "I can't get no satisfaction" hummed on the highway that day!

My band days had also begun! The best band included a wonderful drummer named Joe Burns, Johnny Flagler and I. Joe looked like James Dean so he had that stardom look! Joe Burns could also play Wipe Out. In 2021, I got a message who said he was Joe Burns! He had seen a Face Book posting about Dyre Street and remembered.

Our little group played Beatles stuff, folksy stuff, and others. We practiced in my living room. I had been singing for a while now and my voice grew stronger. We put on several "concerts" at my Aunt Artie's garage and other places. She lived about half an hour away. Aunt Artie had a pack of children and a generous and supportive attitude. As an adult, I talked with one of her children who still remembered those amateur shows.

As bands often do, Johnny Flagler and I eventually parted ways. He got into electric guitar and rock and roll while I tended toward the acoustic, folk side of things. I felt happy however with my choice of genre. Dylan had more profound things to say than AC/DC. Sorry.

My interest in music and singing brought me, however, to one of the best chapters in my life. I moved to Frankford High School about a mile away. We would walk both ways! The school looked like a gigantic fortress, taking up a city block. And it had a choir.

Robert G. Hamilton led the Frankford choir. I tried out my first year and passed the audition and became a 2nd tenor. The large choir sang a Capella, show tunes, hymns, classics, and folk music. Mr. Hamilton would look at me during a performance or rehearsal and point up with his finger, meaning my tone was flat, and I needed to put more chest into it. He taught us how to breathe and sing from our diaphragm. My lack of a big chest prohibited me from putting a lot of air into my singing.

Over the years, I had found singing to be a freeing activity. It sounds corny, but my singing voice connected me with a deeper spirit. To sing brought joy but also a confidence that was lacking in other areas of my life. Singing felt right and resonated with me.

I took a course in music theory from Mr. Hamilton that first year. He taught us about the inner structure of music, harmonics, and the ability of musical sounds to solicit emotions and ideas. For class, I had to write a composition. "Grandma, can I come to your house and use your piano to work on a music project? Thanks." I passed with a C. The song had a simple guitar chord structure. The grade didn't reflect the profound effect that music had on me. Metal on metal, sparks.

Mr. Hamilton one day came to choir. "I want to let you know that I have proposed to the school administration that we take an international trip, singing and touring South America. Here is an information sheet for your parents." I thought it would be impossible for me to go. There didn't seem to be much money. My father would often say, "What do you think money grows on trees?" I recall my father would also exclaim, "I don't have a bucket to piss in or a window to throw it out of." We didn't have vacations or get new clothes very often. We had what we needed, but there didn't seem to be much for other things.

The estimated trip cost was about $400. This seemed astronomical to me. I brought home the information about the trip. "Mom, they are talking about the choir going to South America for a tour. I would love to go!" "Well, dear, I don't think it's possible. How much will it cost?" "Around four hundred dollars." "Oh," grimacing, "Oh, my. That is a lot of money. I will talk with your father about it." And she shrugged her shoulders. A few days later, I sat down with my parents for a sober meeting. My mom talked about the trip, "Your father and I have talked and Steve, this is very expensive." A pause as she looked at my dad. "But we think it'd be a great experience for you. We know you like this new school and the choir. We want you to go!" They met and lived in Panama, so giving their son a taste of that culture probably didn't seem that far-fetched. I felt overjoyed. A harmonious gong sounded.

To help defray costs, the choir raised money for the trip. On a Saturday morning, by school, we met by the empty tractor trailer. "You ready to fill this truck up?" shouted a parent. "Yes!" we all screamed. Soon a line of cars formed and people dropped off bundled newspapers. "I'll get on the truck with Steve here. Throw the papers to us!" Hence began one of the biggest fundraising actions of all time, or at least this side of the Mississippi. We collected $90,000. The work attracted significant community support. With great hope, we were counting down until July.

As the day approached, serious planning began. We would bring our blue blazers with the "Ambassadors of Song, Frankford High School, Philadelphia, Pa." on the vest pocket. Decisions had to be made about clothes, money, cameras, and packing. We had several informational meetings and heard from those who had gone on other trips. Mr. Hamilton sold the parents on the vision of the trip. His naïve and wide-eyed kids all trusted him.

We were ambassadors of song, bringing good wishes from the United States as youth, singing joyously, brightly and reverently. We would fly to Miami, then to Lima Peru, Santiago, Chile, Buenos Aires, Argentina, Sao Paulo, Brazil and, last, Rio. Just the names sparked a deep sense of wonder. The 1967 yearbook said that the tour lasted 24 days, 20,000 miles of travel, 30 hours in the air, and 25 concerts. For me, the numbers weren't important. The trip took this young adolescent across country borders in a whirlwind tour of places and cultures. I drank from a fire hose and didn't want to miss a drop.

We landed initially in the stifling heat of Miami! We took a tour on air-conditioned buses and went past Al Capone's home, among other places of interest. The architecture stood out with bright colors and flowing stucco shapes unknown in Philly. But our excitement rose when we got on the plane for Lima, Peru. I had a seat by the window. I watched the land fall away, watching the moving patterns in the water. The clouds danced and broke up in different striations, like ocean waves. We were on the plane for hours, but the window view never grew old. The landings were uncomfortable with the loss of pressure and the first jerk of the wheels on the runway.

In Lima, I almost lost my life. Yes, full truth. We were walking around the city, probably by the hotel. A group of us were waiting to cross the street. I took a step forward and someone jerked me back. "Whoa! A car!" A speeding little car drove by the very edge of the sidewalk. We weren't in Kansas anymore. I found myself immersed in watching the architecture with its beauty and form and all the people. "Don't you think the people dress so beautifully, Mike? I love all their colors and hats." "It's bright stuff, for sure."

While we were driving in buses past the Palace in Lima, Peru, on the steps were several soldiers with automatic weapons drawn. From my window seat, I looked clearly into the face of a young soldier who pointed his weapon at me as we drove past. The reality shook me.

On a day in Peru, I bought my wooden man statue. He is a foot tall, hardwood and indigenous looking. "How much?" I asked the store owner. He responded in Spanish. I pulled some small bills out of my pocket and showed him. He took a couple and gave me some coins. I have kept that carving on my book shelf ever since. In Argentina, I bought small plastic and cloth Gauchos for my brothers. They had blankets and hats, pantaloons and boots. I bought my parents a bronze-colored metal serving dish.

Mike Agazarian and Bill Hunt roomed with me for the trip. Mike had a guitar with him. At one point, he and I put on a brief show with guitars at a school. We played, of course, Beatles tunes. "She Loves you, yeah, yeah, yeah!" Everyone knew the Beatles. Our singing sounded better than the guitar work. We lived the life and often ordered room service comprising sandwiches and cokes. They sold Coke everywhere.

On one trip to the airport, we were late because of a snafu. Anyway, several of us piled into a taxi. The rain came down hard. The driver spoke poor English, but he drove quick. With the rain getting worse, I held onto the armrest in the back seat. The lines of the street, the traffic lights, everything blurred as it flew by. As we approached the airport, a bus pulled in front of us suddenly, with bright red lights. Our driver braked hard. Unfortunately, it put the car into a spin. We all held our breath, waiting for the collision, expecting to die. The car stopped finally, perpendicular to the bus! We were a foot away from the back of the bus. We could touch it, but that was impossible as our hearts had left our bodies!

We did many interesting things. For one, we went to an ancient burial site in Argentina. We visited the Chilean Air Force Academy and sang at the US Chilean Ambassador's home. In every city we visited, we had a concert. We gave concerts in big theaters and in poor neighborhoods. We visited museums and saw the sights. At a concert, a man threw a big bag filled with a white substance on the stage while we were singing. It looked like a bomb. We were later told that the action was a political protest. It stopped the concert, and the crowd booed over it.

In Rio, several older members of the choir went to the beach. They came back with stories of coming across naked bodies in the sand. We also visited the gigantic statue of Christ that dominates the landscape of Rio. I got to the foot of the statue first, running up the many steps. The Christ figure took away my breath, even on a cloudy day.

I will always remember what occurred when we visited a school in Sao Paulo. One of the girl's families invited several of us to go to dinner and visit their home. We got permission to go through the parents in charge. The opulent grounds were heaven like and beautiful. They had horses, and in the background, the mountains were nearby. "Hello, I am Heloise. And your name?" "Steve, my name is Steve." "Well, welcome Steve. Welcome to our home." "Gracias." I said poorly. We wrote back and forth for a while after the trip. She signed a 100 Cruzeiros bill in Portuguese, "For Steve from your friend Heloise". Printed on the bill was "República dos Estados Unidos do Basil". I didn't know how much it was worth, but I was rich, given the people we met.

The people we encountered appreciated our music. We loved to sing and took care of business. Mr. Hamilton had gotten us to where we were attentive and acted as one voice, if you will. A Capella has been close to my heart since. A beautiful harmony results, glistening with rich tones and syncopation. With a large group of more than a hundred singers, we filled the air with an aroma of musical delicacy that could be breathtaking. At the end, we would sing a prayer that began, "Go forth into the world in peace. Be of good courage. Hold Fast that which is good..." It came from an old Common Book of Prayer. We may have done a version by Mr. Hamilton. He gave us copies of the prayer in gold letters. I have it around in a file here even though it has been 55 years ago. The choir also made an LP. Mr. Hamilton left the choir after our year to begin a new all city Boys Choir. I didn't stay with it after that. The significant memories, however, persist. I grew in maturity over the course of the trip. And I really became a world traveler. Gong!

Back to normal, but much wiser for the wear, I returned to our corner on Dyre Street. While I had already been in a serious relationship (remember sending letters for over a year), I had a huge crush on Rosie from across the street, my brothers' babysitter. Rosie came over regularly. To no avail were my heartfelt feelings of love returned! I don't think that Rosie even liked me. My mom had an awareness of my brother Nicky's limitations.

The neighborhood offered a diverse set of possibilities, some riskier than others. One day, while sitting on my step, three guys came walking down the street. They looked out of place. They were a little older than me. The middle one hauled off right there and sucker punched me to the side of my face. He said, "You gonna do something about it, punk?" With fear and embarrassment, I shook my head, and they walked on, laughing. I had a red mark and my pride hurt. However, I felt guilty for not acting to save my respect. But there were three of them. It seemed like bad odds to me.

One day, a skinny black man appeared and asked, "Hey you all, if you help me paint this house tomorrow, I will give each of you $20. What ya think?" "Sure," we said. The next day, the guy came around like he said. He had all the equipment. We went to this one house, and he opened up the screen door. It made a squeaking noise. He said, "I better fix that." For the next couple of minutes, he got oil from his truck and opened and close the door repeatedly. Getting more dramatic and intense, he pulled hard at the door. Soon, the screen fell out. He repeated, "I better fix that!" A couple more tugs and the metal frame bent. "I gotta fix that." Eventually, the door came off the hinges. He said, "I don't think I can fix that!" as he pulled the screen door off completely. It overwhelmed us with laughter. I had tears in my eyes. We eventually started painting. One of us hung out the second-story window upside down while the other one held his feet. The job was one of the most unusual jobs I ever had. We got our money.

Dyre Street soon changed drastically, which continued my training in catastrophic thinking! Amazingly, Aunt Joyce really owned the property, and she divided the upstairs and downstairs. We had to move upstairs. I had thought that our parents had finally bought their own house. I am not sure if my father knew this at the outset. My mom knew and had said nothing. They were good at secrets. My room became a kitchen.

Our parents sent my brothers and me up into the big attic room at the top of a winding staircase. It gave us privacy. A closet took up half the room. Inside, we soon found a hatch that opened to the roof. Nicky poked his head through the hatch and looked at the roof. "I'm not getting out there!" But I frequently sat on the roof with the world in front of me, heaven above!

As Aunt Joyce moved in the downstairs with our young cousin Tina, there soon developed tension in the house. Arguments between my parents became more vocal. We were all very disappointed. What had been a good life, free of the earlier mistrust and difficulty, soured. It felt almost like Howard Street had invaded Dyre Street. The hammer kissed the anvil with a sudden, mean retort.

Now I loved my Aunt Joyce. But this crossed a difficult and painful line. We didn't stay there much longer. As well, to be perfectly honest, I began to get depressed. This angered me. It felt like we couldn't catch a break.

I have a picture of my smiling father hugging my mom in the backyard of Dyre Street. I want to hold on to that scene. They made a promise at the house on Dyre Street. Indeed, wonderful things happened there, and I grew in important ways. However, betrayal visited as well. So, I took my guitar, a pimple ball, my rough riding skateboard and my Brazilian money and quietly left.

Less

To open one's eyes and not be afraid of seeing
To listen without fear of hearing inconsolable secrets
I reach my hand, out it goes
Yet how quickly I would bring it back at the first sense of heat
My fingers would retract into a fist, a fist of tears and outrage
And out again but less and out again but less
A thousand times, till barely would the fist be opened
I don't know what would soften my muscles
I fear paralysis
As my body silhouette fades into the chair

6 Pratt Street

I said to Tony, "Alright, I'm winning 15 to 8. You got no chance, brother!" I pushed the ping-pong ball a little to the left. He returned it quickly. "Ahh chump," Tony said. I did my best backhand. I knew he couldn't return it. "16 to 8. Meet your doom, turkey!" I served again, but his return ball caromed off the wall. It came back suddenly at a weird angle. I reacted, but it hit the corner of the table. "No!" I shouted in despair. "Yes!" clinching his fist. "Who's the chump now?" my little brother proclaimed.

While Dyre Street had helped us grow, now our family turned to a house not so far away, on Pratt Street. This house would see significant changes in our lives. My mother and Nick would live here for the next 45 years! As we moved, I let myself feel hopeful. Again. Our new row home stood in the middle of the block with four other homes. No step ball here. It was a two story, three-bedroom house, concrete steps, an enclosed porch and a large wide basement as deep as the house. My father put his rusted tools in the closet under the basement steps. Amidst them was a beautiful wooden tool box with "CCHouse" on it.

The basement became our sports mecca. We had a pool table that fitted a ping-pong table on top of it. Playing pool took an unusual skill because the old painted rock walls offered little room. It looked like they were carved out of a mountain. Certain shots were almost impossible. For ping-pong, we played "International rules". This meant that you could hit the ball if it bounced off the walls. Pool and ping-pong became a retreat for friends and relatives.

The upstairs was bright with many windows. The bathroom next to my room had a skylight. Light danced upstairs down the small hallway. If the doors were open, late afternoon saw shadows fade across the top of the steps and down the hallway. This isn't as pretty as it sounds. After a while, the sky light paint chipped off, and it got dusty and moldy. Over the years, that sky light proved to be an ongoing mess, making it, like life, hard to see the sky!

Fairly soon after we moved, we got a 15-gallon fish tank for down stairs. I loved watching it. Tropical fish are so relaxing. I took care of it. I bought cheap fish and especially those that would bear more fish. Occasionally I put money into an angel fish or a discus. I bought an aggressive Oscar once, a cichlid, that ate all my other fish! If you put your finger in the water, it would nip it! I successfully bred zebra danios. "Tony, come here. Look, do you see those little white splotches? Those are baby fish!" I separated the young so they would not get eaten by others.

We also expanded the family with a series of dogs on Pratt Street. They brought warmth with them. Casey Aloysius Kingston the Third was our first. Deagan, a beagle, was followed by Demetrius, an aggressive German Shepherd from Aunt Renee. Walking him one day, he attacked a bike rider who rode by. We had a beloved black poodle, Corky. He became a great listener, sitting at the top of the steps and talking about philosophy and relationships. Dogs can be wonderful friends. They filled the gap when you couldn't approach easily the people you live with.

My parents sold the Chevy Station wagon and bought a 1965 Chevy Impala. My father worked at Boeing, which had a plant in South Philly. He drove to work each day on what he called the "Sure kill" expressway (Schuylkill Expressway). They were making helicopters and as I still built models, I got free kits. My dad worked on the Chinook Helicopter as he had the Sikorsky S 55 in Connecticut.

I bought my first car, a gray 1960 Volvo 122 two door, in 1967 for $500. Aunt Tonia signed for it as I was younger than 18. It had a four-cylinder engine and a stick shift. I picked up driving the stick pretty quickly. I worked at Fitzgerald's Sea Food Restaurant, the last year and a half, so I had money saved up. A cute car, but really underneath the hood lived a heavy clunker. Sitting at a stoplight, one day, gray smoke poured out from under the car. A passing motorist yelled at me. Well, a friend of mine from school knew another student, Billy, whom he described as an excellent mechanic. We got together and talked about the car. "So, it's got gray smoke pouring out from the exhaust. It's running bad too." "I think it could be a ring problem. They go around the engine cylinders and wear out or break. You buy the parts and do most of the labor. I will help rebuild it." It sounded like a deal; however, it would prove intense.

This introduced me to the greatest catalogue modern man has ever designed, the JC Whitney Auto Parts Catalogue. This would be an asset for many years to come. My new friend, of course, had a copy. "Billy, this is amazing. You can rebuild anything with this catalogue. I can finally go out and buy my used Jaguar XKE!" We ordered the parts, and we were off and running. "We gotta pull the engine to get to the pistons and rings? Crap, I didn't think about that!" It would be a long process. However, he had experience and his expertise guided us. We hauled the car to a vacant lot close by. He had an engine lift and other tricks. "Alright." he said. "At first, we disconnect the radiator and all this electrical. The transmission's got to be dropped. This may seem monumental from your perspective. But, wait and see, not that big a deal." Easy to say! "See, these old rings are black. This one is broken. We have to drench the new ones in oil. That's why I brought this pail!" The valves were not that good and so we cleaned and seated them. We completed the entire project in a couple of weeks. The time didn't matter. Proud that my fingernails were black with grime, I felt pleased and successful. We accounted for all the bolts and torqued them. It impressed me the way the whole thing fit together. Welcome to my dad's world! "You ready to start it up? Go ahead, Steve, turn the key!" And it started! From this as well, I bought a toolbox and began to accumulate tools. That alone made the whole thing worth the price of admission. Sound the anvil's voice!

It is interesting how things can spring forth from calamity. I didn't understand what I was getting into, but this began my career changing oil, starters, alternators, radiators, mufflers, and brakes. Of course, I still have that brown tool box. I learned that with the right tool, you can fix anything. I wished it worked that way with people!

While fish and cars were looking up, my parent's relationship was tense. My father drank more. Our crabbing had ended after Venice Park. Nothing like it would occur again. To admit this makes me very sad. I felt a loss then as I do now. I think it was a loss for my father as well. My antidote to despair involved water and especially with my father. I lost that medicine.

Outward conflict would occur between my parents, in frequent, long, vitriolic arguments. They could say mean things to each other. There were incidents of my father passing out and my mother asking me to help him to bed. Several times, he fell down the stairs.

Dinner became intolerable. My father would criticize Nicky for any slight mistake he made. Sternly, "I heard you aren't passing your English. Are you even trying? Are you stupid? Do you do your homework? Tell me, I don't see you bringing any books home!" His face was red with anger. Glaring, dinner became an ugly time. I sat, disgusted, hardly interested in eating. I just asked God for the tirade to end. Nicky just looked at his plate. He didn't deserve this; the assault was unwarranted. He had issues for sure, but this was abusive.

I bet my father's frustrations were related to work, my mother, and money. His drinking only exacerbated it. Home became a battleground, and I found it difficult to be there. I stayed in my room a lot or went to a friend's house. Music became an outlet; my guitar insulated me. My grades suffered. I ended up ranked about 272 out of 312. I bombed high school. That is how this works. When crap is flying in the air, everybody gets splashed.

One sticky and hot evening, my parents fought after dinner. It grew dark outside. The argument went on and it carried the typical cursing and name calling. I won't repeat it. I heard it all from my room. My dad had been drinking. He usually came home with two quarts of beer. He maintained a job, but in the off hours, he drank. They were in the living room and standing facing each other. I came downstairs for a glass of water. As they went back and forth, my father said a phrase that went through me. "I am going to kill you." This represented an escalation I had not heard before. They weren't physically violent; their arguments were verbal but vehement. This grabbed me and, being four inches taller, I stood up between them and looked at my father directly and told him, "You aren't going to do anything like that." A heavy pause stood between us. He realized what he had said, perhaps the line he crossed. He didn't say anything. I hadn't thought about what I would do if it got physical, but I stood between them. My presence said not this night! My mother left and walked the neighborhood. He went upstairs without a word. The hammer spoke to the anvil that night with several fearful syncopations.

We had averted the terrible. For me, this had been brewing for a while. I tired of the conflict. The tension wore me out. My wish for peace and a cessation of the violence arose from deep within. I could not turn back. I sat on anger, sadness and frustration that sought a voice. Enough of this crap and this petty conflict. Enough of this cesspool of argument and posturing. The next couple of days were like the aftermath of a hurricane. The house felt heavy and quiet. A dark air sat silently in the house. Sad sparks flew and tears quenched the forming hot metal.

Beer

His words were beer
His eyes were beer
He moved in beer
He slept beer
The bottles were hung around him like a necklace, like a noose
His chair floated in beer
Going up the stairs to bed, his shoes were awash in beer
And beer distilled his insides until his life was a puddle
That vanished in the heat

On the lighter side, the basketball courts of Penn and Pratt took up more of our time. My brothers and I would often go there to play basketball. I didn't have great basketball skills, but, being reasonably tall, I could play. My weakness involved my inability to palm the ball and dunk it. One time, we played a full court game and a tall black guy on the other team covered me. "I'll take the skinny white boy." It got intense. I dribbled on him and drained a fadeaway jumper. "Try that again, man," he said with a snarl. I did, but this time, he jumped and smacked the ball out of the air. "Hah," he triumphantly said. The guy could jump and he sorely out matched me. We lost. But we lived the basketball life. Having a good basketball and, of course, Chuck Taylor All Stars, black high tops, were all that was necessary.

It sounds corny, but my brothers and I also wrestled a lot. This had happened since they were young. I always won. One time, we wrestled down stairs on the uncovered wooden floor and I got a deep, inch long splinter in my knee. My parents decided I needed to go to the ER to get it removed. I remember distinctly sitting on a bench in a large room with overhanging curtains. I felt anxious. As we sat, a couple with a young child came in and were rushed into one of the curtained areas. They asked the parents to wait in the outer area. As I sat there with my splinter, the doctor, all in white gloves and a mask, moved over the curtain and came out. He looked at the parents and simply shook his head. The parents lost all color and breath. The clear message had a severe impact. That hospital room turned ice cold. I have read about how death always hangs over your shoulder. Death walked by me that day. I heard the anvil distinctly, but those parents heard a repetitive clang for much, much longer.

A guy in the neighborhood, Joe Koenig, and I, became good friends as our time at Dyre Street ended. He lived next to Johnny Flagler. One of the first times I visited Joe's house, we were on the steps and I did my best rendition of the Righteous Brothers. Screaming into an invisible mic, on my knees and with high octane vocals. "You've lost that loving feeling!" His father came out, probably contemplating calling the police. He looked at me with a quizzical and somewhat judgmental look. Great first impression.

Joe was an interesting guy. He had gone to Catholic school but wound up at Frankford, the public school. "They didn't appreciate my sense of humor." Joe had wit and sarcasm, a smart dude. "I'm just waiting for the Apocalypse. Me and Timothy Leary are gonna bring it on!" A little eccentric, he was the youngest.

Now, my mother thought that if you lived too far away from a Greek Orthodox Church, you could go to the Catholic Church. Really, the faiths were very similar, at least until the 10th century! We were in the parish of St. Bartholomew, a Catholic church 10 minutes away. Joe and I would go with my brothers on Sundays. We would go to Mass or stay out front and get a coke and Tastykakes. He did not have a strong faith!

Joe and I had several exploits. At one point, several of us went down to the shore for a fall weekend. The weather had been cold and storms went through. While we were there, we got the brilliant idea to pose as an English rock band on holiday. We each took on English accents. I thought I did a pretty good job. We would go to stores and speak "British". "Hallo there. Just in from London. Looking for fish and chips! We also need some petrol for our motor." We were staying at a small single floor apartment, our flat if you will, by the beach with lots of windows. The people we met, we invited to the house for a big weekend party. During the stormy evening of the big party, we heard a knock on the door. A dad was with his daughter. "Is this where the party is?" He looked around at the disheveled room. Music played on the radio in a dull and somber manner. Dishes were in the sink. Clothes everywhere. "But oh, sorry, not much of a party, huh guys?" They left. Nobody came to our party. I told my mom that the bus had broken down and returning home would be later than I thought. Being a British rock and roll band wasn't so attractive!

Following my long running involvement with electronic gadgets, my parents bought me a Grundig reel-to-reel tape recorder for graduation. At 25 pounds with stereo speakers on the sides, it pointed to serious creativity. Joe and I spent many hours in my room playing music and messing around with this new toy. I had songs to record, creativity to exercise. However, at one point, my mom asked me directly if I was gay. I was stunned and a little angry. True, I did not have a girlfriend. The girl in my English class turned me down to go to the prom. So instead, I went with Billy, the guy who helped me fix my car. He had an extra ticket. However, my suspected gayness was truly remote. I don't think my mom knew about my father's stash of Playboy magazines in the basement!

Joe and I developed a musical connection. He took the part of backup singer, although he didn't like to sing much. At first, we started performing a beatnik kind of routine and made up a song called, "I am a Tree". Part music and part performance art. I was interested in something more serious. I had written music with Johnny. Now, I wrote songs in a Simon and Garfunkel style. We called ourselves, "The Dead Sea Scrolls." Joe said, "It took civilization 2,000 years to find the Dead Sea Scrolls and it will take at least that long for us to be discovered. Our first album will be called, 'Back Again for the First Time' with the picture of the back of us on the front cover!" I wrote half a dozen songs we earnestly rehearsed. We played at his older sister's wedding reception at the George Washington Motor Lodge on the Boulevard. The gig didn't go well. We weren't wedding music. As a sort of whim, we played our senior year at the school variety show. The school yearbook sent me a glossy copy of the picture of the Dead Sea Scrolls singing on stage. I still have that shot. After the show, Mr. Hamilton, my old choir director, stopped me as I walked by. He said, "Nicely done. I didn't know you played guitar and wrote music." It made my day. Sparks.

Significantly, Joe arranged for me to meet a friend of his. His girlfriend and Michelle were friends. "Hi, I'm Michelle. Joe says you play guitar." "Yep, just like Paul Simon…but not as good. You'll love the Dead Sea Scrolls. I bet we could give a free personal concert!" "Yes, I would like that. You guys have tee shirts to sell?" We would soon spend a lot of time together. She was a year behind me in school. Along with Joe, she was an easy excuse to get away from home. She and I had a lot of fun together. She had good grades, was thoughtful, had a good sense of humor and a love of music. "Hey Steve, you want to see Peter, Paul and Mary at the Academy of Music downtown?" "That sounds great. I've never been there." "You'll love it. It is a beautiful venue, and the sound is wonderful." We went to the Philadelphia Folk Festival together, seeing John Prine and Dave Von Ronk. Went to a Sixers game. I fell hard for her. Our circle expanded to Frank and Cindy, and we went to her and Cindy's prom together. Frank and Cindy were married and had a little son, Jason. I knew Frank from school. One time, Frank and I were walking. The track coach caught up to us and asked me, "Have you ever thought about running track? You'd make a good long-distance guy." I simply shrugged. How stupid! What opportunity I nonchalantly wasted that day?

A wonderful phenomenon developed for me, repeated several times over the course of my life. A group of people will form, the guitar will come out, and entertain the group. Joe Murphy lived across the street from Frank and we would find ourselves at Joe's, guitar in hand. "Hey Joe, can I get another beer?" "Sure, in the fridge, but you gotta play another song!" "How about Mr. Bojangles? Now I want to hear some singing." We would drink, smoke, laugh, talk, and sing. The repertoire included the Band, Dylan, Peter, Paul and Mary and others. I enjoyed playing the entertainer. We were friends, getting together and sharing life and love. That's what we did. A sweet high-pitched song of the anvil resounded in my head, intensely marking time and place.

My graduation year, 1968, signified a notable year in the history of the US. I worked at Fitzgerald's, washing dishes and making cups of shrimp cocktails. This rainy evening in April, the radio news announced, "This evening, in Memphis, Tennessee, Martin Luther King was killed by what appears to be a lone gunman. The Civil Rights leader was 39." Later that year in June, we heard about the assassination of Bobby Kennedy. These events jarred me. They brought back to mind the JFK assassination. Double cries of anvil pain!

Philly also saw civil unrest. The Police Commissioner was Frank Rizzo, a heavy-handed authoritarian. My mother liked Rizzo as did many whites who elected him mayor in 1970. After the election, I foolishly told my mother what I thought of her and her candidate. She threw a can of coffee at me and chased me out of the house. I had to stay with a friend.

To further the tension, my father and I had a long and tense argument in the car over the student protests and takeovers at universities around the country. I voiced my views to my parents. I did not favor the establishment.

At the Democratic National Convention of 1968, many anti-war protests occurred, and this brought to a head my alienation from my parents.

Graduation that summer was not the monumental occasion I expected. Being 272nd out of 312, I felt unsuccessful. I had no plans. Almost 18, the draft was about to affect me. I played music and hung around for the summer. My mother got uncomfortable with me. "Steve, here, look at this ad in the paper. The training will help you start a 'wonderful career in the new and exciting field of computers!' What do you think?" My parents saw it as an excellent opportunity. My father was familiar with computers at work. So, I enrolled. It was not a scam, but close. An old man in a wrinkled suit taught an array of skills on old hardware. The class consisted of adults trying to retool and high school graduates, like me, looking for a brighter future. After finishing, I found myself hired as a tape handler by the Penn Central Rail Road in downtown Philadelphia at minimum wage.

A tape handler walked around the computer floor, picking up and delivering computer tapes, like a low-grade mailman. The computer department of the Penn Central Rail Road had many machines on several floors. I worked midnight to 8; at first, I wasn't aware if it was day or night, sleep or awake time.

Late in summer, several people were talking about going to New York for a festival called Woodstock. "No, you can't go." "But, mom." Maybe I burned my prospects by the story of the bus breaking down after our British rock band tour!

The job gave me an income. Michelle and I would go down the Jersey shore and rent a small sailboat. At the end of the season, I bought one of the older sailboats put up for sale. It traveled on top of my Volvo on an old tire. I kept it in the backyard.

There were wonderful people who worked at the railroad. I enjoyed listening to their stories. Interesting for me as well were the veterans who talked about Vietnam. "One time, one guy in my outfit was blown up when he opened his footlocker to a booby trap. I'm glad I got out alive." "I was there during the Tet Offensive. It was horrible man, just ugly." Complicating my thoughts, at the end of 1969, a lottery determined who would be inducted for military service. The lottery selected 156 for my birthday. I was eligible for a year. Frank called me up, "What I have heard is the Selective Service bureau is almost up the 150!" "Crap, Frank, that is close!" My eligibility ended without being drafted and I felt relieved. Just to hedge my bets, I went to the

Navy Yard to look into joining the Navy Reserve. I disappointed my dad again by not enlisting.

One could not avoid news about the war. I thought more about it as my graduation and 18th birthday rolled around. It depressed and saddened me. Whichever way I turned, turmoil existed in the house and in the country. Molotov cocktails, street protests, and the assassinations of King and Kennedy only added to my sense of upheaval. My possible induction into the army worried me. My religious beliefs lead me to see all as loved by God. These ideas put me at odds with the political rhetoric and my parents. I became strongly against the war. I wasn't attending church and felt attracted to pacifist Buddhist writings. The sights of orange clad Buddhist priests immolating themselves against the war however startled me.

Aside from these intense misgivings, my relationship with Michelle progressed. I don't know why, but we bought a car together. We bought a cheap MG. It had a white exterior, a red leather interior, wood grain on the dash, and wire wheels. The engine made a rough purr. Luckily, I had my toolbox. I would need it with this car.

At work, I had a straightforward supervisor, Frank, an Italian guy. He took me aside in the middle of the shift. His silhouette took up the doorway. "House, come here for a second. I need to talk to you." I hoped I wasn't in trouble. "You are a good worker and I like you. You also seem like a smart guy. House, I got a question for you. Why don't you think about going to college?" That simple question reverberated. "Hmm, I'll...think about it," I replied with a nod of my head. There are angels around who say things or do things at just the right time. It is baffling from a secular viewpoint. However, he was an angel, and that moment realigned my life.

Remember that I had bombed high school? Remember that my father wanted me to go to MIT? Remember, I lived at home? Remember the hero who was my father became an alcoholic? Remember, the war going on? Such was the mental context into which Frank gently threw his grenade. The conversation with him was a telegraph message, and life went on. Maybe that is how God works, clear and brief. Waking me up, in my head sounded a loud gong from the anvil that reverberated for a while.

Now, my work life was good, I knew routine. I showed up and put in my time. The future, to me, however, looked vague. It felt a stretch to think that I could get married. The image came with a little anxiety. "What if I turn out like my parents?" I knew there had to be a better life than what I had.

Now don't get me wrong. I ate, had a place to stay and didn't experience frost bite. I don't want to sound ungrateful. My broken family shared love and care as best they could. I had supportive friends, and a job that lent security. I still lived at home, but I knew that would change. But I felt dread concerning the war and my possible induction. I had a negative feeling, not a new one but an old tired friend. It said, "If you go to war, you will die and return in a body bag." However imaginary, the terrible expectation reflected my mindset.

As I thought about it, the local community college seemed like a reasonable possibility. I assumed my fate was to work every day because I got lousy grades and I wasn't that smart. Well, I found myself back at Frankford High School talking with the guidance counselor. "So, Steve, you graduated last year? What have you been doing?" "Working nights at the railroad." "Hmm. Now, Community College just started a couple of years ago. But I have heard some good things about it. Did you know George Allen? He may have been a year or two ahead of you. He's going there. The place started in response to many working adults interested in getting ahead. Maybe married with kids, in dead-end jobs, or with issues with their education." "I think that is me." "Oh yeah?" She handed me an application to the Community College of Philadelphia. "I hope this helps you. Let me know. Good luck." "Thanks." Gong.

Applying, I wondered if the institution could help me? I had learned that in life, you got up and took a step forward, even if you didn't know how solid the ground would be. I enrolled in the Community College of Philadelphia with a spark of uncommon hope. "Can I handle the classes? Will I quit? Can I really pay for it? Stevie, you are an idiot and your own worst enemy. You poison the water with negative beliefs. You need to act, man." My thinking brought me to a Jesus moment. I had to put up or shut up. "Should I do this, whatever it entails, or stay with what I have? That is the question." Shakespeare would have smiled. I have realized that God places doors in our midst. It is our job not to overthink it but to walk through to the room within. It may be locked, just open the next one. That deserves a couple of hits on the hot anvil!

The idea of going to the community college made sense. Of course, the other notable schools in the area, like the University of Penn or Drexel, were scary to me. So, the Community College of Philadelphia stood alone as realistic. No, let me rephrase that. CCP was the place I needed to go. I didn't have the goods and regardless of the stature of the place; I had to prove to myself and others that I could do the work. Questions about my competence and ability to handle the rigors of class work were present. The easy computer school was not a genuine test. Even though just a community college, this meant taking a big step. To my surprise, I got in. It fit my status as a quasi-failed student, looking for redemption. I needed that associate's degree to certify I could overcome my limitations. I had to see myself as more than my lousy student record at Frankford. But the door opened, and I walked through.

The Community College of Philadelphia existed in an old department store, Snellenberg's, in downtown Philly. My biology classroom was located, yes, where lingerie used to be. Right by the escalator! The school was bright and filled with students. I started my first semester anxiously. My first courses were intro biology, English, math. I sought an associate's degree. I could do it in two years or less. The teachers were very supportive. The place offered me hope and a challenge. I brought perseverance and grit!

The classes were interesting but not too challenging; I found out that I could do this stuff. It didn't take a lot of work and I got decent grades. It felt different from high school, but I liked it. Maybe by working at the Rail Road, I had less time at home and its chaos. Maybe I was ready to move out and move on up! But whatever, I learned, and it felt good. A wonderful English teacher revived my interest in poetry. She connected music with literature and brought out the common themes of our aspirations and needs. I wrote a short story based on a man going to work every day. She liked it.

I met a guy named Tim McGrann who took a psychology class with me. "Hey Tim, I got a great idea. Why don't we buy a lab's worth of mice, build some mazes and do research into rat learning? This stuff is awesome!" My mom's clear "no" shredded that idea. I took a practical course in psychology on adjustment, looking at stress, and exploring meditation. A girl in class, Darlene, woke me up as I fell asleep. The class explored common problems people face. I learned words to identify what I had experienced. CCP changed my view of the past and the future. Because I could do the work, I looked for where this would take me.

I realized I took on a lot working full time and having a full load of classes. I took the train to school, attended classes, came home, and went to work. My schedule was crazy. I slept on the train and woke up in time to get off. Michelle's couch was a place I often fell asleep before work. I fell asleep on the job during lunch break.

Working the night shift, I left in the morning for class and came home in the afternoon. Some days I had later classes. I slept sporadically, probably not good for my body or my mental health. But I felt focused and driven. I caught up on my days off. My youth could handle it. I wasn't sure when I would study, but it got done. I had to work to pay for tuition that I needed to go to school so that I could get ahead. It all made perfect sense. I knew that hard work could be done, and that it offered benefits. I liked to put gas in the car or to go to an occasional concert.

Although driven and very busy, I had some downtime. In South America, I got the bug for taking pictures as my latent tourist had come out. I made an overdue purchase of an old Vivitar 35 mm camera. It fit well in an old WWI gas mask bag. I also developed my film with a used photo enlarger I bought. I found I could make black and white photos. Things soon caught my eye, a pretty silhouette of a tree here or a line of cars with reflections just so. It turns out, shape and lines and shading are everywhere! Art surrounds us!

The sailboat kept me in contact with the water and, frankly, my past. One day, my brother Tony and I went out on the boat on the Delaware river. Michelle and I sailed there earlier. We parked the car by a ramp and headed out. An important neglected calculation concerned the wind speed which, for the Delaware that day, hovered at zero! A second troubling fact we faced concerned the tide. The river was flowing out to the bay, then to the ocean. Without wind, it takes anything with it that floats. The river decided we were going south. "Tony, this is not good. Maybe if we don't get wind in a couple of minutes, we should head back." After a while, the captain made the executive decision to head to port. We chose a dock on the Philly side and headed toward it. We used the centerboard as an oar and rowed toward it. The landing included an old wood dock with steps leading up onto someone's property. Tony waited with the boat while I went to get the car. The adventure ended without the police or the owner showing up.

Besides sailing, the MG offered exhilaration. When I didn't take the Amtrak train to the 30th street station, I would drive the MG. The road off of the boulevard that ran along the Schuylkill Expressway called Kelly Drive always exhilarated me. It went along the river, past the boathouses to 30th Street Station. At night, the abandoned road was like a dream. It had several nice curves and no lights for at least a mile. With the top down, at night, listening to the murmuring sound of the MG's four cylinders made for a beautiful hum. I was driving along the Champs-Élysées in Paris!

At the Rail Road, lunch occurred about 3:30 am. I parked in the big lot next to the building. One unusual night, I approached my car to go out to lunch. The lot has tall lamps sparsely lighting it. Off in the distance, I saw an unusual shadow by the car. The vague light just didn't seem right. As I got closer, I realized a person was standing next to my short car, leaning over it. "Hey, what are you doing?" and a person looked up, saw me and started running. I didn't take chase, but went to my car. The person had slit the side of the vinyl black top about a foot long. I was angry. That slit represented money and effort.

Regularly, I came home after school to sleep, take care of any business and enjoy the rest of my crowded life. After getting off the train this day, I walked down the stairs and emerged on to the street corner. I noticed my father leaning against the wall across the street by the Penn Fruit. My busy schedule had prevented much time together. He had been to the doctor and given a diagnosis of skin cancer. They removed a mole by his eye and nothing more was said about it. He continued to drink, although maybe not as much. He still smoked Camels with the Egyptian camel on the pack. I walked over. "I saw you over here. How are you?" "I am tired and don't have much energy." He looked thin and obviously struggled to breathe. He wheezed. I nodded and pointed toward home. "Yeah, I was on my way but had to stop and… catch my breath." "I'll walk with you." We walked slowly the several blocks home. "You're not driving the chevy?" "Your mom took it to go somewhere." He looked and acted tired and old. "I'm taking time off from work. I need to get a paper from the doc for the… union." Our slow trip home took a while. "Michelle and I are going down to the shore this weekend if the weather holds up. We'll take my sailboat. You remember the crabbing we used to do?" I think he smiled. He coughed several times, a deep cough. This alerted me that his health was not good and maybe significantly. We got to the steps. I helped him up. The walk took it out of him. Gong.

My father's illness progressed. The doctor soon hospitalized him at Lehigh hospital, near the old neighborhood. One afternoon, mom, brothers, Michelle and I went to see him in the hospital. I had gone to see him once before. Looking emaciated, he spoke positively, but coughed and struggled. He enjoyed seeing us all. "Dad, the Phillies beat the Mets. Big game." He nodded. "Demetrius misses you, dad." I said. "That stupid dog, don't listen at all!" Nick said. "Shut up," said Tony. "Make me!" replied Nick. "Ok, ok," Mom chided in. My mom and brothers had been there a while. She looked tired. We always meet hospitals at a time of crisis. It doesn't see people at their best. I gave him a kiss on the forehead, "We gotta go, Dad." Michelle waved and smiled. She and I had a date. Her parents would not be home, so we had the house to ourselves. I looked forward to that but felt guilty about it afterward. We said goodbye, a hand on Tony's shoulder, a nod. "Bye Mom, see you later." "Ok, Steve. You working tonight?". "Nope."

A couple of days later, I came home from school in the afternoon. My mother asked me if I would drive her to the hospital to see my dad. It had been several weeks since his admission. She vaguely spoke about his condition. I didn't push it. Getting into the big Chevy, I drove. We conversed little on the way. The trip took about 20 minutes. The hospital stood on a busy avenue. We pulled in and parked. The overcast day fit my mood. We went to the nurse's station on my father's floor and they directed us down the hall. I opened the door. A staff person stood there. The room had no windows. My father lay in the bed, no machines. He had passed away.

I looked at my mom and I looked at the staff person. It turned out to be Alice Reyes, my junior high friend. She pulled over a chair for my mom. I stood. The light in the room felt too bright for me to see what I didn't want to see. I could hear myself breathe. His ears were dark. His eyes closed. "He fought hard," Alice said. "We had to revive him several times, but…" Her voice trailed off. The thick air was silent. I felt stunned, but that didn't quite get it. I really thought nothing, but heaviness went inside and sat on my heart. My mother sat silently. I glanced at her and could not say or do anything. "I am sorry Mrs. House." Alice said. The moment felt slow. My eyes welled up, and I cried softly, my cheeks wet. I don't know what else happened there. I thought I should hug my mom, but I couldn't. We were there for maybe fifteen minutes; I didn't keep track. I allowed her to determine when we should leave. She got up and touched his body, patting it. I leaned over, whispered, "Good bye Dad". A staff person spoke to my mom in the hall. We left and got into the car and drove home silently. My mind was jarred and the reality of my father's death swooned around the tilting room of my life.

Upon getting home, turmoil met us. Yia Yia stood in the kitchen and my aunts stood around. Others, Artie, maybe neighbors, were present. I wasn't sure. "Anna, I am so sorry!" "Well…" My brothers were about. My mom turned to me. "Tell your brothers about your dad." I took them aside and sat them down on the couch amid the stirring household. They were innocent teens. "Guys, I have…bad news. Dad has died in the hospital." Tony put his hand over his mouth. Nicky looked confused. "They said he struggled with it." We all cried and hugged. I kneeled briefly in silence. Why she didn't tell them? I don't know. I worked that night.

As I think about it, my mom knew what awaited us on the drive over and said nothing about it. This pointed to the way things often went. We weren't prepared, and no words offered to help understand, predict, or comfort. Perhaps the adults were so lost in the moment, they could not speak. They thought us strong, or perhaps worse, that we would just deal with it. Perhaps suffering was commonplace and thus needed no acknowledgement. Maybe it is the case that death is lurking over one's shoulder. The best you can do is to ignore it until it speaks in loud and mean terms. However, for us, silence reigned as the standard in all but the most common issues. Death apparently was no exception. But the anvil spoke in its hot and sad tone.

The funeral happened up the street from Frankford Avenue at a small mortuary. My friends came, and I felt very thankful for that. My father lay in the casket in his gray suit that didn't fit well. His thin face looked unusual in a way that the dead are caricatures of themselves. This suit was the same one he wore to Easter and Christmas services.

There were quite a few people in attendance. The Brighindi's were there, neighbors from Connecticut. I don't think my father's mother came. My aunts, Tonia, Joyce and Renee, with their families, were present. The Greek side of the family was present. Aunt Artie with several kids came. The day was a long and a hard one to endure. However, there were positive stories that I heard about my father, work and social life that brought him back to life in a small way.

Now my father didn't practice his Catholic faith. I went to the Catholic church more than he did! They contacted the Catholic church, but they refused to do the service. My father wasn't active in his faith. A Greek Orthodox priest agreed to do the funeral. For me, this left me irritated at what seemed like hypocrisy. In the dire need of a family for spiritual reassurance and hope, the church failed based upon a technicality. This would play a role later in my life, when I could give that spiritual support to a grieving family. I would say, "Yes."

The Greek priest didn't know my father. Dressed in his darkly colored vestments, his presence brought back the image of the priests of St. George. He chanted. I imagine he used incense. However, I will always be thankful for his presence. Sparks from the eternal anvil.

After the funeral, we processed in the rain down to Oakland Cemetery 20 minutes away. It's an old place with a stone wall surrounding it. Cars were on both sides of the small lane. We all huddled around a tree near his grave. The service was solemn and quick. "Be at peace, Dad," I mumbled quietly. Heaviness hung in the summer air. They had a reception at the house.

Prior to his death, my father had missed several months of work and didn't pay his union dues or his insurance policy. My parents had little money for these expenses. The union relented and paid for the policy. This afforded my mother $10,000 or more. As my mother would speak of her ship coming in, the money represented the ship! Out of heartbreak and death came a possible new life. Or so the illusion went.

Over the next several months, things changed. My mother used her newfound treasure and bought the Penn Del restaurant up the boulevard. This surprised me. She had never worked in a restaurant, let alone owned a business. The answer came in the form of a man called "Nick the Greek". Now you had to say, "Nick the Greek" with your thumb, index finger and middle finger all closed in on each other and with flicks of the wrist. In his Greek accent, Nick claimed to make the "Besta pizza in Feeladelphia." So, he convinced my mom that with his skill and her newfound wealth, this would be the time of fulfillment. Things were going to be great!

My father's passing ripped open a wound that stung. Grief would make things rough for me. But as I finished my time at CCP, I applied to Penn State and other teaching colleges. I got in to several places. My grades were good. I had redone my negligent and failed past into a story of success and capability, enough to get accepted. I decided to go to Penn State and major in psychology.

However, my relationship with Michelle deteriorated. We went to the Art Museum one day, a wonderful place filled with beauty and color. "Michelle, you're not too talkative." Looking away, she said, "I haven't been sleeping well. I'm a little tired." She got accepted to Penn State ahead of me and looked forward to it. Feeling her withdrawal, I had become too emotionally needy. Tired and certainly sad, I realized I was not much fun. Toward the end of the year after my father died, she broke up with me. I got the car, the MG, as my consolation prize. Frank and Cindy were very supportive, and I spent too much time over there. About this time, Joe Koenig left for California. It felt like the band had broken up and I didn't know in what key to play the music.

Let me conclude this transition time in my life with my 21st birthday. Mom, my brothers, relatives, and friends were there. The occasion was festive. My mom even bought a cake. She wanted to lift me up. I felt I had to say something. "Thank you for being here." I paused, collecting my thoughts. "I have gotten here not by my doing, but I have to say, through the help of all of you. Yes, even you Tony!" Laughter. "As you all know, a lot has happened over this past year. With school and work, I have been pretty busy. But I want to say thanks for all that you have done for me. Your love and support during these trying times have helped me get through. I am not one to tell you, but let me say that I appreciate having you all in my life. Mom, especially I appreciate all that you have given me. Of course, I think of those not here… I miss dad," a look at mom, "and wish he were here." I couldn't put that pain in adequate words, nor did it get back into the box. "Thank you all and thank you for sharing my birthday!" Brief applause. People shook my hand. I got hugs. Then I began to cry. The tough wall I had erected to keep such feelings at bay cracked. The tears came out in force. I sat on the back steps and wept. After a while, I went with friends for a ride, but the tears, embarrassingly, continued. I felt broken open. Old pain and disappointment, tragedy and grief rose. Loss flowed out of me. Home felt dark and draining, even in the face of celebration.

However, over the next weeks, before I was to leave for Penn State, I felt a glimpse of something else. At one level, I was broken and spilling pain on the floor. But there, amid the wreckage, lay a reservoir of strength. Pain drained out of me but rubbed against an indefatigable spirit, a sense of hope. I wasn't good at hope. I dealt much better with catastrophe! This eruption cleansed me and found its way to an old power going back years. Maybe it was dignity shown to me by my father and grandfather, the men who loved me when I was young. I arrived at a milestone; I encountered a demarcation line. Knowing a truth, I traveled as far as I could here in this place. It was time to move on. The hammer hit the anvil with a long, loud resonance.

<u>Leaving Home for Good</u>
The door closes, light escapes, but in half motion
From the other side, the raucous din of laughter can be heard
The clang of the chains of a swing alone is heard, blowing in the wind
The sound of a car horn blares on the street
One hears the murmuring whispers of children engaged in plots and schemes
A roomful of books is left, used words and diluted pictures, gathering shadows

The guitar sits quietly in its case, asleep and dark
The music is melody fading as the light diminishes
The quiet seeps through the small cracks in the doorway
There will be another morning elsewhere
Leaves shall breathe the songbird's love
The day will speak its endless possibilities to others who can listen
While the door closes on the darkening room, only echoes surround the still air
Echoes become gray and fade and become a still life
Rich colors settle and lose their sparkle
The buildup of years of joy and sorrow push and pull and seek expression
But the memories grow invisible without anyone to recall
They fight the darkening of the light like insistent children
Locked in innocence, they are forever aware only of what is missing
And what they want
The door holds back the old energy, aging the wood in its weariness, frozen in its petrified stance
The unsurpassable skeleton of an age lost and past due
The joyful forces, the carefree energy, the powerful living too big for the room moves on
Its scent slowly dissipates like a cloud burned by the rising heat of the day
In the pregnant moment, the dust entombs, in a quiet dirge, what was but will be no more

7 Penn State University

I found the last room at the end of the third floor. I opened the door with anticipation at the beginning of my new story. The several bags of clothes and stuff I carried were getting heavy. The door opened easily and the empty room invited me in. I didn't have a roommate. Two beds, a couple of dressers, nice wooden desks, a big window overlooking the parking lot and stadium. Sitting briefly on the bed, "This is it, the big Penn State! I am here!" I spoke out loud to convince myself. A lot of noise and shouting came from next door. The door opened, and a guy ducked his head into my new room. "Hey, newbie. Come on over, we're watching the Flyers kick the Redwings." He called himself Wolf. Thus began my time at Penn State.

My first semester began in January 1972. Officially, I entered school as a junior, but really a new kid on campus. The campus at State College, Pa., was by Mount Nittany at the geographical center of the state of Pennsylvania. I drove my little MG to campus, filled with what I thought would be useful. A good pair of heavy boots and a blue parka with a big hood came with me. I had a woolen cap and warm clothes. I packed other shoes. My mom had made me a box of cookies. Notebooks and pens came as I extended what I used at CCP. I included several pairs of jeans, socks, underwear. For sleeping, I packed a pair of thick flannels. Looking like a lumberjack, I brought flannel shirts. The camera came and, of course, a guitar. I brought a picture frame with a page I cut out of a magazine, saying that a man's reach must exceed his grasp. It fit by the desk. I had bought a meal ticket so I could eat. My mother had insisted I take a travel iron and a sewing kit. I didn't use the iron, but the sewing kit came in handy for buttons. I didn't do socks.

The trip took about 4 hours from home. On the map, I penciled out the route. The drive to campus had been cold, but sunny. The little car did well. It felt like a companion. I would make that trip several times and come to recognize the houses and buildings along the way!

The two guys next door would offer more entertainment the next day. After dinner, they called me over to witness Wolf's roommate lighting a fart! The dark room suddenly burst into a spectacular jet of orange lasting but a half second. The room then smelled terrible and pungent.

They were both country guys from the eastern side of the state. At Penn State, there were those from Pittsburgh and surroundings and those from Philly and surroundings. A rivalry of sorts existed. However, for this Greek kid from Philly, this wasn't even close. We had soft pretzels and steak sandwiches. We had Bobby Clarke and the Broad Street Bullies, who had a good season that year.

I prepared well for the weather. The jacket and boots were excellent choices as it snowed heavily several times that winter. Early on, with Wolf, I went to the dairy farm across from the stadium in the cold. We walked there. It had snowed. I took my camera and have photographic proof of the event. The place comprised several buildings, housing equipment and, of course, a big barn with cows. For me, a city kid, to walk around these big and friendly creatures made me feel like I was at a zoo. They mooed their approval.

Nearby, amid the trees, ascending a small road, was a trout stream and fishery. I hit the angler lottery! We were in the hills; the beautiful Allegheny mountains regally stood tall in the distance. There were mountain streams, apparently stocked with trout. An 8-foot-wide stream that ran through the hatchery had many big trout. As well, scattered about were smaller ponds filled with small fish. Eventually I bought a fly-fishing rod and flies and practiced my cast, with success and resolve.

The beginning of the semester saw orientation activities. I met a girl early on who lived in a dorm by the stadium. Our relationship lasted a month, then faded for lack of attention. I wasn't capable, being needy and selfish. Later, I called her and apologized for my selfishness. I don't think she appreciated it.

One time, I went to an ice cream place in town. I shuddered as I walked in. There at the counter stood Michelle, my old girlfriend. Stunned at a deep place, I hurried out. Michelle sightings happened several times around campus. They were not fun, but probably necessary to deal with the trauma of the loss. For me, it felt at that level.

The classes on campus were different for sure than CCP and helped me get my mind out of my emotions. There were more people in class. As well, the classes required a hike all around the campus. The exercise was good. One semester I made the grave mistake of having a lab on Saturday morning. It turned out to be across campus in one of the science buildings. But I relished my psychology classes. I felt an identity with other psych majors. As well, the professors were interesting and knowledgeable. I had one professor who had studied under Carl Rogers, the famous psychologist. That fact impressed us all. However, the class texts were very expensive; I had a limited budget. But classes were informative and fed my open mind. I felt I found a place for myself. Several gongs and sparks.

Now psychology had grand divisions in terms of theory and practice. I had a class taught by a behaviorist that I struggled with. This guy thought, like B. F. Skinner, that mental events were irrelevant to psychology. This seemed like a view contrary to reality, and it annoyed me. With my generally ruminative style, I concluded internal events were significant. To say that reward and punishment were all the explanation we needed to account for behavior felt wrong. You can see I developed strong opinions at Penn State. I wasn't too out of step, however, as the cognitive revolution dominated the field. Strict behaviorism, despite Skinner's brilliance, was becoming passe!

Psychology fit my contemplative nature. I could cut up very well and make people laugh, but my gentler soul rested comfortably in contemplation. At Penn State, I practiced meditation to relax. At first, I wasn't very good at it. As I sat on the floor, eyes closed, thoughts easily distracted me and I ran after them before I could return to my breathing. But I made progress and my anxiety diminished.

I felt I got a poor deal in an experimental psychology course. The grade determined whether you got a Bachelor of Science or a Bachelor of Arts. I passed, but my class project received harsh criticism. I did a questionnaire about attitudes toward war and correlated it with several measures of non-violence. The professor didn't like the idea. It reminded me of my argument with my dad about anti-war protests. A generational dividing line tripped me up. Or at least that is my rationalization for my low grade.

I also took several interesting philosophy classes. This introduced me to Immanuel Kant, the great German philosopher among others. I felt overwhelmed by his intellect. There were also the existentialists like Camus and Sartre. Being and Nothingness was a book on my list to read someday! However, my interest in philosophy waned a little when an older guy in class stood up and quoted Aristotle in Greek! That came a little too close to home. I already had that tee shirt!

My class schedule included several enjoyable hands-on art classes. These instigated my flowing creative juices. While I had experienced mild depression, perhaps more than that, art freed me up. Jill and I worked together at a table. "The discipline of the materials limits you," she started, "but beyond it, the medium calls out for playfulness. Don't you think?" "Yes, I found the same for poetry. There are rules but we can play the edges of these rules to wonderful effect. Pushing these limits, art varies them, collapses them, overlaps them. Art moves the background and the foreground, substituting, cutting off and pasting together again. It is a risky business, maybe turning out well or it might flop." "Woah, you have thought about this!" she said. As a real example, I bought a piece of sculpture from a friend of mine. It started out as a small pitcher that had sagged in the middle and looked wrong. However, if placed upside down, it looked like a wonderful artistic reflection of a brain.

On my first visit home, I didn't know what to expect. I felt ambivalent and different. It wasn't calm, but weird. I went to the restaurant and found my brother Nick delivering pizzas in my mom's car. "Hey Mom, how are you?" "Oh, Steve, what a surprise!" She was busy at the front. Nick the Greek was in the back cooking. I looked through the opening and gave him a salute. He nodded. I felt like the prodigal son coming home. No ring for my finger, though. My mom was working hard at her dream. I asked about how they were doing and she answered, "Good Steve, good. We're busy a lot of the time." It seemed to be fairly busy. "Do you enjoy it, mom?" "We're trying to make ends meet, Steve. Trying to make ends meet." I hoped that the business did well.

To my surprise, I found out that my brother Nick took over my room. I guess no surprise really. He recently opened the door too hard and broke the glass of the fish tank, spilling water and fish all over the place. My old room had newspapers and clothes all over the floor. He had become a hoarder. I made a comment about the mess, but he responded with a shrug. I enjoyed seeing my brother Tony. "Hey bro! Nice to see you. You doing ok?" I asked. "Got a camp out this weekend. I won't be around." He seemed distant, however. Tony was going to a technical high school rather than Frankford.

I would also spend time with Frank and Cindy, visit Joe Murphy and others. It felt great to see them and visit. But the place felt different. I was only a visitor. The place had shrunk.

Back on campus, I always made friends, and in the dorm, this happened as well. We had a wonderful group. I met a very social and fun woman whose major was drama. "Oh, Steven," she liked to be formal, "you psychology types are stuck in your heads! Let it go and be present in this delicious world!" People congregated around her. She wore these flowing dresses and scarves in quite a dramatic way. What gravitas! What persona! Perhaps she was a little like my grandmother. There were also psych majors, the brainy ones who you could come to with issues. They didn't do therapy but were good consultants. There were a couple of science guys. Kodak had a lab on campus in the chemical engineering area. There were Spanish majors. Isn't it interesting that I remember people by their major field of study? From this group, I found several people who would type up my papers. I brought a typewriter with me but I really couldn't type. My skill level took hours hunting and pecking. Luckily, for a small fee or for free, I could arrange for typing services.

In our group were few who cared much about going to the football games. I agree this sounds like sacrilege, but I never went to a Penn State football game. A friend of mine, smiling, nodding out the window at the stadium across the parking lot, "Steve, here is how I look at it. Why freeze our butts outside in the frigid wind of a cold stadium when we could just as easily get drunk inside a nice, warm dorm room?" He had a point.

I took on some challenges while there. I had my guitar with me and, as was popular, the town had a couple of coffee houses. Of course, there would be an open mic night. Once I took up the challenge and brought my guitar to the open mic. I played several songs, folksy kind of stuff, Dylan, Peter, Paul and Mary. This old stuff came from memories laid down from the Frankford days. They told me, "House, you're good. Come back whenever you want." It felt good to perform. I need to say as well that Joni Mitchell got me through my emotional trials at Penn State. Her "Blue" album was the soundtrack of my emotional rehab.

Admittingly, my partying reached a professional level. The school ranked high for its partying nature. Well, in the dorm we tried to keep up the reputation. In the latter part of 72, my dorm room changed to the other end of the hall and I got a roommate. Many of the same people were there.

Marijuana was usually available. For my 22nd birthday, the guys on the floor celebrated. "It is party city tonight! Johnny brought the Vodka. We chipped in and bought some dope just for you, Stevie!" The evening lasted quite a while. We visited several places on campus. I had to be helped back to the dorm. This probably marked as close as I got to develop addiction issues. I felt the not-so-subtle pull of smoking and partying. I liked the feeling of getting high. However, a red flag went up in my head, recalling the damage my father's drinking had caused. I didn't think that smoking harmed me, but a warning went off inside.

In the middle of coursework, the leisurely game of getting high cost me time and focus. As well, it probably incurred brain damage, and focused my mind on really petty things. It could not continue. As I narrated, "You paid for this opportunity to be in college. This time is your chance to avoid the Philly life. You have a ticket and you are squandering it, stupid." You have heard about the best way to cook a frog? Put it in a pan with cold water and then slowly turn up the heat. By the time the frog realizes that the water is getting hot, it is too late, or so the story goes. Well, I sat in hot water. A loud warning kiss of the hammer on hot metal goes here.

On the lighter side, much in the intellectual vein of Aldous Huxley's The Doors of Perception, at one point I conducted an experiment. The conversations that we had while we were high always seemed to be of such great insight, wit, and wisdom. Early in the evening, things were flowing well and so I wrote for about ten minutes everything that people said. The next day, under the more sober light of reason, I scanned the paper I had stuffed into my pocket. I wrote mostly legibly and in sentences. "Grace Slick is a beautiful thing. Can she cook? I can cook eggs, but do I want eggs? You know eggs are nutritional. However, warm clothes ...we need to keep warm. Laughter." The experiment resulted in stunning evidence showing the negative impact of pot on our judgement. This was also the time that the engineer of the group got high for the first time. He noted he felt like, "a three-phase transformer about to blow and the circuit breaker would not kick out!" Pot left him with quite an experience!

I learned here that I could go between being introverted and extraverted. The pot smoking probably increased the introversion. However, I had curiosity, an inventive nature, and a sense of humor. "Karen, I found out about this book called, I and Thou by a Jewish theologian, Martin Buber. He brings all relationships to two forms. I and it, like a machine focused on use, or I and Thou like what God gives us. Is that cool or what? Hey, you want to be my Thou?" "If you'll be my It and get me a tissue over there!" "I'm trying to have a conversation here!" I conversed and had an interest in others. Logical and practical, maybe smarter than I thought, I worked on how people thought and judged. I probably had been working on it for years. I knew I didn't trust easily. Depressed, check, and anxious as well. I had a high tolerance, however, for weirdness. I wasn't one to judge.

While developing friendships, I was on the lookout for a girlfriend. In the cafeteria, I saw a cute woman whom I had to meet. After asking around, I found out I knew a person she knew and so I had a way to get introduced. I could not just go up to her and say hi! Vanelle was attractive, with soft and inviting eyes. I noticed her welcoming smile. She seemed to be a gentlewoman. "Hey, Dave, how are you? How's the project coming?" "Steve, here's a friend of mine, Vanelle." "Wow, that is a pretty name. Are you a student here or is there a beauty contest going on?" "That is the stupidest pickup line I have ever heard." She laughed. "Give me a minute, I got more. How long have you been waiting for the bus, Maam?" She later told me she was attracted to my blue eyes. It must have gone well, after we met, we spent increasing time together.

At one point, on break, I visited her home in West Chester. The beautiful house, on a tree-lined street, reminded me of Connecticut. Her mother had a warm and friendly presence. She generously gave me a beautiful spoon with a hinged cover on it for holding tea.

On another trip to drop her off, we had a very unusual experience. I wasn't aware of how it affected her, but it had a great impact on me. We were going down a hill at night and the dark street had few lights. Halfway to the bottom, I felt a strong urge to change lanes, and I did. This premonition proved significant. At the bottom of the hill, we passed a stalled car with the hood up and people around. Had I continued on in the right lane, I would have crashed into the darkened car or at least needed to engage in a quick evasive action. "Did you see that? We're lucky we didn't hit them!" "I wasn't looking." I did not question this unusual experience, but came to accept and appreciate it. I believe I experienced an example of supernatural protection I have felt at other times. My guardian angel worked overtime that evening! Smack the anvil!

Also on this trip, after dropping her off, my car wouldn't start. I had trouble with it flooding. It had sensitive SU carburetors that I could never accurately adjust. Well, anyway, I went back in and told Vanelle of my car troubles. I asked if I could spend the night there and leave in the morning. Vanelle, although not happy with me, relented. The car finally started the next morning.

During spring break, Vanelle asked if I could take her to Boston. She wanted to see a friend at Harvard. She would buy gas. I really wasn't sure the MG would make it, but it reluctantly did. I feel we annoyed each other however, during the long trip. She excitedly talked about her friend the whole time. "I know all about your friend and how close you are. Can we talk about something else?" "Oh, that's right, it has to be about you." I just shook my head and drove on. However, this was my first time at Harvard. She stayed with her friend and I slept on the floor. I enjoyed walking around the Harvard yard and the Charles River. A mist hung in the air that day, that created a solemn and peaceful atmosphere. I seemed to have the place to myself. The beautiful, old and scenic neighborhood felt gentle and good. I felt moved to write several poems and made good on a lousy situation.

Another time, Vanelle and I had gotten high on a Saturday morning. We began in the dorm and listened to music. I played a "Yes" album. "Hey, can I tell you how this music affects me? I see an epic journey. Can you hear at the beginning the questions hanging in the air? They are just starting." "Now, how about that track? There is tension and conflict. Aren't you feeling a little anxious about it?" I asked. "Well, yes. It was like when my sister and I had an argument." "See, the music is moving ya! The question is, where's it gonna take ya?" "Straight to lunch, I bet!" "Oh, my, you're impossible!" We laughed and talked over the morning. We ended up walking around the campus.

Eventually, the relationship deteriorated. I think I tried too hard and bored her. I felt I was drowning, and she was a life jacket. Not a good basis for a relationship. The last time I spent time with her, another guy came around. After probably too long, I left, feeling angry and disappointed. I can't say that I loved her, but I felt she was interesting. The door just seemed to close.

Being a psych major fit me because I had the skill of listening. I had patience, openness, decent perceptive skills and decent judgment. I forget the specifics, but Dave, a friend of mine from Philly, and I spent time together focused on his difficult life circumstances. His family had seen terrible and violent loss. We spent a lot of time processing this. "Dave, I don't know what to say. You have been through life events that are horrible. I have little advice, but I'd like to hear how you are." However, we talked regularly and intensely for a while. He led, and I listened. After a while, we spoke less. He posited me with helping him cope with the difficulties he faced. For me, I applied listening skills and simply responded with caring, gentleness, and humanity. It would be a skill set that I would later build a career on. Years later, Dave would contact me and we wrote back and forth for a while.

Having an MG made for easy comments and offered entertaining opportunities. The campus had several sports cars enthusiasts who would occasionally have scavenger hunts with their cars. My new roommate, Rob, and I took part in several of these. They would give us a list of clues we had to follow and decipher. "Ok, so the first clue has to do with a gas station on a two-lane road. Looking for a big blue sign. Do you have any idea?" It would last most of the morning. We never got close to winning. But we sure looked good in our MG sports car!

I befriended a local guy, John, who attended the university. At one point, he asked, "I have written a play for a class of mine and I need someone to be the voice of God. I wondered if you could do that?" "Sure John, I know the guy personally!" He thought I would fit the bill. We had fun doing the project, and he got a good grade on it. John knew the county better than anyone, and we took long rides. One such time we ran out of gas. We were probably miles from anywhere. Walking a couple of miles to a gas station, we had to find open containers to carry the gas. Each of us carried almost a gallon of gas. However, by the time we got back to his car, the gas had almost all evaporated. We had enough to get us back to his parent's house. But barely. In a joking fashion, we also made a deal that whoever got married first would buy the other a piece of cheesecake.

After Boston, the MG ran poorly. The emergency brake went out, and the starter failed to engage all the time. I solved the issue by starting it in 2nd gear after a rolling start. That meant I had to park it on an incline. To start it, I would push it with the door open, get it rolling, jump in and stick it into second gear. Voila, the engine would kick in. I had little money, so I had to live thin. Starters were expensive. I know, I had the catalogue! I had saved money working but as it got closer to graduation, I had little extra.

My half working MG ultimately created a significant problem for me. One time, I parked it but apparently didn't set it in gear to keep it from rolling. The car tragically rolled into the old 62 Oldsmobile parked next to it. A friend of mine saw it and rolled it back and set the gear. This happened however after the owner of the other car saw it and left me a note informing me of the incident. My friend told me what he did. But I wrongfully ignored the note. Eventually, he called the campus police, who questioned me about the incident. I had to go to court charged with leaving the scene of an accident. The intimidating courtroom was solemn and heavy. "Mr. House, do you understand the charge you are facing here?" "Yes, your honor." "What do you have to say?" Slowly, "I moved my car. I didn't see any damage, so I ignored the note Mr. Warren sent me." I didn't say anything about my friend moving the car. The judge, looking at me, responded, "Mr. House, I find you guilty of the charge and the court fines you $150. You will relinquish your driver's license for 6 months." I felt terrible and shameful. It felt like a small thing that got out of hand, but the consequences were severe and shaming. My desire to protect my friend cost me. I parked the car, but I took a substantial risk and drove the car home without a license before graduation. My mother drove me and the family up to graduation.

I had hitchhiked before losing the car. But with money in short supply, and no car, out of necessity, I thumbed my way home. It worked out. My hitchhiking days occurred my last couple of semesters. School had an information board about where people were going and when. So, I rode with strangers a couple of times, helping with gas.

Hitchhiking could be an adventure. You never knew what would happen. One time, I got close to the store where a friend of mine worked in a different part of Philly. I arrived around dinner time but he wasn't working that night. So, without the expected ride home, I had to hitchhike again halfway around Philadelphia to get home. The last time I hitched a ride, I got picked by an older gentleman. He asked where I needed to go and I told him to Philly and he told me to get in. It started out well enough. He took me almost all the way. However, shortly after we started, he pulled out a gun from his pocket and laid it on the seat so I could see it. This stunned me. I wasn't sure it served as protection or aggression. He looked at me and said, "Son, just in case." I guess I appeared to be one of those long-haired, college going, drug dealing, violent, hippie types whom you couldn't trust. I would have been fine getting out and walking!

My last semester, I took classes over the summer. Funds were low. Several friends got into an apartment. They asked if I would be interested in joining them. I said "yes," as it would be a little cheaper. We split costs four ways, and we each took turns buying groceries. One guy was a forestry major. One night, he came into the apartment with a bag. "Hey, Rick, what's in the bag? You got dinner for us?" "Well, kind of," he said. "Take a look." I opened up the bag casually. Unwrapping a smaller object wrapped up in paper towels, I exclaimed, "Holy crap!" There in the towel, bloody I might add, I found the beheaded body of a snake. "I brought you a timber rattler we found today and killed. They are decent eating." We fried it up and took the small pieces of meat off the snake's many ribs. When cooked, it turned white and tasted like chicken!

While I had gotten through the draft lottery without being drafted, the war continued to rage. On the route walking to class from the apartment, I passed a TV store. I remember seeing Nixon on the TV several times when I would come past. I had a couple of choice words for him.

On top of the other stresses, my graduation almost didn't happen. I had taken a geology class with a volcanologist. He had interesting stories and spent his free time drawn to active volcanos. The grad student who ran the lab lost my paper. My grade of F stunned me and meant I couldn't graduate. This created a crisis. I had turned in all my work, including the suspect paper. I contacted the department. They contacted the professor who was in Peru. Eventually it got straightened out. I didn't need the upset or the added tension. I felt tense enough going back home with a degree and not much of a plan!

My last semester, I felt obvious turmoil. The protests on campus were a part of it, as was the legal jeopardy I experienced. Breaking up with Vanelle floated around me. But then, I faced the prospect of what to do with my new psychology degree. What doors would open because of my degree? I had thought little about this moment when deciding on my major. My life circumstances, I felt trained me for a psychology career. My plan involved being a therapist or a teacher. I almost had enrolled in education.

I visited an older female grad student I knew. She said, "Steve, I think my dad would like you." "Oh, yeah. Would I like him?" with a little smirk. "I don't know. He likes to plan. Do you really not have a plan when you graduate? What are you going to do?" I think I avoided it. "Going back to Philly." With a shrug. "You know what? I'm hearing some fear in that. I bet you are a little scared. Sorry if that's too bold." "Yeah," letting out a breath. "Doc, you see right through me!" Rolling her eyes, "Oh, stop." I hate to admit it, but she voiced the truth. The exciting jaunt into the world of higher education proved time limited and about to end. And now the real question reared its ugly head. What should I do? The return to the dark and heavy Philly life approached, and no simple plan existed. I had no viable relationship. My bachelor's degree didn't amount to an engineering degree or even a culinary science degree. It gave me general people skills and opened me up to work in a million settings, but specific to none. Driving back home after graduation in the old Chevy, by the back window shelf of the car lay a book on existential philosophy. That would be the question, what would come of my existence? The anvil sings a low-keyed song.

After graduation, I took over my old room again when I got home. For me, this made up a necessary evil. I really didn't want to come back to the old life I left. But I had no choice. I made practical decisions and did what had to be done.

My next move, however, I thought, came from pure brilliance. I contacted an employment agency! I had computer skills from my railroad work and I had a brand-new psychology degree. The computer experience proved more valuable, unfortunately. I went on one interview where the guy asked about how I thought my computer and psychology background came together. My long and abstract BS answer did not satisfy him. The employment agency person asked quizzically, "What did you say to the interviewer at the job site?" I didn't have a good explanation.

I got an interview at an oil company that opened to a job. The company made topographical maps that helped geologists find oil. The small office had only had a handful of employees and several large 8-foot by 8-foot-wide tables. Our job involved setting up the computer, keeping the ink reservoirs filled and the paper tight. The work paid well but could become tedious. I needed funds to make an unforeseen future happen. I decided my time living with my mom had to be limited.

At the job, I met a single woman and her sister-in-law among several other employees. After a few months, we began a romantic relationship. She was Italian, a big woman, and a humble and generous soul. After work, we would hang out and go to bars downtown. I had no other distractions other than work. My mom's restaurant continued to occupy her time. Nick the Greek still hung around a lot. They had their arguments, however. He thought he knew how to run things, but my mom asserted her ideas and will. I felt I had seen this act before with her and my dad. I tried to stay out of it.

My girlfriend and I went to the movies and enjoyed drinking. She had an apartment, and we spent time there. Now she was affectionate and had a playful attitude. Maybe that attracted me to her. We had fun and things were not heavy or tense. She went well with the flow. Now, because her sister-in-law also worked at the place, I got invited to family gatherings. Her tall and older brother was unsure about me. One time we went down to the shore and took my sailboat. At one point, the boom caught him by his shoulders and threw him into the water. I hadn't planned this, and I felt embarrassed. This didn't endear me to him at all.

Now another disturbing thing happened when we visited the apartment of a family friend. They described him as a little weird. As we entered his apartment, things went quickly south. Shutting the door revealed a life-size poster of Hitler on the back of the door! This was too much. Uncomfortable, we didn't stay very long. She apologized several times.

In February, the company said it was moving to Houston, Texas. The office workers would get a small severance pay. The move happened during the summer. I filed for unemployment and again didn't have a plan. My Italian girlfriend and I broke up. The relationship wasn't going anywhere. Later, I found out that her father died and I didn't call her. I added my regrettable behavior to the bag of stupid and insensitive things I had done. The hammer delights in making noise over this one.

I read a variety of books during this time. There was Ray Bradbury, Richard Brautigan, Kurt Vonnegut, Jr., and Carlos Castenada. On top of that were James Thurber, Robert Frost, Alan Watts, Rumi and books on Zen Buddhism. No rhyme or reason. I fed myself an eclectic and weird assortment. I regret to say I drifted away from Christianity. Fantasizing, I decided I would write a novel at some point. The last scene would be me sitting by the side of the road while the MG burned. Such was my mindset. But contrary to this and considering the mysterious power of God in my life, reality would be different.

Walking around down town Philly by myself one day, unemployed, alone, and gloomy, I was on my way to the Franklin Museum. I had gone many times to the magical museum as a kid. Well, I ran into Darlene, my friend from CCP. "Darlene, is that you?" Big hug. "I haven't seen you in years." We sat on a bench. "I just graduated with a nice new psychology degree. How are you and Carol? Still living by the park? Still got the dog?" "Yep. I've been working at an office since CCP. It pays well, but I may be moving out of town." "Yeah?" It was wonderful to see her. I gushed to her about my lack of plans and situation. Like other angels I have encountered, God set up this one. After a pause, she looked at me directly. "There is a school in Michigan that you could probably get into. They have a Master's in psychology. I realize it's late in the year, but I bet you could get accepted for the fall. You should look into it." She told me that Eastern Michigan University was in Ypsilanti, Michigan. She was going for a master's and just wanted to offer it as a possibility.

The great power blessed me again with a profound encounter. As the story goes, I applied and got accepted. Later, I visited Darlene in Ypsilanti a couple of weeks before school started. I took the trip to find a place to live. I found a small room rented by a pleasant couple, cheap and close to campus. The anvil and hammer were busy. Joyful sparks were flying!

I met a woman at a Philly bar maybe two weeks before heading out to Michigan. We got a booth, talked about psychology and many other things for several hours. We shared our histories and dreams. Walking her to her car, I gave her a quick kiss and said that I would probably see her again, but neglected to exchange phone numbers. I really had it in the back of my head that I was leaving. It probably could have been a great relationship. "Here's looking at you, kid!" I will never know.

Come the end of the summer, I packed all that I owned into the MG. I brought a small, foot tall palm tree, my tools, my unused typewriter, clothes and a sewing kit. My turntable and two small box speakers came with me, as did a guitar. The trunk was full. With a face like flint, I took on the wiry future. I hugged my mom and brothers goodbye. I drove west to who the hell knew what.

<u>The Turns in the Road</u>
Do not look to where you've been
It's done and spent, old paths, used steps
If it brings joy, then all the better
To have it once and again, to remember
Instead, look forward to turns in the road
To where your path meets open sky,
The dips and rises in days to come
A friendly wind in your face to guide
And place your hope and direction there
The past a comfort can only be
For truth be known and truth be said
Challenge comes from future's promise
And future's gifts all lie ahead

8 Ypsilanti

My dear, four-cylinder friend made it across the US to Michigan. Along the way, I followed another sports car and shadowed them. We waved. They got off in Ohio. I felt enthusiastically free. I had been to Michigan only once. Luckily, I had warm clothes, good boots and a friendly attitude. This felt like the start of the rest of my life! It felt good to leave Philly. Really, you could call this an escape. I was treading water in Philly.

I rented a medium-sized room on the second floor of a small house just off campus. A tall guy with a beard occupied the back room. He didn't say much. I introduced myself. "Ray," he said, not making eye contact. We shared the bathroom. I set up my stuff. It was late summer and Michigan felt several degrees cooler than in Philly. The landlady did not want me to have a hot plate. But the university had a cafeteria, so it would have to do. I could get a refrigerator if I wanted. But that would cost. I saved only so much from the mapping job. I had to eat enough to stay alive while working on my master's degree. That sounded formidable, but kind of cool. I took to this college thing. Sparks.

I had several days before classes started, so I explored. Campus was a short walk away. Darlene and I met up, and we went and ate. I didn't want to bother her too much or seem dependent. "Darlene, I don't know, but Philly has been tough for the past year. Driving here, I felt released from the pressure. I felt like I was suffocating." She smiled, thumbs up, "Good for you!"

Eastern had a fairly large campus, not by Penn State standards, but bigger than a one building department store! It had been around for a while as there were grown trees around. There were new buildings as well, pointing to recent growth. As I approached the campus from the street side, West Cross street, a large concrete tower, probably 100 foot tall, caught my eye. It had girth to it. Maybe it served as a water tower or a communications building.

The town of Ypsilanti, Michigan, had a unique history. A marvelous story originated at the state psychiatric hospital there. Milton Rokeach, a social psychologist, had written a book about it in 1964. It concerned three delusional individuals who all thought they were Christ. Rokeach, who worked at the hospital, attempted to manipulate the interactions of the three in order to stop their delusional thinking. It did not work. However, being confronted by the others, the men developed ideas about who was the true "Christ". I felt certain psychology was my true calling.

I walked the streets a lot those first few weeks, getting acquainted with the place. A Catholic church, Holy Trinity, a tall A-frame building, stood on a corner of the other end of campus. There were advertisements about upcoming events. I made a mental note. I enjoyed going to a Catholic Church. That little church would play a big role in my stay at Eastern. Fr. Bob Kerr was the pastor, the sign said. I didn't attend to the hammer sound, faintly echoing in the air.

The University of Michigan at Ann Arbor was down the road. I took a trip over there and it seemed very much like Penn State. It had a large campus and lots of buildings, with many students milling around. I felt content at my middle of the road to school. What made the trip was I found a Dairy Queen on the way!

I had calculated four semesters, with maybe a trip or two back to Philly. Money was tight and would hopefully cover. Out-of-state tuition costs were high. Perhaps I could get a job in the department. I could probably find a computer job, but I had to be careful about working while going to school. Did that and got the tee shirt, thank you. I could handle the tuition, and I lived off campus in a fairly cheap room. It felt like I acted prudently.

One of my first classes, a guy in the back, sat next to me. I didn't like to sit up front, maybe junior high Spanish class trauma! He was about my age. "Hey, how are ya?" I said, looking over at him and extended my hand. "I'm good," he says. "Bob Bates." "Nice to meet you, Steve House. I just got here from Philly." "Oh?" he says, "You are a way from home. I'm from further north, Flint, Michigan." He opened his hand and showed me where home was, pointing between his fingers. "Huh," I said, "that's the state of Michigan?" "Yes, right up here in the middle is where I am from, maybe an hour from here." Interesting indeed! "I will get to explore when I can. Right now, I am trying to figure out where my classes are." A smile, "You shouldn't have much trouble. Campus isn't that big." The professor began the class, so we stopped. After class, I nodded, "See you around" as we left the classroom. I felt good to know another person in Ypsilanti.

Other than class, I had little to do. I bought books, as many used as I could. I played guitar and listened to music. The folks down stairs were friendly, but they honored our privacy. I decided I liked the idea of just going to school. I kept my eye open for small job opportunities while I relaxed just doing classes. The texts and lectures were interesting and the variety of classes engaging. The focus was not overwhelming. I liked that feeling of growing. Maybe that is what I missed in Philly last year. Nick the Greek making pizza didn't do it for me. Neither did the job at the oil company. I felt the old need to venture out and fill up my tank.

I did struggle with the question of purpose. Not working a job or making money sat heavy on me. Academia wasn't regular life work, like at the railroad. I often had this tension between the academic focus on books, professors and ideas and the practical world of making money. I wasn't so worried about relationships, for they seemed to just happen. At 23, I wondered where this would go. What sort of psychology job awaited me at the end of this rainbow? I had packed all that I owned into that little car and driven to the middle of the country with a two-year plan. This felt like my best shot. Vietnam was still on. My mom and brothers still lived in Philly. Everything that had been was still back there. I didn't engage in drinking or smoking. My sobriety said I was in a good place, cold but good. Taking the adventure day by day.

Well, as fate would have it, things were about to change. God's hand, as usual, was at work. I went to the cafeteria at the student center to get something to eat. Walking through, I saw Bob sitting at a table with a woman. I looked at Bob and he motioned for me. "Come, sit down." I took my tray and sat down. "Hey, how are you?" "Good, and you?" I nodded. "This is a guy from Pennsylvania," he said to the red-haired woman he sat with. "Steve House," I said, smiling. "This is my friend Rochelle. We went to high school together." "Oh, up there," and I motioned with my outstretched hand. She laughed, "Yeah, right there." She pointed. "Are you a psych major?" I asked. "No, I'm in Special Ed. Bob's a year ahead of me. I'm an undergraduate here."

"Well, cool." "Rochelle is a pretty name." "Thanks, named after St. Roch." "So, you survived your first couple days of classes?" Bob asked. "Fine, good stuff," I replied. "I really like it. Good classes. The weather seems to get cool at night fast. Maybe it's me." Rochelle had long, reddish hair and a pretty smile. "Different from Pennsylvania?" "Yeah, I'm from Philly and it's a little warmer than here." I found her attractive. She laughed easily. She seemed tall and fairly thin. I had a crush on a red-headed girl in my homeroom in high school. I must have been a dork back then. Not the college graduate stud I was now, or so my fantasy told me. "So, you're from Michigan, yeah? You guys are called Michiganders?" She laughed. "I haven't heard that in a while. Yep, I'm a Michigander!" She exclaimed. "I have lived here all my life. My family is big, 8 brothers and sisters. I'm the oldest. We're Catholic." She looked at Bob. "Yes, it is a big family!" he said. "Well, that's interesting!" I said. "I just have a couple of brothers. But I'm Greek Orthodox although I like to go to the Catholic church. I walked by the one on campus, Holy Trinity." "Oh?" she said. "I'm sorry," she inquired, "so, where is Philly in Pennsylvania?" "I grew up over here." I pretended to outline the state of Pennsylvania with my two hands. "It's right here in the corner of the state." She laughed again. "Never been there." "Well, they got the Liberty Bell and Betsy Ross's House!" "We just have Buicks. Our town has a big Buick plant." "Do you own a Buick? I hear they are really cheap in your hometown!" She smiled. The conversation stalled a little after that. They finished their meals and got up to leave. "Nice to meet you," I said to Rochelle. "Bob, see you later." "Yes, nice to meet you." I felt good about our pleasant conversation and I felt good about expanding my social network. I made a mental note to be continued. The anvil sent out a loud percussive echoing volley. I heard it.

The next time I saw Bob in class, I asked him about Rochelle. "Maybe we can get together." I told him. They seemed to be friends, and I didn't sense a romantic connection. He said, "If I see her, I will ask her." Later, he said that she invited him and me to her house. She lived with 4 other girls right off campus. So, we set up a time. I didn't have a phone in the room.

Bob and I met on the weekend and drove over to Rochelle's house. I got introduced to all the others. Carolyn and Chuck, her boyfriend, were an odd couple: she was 5-foot 5 inches, he stood 6-foot 3 inches. They were friendly people. I found out Jill played the guitar. Another of the girls had significant medical issues. One girl bubbled and talked. I knew little snippets of their lives. It probably felt good to Rochelle, who came from a household of kids. Luckily, the house had a lot of room. "Hey, anyone up for some football?"

Across the street was an open field between houses. "You up for it?" I motioned to Rochelle. "Sure," she said. One other girl volunteered. Rochelle and I versus Bob and the other woman. The light-hearted game went quickly. It's a simple game with only two on a side. We won and there were high fives and hugs. That was a pleasant surprise.

A couple of days later, I saw her on campus and we arranged I would come over. I could walk to her house in a couple of minutes. I put the top down on my car. While the sun went down, the sky had beautiful mauves and pink. I went up to the door and knocked. She answered, smiling, "Hi, nice to see you. Come on in!" she motioned. I told her, "First, I have something to show you in my car." We walked down to the car at the curb. I opened the passenger car door. There on the seat were two Dairy Queen sundaes. She giggled and said, "Oh, what a treat!" "Yep," I said, "I thought you might like one. There is always room for ice cream, huh?" We pleasantly strolled around the neighborhood while the sun went down. "I don't know a lot about special ed. Tell me what that is about for you?" "For me, I have a place in my heart for those special kids who can't quite make it in the regular classroom. They need help to …succeed, you know? Eastern has a highly ranked program, maybe even better than Michigan. What I would like to do is open up a school for disabled children where they could receive an education up to their abilities. They need to be respected!" She said it emphatically. "You are going to be a psychologist, right?" "That's kind of the plan." "Maybe you could work at the school I'm thinking of starting." She looked at me with a little smile. I tilted my head, "Maybe." It seemed a little presumptuous. Frankly, I hadn't thought that far ahead, but I would entertain any offers! It showed how thoughtful she was. She planned things and considered other's needs. My mom had a giving heart, and this was not unlike her attitude toward others. The plan felt concrete and doable. I thought to myself, here is a strong woman with ideas. "What do you like about psychology?" "Well, let's see, it's a great mystery how the brain works and how our behavior and thoughts come to be. It's like a gigantic puzzle. For instance, what caused you to ask the question? People have ideas and images, feelings and behaviors. We can reason, plan, and we can feel. Our personalities come with tendencies to act this way or that, to feel this way or that. We get depressed or anxious. Or schizophrenic. We also can imagine and project into the future and remember the past. We can plan and expect." A pause, "I just love the depth of it all." Pointing to my head, "This 5-pound brain holds all these secrets!" She responded, "You're pretty enthusiastic about it!" I shrugged my shoulders. We strolled back to her house.

As I drove away, I said to myself, "Well, Mr. College Stud, what are *you* planning to do with your life? Hmm." Looking into the mirror, "A vacant look. Just what I expected!" The words, like smoke, hung in the air. I had escaped Philly, thankfully. But the next step hadn't been that well-articulated. It sounded like work needed to be done. The hammer replied with a "yes".

Rochelle and I visited frequently. The people down stairs liked her. Pleasant and friendly, she brought a calm and positive presence. As we talked, I shared about my father's death, my mom and Nick the Greek. These were difficult things to talk about. I shared my pain and my loss. "I don't know what to say about my mom. She defies easy categorization. I love her. She's kind of quiet, loves to cook. Can be strict. Had a tough relationship with my dad." "Your brother?" "Nick is...special, maybe autistic? Has social issues, clumsy. He's got friends and works, but a little weird? I know that's a lousy description." We also talked about politics and war. We had similar views of the foolishness of conflict. She had gone to protests against the war. "At one point, I put flowers in the gun barrels of National Guard soldiers. I have strong feelings about the war." That seemed like a ballsy thing to do.

Religion came up. She felt distant from her religion. "For me, Rochelle, I know God exists and is loving. But I'm not sure how to respond. I don't pray well. The poor examples of trust I saw in my family make trusting in God difficult. You know what I mean?" As we spoke and shared opinions on subjects, I encountered a mixture of common ideas and differences. My family's swirling, out-of-balance dynamic certainly gyrated much differently than the steady, predictable pace of hers. Her Dad worked as a financial guy for a natural gas company, an accountant. She came from a "normal" family from my varied perspective. Her mom stayed home to raise the kids, but was a teacher by training. She had several sisters, a couple of them young. Her brothers did guy sort of stuff. One had a motorcycle. They were good Catholics, went to Mass, said the rosary.

As I walked home, one day, I ruminated about where I had been. The last half a dozen years had seen a substantial change in me. Education and making money had changed and broadened me. Perhaps I felt more independent. I liked that. I didn't have much, but I felt independent. Philly had left me feeling dark and weak. I was only starting to breathe. Here, I felt a participant in this life. The relationship with Rochelle felt good. Since high school, I felt better at the game of relationships. I had learned the give and take. God knows, I didn't have the best teachers in this realm. In fact, I knew more about what I didn't want than what I did. The meanness and negative energy in my parents scared me, and I firmly committed to avoid it. I had been on that emotional roller coaster that if it didn't throw you off the ride, it certainly rattled your teeth. I didn't want that relentless cycle of acrimony, casting my spirit into a mean snarling dog of a being. Gentleness and a caring peace attracted me. I certainly had my own demons of energy and confusion. But I saw a crack in the door that opened to a better place. Rochelle opened up possibilities for me with her gentle and caring demeanor. I thought about her often and enjoyed being around her. She made it easy to be with her.

Sweetness
For sweetness comes infrequently to this life of toil and pain
And when one can't predict it so, a sweet presence will invite again
But on the ready we must be with warm embrace and open heart
To lift our head and watchful see, to speak the humble words of love
When life is effortful again, we remember when all is still
Lovely, lovely sweetness, that we were touched by sweetness
By which our heart and soul were filled.

On the next weekend, she asked if I would be interested in meeting her parents. I said yes, although a tinge of anxiety went through my chest. Later, driving north with her to meet them, I felt anxious about it. I could usually count on being charming when I needed to be. Smile, don't fail me now! They met halfway to give her food. She thought it was a nice way to introduce us. It seemed like the next thing to do.

Now, I am a mildly long-haired individual; my hair went to about my shoulders with a moustache and a goatee. I didn't bring dress-up clothes. I didn't iron. There were many button-down shirts in my closet, so I decided on one to go with my jeans. My saving grace was in my beatnik but comfortable suede loafers. I just loved those shoes. I wondered what she told her parents about me. We chatted about it along the way. "So, your dad is an accountant?" "Yes." "And your mom is an ex-teacher who runs a household with a slew of kids. Was your dad in the military?" "Nope. I do have cousins…" This felt like prepping for an exam. The radio's music narrated our fairly quick trip. She pulled the car off to the side of the road in a restaurant's empty parking lot. I breathed deeply. Her parents were waiting for her. They hugged. "Mom and Dad, this is Steve. He is a friend of Bob Bates

I told you about." Her dad reached his hand over and I shook it. Her mom said, "Nice to meet you." The conversation quickly turned to Rochelle and how she and the girls were doing. She had an exam, and they asked about it. They were gracious people, well dressed. They had a big, new American car, maybe a Cadillac. The dad looked like an accountant, if that is possible. Rochelle favored him. He had an amiable smile. Her mom had her reddish hair up. The dad asked where I was from, "Philly," I said. "Oh", he exclaimed. "What are you working on in school?" "I am in psychology, working on my Masters." "Hmm, sounds interesting" he responded. I am sure many questions ran around his accountant's head. Maybe he tried to calculate how likely I was to have a viable career. We had a couple of minutes of conversation. The mom noted, "Sorry, but we have a bag of meat in the trunk that I don't want to go bad." They opened the trunk and handed her a bag of groceries. "Here you go, dear." How's everyone at home?" "Everyone is well and send their love." "I will call you tomorrow." Hugs. "Nice to meet you, Steve." A hand shake and a nod from the mom. "Nice to meet you guys." And back in the car. "That wasn't so bad, was it?" she asked. "No, that was fine. Your parents seem like gracious people." "You have your dad's smile." "Thanks." As we pulled out, "You guys do this every couple of weeks?" I asked. "Yep, it helps with expenses." "That is very kind of them. They take care of you." She nodded. She also confided in me later that her mother told her she wasn't going to bring any more food if it meant feeding "that hippie!" Meaning, of course, me! I eventually won her over. But the long hair served as an initial impediment.

Let me tell you the first time we went to Flint to meet her family. We rode up on a nice cool Michigan day. Walking up the path, I paused and looked to the sky." I gotta do this!" The door opened. Her siblings were by the front door and in the living room. They were an even dozen I thought and ranged in size and age. "Oh, hi. Are you Rochelle's boyfriend?" said the small one. "Susy, be quiet!" a sibling said. "He goes to her school." "How are you guys?" I asked. "Are you all related?" "Yes!" they said, smiling. Rochelle introduced me, resulting in a round of hellos and nods. Stanley, her next oldest brother, wasn't there. Rochelle's mom came in and greeted me. Rochelle seemed pleased at the spectacle. For me, I felt overwhelmed. She went through her siblings from the top down. Of course, I didn't remember much. The mom joked, "Before you can leave, repeat everyone's name!" "Oh, Mrs. Zochowski, my memory can't do that!" Nine kids in fourteen years. Quite an achievement. I gained respect for her mom! Sparks.

While the mom prepared dinner, I had a tour of the house. Upstairs, they showed me where people slept. I saw their stuffed animals. They followed me around like a doctor doing rounds. I wondered if Rochelle had any other boyfriends or if I could be the first serious one. Maybe my reputation as a long-haired hippie had preceded me and they wanted to see what one looked like and if I would try to sell them drugs?

When I got downstairs, the father had come home. "Nice to see you again," her father said. "Yes, sir." I responded. "You have a large family." "And a good one", he assured me, "and a good one."

We all sat down in the big dining room. I sat next to Rochelle. The meal started with grace, "Bless us, O, Lord, and these thy gifts…" Her mom made a wonderful and filling meal. And we had plenty of it. During dinner, we engaged in a light conversation with her parents, asking me questions about my background. My answers were short. I found it uncomfortable to talk about myself. "Philly is a big city like Detroit. My family lives in a row home. Anybody know what that is?" Open looks like I was going to tell them where I buried the treasure. "Well, it's a house that has other houses right next to it, with the same wall. And you know, you can hear everything that they say in the next house!" "Really?" "No!" "No, I'm lying, You can't!" I tried to make simple jokes that the younger kids responded to. What I saw here seemed vastly different from my style of family. The family had a gentleness, a flow, yet clear rules, with people getting along, talking, laughing, sharing. As a result, I relaxed. These were nice, friendly, easygoing people. Light-hearted banter floated around. Laughter came easily to the family. The mom, however, governed the place. They were probably on good behavior. But for me, far from home, and a different home for that matter, this created a welcome respite. It beat the cafeteria food by a mile and the pleasant conversation welcomed me. The visit left me with a warm, good feeling.

At Eastern, I had enrolled in a 45-hour Masters, covering the major areas of psychology. The program required a thesis and a comprehensive exam to be taken. Bob Bates did the specialization in clinical psychology. He would open up a practice in Michigan. My plan focused on getting my masters and seeing what opened up. Teaching still attracted me.

The classes at Eastern were broad and informative. I took an important class from Dr. Beecher, the physiology guy. I talked with him in his office about a thesis topic. "Dr. Beecher, I am not sure what to do about a thesis. I am thinking about it. I enjoyed your class. Brain studies and cognition are fascinating to me." I explained. "Do you have any suggestions?" Well, "he said, "my research concerns hearing, which would be a hard thesis topic. There is interesting work with divided attention and hearing." A pause. "You know…there is an old EEG machine in the closet. Take a look at it. How are you with electronics? There is probably an instruction manual around. It hasn't been used in a while." That got my interest. Remember my amplifier and stereo tape player? An EEG machine couldn't be that much more complicated! "Sure, that sounds good. Let me look at it." We found the thing in a box, an impressive piece of electronics. There were wires and plastic packets of small metal cups. We found an old printer apparatus with reams of graph paper. We didn't find the handbook. For the next several days, I played with the thing and got it to work. Calibration had to be figured out, the attachment of electrodes to the scalp, the printing of the recording. I researched the EEG. Upon Dr. Beecher's suggestion, I also visited a helpful woman at the University of Michigan hospital who worked with EEGs. She clarified several points concerning the machine.

Exploring the device, Brian Brereton, a fellow psych student, and I got it working. "OK, turn on power. The recorder has ink and is working. Sensitivity at zero. Leads in." "Looks good." He said. "Let me take this, use some of the connecting goo and push it against my scalp. Anything?" "Wow, look, we got squiggles! Those, my dear friend, represent brain waves!" "Awesome!" Small but significant steps. Now, I had to tackle the next really important step. What to do as far as an experiment? The machine measured the minute electrical variations emanating from the brain and opened up access to the brain. I just needed to find a question.

Things emerged, given my interests and classwork. My interest in thinking took me to a researcher named J. P. Guilford, who sought to classify intellectual processes. His model, called the "Structure of Intellect model" reflected a periodic table of intellectual processes. He attempted to classify and organize a lot of data into a coherent scheme. It offered a big view, like looking out on the roof on Dyre Street. I took distinctions he made and tested whether an analogous difference existed in brain functioning. Yeah, and with an old device that collected dust in a closet for ten years, a piece of cake! Well, the model proved useful. The machine gave up brain secrets, and I finished an 81-page thesis, although no one considered the Nobel Prize!

I saw an interesting result however of my experiment every day in class. My fellow grad students who helped had two electrodes held on their heads with a gooey substance. I could tell who had helped me out by the grayish circles of gunk in their hair. Ah, the progress of science yields nothing to fashion! Chang.

Brian Brereton became a good friend at Eastern. One time, he invited us to his home for a weekend. "You guys up for a sailboat race?" "I'd love that!" I said. It was great fun, but Rochelle seemed less than enthralled. She said she had an accident several years earlier where she found herself under a tipped canoe. As a result, she developed a fear of the water. She courageously went out in the boat. She probably felt that we were about to tip over. Rochelle found it a grueling experience. I fondly remembered my old Sunfish.

We also went to the Stratford Theater in Ontario, Canada. Northeast of Detroit, the beautiful Shakespearian theater offered an excellent production of Macbeth. We enjoyed each other's company as well. The well attended festival brought me back to high school Shakespeare. Not a great fan, but seeing it on stage brought it to life. Rochelle really liked it. She had been there before. The theater won her heart.

At school, I had a small paying job as a statistics tutor for undergraduates. With my money draining, I needed more. In Philly, I had worked briefly as a shoe salesperson. Of course, the lady who would come in to try on dozens of shoes made the job difficult. Tolerance and patience were required. In Ypsilanti, I took a job at a local shoe store, Willoughby's Shoes. Mr. Willoughby, a guy in his 60s, had owned it for years. He hired me because he needed the help. The hours were not bad; the conditions were clean.

One Saturday, a guy came in looking for a pair of loafers. I figured him to be middle-aged. He tried on a couple of pairs of shoes but wasn't pleased with them. As he sat there and I kneeled on the little footstool in front of him, he took off his hat. It had aluminum foil in it covering the inside of the hat. Of course, my curiosity pushed me to ask him about it. He replied, "I keep that in there so the FBI can't read my thoughts." So, this was the guy the FBI had been investigating! This example always grabbed attention as an example of pathology when I taught psych classes.

Now Rochelle and I were getting serious and spending a lot of time together. We began to encounter everyday things with each other. One day, Rochelle baked a cake for a friend's big birthday. "Hey, that smells good." "Yes, it's a cake for my friend Tina for tomorrow." In the morning, as we got ready, "We need to get going. You have pants other than jeans?" "Ok," I said grumpily. "Can you grab the cake? I don't want to be late." "Sure." The beautifully decorated cake sat in a plastic container on the counter. As we headed out the door, I helpfully picked up the container. "Got it!" Except, I grabbed it by the upper part of the container, not the bottom piece. As I lifted it to go on out the door, the unsupported bottom gave way and the beautiful cake fell on the kitchen floor in a splash of epic proportions. "Oh, crap!" I uttered. "Oh, no…no" said the shocked and disappointed Rochelle. Mr. Helpful quickly became Mr. Schmuck! However, the dog liked it.

Another time, her parents came over. Because I spent a lot of time there. I had some clothes in the closet. As they sat up in her room to talk, we both feared that they may look in the closet!

Around Thanksgiving, Rochelle invited me to go to Thanksgiving dinner with her family. I said yes and felt optimistic about it. It would be nice to see everyone. This time, I met her brother Stanley and his girlfriend. Tony and Stephen, her other brothers, were both tall. The younger Stephen seemed like he would grow to be a giant. "Stephen, do you play basketball?" I asked him hopefully. He said no, and I thought, "All that height is going to waste!" I could barely dunk the ball, but I bet Stephen easily could.

The feast of a meal was a delight, and the hospitality was warm and relaxing. I began to tell the siblings all apart. Susan, the youngest, probably five or six, seemed a little hyper. Tony seemed to be the most serious. The young girls, Mary and Laura, had a tendency to giggle. Helen and Teresa seemed a little more aloof. Rochelle's mom slowly warmed up to me, I hoped. I had tried to be attentive and to counter her feelings about me being a drug abusing hippie, stealing and ruining her precious daughter! I shared my suffering with my Philly football team as we watched the Detroit Lions on the TV. Rochelle's father went through the same thing. I missed football.

As winter proceeded, a great snowstorm came down on us. I had snow at Penn State and certainly growing up in Connecticut. I loved the snow. Well, that Thanksgiving it snowed and reached a record of 23 inches for that time of year. Rochelle and I walked around after the snowfall and experienced the sublime beauty of it. "Isn't it beautiful?" she asked. "I love how quiet it is." "Yeah, it's almost silent." I said. "Did I tell you I can't find my car? It's buried somewhere on the street! I won't drive it until next June!" The sun came out after the storm and glistened off everything. You could see your breath in the bright and clear air. The snowplows were out, clearing the big roads. "Oh, look at that. That's a magnificent picture." I said. "How about we make us hot chocolate when we get back? You up for that?" she asked. Of course, we had a snowball fight later that day! As the snowballs flew, the hammer fashioned the hot metal, forming friendships with its loud kiss of the anvil.

Over time, I became acquainted with the Catholic church on campus. I began to attend regularly. The church had a beautiful wood interior. The pastor, Fr. Bob Kerr, was welcoming. After Mass we would talk. "So, you're from Philly?" He asked. "I have a cousin who lives in Upper Darby. Tell me about your family back there." My tale of loss probably wasn't what he expected, but it had a good helping of God's presence. He listened well, and I enjoyed talking with him. When Rochelle found out that I was going to Mass, I asked if she would go with me. I didn't have to push.

At the church, I saw an ad for an upcoming staging of "Godspell". The musical had been around since 1971. It musically retold the Gospel story. We volunteered for jobs on the crew that needed to be done. The show needed a Shofar, a Jewish ritual horn. Father got us in contact with a local Jewish synagogue. "Rabbi, we thank you so much for letting us borrow this." As he gently handed the little bag with the horn to us, he said, "Now remember, that is a precious item. Please, please keep it safe." "Rabbi, you have our word." We returned it after the show and he was thankful. For the upbeat production, a bigger movement was in process. I have seen that God works in mysterious ways. How is it that a Greek kid from Philly should be the way a lifelong Michigan Catholic girl gets back to the church? There were angels afoot. Her mom liked the renewal of her daughter's participation in the Mass. Maybe it helped to see the hippie on better terms?

For Christmas, I went back to Philly when school shut down. I spent that first Thanksgiving with Rochelle and her family, so it seemed natural to go to mom's for Christmas. I entered the house and there by the side wall stood a tree as tall as the ceiling. As tradition, the tree was illuminated in lights and, of course, tinsel. Colored lights hung across the living room. Along the banister going up the steps were lights. There must have been lights out in New Jersey because all the electricity fed 1891 Pratt Street! My brother Nick and mom greeted us. He reveled in the lights. It felt good to be back. I missed them. This must have proved that Michigan was good for me and the wounds of Philly were healing!

Now I am not sure how it happened. February came around and Rochelle and I were doing well, doing college and enjoying each other's company. It felt like the two of us fit well together. Her calm temperament and beautiful soul supported a welcoming smile and bright presence. A crazy idea entered my head. I should ask her to marry me! Now really, this was as risky as a flamingo living in Antarctica! We had engaged in a quick and fast romance. Was I sure about this? Did I know my heart? Was I afraid of losing her? Now, I had losses in relationships, so I knew there were risks. No. It seemed to me that I had found a special person, different from the others. We had a deep connection, a deep resonance. She had a pretty traditional view of things and came from a traditional family. I did not see myself in those terms and wondered if she would accept my offer or if I was about to make a folly of a decision?

Because of my interest in macrame and having no money, I decided I would make a ring out of tough string. I chose a subtle orange color; it took me a week. I made a nicely braided circle about the size I thought of her finger.

It took time to get the courage to ask. I probably dabbled too long in my anxiety. So, one evening, when we were alone, I built up my courage. I had the ring in my pocket and could feel it between my fingers. I saw a chance and got down on one knee and pulled out the little ring. Quietly, I asked her if she would marry me. I looked expectedly at her. She said, "Yes!" and gave me a big hug, almost knocking me over. There were tears. The ring fit. I took a triumphant sigh of relief. We became engaged and life started moving fast upon us. The girls in the house were excited. That day saw metal formed and sparks flying. The anvil's work took on a deliberate demeanor.

That spring, we decided that the two of us would go to Philly to see my mom. I had run into Darlene and she would go with us. When the time came, the trip going out was easy. We drove Rochelle's big Chevy with plenty of space. On the way in, she drove by the big sign that welcomed you to Philadelphia, the city of Brotherly Love. At that moment, a car cut her off, and she had to brake quickly. We dropped Darlene off and went to my mom's. My home in Philly probably shocked Rochelle. I don't think she had ever seen row homes before.

Nick opened the door. "Hey, bro, how are you?" He yelled inside, "Steve's here. Is this your girlfriend?" He hugs her. She wasn't prepared for that. "Rochelle, this is my brother, Nick." As we entered, Tony came down the stairs. "Tony, this is Rochelle." "Hey, nice to meet you." Mom came in from the kitchen with an apron. "This is my mom, Mom, Rochelle." "Oh, Rochelle, nice to meet you, dear. Sit down, please. I'm making dinner. I wasn't sure when you would get here. Nicky, get them some water. Well, tell me about your trip. How long did it take?" "We left early this morning. We dropped off a friend of mine." Rochelle didn't say a lot but smiled. Maybe she was in shock! Mom was friendly and talkative. Of course, she made a lot of food. My brothers seemed excited. I thought my family tried to leave a good impression. We took pictures. The visit went well. It was a good start. However, the place was familiar but had lost the sense of home. I had found a new home with Rochelle. Coming back to Michigan, we encountered a snowstorm of epic proportions. The interstate closed down in Ohio. The snow had overwhelmed the snow plows and they couldn't keep up. We eventually found an open motel, and we all stayed in a cheap room. Gong.

We decided to get married fairly quickly in August 1975. We just found no reason to wait. While it left little time to prepare for a wedding, ours was of small proportions. We rented the church basement. People brought in food. We hired a DJ to play music. You remember, Rochelle had a large family. She had dozens of second cousins who all lived in Michigan. My family had two brothers and a mother. I had a couple of aunts and a grandmother, but only my immediate family came out to Michigan. I knew only several friends in Michigan. Frank, my high school friend, was my best man. Joe Murphy came with Frank and Cindy. What I am saying is that the church literally leaned to the right with all the people on that side!

She and I put together our program. Ours was probably the only Catholic wedding program that had the Ying and Yang image on the cover, not exactly a Catholic religious symbol. I hope I did not offend God. But it stood for our differences and how those differences melded together. I am sure Rochelle's mom had things to say to her husband about that hippie insignia! We wrote our own heartfelt vows. We were very sincere about God taking part with us in this matrimony endeavor. I had the example of my parent's tenuous and tense relationship as a model in my mind. I needed God's help to make this work.

The August day found the weather warm and muggy. Frank and I sat outside before the ceremony, chatting. "You look good," he said. "She is quite a person. You found a good one!" "Hey, I really appreciate you doing this for me! I am so glad you guys are here and Joe, as well." My tan suit with a bowtie compared well to the wedding party men in blue. My brothers stood in the wedding party and looked snazzy. Frank's little son Jason carried the rings, and he stole the show. My friend Tim McGrann had made them from her grandmother's ring and my high school ring. I was a poor college student! Fr. Bob spoke warmly and caring, which extended the wonderful feelings I had about the whole thing. One of her roommates, Jill, played Paul Stookey's Wedding Song. Rochelle looked beautiful and happy.

We had a grand party, if I don't mind saying so myself. We danced and laughed. Her many relatives loved her and showed it. They all wanted a picture with her. I got in some of them even. Her parents and family danced many polkas. We ate well. Food was plentiful. My family had a good time. At one point, I saw my mom talking with Rochelle's mom, smiling and conversing. We stayed a long time because we couldn't stop celebrating. Easy, abundant sparks rose to God that evening!

Now we encountered a big problem when we went to the hotel. Catastrophe starts with a capital "C". "We don't have a room under your name." "What? We just got married!" "We can offer to put down a mattress in a conference room." "Uh, no!" Thankfully, Frank came to our aid and gave us his room. They stayed with Joe Murphy. I also later found out that Joe, a firefighter in Philly, had switched with another firefighter to come to the wedding. That colleague died fighting a fire that evening.

The next day, we got together for breakfast and enjoyed the family's tradition of opening up gifts. We got tons of stuff from pots and pans to beautiful bowls. One thing that we received became very special to us. Rochelle worked at the business office at Eastern and loved her Taiwanese boss. A Taiwan tradition is to put a picture of the newly engaged couple on a small plate. Her boss took our engagement picture and sent it back to Taiwan to have it created. We still have that aging plate. Chang, sparks.

Before the next semester started, we took a little honeymoon. We didn't have much money, so we drove to Canada through Detroit and camped out. The nights were getting cooler. One morning, a nice Canadian couple who heard us come in brought over coffee and doughnuts. You could see your breath. We drove to Toronto and spent a couple of days there. We wound up at Niagara Falls, which from the Canadian side excited us. Making our way through Buffalo, we went on to Philly. When we arrived, Rochelle did not feel well. I went to visit Frank while she stayed at my house. That was a poor decision. My mom and Nick the Greek got into a big shouting match while she lay on the couch. She had witnessed nothing like that before. It was a sad welcome to the family. I shouldn't have left her. We eventually made the rounds and visited my family.

As we planned for our next steps, I decided I had to sell the MG. I loved the car, but I needed tuition money. I sold it to the guy who shared the upstairs. He got a deal; I am not a hard driver. He moved out shortly afterward, and I saw the car around town painted red! Unfortunately, the paint brush job was ugly. That made me sad. On top of that, he stole a couple of my records. The money helped, however.

Rochelle and I promised her parents that we would finish school and that the wedding would not impede graduation. We found a small apartment and resumed our student lives. It is strange taking on the new role of husband and wife. They should warn you about it! After marriage, there is a big change in how you relate to one another. Old patterns come out. "Steve, we have a hamper for your dirty clothes. They don't belong on the floor!" "Gotcha!" Rochelle liked things put away. Rochelle cooked food with a lot of oil and I felt heartburn so badly that I went to the nurse to find out why my chest felt so uncomfortable. "Do I have heart problems?" I asked the nurse. "No, it's just heartburn." But we adjusted and prospered.

We had a few pieces of furniture. For a table, we had a large mirror on a tree stump. This made for a cool and earthy kind of decor. Really, the furniture was cheap and all we could afford. One evening, while watching hockey, I hit the mirror rather hard in anger at my crappy Flyers. The thing broke into many pieces. Such were the trials of a new life together! I don't believe in the superstition about 7 years of bad luck.

As time went on, we thought about next plans. The option I dared to think about involved getting a doctorate. Given my history, it was an outrageous possibility. I am not sure desperation or unbridled idealism prevailed. But I applied to several places, Tennessee, Texas, and Pennsylvania, for doctorate programs. The distance from Michigan was a strong consideration. Rochelle had not lived very far from her family and so distance factored into the equation.

In my better thoughts, I asked myself what the hell I was doing? Did I really think I could pursue a doctorate? Come on, I recently attended a community college. My, how my horizon had changed. The boy had become a man; and the naïve one, more competent. Anxiety had abated. I was more confident. Is that what love does? Does success work this way? Is that what a smiling God does? My attitude said, "Put on your glove and take the field." This game called life required that you say yes and show up. I had support and a crazy feeling that it could be done. The anvil sang. It liked the heat.

After waiting with uneasy breath, Peabody College in Nashville, Tennessee, accepted me into the Ph.D. program. A professor had an interesting research program, and I looked forward to working with him. Now the only obstacle concerned paying for it. We figured Rochelle would work as a teacher and I would get an assistantship. Such paid work was available.

For this city kid from Philly, Michigan proved to be a true adventure. My time there was profound and its impact on me was significant. I found a loving person who melted my heart. I felt my past wounds healing. Our partnership offered me more peace and security than I had known. I saw more future than I had ever reasonably expected. This only could have come from God. I had seen too many human plans fail. My joyous world expanded before my eyes. Tennessee, ready or not, here we come!

<u>To Adventure</u>

To adventure!
To escape!
To enthusiasm's keeper!
To release from the forgone, to jump out of frame, glance the ordinary, foreclose on the usual thing
Be time unlimited and vision unreflected
Dance the unheard tune: sing wild, exotic and loud
Carry your bones to a different stance
To hypnotism that reaches the corner of your lungs
Rejoice!
Adventure comes to bargain your quietude, put rings on different fingers, and tilt your hat on your nose
Open those eyes grown restless, the voice that quivers in renunciation
Stand up and shake off the residue of yesterday's convictions
The mountains approach to grab the dullness that has slept too long in your guts
Grab the wine, yes the opportunity, and embrace the breaking of the crocks
Adventure has no patience: throw it in the fire
Plunge the gorge with one hand waving free, till your mind and body are out of balance:
To adventure!

9 Nashville

It is called Music City. If you want to make it in country music, you go through Nashville. In 1976, Nashville had its reputation. The downtown area bustled with activity and growth. A fair number of music stores and recording studios existed in town. To buy a guitar, you were in the right place. You could find music everywhere. Outside of town, there were homes of the country music stars. The Grand Old Opry, the Mecca of country music, was at the Opryland theme park. It had been at the Ryman Auditorium but recently moved. They built the Country Music Hall of Fame in Nashville.

Besides music, Nashville existed in a natural meeting of interesting geography. The Cumberland River flowed through it. Nearby existed a large reservoir called Percy Priest Reservoir. To the east were the beautiful Smokey Mountains and the Appalachian trail. Interstates 65 (north and south) and 40 (east and west) tangled around Nashville.

Nashville also had a religious and educational core. Churches existed on every corner of the town. Higher education also garnered a sizeable presence in the town. Nashville claimed home to several colleges and universities.

This will be the longest of my academic stays, but not the easiest. There will be trials and unexpected joys. Rochelle and I will develop a strong bond. Family will grow, school will be engaged, work will be productive and tasks achieved. We shall flourish. The years will test us but find us able to succeed and persevere. But let me not get ahead of myself. Nashville stands as a great chapter in the life of Stevie House! So let that hammer ring.

My first encounter with Nashville left me unpleasantly surprised. We moved from Michigan where it is cool and low in humidity. The first time I opened the door to Nashville, I got blasted with thick humidity and heat. It felt like I had walked into a thick, hot, heavy fog that stuck to your clothes and filled your lungs with warm sauce. This was not clean mountain air. I didn't walk but swam through it.

Rochelle and I got an apartment on Belmont Avenue, down from Belmont College. The brick apartment building had an old stately feel. Surrounded by a courtyard, brick wall and well-kept bushes and lawn, our good-sized apartment had a hidden Murphy bed in the wall. Rochelle's parents and family helped us pack and move. They brought frozen cake from our wedding. "Aw, mom, you brought our wedding cake!" Rochelle exclaimed. "Had to dear, it's a year today. Let's celebrate! We have enough for everybody." "I'd like a big piece!" "Steve," with a look, "now you must share," mom said. "Wasn't it a fun party? I had fun," said Rochelle. "Except when they gave away our room!" I chimed in. "But you were beautiful!" said mom. "Oh yes!" added everyone.

We had kind, elderly neighbors who often checked in on us. Our only surprise came in the inch long cockroach in the drawer. The accents of the locals took practice to decipher. I felt embarrassed going to the store. I had to ask several times for the cashier to repeat herself. After a while, I found it a little twangy but acceptable to the ears. The people were certainly friendly.

Moving away, Rochelle intensely missed her family. The first year in Nashville required great adjustment for her. "Rochelle, I don't really understand, and I can't make up for your family. We will go visit your family soon, ok? We're not that far away. But you and I are a team now. OK?" I tried to comfort her. "Thanks," between breaths and tears, "I just miss being around them. It's not the same!" More tears. She ruled as the oldest of 9 and had played the role of surrogate mother. It got to me as it could be intense and I couldn't do much to make up for her loss. We took trips back to Michigan, certainly more than going back to Philly. Really, she needed that.

Rochelle quickly got a job as a Special Ed teacher at a little school in the country, called Pinewood Elementary. She had a small class of special needs kids with an aide. A nasty surprise awaited her, however. The folks at her work were mostly fundamental Protestants who believed that interacting with a Catholic would send them to hell. Aside from her aide, people didn't talk with her and otherwise showed her the ugly face of religious discrimination. Eventually, she changed people's minds. Of course, she was a competent teacher who loved her kids. Luckily, Rochelle's good nature and gift of love shone brighter than the dark discrimination she encountered. Chang to that! People eventually saw that.

Shortly after we arrived, we traded in the big Chevy and, with her new teaching contract in hand, bought a green Datsun compact. The car had a stick shift. That latter fact is important. Rochelle didn't know how to drive a stick. So, we went to the empty parking lot of St. Henry's Catholic Church and practiced. "Ok, put in the clutch with your left foot. You can change the gear!" "Steve, I am afraid to do that." "Yes, you can, you'll get it." Nashville is hilly. Soon Rochelle drove to work and got stopped on a hill. As the light changed, she tried to get the car in gear but couldn't. A truck sat right behind her. The guy behind rolled down his window and told her, "Lady, put it in neutral!" He nuzzled her up the hill and through the light. She then got it in gear and moving. She came home, however, afraid that I would be angry with her for scratching the new car. I could only laugh.

Another significant thing that happened in Nashville concerned my brother, Tony. We went to Philly and brought my mom and brothers to Nashville to see it and visit. We had a pleasant visit until the end. Preparing to go back, Tony strongly insisted that he couldn't go back to Philly. After a hard and deeply felt discussion, he stayed with us. Nick and mom left to go back without him. This made for a good move for Tony. "Steve, I gotta tell you, I felt abandoned in Philly, if that's the right word. I had little family support." As he said this, I understood. "Dad died a couple of years earlier, although I didn't have a great relationship with him. I was only 15. You moved out right after. Now I played sports and did Boy Scouts, but I didn't find any real male family support. I looked up to my scoutmaster." We were not a family that identified emotional needs, talked about them, and supported them. We were a family of quiet desperation where the surface waters deceptively hid the tumultuous currents deeper below. "Tony, I am surprised neither of us developed substance abuse issues or some other dysfunctional stuff." Sometimes, it looked like it could go that way, but we survived intact. Nick had his issues and latched on to our mother as his security. For me, I had healed from the hard loss of my father to an extent. I had grown through school and Rochelle. The loss seemed to be still raw for Tony. Coming to Nashville reflected a new start for him. Sparks and the healing metal takes shape.

It got interesting, however, when my wife insisted he get a job. "Tony, you can't just hang out here all day. I bet you could find work in the city, don't ya think?" I agreed. He was young and capable. He had good technical skills. In fact, he quickly found a job with a land developer. He worked as a draftsman and surveyor. Nashville was booming, so the company had plenty to do. He later met a woman in the apartment complex where we lived. Ruth had a couple of kids and they eventually married. They were happy and after legal issues, Tony adopted her children, Amber and Erik. He and Ruth are still married. He still lives in Nashville. Isn't it interesting that what seemed like a spur-of-the-moment decision lasted a lifetime? A life grew around that decision and people's lives were seriously affected. Like the Robert Frost poem, that path made all the difference.

Nashville found me looking up and expecting good things. This was, as you should know by now, an unusual thing! When I first saw the Peabody campus, it had an old school charm. It had a big green quad, crisscrossed by wide pathways. Several large buildings, each with white steps and roman like columns, surrounded the area. A more modern building on campus called the Kennedy Center for Human Development was where my office would be. In the foyer stood a large bust of JFK. The Kennedy family supported the center's research into special needs populations and service initiatives. I felt ready to take it on.

A negative quickly emerged. "Steve, the professor whose research interested you, Dr. Williams, has taken a job at another university. However, Dr. Paul Dokecki will become your advisor." He would lead my dissertation committee. I would work with him on several projects. I also got an assistantship, helping Dr. Howard Sandler on a research project.

The gathering area for us graduate students in the Kennedy Center was a room we called the grad ghetto. It was a busy place with people in and out for class or work. We were at different points in the journey, finishing up studies and students like me, just beginning. It was about evenly split between men and women with Ph.D. and Master's level students. However, my fellow graduate students were impressive! They were an eclectic bunch. Many of us were thinking about human development and how it intersects with medical, parenting, social, school, and therapy issues. "House, what are you interested in?" "Well, cognitive processes, thinking, memory. How it changes. Heard of Piaget?" "Sure, Swiss researcher." "Yeah, that kind of stuff." We discussed memory, attention and brain process. Piaget, Kohlberg, Erickson, Freud, Skinner, Bowlby were names kicked around the table. We discussed issues peculiar to our research interests, things brought up in class, and more global research issues. The rich experience made me feel like a flag in 40 mile per hour winds. The subject was important and deep, but also created a fun engagement. They were some of the most logical and argumentative individuals I have ever known. These students were also knowledgeable about many other things, not just psychology but world events, travel, medicine, wine and music. They were from different parts of the country and overseas. The grad students shared an intellectual culture. For instance, in 1980, Jean Piaget passed away. The mood was sad in the grad student ghetto. "Everyone, can I have your attention? I have just found out that Piaget has died in Switzerland." "Oh no," said the crowd. "Let us have a moment of silence!"

Now I have to say that this was the big leagues. We all were looking to get a Ph.D. We had high aspirations. Sometimes my confidence grew thin. This didn't happen very often. I usually felt passionate about my studies and, like a kid, excited about the candy store with my nickel. But as time went on, I had that nagging sense that I could be more practical. We were surviving mainly off of Rochelle's salary and my meager income. I wasn't sure my dad would approve.

There were a couple of department parties early in the semester. One professor held a party for us. I am not a great party goer as I am shy around people I don't know. Here, I knew a couple of grad students but of course not very well. Rochelle was with me. "Hey Laura, this is my wife, Rochelle." "Hi, Rochelle. That's a pretty name!" "Thanks. Named after a Catholic saint, St. Roch." "Didn't know that." "Where are you from Laura?" "I grew up in Columbia, South Carolina." "Oh, so you're not too far from home." "And you guys, Pennsylvania?" "That's Steve. I grew up in Michigan. A little cooler than here." "I bet it is a change for you, huh?" "Let me tell you, yeah!" "What kind of work do you do, Rochelle?" "I'm a Special Ed teacher at a little school south of Nashville." The conversation got around to the experimental school on campus focused on children with disabilities. The school was a demonstration project of Dr. Susan Gray. "Dr. Gray is such a great person. I bet you would find it interesting with your Special Ed background and your job." Looking bored, I said, "I'm gonna talk to Ed. He owned a Triumph Spitfire." This seemed to be the very school Rochelle dreamed about starting.

By the end of the year, I got into trouble working on the project for Dr. Sandler, who was head of the department. Dr. Dokecki arranged the job for me. One time, Sandler's wife was coming through the office. She asked me a question about part of the analysis being due soon. I told her I would get to it, but I quickly noticed it wasn't the correct answer or she didn't like my tone of voice. My Philly attitude can come out. Probably not a good thing in genteel Tennessee. I heard quickly from Dr. Sandler that he was replacing me on the project and that I needed to get my portion of the data analysis done. The response surprised me. There were rumors among the grad students that Dr. Sandler preferred female grad assistants rather than males. He could be a touch arrogant. I heard several times how he went to Johns Hopkins University. He thought I shouldn't have been admitted, having come from a school which only offered a terminal Master's degree. It could be ugly. I finished my work on the project and became unemployed again. Seeing Dr. Sandler the day of graduation, I nodded hello. I don't think he remembered me. Also, I taught a stat course later and used one of his books as a required text. I guess I tried to make up for whatever wrong I had done.

Rochelle and I had a significant life outside of Peabody. We were going to a Catholic church called Holy Rosary. We got to spend time with the assistant pastor; a young guy named Fr. Steve Stolowski. Rochelle and I have always been supportive of the priests we have known. People expect them to be on at all times and to play a variety of roles. They come home to empty houses. Fr. Steve was a good and gentle man. Early on, we invited him over to our apartment for dinner. "Father, you know anything about cars? I got to change my oil." "Sure, I'll help with that. A little different from the hot rod I owned as a teenager!" As well, while waiting for dinner, he fell asleep on the couch. Of course, we let him sleep.

At church, we joined a group that would have a great impact on us. Rochelle and I got involved with a group called Marriage Encounter. It provided a spiritually focused program aimed at keeping marriages alive and in the faith. It began with a weekend experience going over topics of significance to marriage, such as communication and sexuality, kids and money. Rochelle and I had been married maybe a couple of years at that point. It spoke to us and hit upon issues that were percolating. We weren't on the verge of collapse, far from it, but the relaxing and informative weekend helped us with our communication. The program had small groups of couples meet regularly after the weekend. The core activity concerned writing each other love letters. These would be on a relevant topic and involve 10 minutes of writing and 10 minutes of sharing. We joined a group (as we have joined things ever since) and made incredibly supportive and loving friends. "Here is our question for tonight," said Cathy. "What is the hardest thing to share with your spouse and why. 10 minutes to write, 10 to talk." We met the Pfleigers and the Colclasures among others through the program. Rochelle and I were far away from our families, and this group met those needs. "Guys, we thank you for taking us in. We feel you all have adopted us!" Christ speaks of loving God, but also of loving each other. This powerful program reached that end for us. The hammer forged a significant piece here.

Besides Marriage Encounter, we had a social life! A wonderful Mormon couple lived next door. We would visit often. The wife told us one time we were so nice, we would make great Mormons! Down the way was an Iraqi family. The husband, Tariq, was a talker! "Mr. Houze, come over and I will make you a cup of coffee you have never had before." He brewed the stuff thick like hot syrup in these small cups. If you had a full cup, it would kill you! We went tubing down a couple of the rivers around Nashville with fellow students. Rochelle's sister, Helen, came one time and we saw Dave Van Ronk, whom I described to them as a founding father of folk music. He did not impress them. As well, after a time at a local bar with Tony and Helen, we came home, and I played my guitar. After I forgot a couple of words, I hit the guitar in irritation. However, the beer must have given me strength I didn't know I had because the neck cracked! I was without a guitar for a while. But, hey, I was in Nashville, home of many guitar stores! While living here, we drove to Michigan to visit family. We also made time to visit the Smokies not too far east. We would stay at the slow end of the Smokies rather than the tourist crazy Gatlinburg. I would have to say that the fairly slow pace of life in Tennessee was a good speed for us.

In 1977, we had decided we wanted to start a family. We felt comfortable. Rochelle enjoyed her job very much. I felt settled into grad school. We had a routine going. Peabody was expensive but doable. I got loans and found jobs to do. Well, it so happened that Rochelle missed her period. This did not go unnoticed. We got excited about the possibility of being pregnant. When it is early, you don't say things to people. Sadly, Rochelle miscarried the growing child after a short while. It devastated us. It took a while to get through that loss. I held her and told her we would get through together. And we did. Sad and wilted sparks from the anvil that day.

We thought we would try again as soon as we could. We were both first born and strong willed. Shortly after New Year, we were again counting days and hoping. This time, it became very clear that Rochelle was pregnant. Rochelle is not a heavy-set person. What this means is that when she put on weight in a unique sort of way, you noticed. She felt especially miserable, however, being pregnant in the summer in Tennessee.

We went to classes and worked on coaching her breathing. "Steve, help Rochelle get into a rhythm of slowly breathing in and out. Focus on your breath, Rochelle!" There are also all the preparations that must happen. Setting up the room, having a baby shower, etc. Her family, her work and the Marriage Encounter folks got involved. It became a big love fest for sure.

In September, the time arrived to give birth. We encountered a slight complication. Not really a problem for us, but for the doctor. He scheduled a vacation for our due date. To satisfy the doctor, he medically induced delivery. It did not result in a pleasant experience. The contractions occurred painfully and quickly. In about an hour and a half, we met our son, Paul. I had the great privilege of being in the room. Hear the smiling gong.

You are aware having kids is a wonderful thing on paper. It is necessary for humanity to progress. It is wonderful as your family grows. Kids can be fun. Watching them grow is delightful. It is also a challenge as your life changes before your very eyes. "Paul, a poopy diaper at 2 am? We have to talk about your timing, young man." "Rochelle, wasn't life better before this?" "Steve, this will pass!" "By the time he is 18?" However, the most terrifying thing is leaving the hospital. The nurse takes you to your waiting car, helps you out of the wheelchair, and says, "Bye now, good luck dear" and closes the car door. You look at your wife and the little baby and you wonder "Oh, my, now what?"

Of course, that first couple of months, you check on the baby every hour to make sure the baby is still breathing. You struggle to get sleep when you hear a little cry. Their hands are so small and delicate. Their feet are so cute with their little toes! It's a wonder you had a part in creating this little thing. You thank God a million times for so great a gift. Looking at your wife and she at you, you say the word, "Daddy" and "Mommy". The house is baby proofed. You buy diapers. The new world has gone upside down with no promise of when it will get upright again. You adjust. And you smile.

Now Paul tested us early because he had colic and cried a lot. "Ok, I have rocked him for 20 minutes. I am going to lay him down." Wahh! I had a special shoulder and a rocking chair that, when employed together, could rock him asleep. But if I laid him down, he would wake up and cry. A short car trip would help, but we still had the problem of the transition to bed. This tested our early patience. Rochelle, Tony and I didn't sleep well. The crying eventually ceased, but those first few months were tough.

Having a newborn in the house, however, proved to be a nice experiment for me in child development. My schooling allowed me to map out what new things we saw in his behavior, physical abilities, and cognition. To realize that this little creature had our genetic makeup was a powerful testament to our impact on the world. We were not two separate and independent people but a family of three, with the third a view of God's marvelous handiwork.

Rochelle befriended a young woman she worked with. Her husband was a photographer, and this led to a photo shoot with Paul during this time. The little guy had grown into a cute and smiling boy interested in everything. "Rochelle, sit him down over here. Yes, yes. That's the smile cutey, yeah, keep that pretty smile!" Because of this, we have a million pictures of Paul.

The early days of family life were a blur. Perhaps the lack of sleep affected us! But Paul made life interesting. He even asked questions after a while. Fun to play with, he traveled well and loved the out of doors. He got into books early on and it became a joy to open up the world to his little mind. It became our role to protect him and to show him around the place. "Rochelle, how are you doing? You know, I gotta tell you, I really enjoy being a dad. Thanks. Big hug!" Maybe it took me back to my brothers. Our families loved him. I got a clear sense of the web of love and care a family can be. I felt sad that my father wasn't around to meet my family.

While I continued in my studies, Rochelle took time off to be home with our new child. We, however, still had bills and so we looked into working as house parents at a group home. A company called Serendipity House administered several homes in the area. They always were looking for people to live and supervise the residents. We interviewed, and the company hired us. We had to solve logistics problems, and we had a little baby. But my brother who lived with us could stay in our apartment while we worked.

Our large group home sat in a pleasant neighborhood outside of Nashville. We had 6 clients. The troubled girls we served had many issues. Most had experienced abuse and neglect. Several had run away. Others had mental health issues and were coming out of hospitals. We had a strong behavioral program, therapy support services and social worker guidance. Having a little baby proved to be a positive. The girls just loved small and cuddly Paul. We had limits and rules. Rochelle had skills at that. For my role, I represented the non-abusive male, the one who didn't yell, hit, or get drunk. My gentle presence and sense of humor helped to keep things light. We also had a terrier named Jessica, who had a therapeutic role as a gentle and easygoing pet. Unfortunately, one day a girl ran away from the home. The dog followed her. While gone, a car hit the dog and killed her. After they found the girl, we had an idea what happened. The girl sent us word she was sorry. We did this job for more than a year.

Following church teaching, we used Natural Family Planning after Paul as a means of birth control. This was difficult. We certainly were not ready to have another child. NFT involved Rochelle measuring certain biological signs of fertility, such as her temperature. We would avoid sexual relations during fertile times. It allowed her to get to understand her body better. It also forced us to experience intimacy in other ways. We made a good team, and it surprised me at the gentleness that it pulled out of me. Rochelle liked a schedule. She knew well the dynamics of family interactions. I went with the flow more than a map. "Paul, sit on my lap. Let me read Green Eggs and Ham again. You ready?" I offered an easy and gentle demeanor to interact with. I became the more spontaneous and playful parent.

After Paul was born, "Hey, Rochelle. I was thinking. In the car, I decided I want to convert to being Catholic. What do you think?" Surprised, "Steve, that is wonderful. Oh, I am so proud of you!" "I think it will help the unity of our family, but also, I have seen the goodness and love in your family. Whatever you guys are drinking, I want a jug of it for our family!" Now, my father was Catholic and becoming a Catholic also rested on the excellent models of Fr. Bob Kerr and Fr. Steve. I went through classes at the parish to join the faith. I asked Rochelle to be my sponsor. We went over many theological and church topics. We both got a lot out of it. Gong and sparks.

Now minor problems arose with the ceremony, however. The first time I went to the ceremony with the bishop, I misunderstood what the priest told me. So, after just a profession of faith, we left, thinking that I did what I had to do. However, that was not the case, and I had to go again to a different church to follow through with the rite of confirmation. I felt wonderful the second time. The Pfleigers went, a couple we met through church. They also came back with us again the second time the dear people. I didn't tell my grandmother, however.

It would be years later that the wise Fr. Bede, a wonderful Benedictine priest and monk, told us I didn't need the whole ceremony, anyway. My Greek Orthodox rites I had as a child were sufficient and I only needed a profession of faith!

School was progressing. In the program, you could have an extensive exam or write an area paper. The latter reflected a large review of the research and would act as the first chapter of a dissertation. I took the area paper option and wrote about the area of learning disabilities. This educational construct connected with brain processes, cognition, clinical treatment, age related phenomena and others. I spent quite a while in the library and came to love the smell of libraries. I explored the interesting geography of the learning disabilities literature. However, my idea of the space proved to be a little different from Dr. Dokecki's idea. I intended to cover it well and fully. I came back after a year of work with a 100 plus-page paper! His expectation, I found out, was to produce a moderate 50-page paper. I camped out when I was supposed to only drive through!

My research journey left me excited and intellectually fulfilled. I would get excited searching for an important article in a journal, invading the stacks at the Peabody, the Vanderbilt or the Medical libraries. One day, while doing my research, I realized I had made a wrong turn and found myself in the Russian section of the Vanderbilt Library. It took a little while seriously to find my way out. All the signs were in Russian!

The number of books I bought soon became a problem. We had no place for them. So, I built a large bookshelf even though I didn't have a workshop, and I didn't even have many tools. I brought the wood and hardware home in our little car. I built the thing on the front steps with my father's electric circular saw. This bookcase stood 6 feet by 10 feet wide, made of pine. To this day, I still have it. Flying sparks reveling in wood and tools!

The Marriage Encounter community was a gift to us. For instance, they would watch our little one while we went out to dinner for our anniversary. You don't allow just anyone to watch your baby! We usually enjoyed going to a nice and inexpensive place called O'Charley's. However, our buddies recommended another place for our anniversary. We made reservations and had a wonderful dinner. It shocked us, however, at the end, for the cost of the diner was a little over $50. But the server with the white cloth on his arm and the French accent made it all worthwhile. Oh, yeah, the food tasted pretty good as well.

I had seen this restaurant on my paper route. Yes, that is correct, I had a paper route while I attended grad school. It paid little, but it took less than a couple of hours a day. I guess if you want the dream, you have got to pay the price, and sacrifice! This job left me with issues with my right hand, probably because of injuries throwing papers out of my car window. Anyway, on one part of my route, I had to turn around. "Oh crap, what was that?" Opening the car door and walking around the back of the car, there lay a guy's mailbox on the ground by the wheel. I left him a note. The timing sucked because that month, we were short of money for rent. We could have gotten the money from Rochelle's parents. However, God had a unique plan. Things moved quickly, and we got an insurance check for almost the amount that we needed for rent. Could it be just a coincidence? No, God kept us in his care, even when I, in my great faith, doubted that we would survive. Holy sparks this time!

Over my several years in grad school, I went with my colleagues to several conferences of the Society for Research in Child Development. They held the conference in 1979 in San Francisco. There were brilliant speakers, and the conference held a job fair on site. After having a son, I strongly felt the urge to get done and get a job. I still had classes and the dissertation to do, but I felt antsy about staying in school. During the conference, we enjoyed the sights of San Francisco. These were many places a good tourist had to see. But I came also with expectations of finding a job. Well, I had only a couple of interviews. These didn't go anywhere. The overall lack of job bites felt discouraging.

The last day of the conference, a Sunday, I walked around the concrete plaza area around the hotel. There were steps and people going down. It opened up to a large area with an array of chairs set up. I sat down, contemplating my future. "Well, Stevie, this hasn't been the experience you expected." Feeling discouraged, I sat and just watched the people. I noticed people gathering and then standing. Behind me, there appeared a person with a cross and then a priest in procession. I had stumbled upon a Catholic Mass! Along with my surprise, I felt reassured and comforted by it. By this action, God told me that things would be ok. The conference ended without a job. But I felt satisfied. It would be a while before I would complete my studies and the requirements. I continued to pull the line up slowly. I got the message to hang in there!

In the fall of 1980, Rochelle and I decided to have another child. It had been several years since Paul's birth and we both thought that having children a couple of years apart represented an excellent strategy. Close enough to have relationships but far enough apart to have their own friends and identities. Being pregnant during the winter meant new winter clothes for the fat lady! We easily decided that we would not go through another induced birth and focused on a natural birth. The hospital had a quiet birthing room.

As the day approached, Rochelle and I felt well prepared and ready. We were at big Centennial Park, a beautiful green space in the middle of a city, having a picnic. I took Paul to the big locomotive at the back of the park. "Go on train." "Sure buddy, climb up." He liked to pull the levers. "Toot, toot." He said. Rochelle called to me, "Steve, Steve! It's time!" "Huh?" She said, "We better get going to the hospital. My water broke. It's happening!" "Paul, we have to go." "No, stay!" "Sorry." I picked him up. We quickly found the car and headed out. We dropped Paul off with a neighbor and went to the hospital. They got us a room while we waited for the birthing room to open up. "Nurse," I said. "Not sure we are going to make it. We don't have time for messing with that. This baby is coming now!" Rochelle was well dilated. Memorably, she started gagging as I sat next to her. I quickly opened up a drawer in the cabinet looking for a pan, but I acted too slowly. She threw up in the drawer! Thomas arrived quickly after, not waiting for things to be ready. And so, we had another beautiful little boy. Two gongs, a couple of changs and lots of sparks!

Then there were four of us. An interesting thing happened when we went to baptize Thomas. We asked Fr. Steve to do the baptism, and he agreed. We met him at the church but encountered a problem. "What's wrong Father? Can we help?" The church was locked and, being fairly new, Fr. Steve didn't have keys to get in. "Well, my solution is that we go to your house and baptize Thomas in your sink! I've got the oils." Our day turned out to be special and wonderful with those in attendance huddled in the kitchen! Thomas had a much milder temperament than Paul had. He proved to be a calm baby. He slept well, ate well, pooped well! But unfortunately, he didn't get photographed near as much as his older brother! I have no excuse for our parental neglect!

Around this time, my dissertation was all that stood between me and graduation. I asked several faculty members I knew from the department to be on the committee. My study concerned the attentional skills of good and poor readers at different ages. With 80 students all together, selected from a larger pool, I put in many hours of work, with a couple of my fellow students helping as well.

After a time, I reached the very exciting part of doing the analysis. This is where the rubber meets the road. Did my hypotheses find support in the data? As I would later tell my intro psych students, "Research concerns building a wall of scientifically proven facts one brick at a time, each brick resulting from a well-designed and understood study, giving us valid and reliable information." My research didn't prove a lot. Several of the hypotheses found support, several did not. However, I had things to talk about. While I had to finish writing, and have my dissertation defense, my need to make money and contribute to our growing family became intense. I decided to find a job and to finish writing later. I would come back to campus for the defense. Not the best situation, but doable.

Our time in Nashville was ending. It was a good place to live and work. This was the place our family began, and we were blessed with two beautiful boys. Our marriage grew as we worked out the kinks, taking off the training wheels. We developed friendships that were authentic and caring. Our relationship with the church grew into a source of spiritual nurturance and faith. My relationship with my brother would always benefit from the heartfelt connection we made in Nashville. The mountains were impressed upon my heart during our stay here. Personally, I left Nashville with greater confidence in myself and a deeper investment in my career. Life still took charge, problems still arose, but this energized southern metropolis was kind to this Philly kid!

Moving kicked in a serious and sobering job search process. Resumes started going out. I felt a certain urge to get it done. I needed a job! The time at Peabody took longer than I had planned. By my schedule, with two children, time on the meter had expired. I had several interviews at Corpus Christi and James Mason in Virginia. They offered a job of running their rat lab and teaching. Maybe not my best decision, but I decided against it. I also went for a sabbatical leave replacement job, teaching at a place called Hanover College in Indiana. The limited teaching job was only for a year or two. The professor would return and I would be back looking for work, although they could hire me on full time. However, the job brought us closer to Michigan. The trip to visit family would be much closer than Virginia and certainly Texas. After the discussion, I took the job in Indiana. It would be difficult to leave Tony, his wife, and their kids. They seemed happy and settled.

As we prepared to move, our Marriage Encounter friends threw us a party. "Houses. we have known you all for probably five years now. It has been wonderful supporting you, getting to know your story and your family." The group taught us about marriage, how to love each other and how to be parents. They showed the love of God to us in their caring attitudes. They had become family. "It saddens us to say goodbye, but we know you have to leave." Mary started. "We hope you will never forget us! Well, you can forget Bill, but not the rest of us. But so, you won't forget, we have a wine bottle with things that we hold dear about you two." She handed us a wine bottle pasted with sayings and meaningful words on the bottle that connected us. We still have that bottle on the shelf of the big bookcase. It represents friendship and love and how we see the face of God through others. The anvil gives off well sounding gongs as it honors genuine friendship. Gong!

Dance

Dance and let your muscles sing the music
Move with joy to the spirit within
The spirit that loves to energize
The spirit that says don't be calm, don't be sublime, don't be controlled
Dance and spin like the uninhibited earth, crooning the stars with its green blue smile
Dance like the universe was watching in envy and hidden desire
Dance and speak your spirit to the moon
Dance and show God you accept his challenge to live

10 Hanover College

If you had asked me growing up to point to Indiana on a map, I would have pointed somewhere around Idaho or maybe north of Colorado. Yes, I didn't have a clue. But here we were in the great state of Indiana, the Hoosier State. This comes from the response of state citizens to a person knocking on the door, "Who's there?" I guess they had a lot of traveling salesmen. And several corn fields.

I took a job at Hanover College, a place difficult to find. It is just off the Ohio River, across a bridge from Kentucky. But you can't get there from here. We rented a truck and with the help of Rochelle's parents, we moved all that we owned to this middle of nowhere place called Hanover College.

Hanover is a small rural town. Agriculture is probably the major industry. Supporting the college is a secondary industry. Farms surrounded it and, of course, corn. If there was a wildfire, popped corn would fill the fields for miles!

As we got on campus, a long snake crossed the road. We weren't in Philly anymore! We had half of a small duplex on campus next to a communications professor named John Schorr, his wife Susan, and a couple of older kids. "Welcome to the neighborhood, you guys. We got here when our kids were about your sons' ages. If you need anything, just let us know." We arrived with Paul, just a toddler, and Thomas, just a couple of months old. A prized sandbox was in the yard. The campus had open space and lots of trees, tall, old trees that gave the place gravitas. Associated with the Presbyterian Church, the college had existed since the early 1800s. Enrollment was about a thousand students.

The psychology department took up the second floor of a large building in the middle of campus. A huge half round window looked over the center of campus and dominated the office wall. Several paths crisscrossed across the open green space before me. The campus had a little of Peabody's peace and beauty. Dr. Alan Berg led the psych department. A clinician who also headed up the psychology department at Madison State Hospital, a psychiatric hospital up the Ohio river in Madison. Dr. Berg had a tall football frame. The faculty included Dr. Roger Terry, a social psychologist and several others. I got a sense of collegiality from them that felt good. It fed my need to belong. I felt part of a team. The place didn't have a cognitive psych person, and I felt I could fill a gap in the curriculum.

Now, I replaced Harve Rawson, a guy who went to Bahrain for a year's sabbatical. He taught developmental psych and statistics, among others. He also ran a summer program for special needs kids at a nearby camp. "You have big shoes to fill. Everyone loves Harve. He has a great reputation and has been in the department for years. He deserved this sabbatical." Dr. Berg told me. I finally met Harve in my second year.

I had a teaching load of several classes. It felt like I had won the lottery. Sprightly walking around the campus on the airy grounds, I began my new job with optimism and enthusiasm. I bought a leather satchel to carry my notes and looked very professorial. "Good morning, everybody. Another beautiful day in Southern Indiana!" We wore suits and ties.

While I taught, I also endeavored to finish my dissertation. Frankly, the task was mostly done. I completed writing it in good time. I had to schedule the dissertation defense and then prepare for graduation at the end of the school year. Rochelle was happy. She told me she was tired of typing up my papers. I understood and I will always be indebted to her for this great service. I don't think she realized how important it was to me. She would always say, "I got a Ph.D. too, Put Hubby through his doctorate!" and in fact that is the case. The anvil's work loudly sparked. It liked dedication and typewriters.

A lot was happening, but finishing and defending my dissertation occupied my mind early on. I don't think you can plan for your dissertation defense. Your committee gets together and they can ask you anything about your research or probably anything else. I went into it with the idea that I probably knew more than the others in the room about the topic. "Now, Mr. House, tell me how you came up with the study's design, and especially the analysis you ran. I have some questions about it." "Can you say something about this Smith, et al. study, 1978, page 43?" They did not make it easy, however. I had to do some intellectual dancing. At the end, they shook my hand and said, "Well done, Dr. House!" It sounds weird and unsettling at first. It is why you put in all those hours, the notes by the bed that you scribble at 4am. For me, I completed a long task that represented persistence and achievement. Graduation would follow. Of course, the hammer and the anvil found sparks. They know hard work.

Getting back to Hanover, the job challenged me to be in a room with a gaggle of mostly eager students with their pens ready and their expectations high. I made words happen, and they were in sentences even. The situation felt probably not unlike combat. You are fighting ADHD and boredom. Their eyes tell you whether you are winning or losing. I enjoyed teaching, and I was developing skill at it. My job was to give my students a sense of the mystery and grandeur of our psychological being. I had developed good notes, and I tried to keep it interesting. "Let me tell you about Watson, the great behaviorist. He had a cush university teaching job until he messed around with a senator's daughter and got fired! However, he went to Madison Avenue and made millions. Now in tv commercials, we are conditioned to connect beautiful and happy people with a soft drink product!"

A couple of interesting things happened that were unexpected. One situation found a female student in my office. She approached me about her grade. She had a C. She was young, and she noted, "My parents will be very upset with me if I get a C. I need to get my grade up. Is there anything I can do to improve it? *Anything*?" She had a desperate look in her eye, almost in tears. She also meant anything! We decided on doing extra work for extra credit. Her desperation felt heavy.

Another incident occurred shortly afterward. A group of several students came to the house insistent that the light workload in the statistics class did not meet their expectations! They also had talked to the department about it. This stunned me. It also showed that maybe I needed to be more rigorous. It showed that the guy on sabbatical had a reputation for being hard on students in statistics. So, I set up the final to be a hard exam. It took the students three, almost four hours. I felt vindicated. I hope the students felt they got their money's worth!

Early in the semester, the administration invited us to a dinner party at the home of the College President, Dr. Horner. They invited all the new faculty. "Yes, President Horner, I love psychology. I enjoy sharing with these young students the dynamics of psychology in their lives. Like… the idea that basic needs for food have to be met to get to higher-level social needs, Maslow's hierarchy of needs." "You sound passionate about it," he said, nodding his head. The purpose of the dinner was to get acquainted with the new people. My wife showed her charm and confidence. I am not sure how well I performed. The evening felt pleasant and relaxed. However, an offer to stay on the faculty wasn't made, so I assume I didn't do well at dinner. That was a tough hit. I second guessed whether Hanover was my best choice. Running a rat lab looked more and more positive!

Now the school allowed us to stay in campus housing into the second year. I taught a course or two for the college the next year. I felt pleased to teach, but the prospect of getting back into the job search game felt like more drudgery. For the second year, we moved to a different house on campus. The task took on emotional weight after we made friends.

One such relationship included a couple we came to know, Margie and Ron. Margie taught English and had a strong feminist attitude. Ron didn't work for the college but had training as an agriculture specialist. He also had lived in Philly, so we shared an immediate bond there. They were older than us and just loved our kids. They had no children themselves. It was interesting to interact with educated and erudite individuals. It was like Peabody. We befriended another professor, Ruth Turner, in the political science department. She had a liberal bend, and she and Rochelle got along well.

As the second year at Hanover proceeded, Alan Berg and I talked about what I would do for a job. We got along and he seemed to like me. He had a couple of suggestions. "As head of the Psychology Department at Madison State Hospital, I may have an opening you could fill. I will know in about two weeks." Madison was one of several state hospitals that housed the seriously mentally ill. "It's a small department. We offer psych testing and program planning for the various hospital units. The adolescent unit might be a good fit for your knowledge and skills." "Let me talk with my wife about it. Thanks." We also had discussions about the possibility of opening up a psychology practice in Madison.

As I look back on this, these decisions outlined the broad choices I had before me. I could pursue an academic position requiring a job search. I enjoyed teaching, and with the Hanover job, had developed teaching skills at the college level. The second possibility involved going for a more clinically oriented job. My training and experience, I felt, would be helpful here. The group home experience had pointed out to me I had personal skills that were useful in helping others. I had learned the importance and power of having a calming presence, coupled with a gentle and inviting voice that helped others explore issues. Certainly, I had a sense of the factors that contributed to stress and factors affecting development.

I decided in discussion with Rochelle that I would pursue the state job. It had security. As they say, a bird in the hand. "Rochelle, at this point in my life, job security feels important." "I agree completely." "We have two kids. I can't just mess around and travel the country looking for a job. The state hospital job seems intriguing and challenging. Alan Berg said that he had an opening and I could start right away. I'll apply and see what happens." I went through the process and got hired. However, a minor glitch appeared. In 1983, the governor of Indiana put into effect a job freeze. This would last the whole long summer. Sparks flew no doubt from the mouth of the anvil, but they were for patience and peace.

In a practical move, I also applied to Indiana University for an adjunct teaching position. Near to Hanover was located a local campus of Indiana University. Adjunct professors are a backbone of the university system. I have taught my entire professional career at the hefty clip of one or two classes a semester. Metal on metal. Tat di tat.

Because of the changes in my work life, we found an old house in Madison, a two-story brick house. They built it when my grandfather was 10. The house needed repair; hence we could afford it! With a huge octopus-like furnace that took up an entire room, the ancient house probably had dementia. The old wiring, not up to code, must have been an inspector's nightmare. Each room had a disappointing bricked-up fireplace. The thick wall paper came in layers. We removed the first five layers, revealing along the way a chronology of the house in bright and stark patterns! We removed it, I should say, and we continued to be married. Like my old Volvo, the Madison house taught me a lot about house maintenance and repair. It was like a cadaver that med students practiced on!

The windows of this house were large, as were the doors. Upstairs, the bedrooms had high ceilings. The boys shared a room. The crooked, poplar floors allowed the boys to have marble races in the grooves between boards. It had a small backyard which could sustain a small garden and room to play.

A turtle would show up from time to time. Maybe it was my lost turtle, come by to say hello!

At one point, we painted the exterior. We chose a bright brownish orange color. Rochelle's parents came to help us. They enjoyed getting involved, and they loved our kids. The old bricks of the 2nd Street house were made in a curious way. The hard external skin of the brick protected the somewhat soft interior. The bricks were now soft, so painting them meant almost painting powder. Anyway, I finished up the chimney painting. Rochelle called up to me, "As soon as you finish with that section, we need to get ready for church. My parents are going to drive back and want to get on the road." "Ok, I'm coming." It took me a couple of minutes, but we made it to church in time. While there, I heard terrible sounds. It began to rain! As we got to the house, running across the sidewalk and down the gutter was a long river of bright brown orange paint. "That paint is supposed to be up on the chimney!" I said in disgust.

The old river town of Madison had a charming and quaint feel. We lived next to the Star food store, an old and iconic grocery store. A single school teacher from New Hampshire named Melanie lived across the street. She and Rochelle became good friends. The town boasted a real-life hamburger joint dating from the fifties. It had an old, beautiful mansion and a historical society. A big energy plant sat west on the Ohio river. It even had a stop on the underground railroad, because of its proximity to Kentucky, across the river.

An interesting surprise during the summer occurred when the town hosted an unlimited hydroplane race called the Madison Regatta. A movie in 2001 called "Madison" dramatized the story of the hydroplane race. The town had its own hydroplane, U58, that competed against the big boys, Miss Budweiser and Universal Van Lines. These latter boats had Lycoming jet engines from helicopters rather than the U58's old Merlin engines from WWII airplanes. The Merlins, however, had a more iconic sound.

Our kids loved to visit Clifty State Park. The nearby park had a huge 100-foot waterfall. You could usually walk around the rocks at the base. The park had camping grounds and trails. It offered fairly strenuous hikes. We camped there many times. We enjoyed getting away even though the place was close to home. Paul could be hard on us in that he got excited and liked to annoy his brother. This became especially difficult in the closed environment of a church pew. But camping, the boys could find a stream and get muddy and find crawdads. We found the park to be a special place. An apple orchard right outside the entrance to the park also offered a relaxed opportunity to pick apples in season. The park connected us to trees and streams that nurtured us.

Thankfully, the job at Madison State Hospital eventually came through. The grounds of the state hospital were beautiful and big, filling a plot of land on a bluff overlooking the Ohio River. The Superintendent told me, when he found out I had taught at Hanover College, the difference between the two institutions. A resident of the hospital, he said, as compared to a student at Hanover, had to achieve goals and be successful in order to leave!

The old hospital grounds had several buildings. One building housed the more violent residents. Other units existed for different populations, one for adolescents, one for older residents, a unit for men and for women. When I arrived, there were more than a hundred residents.

The hospital used to have a dairy farm and cows on the grounds. Patients worked and had productive lives. A graveyard on the grounds held the remains of many residents who died while in treatment. The history of the hospital reflected the history of mental illness and its treatment in the US. It had been open since the beginning of the 20th century. There were probably fewer hospitals now than before because of psychotropic medications. We got a taste for the history with old records in the hallway. The hospital admitted a woman on the conflicted information given by her husband; another admitted for excessive masturbation. As psychotropic medicine developed, the need for state hospitals lessened. Mental illness became an issue dealt with in the homeless population and prisons. The hospital served as a placement of last resort or for only the most severely disturbed individuals. Today, the state hospital facility also houses a woman's prison.

As we had talked, Dr. Berg assigned me to the adolescent unit and the unit with the senior residents. I did psychological testing under Dr. Berg's supervision. He proved to be very helpful and instructive. My Ph.D. had bearing on my salary, but I couldn't work as a psychologist without a license from the state. We had a small team of mostly young people. They all had Master's degrees. My Ph.D. stood out.

However, the actual power on the grounds resided in the nursing department. I realized the nurses made things happen. I became familiar with the head nurse and the nurse on all the units I worked. They had their ethics and their way of doing things. The psychiatrists also depended on them. Of course, the psychiatrist had the ultimate say, but the nurse had a significant influence.

I learned this lesson clearly on the adolescent unit. We had an art therapist as part of the treatment team. She and I worked together on plans for the kids on the unit. I am not sure that the nurse felt she contributed much and tension existed. One issue of a teen came up specifically. "Based on my training, it is my opinion that William here is at risk of suicide. The various factors in his drawings are pretty clear. I believe we should put suicide precautions in place." The nurse pushed back, "But Holly, that is all the evidence we have. He seems to function well and is not showing signs of depression or expressing ideation in any other way. I don't think we need precautions." I wasn't convinced either. Nursing made the final recommendation to the psychiatrist, and they put no precautions into effect. The therapist did not like the outcome.

On the adolescent unit, we set up a behavioral program tied to activities and privileges. The teen moved up and gained privileges dependent upon how they worked on treatment. We posted the privileges of each person each week. "Guys, no pushing. You all can see the board. This is this week's ratings. Billy, great job in moving up." It had a significant effect on the resident's behavior. I would report this in the weekly meetings with the psychiatrist. "Ok, John, tell Dr. Love what you told me about how you are feeling. He wants to help you." In individual therapy, we would discuss their symptoms, medication, family issues and their behavior. In the group, we would share information but also focus on the social skills of members.

I felt concern during therapy only once. An angry kid, fairly new to the unit, became agitated as we talked. He picked up a chair and threatened to hit me with it. I deescalated the situation, and we processed it. The nurse didn't like the potential for violence. For a while, we had a tech sit in on the meetings.

Now the techs we had on the unit were very good. A big man who had served in Vietnam worked the teen unit. I enjoyed getting him to talk about the war. But as a staff person, he had a great rapport with the kids and had their respect. He was the champ of foosball. However, he also would stop a game and talk with a resident if a therapeutic opportunity came up. The staff were all caring, although some were more than others. Not everyone could work the adolescent unit.

A resident that stands out is a little guy I will call Harry. We talked about him even before he came. He had failed several other placements. As he first entered the dayroom, he ran over to the windows, looking out on the grounds. He shouted, "Look, look, see it, a tornado is coming. I can see it!" He charged under a chair. It took several people to hold him down when he became agitated. We often restrained him and he couldn't take part in programming. I talked with him while they held him in restraints. It saddened me to see him. Talking did little to alleviate his symptoms.

Now I also worked on the senior unit. Here there were several interesting people. One person had gotten out on his porch and started shooting at passing motorists. The police came, shooting at him about 30 times, missing him each time. Eventually he came to the state hospital as floridly psychotic. He had been there for several years.

There were others. One man I worked with told me he had a career as a nuclear scientist. He had diagnoses of psychosis and depression. He had asked one of the staff people to hold his head under water in the sink so he could drown. I didn't argue with him about his scientist claims, but tried to work with him on depressive thoughts. One day, "Come, I want to show you something." He pulled out a piece of luggage and opened it. "Here, look at this." He showed me an article he had published in a journal from a scientific society of nuclear research. That convinced me. It pointed out as well the closeness of genius and madness!

Another assignment found me on the unit for substance abuse. I led a group of those who were chronically abusing substances. There were several residents on this unit. In one group, I taught meditation to deal with stress. I attempted to give them skills rather than just house them until they got clean. This opened up a relationship with the nurse on the unit who sought further training. She and I went to a couple of substance abuse trainings put on by the state. She worked toward a certification as an addiction's counselor. I could have pursued it as well, but I wasn't sure I wanted to work with this population. Perhaps echoes of my father and his issues came to mind.

Another resident came back a couple of times, sent by the court. He had promise. He had a personality that drew you in and elicited your desire to help him. The last time they admitted him, "You know what Dr. House, I think I would like to do what you do." "Oh, yeah? It can be rewarding." "But I know this stuff from living it." With his experience and enthusiasm, it didn't seem out of the question. Many took this route to deal with their own addiction and to help others in the light of the 12 steps of AA. However, cruelly, he developed lung cancer. Later, we got word that he passed away. When you get close to people, you see them as human beings and not just as patients or as diagnoses. Chang and chang.

One story that I heard, I am not sure how true it is, concerned a staff member. In the old days, a common treatment involved electroconvulsive shock treatment. It involved conducting an electric current through the brain in order to disrupt and change mental functioning. The story goes they set a man up for shock treatment, although he complained he worked as an employee. The staff person didn't believe him. He gave him a round of ECT. The treatment often resulted in the person having a seizure and shaking behavior. As this person shook with a seizure, keys fell out of his pocket. This showed that he was, in fact, an employee! The unit staff he worked with said that treatment improved him!

An interesting man I met, a consultant to the psych department, was Dr. Eugene Levitt. He had worked for Indiana University and had expertise in the Rorschach Inkblots test, having written a book about it. He taught us what he saw as the value of the Rorschach in working with seriously disturbed individuals. Years later, I had heavy discussions with other clinicians about the usefulness of the Rorschach. I had Rorschach cards and used them.

On the senior unit, I started a successful group focused on helping people reminiscence about their lives. "Ok, Joanie, what do you remember about the war?" "My father was a farmer, but he had a brother killed in Sicily." Many were experiencing dementia. However, they would readily talk and share about the old days. I felt privileged to be a part of it and to witness their stories and sharing. That this is a privilege has stuck with me throughout my career. It has been a privilege to hear patient's stories and witness to their personal and deeply important life events. People need to be known, maybe to feel worthwhile. Maybe that is why I am writing all this stuff down. Gongs to that!

The hospital required regular TB tests. After I had been there for a while, my test came up positive for TB. This concerned me. I had pneumonia several times as a kid and they said my lungs were weak and prone to issues. They prescribed me medication for a year. I had no symptoms other than a positive test. The doctor surmised that someone on the senior unit infected me. I chalked it up to an occupational hazard.

While I worked at the hospital, Rochelle got a job at the DTC, Diagnostic and Training Center, on the hospital grounds and run by the school district. She had kids from the hospital and the community. An amazing thing happened to her once when a kid pulled a knife on her. With her best teacher's voice, she told him, "Put that down!" and he did. I guess sometimes we act without concern or even awareness of the consequences. During this time, she also worked on a Master's degree from IU, where I taught. I did the parent thing while she went to classes. She received a Master's in mental health counseling. Later, this would open up doors for her.

As far as my being licensed in the state of Indiana as a psychologist, Alan Berg thought it would be a straightforward process. Roger Terry, a social psychologist at Hanover, had a license to practice in the state. So, I applied and prepared for the exam. The general exam took four hours. Before I could sit for the exam, I had to be interviewed in Indianapolis at the monthly state licensing board meeting. I didn't know what to expect. Well, I had not prepared for a nasty meeting. "Please, Dr. House, sit." Before me were several psychologists at the table. "Your degree from Vanderbilt is in developmental psychology?" "Yes, I have specialized in working with learning disabled children. My dissertation was with good and poor readers. I also have worked at a group home for several years while working on my doctorate. I am currently in a position working at a State Hospital with adolescents. I have developed clinical skills, I believe." He asked me to elaborate on the clinical needs of teens and I responded with some brief comments. After a pause, "In our view," he looked around the room at nodding heads, "you lack a specialization in clinical psychology. We can't allow you to sit for the licensing exam. We believe you are acting in an unethical manner that could cause you to be sanctioned." I felt like a criminal, harking back to Penn State, trying to conceal an attempt at grand larceny!

I reported back to Dr. Berg, who was very surprised. It didn't affect my job status, but it left a foul taste. He and I later developed a plan to make the work at the State Hospital function as a preceptorship with his supervision. As well, I spoke with the faculty of Spalding University in Louisville, Ky., about their post doc training programs. While I felt I was being sensitive to answer the concerns of the board, it didn't remove the guilt I felt. I have probably always felt a sense of being on the outside. From living with grandmom to bombing high school, I have been behind, a dollar short and a day late. This fed into that feeling.

For the next couple of years, I, the art therapist, and another therapist made our way to Spalding University in Louisville for our evening classes. We enjoyed each other. As well, the coursework proved interesting. I worked with a priest for one of my class assignments, interviewing him and talking about issues for several sessions, afterward writing it up. These classes were a good, quick immersion in clinical psychology. The staff were supportive and practical. Many of them, similar to Dr. Berg, felt that the Indiana state board had been too restrictive. The head of the department at Spalding felt that after my courses, I should be able to reapply for licensure.

My continued teaching at Indiana University Southeast got interesting around this time. A nuclear reactor was being built by the Ohio river called Marble Hill. Employees of the company building it requested to have college level classes on the grounds in the evening. The school asked me if I would be interested in teaching a developmental psychology class on the grounds. So, I drove through open acres of machinery needed to build a nuclear power plant. My class was mainly middle-aged workers looking to get ahead. I enjoyed the class but they could give me grief. For instance, I talked about Piaget's theory of cognitive development. "Dr. House, I disagree with this guy, Piaget. My granddaughter doesn't follow any of these trends he described. He is just wrong!" Well, that was how class often went. Their kids were all, like Lake Woebegone, above average. At the end, however, they were appreciative and recognized how hard a time they gave me. As a thanks, I flunked them all! Not really.

The town of Madison had a Catholic church in town that we joined. This would, of course, be our home away from home. I began to participate in the liturgy by reading during Mass. I had a pleasant speaking voice and felt comfortable standing up in front of people. However, one week I embarrassingly read the wrong reading!

We also joined a group of young couples in Madison involved in Marriage Encounter, similar to the group in Nashville. There were several couples who met, Mike and Cindy, Paul and Rosie, and several others. "It is so nice to be here with you guys. We belonged to a Marriage Encounter group in Nashville. This feels like old times. Thanks." "You're welcome. It's great to have you!" These were good people who wished to live out their faith in the best way they could. I must note a member named Paul. He did birthday parties for kids dressed as a clown or a gorilla!

This group helped me realize my "masks". "This topic of masks is a hard one for me. I have put on masks since I was a kid. Honestly, I can play the intellectual or the therapist. I hate to admit it, but I can also play the know it all." "Steve, nobody here is perfect. We want to accept you for who you are. And besides, we don't know too many Greeks!" I admitted that my defenses protected my wounded boy from threat. Maybe I am being a bit too deprecating. As I trusted the group, I shared my hard reality and communicated honest meaning. I was raised to be nice, gloss over the pain, and not express what I really felt. This, of course, did not contribute to the group process or to my wife's understanding of who I was.

Another wonderful defense of mine involved humor. It always distracted and had a social value in that it made people laugh. However, it served as a great balm to protect soft spots. It was fun to play around with Paul. "Paul, I was thinking that gorilla outfit must make your married life interesting!" "Especially our sex life. Rosie loves to pound my chest!" Rochelle, on the other hand, had a straightforward style in that she spoke honestly and readily about what she thought. She enjoyed social interactions and had a groupie heart. The group experience worked for us because we incrementally progressed toward honesty and greater intimacy. The hammer likes this and forms metal through hard, bright and spontaneous strokes.

Our religious life continued to be strong and, at one point, brought us to St. Louis for a National Marriage Encounter conference. Rochelle's parents came to stay with the kids while we went. Going to the conference counted as part vacation and part retreat. We heard talks by noted speakers, especially Fr. Chuck Gallagher, who founded Marriage Encounter. We got hugs from him in the hallway of the Convention Center. That thrilled us. The biggest thrill of the entire weekend came at the Mass on Sunday. It outshone seeing the St. Louis Arch! There were many priests there. We were standing up in the balcony along with thousands of other couples. As the priests came in procession in their vestments, probably 40 or 50 of them with several bishops, the crowd broke into a chant, "We love you, we love you!" It felt like we were at a Phillies game, cheering on the team!

This love originated with the many priests we knew who were supportive, open, and engaging. In Madison, we came to love the pastor, Fr. John. He asked us to help with the marriage preparation course. Our Marriage Encounter experience was very helpful. We talked about communication, the sacramental view of marriage, children, sex, money and natural family planning. Fr. John took part with us and with several other married couples. We met engaged couples and educated them from our perspective about marriage. We felt the experience gave the couples a genuine look at marriage and family.

Through this and other church activities, the priests supported us in our vocation of marriage as we tried to juggle job, relationship and family. God had given us opportunities to be with priests, to get to know them and work with them. We supported them in their religious vocation. Over the years, we have adopted priests, and they have adopted us. I realize we had a common goal with priests we knew. Father John would say, "We are all interested in getting to heaven, but also, we have to face the world. This requires that we figure out how to live in the world but also be separate from it. You know, the world can be uncertain and ugly. If I support you in your marriage, and you support my priestly vocation, then we can all be more holy. Let's pray for each other and for God's protection." "Yes to that Father!" That will always get a chang on the anvil.

While we tried to live out our marriage in a just and loving way and to deal with our kids with respect, fairness and reason, they tested it. We had a babysitter in Madison who had had an unfortunate incident with the boys. I worked with her mother. This incident may have ruined her for life as a babysitter. One night while she watched our kids, the boys upstairs had a contest. They stood a couple feet away from the small trash can in their room and tried to hit it by peeing into it. Of course, they got close but missed as well. Imagine the surprise and consternation of the sitter charged with keeping them safe and in good behavior? "Boys, what were you thinking?" "I don't know." Came the meager response. I could only laugh. She, however, was devastated.

At one point, a very dire situation developed. Thomas and Paul were playing out back on a nice summer day. We had the regular door open and the screen door shut. A row of rocks surrounded our small patio outside. Apparently, they walked on the rocks. As they were doing this, we heard a loud gasp, and a muted cry of pain. I went out and saw Thomas on the ground, crumbled up. I picked him up and brought him inside. Asking Paul what had happened, he said Thomas had fallen off the rocks. We laid Thomas on a chair and decided that we needed to go to the hospital. He had passed out, so this got serious quickly. I got frightened, as did Rochelle. We got to the ER quickly. We heard Thomas crying out loud while they worked on him and took x-rays. It turns out he had a spiral fracture up his leg. This occurs often when a child is physically abused, we were told. We denied we had hurt him. Shortly afterward, a caseworker from the Welfare Department came to question us about what had happened. They separated us while they questioned us. This scared us both. We both had reported child abuse through our jobs. We just didn't think it would affect us personally. Well, it finally got straightened out, but not without concerns, wondering if they would take him and Paul from us.

The treatment for his leg break involved a long body cast. He could not move on his own, but had to be carried for the next couple of months. We were happy to get him back home, but rearranging the home had to be done quickly. We developed a new routine in the household while Thomas healed. I have to say that he showed great strength and courage. He didn't complain, but smiled his way through it. He had a better attitude than the two of us.

We all know that life doesn't go by a timetable. Around this time, Rochelle got pregnant, probably signaling our satisfaction with our lives. It felt that things were settling in to a pace that felt comfortable. We didn't make enough money, of course, but it paid the bills. We had friends and a church community that fostered rich connections. The boys were doing well, mostly after Thomas got out of his cast. For a while, one leg was longer than the other.

On a chilly day in March, I got called that told me to come to my office. My wife was in the throes of labor and needed me to come home as soon as possible. As we got to the hospital, we told the person at the desk that labor and delivery went quick for us. They called the doctor. We were in the waiting room filling out forms. We didn't make it to the delivery room, but found ourselves again in the labor room when our daughter was born. But we had the doctor present who reassured us that all would be fine. Little Catherine was born in under 30 minutes. Rochelle had an epidural, but it didn't matter.

We were both thrilled to have a baby girl. We knew how to do boys. It would be interesting to see how girls do things differently than boys. My father-in-law with 9 children thought boys were easier to raise than girls. With two children, you each have one, but with three, what happens? You might say our hands were filled! But we filled them with a beautiful baby girl and all the aunts went, "Ahh!" The hammer sprang into action this day.

I hate to admit it, but I got a desire to do more than I could at my work. The residents were pretty limited because of the high degree of psychological insult they experienced. The oppositional and disruptive behaviors were considerable and the insight and desire to improve fairly low. As well, after a couple of years, Dr. Berg moved on and I became the interim head of the Psychology Department. The limits of my job became clear. I wanted to deal with more common, less extreme, and chronic instances of mental health issues. Dr. Conway, a psychiatrist, told me of an opening at the hospital associated with the mental health center in Columbus, a bigger town south of Indianapolis. He thought I could do well in the position. Chang.

So, I would soon leave the hospital and take a job at a mental health center, coinciding with the end of my time at Spalding. The director of the program regrettably told me she wanted to talk about hiring me to teach at Spalding. However, at that point, I had already taken the other job.

Hanover and Madison left important lessons. Hanover held a promise that wasn't realized and it left me disappointed. Doors opened, however, and we walked through to the State Hospital, bringing me more lessons about pain and suffering. Here came the clear awareness that I could play a role in recovery and healing. I found a niche beyond the Psychology Board's chastisement! We continued to grow as a couple, as a family, and in our faith. These carried me and proved to be sources of great satisfaction. We weathered serious issues, but with the support we had from family and friends, we got through without a lot of damage. Jobs could be tough, family overwhelming and house stuff a pain. But we found a balance, we persevered. Rochelle liked that, and we both found it diverse enough to be interesting. Rochelle and I talked. "My expectations to be blunt are not really high, Rochelle. I don't expect to be rich, to entertain every weekend, or to be at the top of my field. This has taught me I can help people. I feel blessed. I love our family and you!" Big hug. No matter what, we would make good come out of whatever we were given. Hanover and Madison opened up a more pastoral, rural setting. I left with more skills in my pockets and new friendships in my backpack. With a wonderful wife and three beautiful children, I was indeed blessed. Indeed.

<u>We Have Rested Our Dreams, for Catherine</u>
We have rested our dreams upon your shoulders, precious one
The dreams that carry the words of our hearts
When you sleep, you rest with our hopes upon you
Your little eyes look, we hope, to the peace of tomorrow
In your hands, you grasp what our desires hold
Your presence marks the day we looked beyond ourselves
The day we gave to you the heavy gifts we longed for
You lay not alone, but are with the angels we prayed for

You sleep with God's promises enveloping you
We have rested our dreams upon you

11 Columbus

The meeting represented a unique congregation of the Quinco therapists and staff. Our group, the Reunion staff, who worked with teens and their families, were to present an overview of our work to the larger company. I made videos for my supervision with the Bloomington group, led by Dr. Steve Greenstein. I suggested that as part of our presentation, I would present a video of family therapy in action. Really, I put together a staged vignette of my family, as told before and after family therapy. The before therapy scene looked like this.

"I don't want to eat dinner. Your cooking sucks!" said the 10-year-old with a loud retort. "Don't talk to me like that. I am your mother!" the frazzled mom said. He grumbles under his breath. As the mom speaks those words, the 4-year-old comes tearing into the room, screaming that her brother tore up her clothes again. In tears, carrying a dress and a doll, "Ahhgh! My favorite dress! And he pulled off the head of my doll!" Just then, the middle child comes into the room with an evil smile, stops and mugs for the camera, brandishing a pair of scissors. "I will cut off your head next!!" The father stands up and, almost tackling the running child, takes the scissors away. "Not in my house, you will!" The child breaks free and running out the room, shouts, "I hate my life!!!" The father shakes his head, looking into the camera, "What can we do?" Mom says, "I'm going to call Reunion!" Dad shrugs agreement. The screen goes black. A title, Post Family Therapy. Sitting at the table, the boys have ties on and are upright and quiet. The little girl is smiling and holding her doll. The father says robustly, "The therapy we went through was wonderful! Reunion really helped us! What do you think, Johnny?" The ten-year-old says, "Yes, father, I feel so much better!" The middle child says,

"I don't play with scissors anymore! Mother, are we having Brussels sprouts again?" As the scene closes, they all look into the camera and give a thumbs up!

As the several credits rolled, the crowd applauded at the obvious, over the top depiction of mental health services. Unfortunately, I recorded over the actual fun filled drama with real therapy sessions and so lost it to posterity. But I am here to verify that the above accurately reflects the video that was presented to the entire staff!

As I write this chapter, I feel it reflects a time when I feel confident, comfortable and solid in myself. No longer a naïve practitioner of his craft, I have had experience and developed my skills (playful videos to the contrary). I have taught and worked in the field for several years. I have seen up close the ravages of significant mental health issues. Having my own emotional pain, tempted by the promise of substance abuse, and going through periods of anxiety and depression, I have endured. Simply, I have seen some stuff, done some things. As well, I am now the father of three, no minor achievement. My marriage has lasted for ten years and we still sleep in the same bed and talk to each other even. Our children are cute and probably above average! Financially, we are gainfully employed and solvent. The Catholic church is a comforting place for us, both in terms of belief and community. The larger family ties we have are stronger on Rochelle's side than my own. We have lost track of my mother's family, except for the funerals of my aunts and Yia Yia. Tonia has gotten divorced. My mother, however, continues to send birthday cards religiously, even sending two, signing them from her and my long-deceased father. Tony prospers with his family in Tennessee while Nick, it seems, is stable with steady work in Philly, although he still lives at home. We have left friends in several places and now have a long list of Christmas card addresses. Sparks in red and green!

My work calls for a significant amount of energy and focus. I face the storms of mental illness and the living issues that my clients bring. They are intriguing problems to be understood and addressed. This is a task with serious consequences. I always knew that I didn't make widgets for a living, but dealt with human pain and suffering on a grand scale. This feels right, challenging, but right. I am called to offer attention, care, and presence. Probably, this is also a task I have practiced since I was a kid. I have lived with conflict and anger. My work and skills have allowed me to respond seriously to conflict and difficulty. As a child, I felt powerless to intervene in what I saw. However, now it is my job to intervene and I bring tools to use. My ship runs well through the waves of pain and suffering.

Shortly before we moved, I started working at Quinco, the Mental Health Center. In the mid-80s, Quinco was a mental health services organization that provided services to five surrounding counties. While living in Madison, I drove the hour to the big town while we looked for a place to live. This occurred in May and we moved in August.

The hospital at Quinco found itself in an interesting building situated over a creek. It called up the image of a bridge over troubled water. This showed the architectural expertise of the town of Columbus.

Growing amid the cornfields of Indiana, Columbus had a big heart and a large identity. A bustling international community of 30,000 people, Columbus stood as a unique jewel. The Fortune 500 company, Cummins Engine Company, had their headquarters in Columbus.

A chauffeur, Clessie Cummins, started the company in 1919, building diesel engines for trucks. He loved to tinker with machinery as a farm boy and mechanic. His reputation got him a job on the Harroun car racing team, which later won the first Indy 500 race. He teamed up with a banker, Michael G. Irwin, and built a solid and profitable engine company. In the 50s, Cummins became an international venture. With the aid of J. Irwin Miller, a relative of the banker, it continued to grow, making well-built and reliable truck engines at several factories in town. It also began a foundation, and this is where Quinco comes in.

The Cummins Foundation paid the architectural fees of world class architects who then built several renowned buildings in town. One could often see a group of architectural students walking around taking pictures. I worked in the concrete and glass masterpiece of a building located over Haw Creek.

Besides the famous buildings, the town met our needs. There was a beautiful community park for walks and a playground. The mall had stores. A bookstore offered a cozy environment. An exclusive neighborhood existed with large, beautiful homes not unlike in Connecticut. A must in a prosperous town, the community had a wonderful library with its large plaza. There were several golf courses I would play. Of course, several churches dotted the area, including two Catholic Churches. An old Army base, located further out of town, would play an interesting role later. It boasted a small prisoner of war camp for Italian soldiers who built a small chapel there.

Before being hired, I went through an interview process with a psychiatrist, Dr. John Holdread. He was not confident about hiring me. I am not sure what issue concerned him. But he and Dr. Conway talked for a while after my interview. I felt a little uncomfortable. However, eventually his concerns were resolved, and I got the job. Other than my poor first impression, Dr. Holdread turned out to be a very instructive and good psychiatrist with which to work. I learned a lot from him.

The small hospital unit housed adults and adolescents. Similar to Madison State, it admitted people who were experiencing significant mental health issues. We had teens who were very oppositional. One girl we rolled in a blanket to control her as she hit, slapped, kicked, spit and bit us. Sitting with her, talking with her, trying to deescalate her, she spit many times at me. One man who had been on suicidal watch got a running start and flung himself at the large window. The glass held. They admitted a girl I worked with several times because of suicidal attempts. With her last admission, she told the truth about being sexually abused and, hence, began actual progress. Another humorous case involved a man whose rapid thinking and poor judgment led to all kinds of issues. However, in a calmer moment, he called the local supermarket and ordered three large event cakes, probably two feet by two feet a piece. The store called the unit, apparently thinking something wasn't right!

Treatment on the unit involved medication, group, and individual therapy when appropriate. The psychiatrist, therapist, nurse, and other staff would meet in a side room for a weekly staffing. "OK," the nurse would begin, "let's go down our list of patients." I met with families as I worked mainly with adolescents. Focusing on the resident, I helped them put into words what they were thinking and feeling. Like a sleuth, I tracked the development of the problem and what factors contributed to it. Seeing the family, when possible, I looked at the dynamics and issues of the family as much as they allowed. I listened. I was good at listening.

As I had experienced before, the people who worked there created a team of professionals. Dedicated and competent psychiatrists led the team. Dr. Holdread and the older Dr. Weinland offered professional skills. Later, Dr. Vinita Watts, a child psychiatrist, joined the team and added her special skills and warm attitude. Caring and competent nurses carried out treatment plans. Therapists, psychologists, and social workers added their expertise. Drs. Ben Sklar and Ken Beavers were colleagues enjoyable to work with. There were also techs who had therapeutic skills themselves. Jack was one, for instance, who had good therapeutic skills and dedication. All worked together to create a team, ensuring that we carried out treatment plans and created a therapeutic environment.

The Center represented a respite, a calm place amid a firestorm. It proved to be a first aid station in the middle of a battle, not unlike the TV show, MASH. The staff brought needed sutures to the pain, hurt and brokenness that life and mental illness conspired to create. Our tools were not exacting, our words proximate and our actions attempts at pointing things in the right direction. We were a passionate and caring group of people who used what we knew and what our creative juices could bring to bear on issues. The anvil joins with sparks. It knows the truth of what I say.

Dr. Holdread would say, "We don't do miracles. But we are successful more than not. I think we improve people's situations in that suicidal urges after a while subside, replaced by hope to try again." A better attitude and improved sense of being often resulted from treatment and medication. A heavy intervention, hospitalization was the ultimate step in tamping down the fire of ill health that raged, burning up one's life. Yep, we were firefighters, dedicated to it, focused on it, and fiercely passionate about dousing the flames. Although Dr. Holdread felt hesitant at first, after working with him for a while, we developed a good relationship. At one point, he and I, with our wives, took a trip to Chicago for an adolescent psychiatry conference. We had a great time. I found him to be a gracious and kind man. I always had respect for him.

An older psychiatrist, Dr. Weinland, worked on the unit as well. He was a kind man and a knowledgeable professional. At Penn State and at Madison, there were older guys around who carried a history with them I enjoyed hearing. "Dr. Weinland, how was it different back when you started?" "Well, it was hard before Thorazine and Haldol. We housed people, but progress was slow. We had electroconvulsive shock treatment. Also, we had others like barbiturates. Tricyclics treated depression. With some success. It was very different."

Over time, I saw the terrible impact that mental health issues had on lives. I knew a brilliant med student who developed a psychotic disorder and later committed suicide. A depressed woman found her husband's gun and killed herself. A woman in the throes of mania almost had an accident with her kids in the car. The lives I encountered were often tragic. A significant mental health issue could exacerbate and lead to job loss, marital discord, or tragic decisions. Chronic situations reached a level that broke open, sometimes in a violent or extreme reaction. The worst of human coping, the nadir of healthy behaviors, the accumulation of years of unsuccessful living could come to a head. This job was an education in the power of frayed living that blew up in one's life.

As time went on, at the hospital, I developed as an individual and family therapist. Services for adolescents were improving. An extensive discussion concerned separating the teens from the adults. A schooling component also developed so that kids in the hospital would not be so far behind when they returned home. I did family therapy to deal with home issues more effectively. I would also follow adults in treatment as staffing needs varied.

About this time, I heard from a psychologist I had worked with from another county. Howard Simmons was unique and had a Ph.D. from MIT. Howard's phone call would change my life. Over the years, the rejections by the State Psychology Board had produced several lawsuits against their flawed process. The legislature in response passed a law that revamped the licensure process. An option opened up for me to try again to be licensed. Filling out the paperwork, I contacted Dr. Berg concerning my work at the State Hospital. I took the licensing exam and the Indiana state psychology exam. After waiting, I found out I had passed and I became a licensed psychologist! Belated sparks of success.

Seeking to improve my family therapy skills, I attended a supervision group in Bloomington with a master therapist named Steve Greenstein. I applied for licensure as a Marriage and Family Therapist and, with his supervision sign off, I received this license as well. The metal forged here accumulated. Steve had a clinical Ph.D. and ran a supervision group for therapists in Bloomington. Based in Virginia, he had these types of groups across the country. A tall (probably 6-foot 4 inch) Jewish man with curly hair, he left a powerful impression. "I have worked with Salvador Minuchin at the Philadelphia Child Guidance Clinic in South Philly. Sal is a major figure in the development of family therapy and, specifically, Structural Family Therapy. We look at the persistent dynamics that occur in families that are often the source of problems. For instance, a mother always deferring to the father can create issues. I worked with him starting around the mid-60s. It was exciting. Sal was at the center of significant advances in family therapy through the clinic. He trained many therapists, and I worked for him as one of his students." The supervision group met once or twice a year. It involved maybe twenty therapists from Bloomington, but also from the greater area. Diane, a social worker I knew from Quinco, spoke about it. I wanted training in family therapy and she suggested I contact Greenstein to join the group.

The supervision group became a wonderful training ground for me. Therapists would bring video tapes of sessions and present them to the group to be analyzed and critiqued by Steve. He had a formidable range of experience. As I became acquainted with him, his style seemed like that of a surgeon. He made comments that were concise and clear but supportive when needed and confrontive when needed. His insight, knowledge and experience made him a master therapist and thus he knew the game, the language, the ins and outs of therapy. He would pinpoint issues quickly. It seemed almost to be a situation where he could name that tune in three notes! He spoke to the case and to the therapist. And both he did, with wisdom and caring.

The first case I presented didn't go well. He basically told me I needed to change my voice from an ineffective neutral to a more caring and involved one. He correctly identified my anxiety and the poor rapport I had with the family. His comments were right on and even though I felt essentially criticized, I left with a mission to put into effect his suggestions. The next time we met, I presented another case. He noted how significantly different I was in the therapy room. He felt an improvement in the power of my presence.

Perhaps that is what I gained from working with him, a sense of the power of presence and the use of self in therapy. What the therapist attended to and how the therapist spoke, influenced what the client saw, attended to, and thought. A secondary benefit of the group concerned seeing the work of other therapists. Some of these therapists had great tools and skills. To see a variety of cases and to hear the feedback and discussion felt like doing rounds at a hospital. We followed the eminent surgeon and listened to his concise wisdom.

We would meet at a hotel and use a conference room set up to project our sessions. The cases we saw had great diversity, as were the practices of the therapists of the group. There were cases of families and individuals. We had permission from the clients to present their session. Most of my clients were very open to it. They would be eager to hear what the good doctor had to say. I also saw therapists shaken by insights offered. The therapeutic wisdom in the room meant drinking from a fire hose, and I could hardly take it all in. One simple intervention suggested that the client bring in pictures of themselves with their family of origin. It felt like a simple but powerful intervention that touched on my own issues. Several clashes of the anvil.

One session proved to very difficult. While driving over, I had encountered a terrible thing along the way. I made a turn to get to the place where the meeting occurred. There was a car on the side of the road by the intersection. On the corner where someone would find it lay the body of a man lying face up on the ground. A shotgun rested between his legs. He had shot himself in the head, which glared red and looked like a piece of meat and bone, violently rent and torn. I parked the car, got out, and walked by the body. I stood there briefly, as if to reassure myself that this was what I thought. As I did so, another car came by and stopped and the guy rolled down his window. The stunned driver asked, "Is that what I think it is?" I looked at him and said, "Yes, he killed himself. I will go to that house over there. You wanna stop at the store and call the police?" He drove away. I went up to the house and knocked. A lady half opened the door. "A man has killed himself on the corner. Can you call the police?" "Oh, my." She replied. I waited for a little while. A police car came fairly quickly. He told me to move on. In the paper the next day, I saw an article about a distraught banker from Indianapolis. Late for the Greenstein group, I told the story. During the morning presentations, I sat, kind of stunned and out of myself.

A suggestion from Steve led to a significant experience for me. I had limited group therapy experience at Madison but abundant church group experience. He advocated I take part in a group to understand the process better. This occurred maybe in the second or third year I attended. I took the opportunity offered. There were two Bloomington therapists, Gates Agnew and Colleen Cleary, who ran a group. They were open to me joining if others in the group agreed. We settled on a cost that would be doable and for about 6 months or more; I went to Bloomington once a week for group therapy. This acted as a training exercise to help me learn about how the group worked, but also benefitted me psychologically. Of course, I had issues to discuss. "Guys, my father's death had a big impact on me. I grieved his death for a while and that of my dear grandfather. Losing relationships over the years has left emotional remnants. My family did feelings in a weird and unhealthy manner. I could use help to figure it out." The family stories of others in the group provoked my past family experiences. I found it useful to share. There were maybe 6 of us in the group and we all had issues. I enjoyed supporting them and exploring things with them. The experience proved very helpful. I came to love Gates and Colleen for their insight, their warmth, and their skill. After the group ended for me, Gates and I went to several Indianapolis minor league baseball games. Colleen regrettably died several years later from cancer.

Steve connected with us and helped us connect with each other. For instance, we did meditation and practiced other methods of relaxation. We were guinea pigs for new ideas that a participant brought in. For me, I let it slip that I wrote poetry. He asked me to bring a poem or two the next time, and I did. I found it a useful experience to read it in front of the large group. But from that point on, I would bring an old poem to the group. Steve wisely suggested, maybe quoting Rumi, to read the poem twice out loud. The first time for the head, the next for the heart.

Overall, I found this one of the most important professional activities I engaged in. I felt valued by the group and I learned so much. Steve became a mentor and a friend. He got married several years into the group experience and I wrote him a poem for his wedding. I certainly became a better therapist because of this group, but I became also a better person because of it. A brilliant teacher goes beyond a subject, opens up the depths of truth and speaks to your heart. Steve Greenstein did this for me. I eventually published a book of poems and I sent a copy to him. Tat a tat, chang.

My new psychologist and MFT credentials opened up for me the possibility of working in the Quinco outpatient service. I had been consigned to the inpatient service up to now. The adolescent services were being organized and codified by the agency, and I became a part of that development. They gave the unit of outpatient adolescent services the name Reunion. These were exciting times.

I also became a member of the crisis team. This meant I had a regular weeknight shift and then did a weekend stint from time to time. The job required being available for the Emergency Room of Columbus Regional Hospital when an ER doctor needed a mental health consult. We were the liaison with the psychiatrist. The interesting work varied. You really didn't know who you would see or when. It could be a teenager after a suicide attempt, an alcoholic picked up by the police threatening to kill somebody, a person walking down the road naked, or a manic person brought in by a concerned spouse. If no beds were available in the hospital, a tough and frequent situation, an alternative placement had to be found. The hospital might send the person home with an appointment for outpatient therapy. If we suspected child abuse, a case had to be filed with the Human Services Department.

The interview could be tricky. If I saw a teenager, I might interview parents and the teen together, then meet with the teen alone. "Ok, so that is what your parents think. Where are you?" I might ask. "They are full of BS. They just want me to be like my goody two shoes sister. Ain't gonna happen!" I have seen parents who were angry, and I had to get them out of the room to get the information I needed. I would avoid making promises not to tell as that could bite you later. But I would try to be supportive and open.

A cool head was necessary to handle the midnight appearance in the ER. I would seek to be clear and calm in gathering information. Getting called could annoy me, but then I would fall into my therapist's role in meeting the patient. The therapy voice would come out and I would ask the needed questions. People would deny what the police officer said or what their spouse told you. Becoming a good evaluator meant developing a gut sense. I honed in on the words and the non-verbals, coupled with a sense of mental illness and how people acted.

I have to say that dealing with angry people could be a challenge. We interviewed people with the door open and a person outside the door. One time, a man who was experiencing mania became more and more agitated. He talked fast to begin with, but then he escalated and became threatening. Luckily, help was readily available and waiting. They trained us to position ourselves by the door and not allow the person to get between us and the door. I had an interesting case with a depressed woman. I asked about the means she had for harming herself, and she innocently pulled out a small gun from her purse and handed it to me. Whoa, that got me going!

As I took part on the crisis team, I encountered various interesting situations. I visited the jail because of their need to determine the suicidal potential of an inmate. I thought some could talk through things, others were seriously in a state of suicidal ideation that warranted interventions by the staff. The staff took away their belts and shoelaces, for instance, and checked on them at regular intervals.

My relation with a local judge opened up the assessment of violence potential of inmates convicted of sex crimes. Indiana enacted a law that required this. They would use this information in sentencing decisions. After going to several forensic psychology trainings and conferences, I put together a packet of tools to answer the court's question of violence potential. It is not a clear or easy question to answer. Probably the major factor is past violence. The trainings were interesting, for instance, listening to FBI agents talk about the actions of sexual predators. As well, sex offenders had a selfish mindset. In one case of a convicted offender, he told me how he knew this young girl "wanted to have sex with me. I knew it how she was dressed. She smiled and wanted to talk to me. These were her signs." He interpreted these in sexual terms, and significantly, he felt no guilt at all.

The effects of violence and dysfunctional relationships became clear to me when they appointed me to be on the child protection team through the Human Services Department. I took part in oversight of the department's handling of abuse and neglect cases. It could be a bed bug outbreak or a lack of adequate food in a household. There were horrendous situations of abuse. Seeing the pictures of the impression of the belt buckle on the naked back of the child made me sick. One case had a boyfriend throw the child against the wall with substantial force. The child received brain damage as a result, became blind, and could not speak. I felt privileged to work with the social workers of the department. These dedicated people received too much negative feedback for doing their jobs.

Since our move to Columbus, my college teaching continued. Jacqueline Franz, the wife of a psychiatrist, connected me to the local college administration. This joint venture of Indiana University and Purdue University, called IUPUC, provided classes sanctioned by both universities. I had a track record of teaching and they hired me to teach psychology. Over the years, this would expand to a good repertoire of classes. Later, I received a distinction for teaching at IUPUC for 15 years. I didn't teach more than one course a semester as an adjunct professor, but I came to enjoy the interaction with students.

Probably the high point of my teaching or at least the class I had the most fun with concerned the learning class. I used a software program called Sniffy the virtual Rat. Since I turned down a job running a rat lab, the prospect of rats running in mazes has haunted me. At the group home, at Madison, and now in Columbus, I found behavioral techniques useful. It only made sense that, in teaching undergraduates, I would have a rat-oriented program illustrating behavioral techniques! I couldn't get away from it. "Let me tell you about the software we will use in this class. Sniffy is a hoot! It simulates a rat in a Skinner box with reward and punishment built in. You can zap Sniffy with a bolt of electric shock, or reward him with a food pellet. The visuals are good and the presentation of Sniffy impresses you with his reality. If you get good at commanding the controls, you can even get him to roll over! Extra credit for that!"

One necessity of a professional career is the need for continuing education. I can't calculate how many conferences or day long workshops I have attended. Quinco had a Solutions Training Institute that conducted trainings and so we got a pleasant break on the cost. It would require that you take off the day, but the training was excellent. The good ones would leave me with excitement.

One conference, held every five years starting in 1985, included the biggest name therapists, researchers and theorists in the field. The conference was called the Evolution of Psychotherapy Conference. Bob Siegmann, a social worker and I went twice. He ran the Quinco institute that provided speakers for local conferences. The first time, we went to Anaheim, California, where he grew up. We visited his warm and gracious parents. They lived in a finely appointed apartment. It felt like a visit to a palace. And they certainly loved their son. We also visited Hollywood with its Lamborghinis, Rolls, and beautiful people.

The second time, we went to Las Vegas. Of course, we did some gambling. But the speakers were none the less impressive. The Hoover Dam and the mountains were also a treat.

Many famous practitioners gathered at these conferences. I taught about these individuals and felt overwhelmed to be in their presence, like royalty. I walked around and passed by two old guys talking on a couch. Their name tags said "Aaron Beck" and "Irvin Yalom". I walked by twice to make sure. I almost asked for autographs. Seeing such people gave me a boost in enthusiasm and I impatiently wanted to get back to my cases and try out the ideas I excitedly heard about.

Let me share about another Quinco adventure with Bob that occurred around this time. I am not sure how it started, but the idea of going rafting on the New River in West Virginia made the rounds at Quinco, looking for takers.

The New River cuts through the New River Gorge, West Virginia, for 53 miles. It is a twisting, fast-moving river which affords wonderful views and whitewater rafting on its turbulent waters. We drove down to West Virginia, stayed at an inexpensive hotel and hired an outfitter to get on the water. Over the river loomed the spectacular New River Gorge Bridge that spans the Gorge.

The drive down took most of the day. Getting to know Bob and Ben better was nice. I didn't know that Bob grew up in New York and had a couple of grown kids. Ben from California, also had a couple of children and been through a divorce. Driving on a trip brings out the stories. Roger, a social worker from the crisis team, and I had a connection in that we worked at Hanover College around the same time. We were all excited as this would be the first trip rafting for each of us. Little did we know the trip that awaited us.

Rafting started out early. Taken to a beach area, we found large rafts waiting for us. We got on our wet suits and put on our life jackets, making sure that they fit. These were not for show. We got paddles and blue and yellow plastic helmets. The paddles were single oars with a tee at the top to hold on to.

Getting into the boats, the dirty brown water flowed quickly. We tucked our feet into side ropes and sat on the edge while we paddled. We received instructions from our guide, Randy. He sat on the very back and had a large paddle to steer, and showed that we had to work as a team. He gave us orders about paddling. "Now, you on the right side, I might call on you to paddle only or you all on the left, or maybe I will yell at everybody. I might ask one side to hold paddles in the water to slow us down, while the other side will paddle. If I yell, "dig", that means you bunch better paddle as if there is a beef brisket waiting for you at dinner! Now, you get tossed out of the boat, take a sitting position and face downstream. Let us work together and have some fun!" We clicked our paddles in the air!

It took some skill. I sat in the front. Twice I got pushed into the boat by a wave or gyration. Starting off, Randy practiced with us, calling out orders and us responding in our inept and amateurish manner. We were there to have a good time not to work. We then hit a run of small rapids. There were rocks on one side and we steered away from them. We were excited but also felt a sense of the seriousness of the job we took on as we watched the rock glide by us. Strongly jostled, we got wet. I almost lost my paddle when a small wave splashed me.

The walls of the rock edges were beautiful in browns and greens. The sun came out and glistened on the water. Big outcroppings of stone passed by. We passed sandy areas and those with tall rock facings. But I didn't have time to watch the pretty scenery; I had to paddle. We found a small clearing to the side, and we paused. The guide asked us how we were doing. Everybody nodded. "All right," he said. Maybe in his mid-twenties, a surfer looking guy, he had a ponytail, bare feet. "I have been doing this for maybe five years. I attend school in Colorado and this pays for it. Let me remind you, you can tip me if you like my stories. They are all true!" He told us about the Gorge and the names of some rapids we would encounter. I couldn't hear what he said. When he yelled orders to paddle, I heard that!

As we moved well down the river, there were rafts ahead of us from our group and several others further back. The boat would drift to the left or right if we didn't pay attention and Randy would get us to go straight into a rapid. He didn't like sideways. When the action hit, I couldn't look back but only listen for his voice.

After a period of calm water, we encountered rapids again. This suddenly changed as we followed a light turn into the river. Randy instructed us to get to the center of the river, and we did. As soon as he said that, we hit turbulence that surprised me. The raft buckled and we on the right went higher than the guys on the left. No worry, in a second, they were higher. We got pelted with waves of cold water. For a second, we were going to the left, then we got pushed and went right. A rock loomed in front of us and we were told to push left. I swear I could have touched it as it went by. A huge rock wall stood menacing on the left. For certain, he didn't want us to have any of it, so we aimed right. A movement of water helped, but pushed us down as well. It almost felt like we were being sucked into it. He shouted more commands. Around it we went and then we were calm. We pulled off to the side. "Ya'll, ok?" he asked. "A little wet, huh?" He got nods. "My ass is so tight," he started, "you couldn't drive a 6 penny nail up it with a sledgehammer!" So there, that is how we all felt. Tight butts, all.

As the day went on and we floated down the river, the overhead clouds moved across the pretty blue sky. Occasionally, birds flew overhead. We stopped for lunch by a beachy area with food and drink waiting for us. Not stopping for long, we jumped into our rafts by the quiet water by the edge.

As we proceeded, the rocks got more prominent. White water gurgled more, and the gyrations were more expressive. The bronco came alive. We entered one set of rapids, called the "School Bus rapids". They tossed us back and forth and the boat felt like it wiggled on the water and under us. Maybe it laughed at us. The rapids pushed the raft in front of us almost sideways.

One end flared up and a middle person fell to the inside, their paddle going straight up, almost hitting the person next to them.

Then we got our chance. We hit it further left than they did, but it still caught us and pushed the other end up out of the water. I could hear the guide yell, "Whoa there!" as he slapped his oar in the water to correct us. We went sideways and just a tinge of fear went through me. He yelled for the other side to "Dig it, DIG IT" and the raft straightened slowly, like in slow motion. Then we were out of it. "Thank the Lord!" I heard from the back of the raft.

It got colder as we continued down the river. A breeze developed, moving the trees, going over my arms and face. We went a little further, but then we pulled off to the side. This time, however, we stayed and circled. The other rafts from our group had also pulled to the side. We took a break and got out of the beached rafts. I felt exhilarated, breathing in the cool air. The guides got together and consulted each other. We didn't understand what had happened, but it didn't feel good. Randy said little to us. A helicopter flew by rather low and stopped down the river. It paused a way behind us. You could see the water vibrating under the helicopter's blades. As we watched, sharing odd looks with each other, a single paddle came floating down. The handled part floated slowly above the waterline. It bobbed up and down slightly as it went by us. I am not sure all saw it. It looked like a cross.

After maybe 30 minutes, we got started again. One of the group asked Randy what happened. He said in a much lower tone, "A person in a raft back there fell over and drowned. The helicopter came to recover the body." He gave us just a brief report, but a chill went through me. We hit the rapids as we continued. However, the trip, it seemed to me, felt essentially over. As we talked on the bus going back to the camp, we called this the river of death. We knew it could be risky. However, until you face it directly, it simply lives in the back of your head, unrealized. We thanked Randy and yes, we gave him a nice tip. Subdued sounds from the anvil, working, but solemnly.

An interesting character who worked at Quinco was a guy named Dugan Mershon. A social worker who worked in the Addictions service, Dugan had a loud presence in his 6-foot 3-inch frame. I worked with his wife in the adolescent service. Dugan invited us all to come and watch him try his hand at stand-up comedy. Several of us went and saw him as he took the stage at an open mic in Bloomington. "I'm Dugan and a therapist by day." "Sorry!" somebody shouted. "Let me tell you some mental health stories. But first, I need your insurance information and driver's license!" I don't think it went well. Dugan played a role in several group activities.

The Indianapolis 500 had a mini marathon a couple of days before the race. Several of us ran the race. The race ended at the 500 track. The last couple of miles were around the 2 1/2-mile oval track. You can't comprehend how steep it is or how long it can be until you try to run around the track at the end of 12 miles. From Quinco, Bob took part on the "race team" as did Roger and Dugan. Quinco gave us red and white "Quinco Running Team" shirts. Roger and I would train around Columbus. We would tumble down a long stretch of road over several months, running every couple of days, increasing the distance as we progressed.

The race itself went around the downtown area of Indianapolis, starting at the big circle. Thousands of runners, stretching, sprinting and talking in little groups, were present at the start. The air felt electric as we got ready. "Roger, you ready for this?" "As I ever will be. Do you think we trained enough?" "No, but it doesn't matter now!" "How are you?" "Good. Let's do it!" High fives! Others inevitably passed us up rapidly, and we wound up with very slow but satisfying times. I would achieve a comfortable pace and keep it up for the first 4 or 5 miles, then slowdown in the middle, only to push myself toward the end. My time didn't really matter. The camaraderie and the exercise were enjoyable. I ran it maybe 4 or 5 times till my body said, "Enough!" It wasn't a full marathon, but it felt like a Ph.D. of a race. So, I got my degree and moved on.

Given my stellar baseball career as a youth, when Quinco needed softball players, I jumped at the chance. Dugan coached the team. While we had played volleyball for several years at a local armory, the softball team stood out because it had, at least for a year, a good bit of success. I played third and shortstop. This year, we won the over 40 league hands down. The grand prize included, of course, a picture in the paper. I'm sure we got a trophy and I'm sure they put it in the trophy case at Quinco with all the other sports trophies the Mental Health Center accumulated over the years! We got winning blue tee shirts, which I could probably find around here at the base of the closet.

Another service project I did with Dugan concerned meeting with poor youth. Through my contacts at Human Services, I took part in a conference for boys called Boys to Men. It sought to help boys learn to treat girls respectfully and non-violently. It was an informational and skill building effort. Dugan and I worked the weekend retreat with several others. "Come on, Mr. Dugan, dunk the ball!" With food, music and basketball, we tried to have fun with a difficult topic. We focused on respect and communicating honestly, hard topics for some boys whose homes were violent, negligent or with absent fathers. The yearly conference went on for several years. It felt like worthwhile work.

Because of my work at Quinco, my developing reputation in the community was good. I approached the job with a level head and I had reasonable success. In the therapy business, there will be cases where the relationship between the client and the therapist doesn't work. I had enough of those cases to keep me humble. I also had cases I knew were successful. At one point, I saw a man whose wife committed suicide. We worked together for about a year, talking on a weekly basis. We got through his intense grief and guilt and brought him to function again. I saw a young, significantly disabled client. We met off and on for a long time and eventually he signed up with the Special Olympics and did things he could not dream of doing early on. The treatment could be tough and difficult, but I look back on our work with pride. He found a life, and I helped to mediate the change. God struck those anvil blows.

I spent a decade at Quinco. One year, there were promotions and they passed me by. This got me to thinking about other opportunities. I knew people who had a private practice. We talked, and I thought a change of job might be a good thing. Private practice seemed to be the next step after working at a big agency. It could also be more lucrative.

Private practice had its pros and cons, but the pros won out and I moved to a small practice with five other therapists. I knew several of the therapists and the atmosphere was friendly and collegial. As I always did, I prayed about it. I can look back and see many occasions of divine intervention. I thought it only natural to ask for God's help in making this change happen and to have it be a good thing for me, my family, and my clients.

There were other opportunities that came up. I took a contracting job with a private hospital to conduct psych testing for their adolescents. Over the years, I probably did tens of dozens of interesting assessments. Other contacts flowered into an opportunity for doing supervision with a practice in town. The therapists were all social workers and very competent and experienced at that. They simply needed my signature to verify treatment needs legally. The agency helped the poor in town.

In private practice, I found it important to offer services to low-income clients who were on Medicaid. These clients were more chronic than others and the resources of the family and the client were usually low. Abuse, trauma, family difficulties and addictions were typically present and made for an uphill battle.

I spent several years at this private practice until the owner decided she wanted to sell the practice. Several of us got together, however, and talked about opening up another practice. We had surreptitious meetings at a local restaurant. But we figured we would take the best of what we saw and drop or improve on the poorer aspects of the business. This is when the Columbus Counseling Group came into existence. We found a modern and clean building and hired a bookkeeper and a receptionist. The four staff, three psychologists and a social worker, opened the business. Kelley, Susan and Megan and I were a good fit for each other. I counted as the only guy. But hey, my masculinity could handle it. I have worked with many strong and articulate women professionals. I gladly and rewardingly worked at the Columbus Counseling Group for a number of years. Loud gong.

I had a conversation with a young relative one time who told me he wished to make a million dollars by a certain age so that he could retire young and enjoy life. He said he knew my lifestyle and that my motivation differed from his. He said he admired me for giving to others, but it wouldn't work for him. I had known this for a long time, but it surprised me when he said it. In response, "My social awareness and concerns lead me to seek opportunities to help others. Rochelle is the same way, if not more. Accumulating money is nice, and it makes things happen. Good luck to you, but it is not a primary reason to live for me. Since a kid, I have enjoyed watching people and involving myself in their lives. Hearing about pain and suffering does not turn me off, but opens up my interest and curiosity, my sympathy and attention." "I don't understand it, but I respect it." He said.

One time in Walmart, looking for an item, a young man walked by and in the next aisle, approached me. He asked, "Are you Dr. House?" I said, "Yes." "I don't know if you remember me," he told me his name. I didn't. "But I saw you for a couple months three years ago. I thought about killing myself and talking with you helped." He nodded his head. "Well, that's great, Brian. Thanks for that. I'm happy I could help." He hurried away. That one interaction shows me that my career with all its difficulties had worth. My time in the chair was a gift. Making a million widgets wouldn't compare. Sorry to all you who are widget makers!

The Next Scene

In the serendipity of life, we discover the rich scenery of our drama
It carries us from day to day
It is the chance occurrence, the unlikely occasion, the twisting possibility that guides the vague path we reluctantly follow
This is the act in which we play, the characters we meet, the script that yields our words before we speak them
Our theater creates fear and joy, inducing the satisfactions that make up our blinded experience
We do not plan where things will take us
We do not have control (though try as we do)
It is that unseen hand of God that opens the surprising door
We move from moment to moment in the opportunity that arises unforeseen, the unpredictable conversation, the impulsive thought, the chance encounter
Do not fear the dimming of the lights
It is God's gift and will contain the next scene that upholds your time's pathway

12 Waycross Drive

Let me share one of those times that just happens, a Zeitgeist kind of thing. I contributed to the decision, but I wasn't prepared for this. The kids were fairly small. I worked at Reunion and came home one day. As I entered the front foyer, I saw everyone sitting unusually in the living room. Besides that, they were all smiling and giggling. As I walked up the steps, they all shouted at once. "Look Dad, we got a dog!" Sure enough, among them, jumping up and down and falling over himself to a cascade of giggles, sat a small brown and white puppy, a border collie mix. The cutest little dog, full of energy. He had certainly found the correct place. Loud peals of joy responded to his every little move. "What's his name?" I asked, assured that if he had been there for half an hour, he already had a name. Thomas said, "It's Alex". From that moment on, little Alex would be a part of the household. How he did it, I don't know, but he won over people in a second and we never looked back. He loved to run and play. I am not sure that I ever heard him growl, except playfully. He became the perfect friend who added a certain heart and warmth to the house. The place became more of a home with Alex.

We have a favorite picture of Thomas as a very young boy sitting on the couch with Alex. He grew fairly quickly but stayed at a good weight and size and continued to be a gentle dog. As he grew, he also increased in the speed with which he could run around the yard. He loved chasing the rabbits that liked our yard. He had little guard dog instinct, but loved to be a part of things. For maybe 14 years, Alex added to our life, a superb listener, confidant, and play buddy. I am fond of that picture of him and Thomas.

When we moved to Columbus, we at first lived in an apartment. This helped us to get our bearings on the new town. It was a place that really fit us. Within a year, we moved into a split-level house. I am not sure that Rochelle loved it, but we could afford it and the house was in good shape. The woman who owned it raised her family there. She cried at the closing.

Our new house was on Waycross Drive. A fitting name, it is how we made our way cross the years! Up to now had been preparation. The other dwellings I lived in kept me out of the rain. But this house resonated differently. I have been in many rooms, looked out many windows, walked down many hallways, and proceeded up and down many flights of steps. My clothes have hung in way too many closets. The several houses in Connecticut were like acquaintances, giving of themselves but not too deeply. They offered joy and living, but soon departed. Atlantic City had adventure all over it and we laughed so much with that house, but then it crashed upon us. My grandmother's house in Philly did not belong to us and treated us like strangers. It amounted to a bus stop, really. Dyre Street wanted us to be happy. It really did, but it couldn't give what it didn't own. Pratt Street was the scene of too much drama. That house was real life, but raw and difficult. Ypsilanti put a spell on us, but it was short-lived. We went to Nashville for life training. It took a while to learn the language. The Madison place came closest to giving us life. It gave us its fullest effort. But that house sagged with age and couldn't keep up with the energy. This house, the way-cross-our-lives house, did us a service. It gave up itself for us, from its heart, and we returned the favor and gave our lives back. This became a love affair. It knew how to do families! Here we encountered the marathon race of raising children. No, it wasn't a sprint! But here also, my heart could rest. Sit and stay a while, I heard the walls say in a quiet invitation. You have found a place of respite, a space that allows the deep breathing of love and life, a place that may grow old with you.

Until now, I have lived in transit. However, in Columbus, we encountered our destination; we got off the bus, and it became a home. It happens when the time is right, the vibe resonant, the mood comforting. God says this will be the place where life will grow, memories made, and moments shape into character. Here the light from the windows is joyful and relaxed. The walls ask how can we help you celebrate? The floors ask how they can support the dance steps. You can stay here and this will be your brightness and your love, said the house. Here you can stand with your imperfections and we love you, anyway. Rest with those crooked bones bent by the lessons of the wind and the waves battering your ship but not sinking it. Here is your harbor.

In bed, "Rochelle, because of my past, I feel an almost unconscious imperative." "What?" She frowned. "I want our family not to endure violence, verbal or otherwise. I can't support displays of rage or disrespect. Ideally, I want to offer honest relationships to our kids, calm, and trusting. Expecting our kids to be silent and out of the way is not my style." "Nor mine!" she said. "I want us to be active, communicative parents, Steve, concerned with what they are doing and experiencing." "My parents did the best they could. But I desire better." I said. "How can I be authentic, real, direct, and respectful? I want so much to raise good human beings, knowledgeable and caring." It felt clear as day to me. "Hey, I don't want my kids to experience my suffocating upbringing. Here it should be different. I lock the door at night and I have influence over dinner choices. Of course, it would probably be more realistic to say that I get to choose between hot dogs and mac and cheese!" She laughed. But I had some power and felt some influence. I wanted to support these kids finding their own voices but not drown them.

I joined the woman with whom I shared these responsibilities. She proved a wonderful partner who gave me a voice as she herself wished to have a voice. Three young kids are a pack of cats and herding them is a monumental job besides trying to turn them into good human beings. There were rules and structure, but we loved these kids and sought their growth and development. Now, we had our moments of doubt and testing. Don't get me wrong. But I look back and see a wonderful though imperfect dance. I would do it again, although I have nowhere near the energy! These next couple of chapters narrate the unpredictable, mundane and marvelous journey our family took. This was our life in the raw. Yet, it shows the simple acts of presence, care, and attention we gave each other as we were molded into a family! Gongs for that!

Let me share where we were. Paul presented with a strong will. He verbally expressed himself very well. He got an award for writing in third grade. But he needed our care to direct him, for he had an edge. Thomas took the middle child role and fit in wherever he was. He didn't clash with Paul, but played the mediator. He looked up at Paul and followed to an extent. However, he had his own unique style. Thomas flowed and had an uncanny comfort with himself. Catherine gave us her young but beautiful presence, the little smiling girl with curly, blondish hair and a beautiful spirit. She had an innocent, beguiling smile and gentle blue eyes. If this family was an ice cream sundae, she would be the cherry on top. Rochelle blossomed into a mature, wise and confidant partner. She held the practical, money smart role and yet had perseverance and a worker bee mentality. We changed the sheets too often, but we maintained order and decorum. To my core, I mostly felt like the Philly kid I grew up. Not too far removed from shouting at the TV at the dumb Eagles or Sixers, I could be rough and intense. But I was observant and had a presence. I enjoyed a sense of humor, playfulness, poetry and music. Appreciating the gift of my life, I took care of business. I was holier, more discerning, and more trusting. In the mid-west, Philly was a couple of chapters back!

Rochelle and I saw an important course correction in our relationship around this time. Rochelle and I had a fairly good relationship. However, there came unforeseen bumps in the road. Rochelle got riffed, and she lost her job at the middle school. This affected us as we needed her salary to complement mine and pay the bills. Our communication became strained. We did not outwardly argue or fight, but I felt the significant tension in our relationship that needed to be addressed. I asked around and got the name of a therapist in Bloomington, Elvie Dublin.

I recall the first time we went to see her. We came to her small office just as you got to Bloomington before campus. The short and older therapist had a slight accent. But her voice had a gentle and accepting quality. She listened and allowed us to share the tough stuff. "Elvie, we are not in a good way. We are irritated more often. I am feeling," looking at Rochelle with a sad and regrettable look, "unhappy and tired. The kids are stressing us out." The pain came out. Together, we laid out our family and marital issues and malaise. Elvie presented as just the warmest and most insightful person. We lucked out when we saw her for therapy. We explored several issues and their background in our lives growing up. Working with her, we learned to connect again and restore our tempered trust. She had little coasters that she would fling on the floor. "Rochelle, say something to your mom about how you are feeling." "Steve, here," tossing a coaster, "speak to your son, Paul." She interpreted and made suggestions, but also brought issues and people into the room which we had to address. We ended therapy with both of us feeling release, insight, and hope. Sparks.

Around this time, Rochelle worked in a different county with a different spring break schedule. I felt confident in my role as dad and so I took this little band to Philly, where we headed for spring break. The packed car had clothes and all the stuff you need for an enjoyable weeklong vacation. Paul rode shotgun and kept the map (although we had done the trip many times). Paul also had the AAA book of attractions. Philly was the goal, but we would explore. Thomas and Catherine were in the back, separated by book bags.

On these kinds of trips, we always brought kid's books on tape. The Lion, the Witch and the Wardrobe by C.S. Lewis accompanied us. We had Winnie the Pooh, Charlotte's Web, and Robinson Crusoe. Our kids did not starve for good books and stories. C.S. Lewis always delivered!

They were 11, 8 and 6, with fewer episodes of anger or irritation. The occasions of conflict usually meant they were tired, bored, or hungry. We brought snacks with us to take care of most of their needs. The tapes helped keep the boredom down.

Because we called this spring break, we packed summer weather clothes expecting to have fun in the sun. Our miscalculation became clear when we went to Gettysburg for a tour of the battlefield. I hadn't been there before. We turned off and made our way to the small town of Gettysburg. We talked about the battle and the Civil War. I almost felt them getting excited to see the place. They were not ignorant of history nor of significant places that needed to be seen. We had instilled a good desire to explore.

We stopped for gas and I asked how close we were to the battlefield. The man at the station looked at me, a little puzzled. An older man with whiskers and gritty hands. He looked in the car and surveyed my kids. "I wouldn't take them to the battlefield, son. The place is all under a couple of inches of snow. You can't see anything." "Really?" Shaking his head, "Yeah!" "Well…thanks." I made a sound of disappointment. I had lived in Philly for most of my life and had never been to Gettysburg. It reminded me of not seeing the Liberty Bell until late in my twenties!

Now what, I thought? Like the battle, would this be the turning point of the trip, disappointment and failure? "Hey, kids, we can't do the battlefield. You heard the guy. There's snow." "So where are we going?" asked Thomas. The travel book talked about visiting Hershey, Pennsylvania, not too far away. "How about some Hershey kisses?" "Yeah!" from the back. Sweets would always take their disappointed minds off being bored.

When we arrived, we discovered we had found a full-blown amusement park that wasn't open. But we could tour Hershey's Chocolate World for free! We parked and went in and I felt a certain relief as it gave us something to do. There was an exhibit about the history of the company. I noticed there was a ride of sorts. But the best thing was the gift shop. Paul said, "I want the 12 lb. Hershey Bar!" Of course, the answer to that question was clearly no. Catherine liked the intriguing white chocolate. She wanted the big Hershey kiss. They gave us free small Hershey kisses, and we bought a big bag just for good measure! You could always bribe the kids with food, especially sweet food. They weren't marvelous M and M's, but they would work as small delectable pellets of reward, conditioning smiles and good behavior!

You know how there are moments that seem to define an occasion or an event, like the screaming fans at the Beatles concert? This moment made the trip for me. As we drove to Frank's, my friend from high school at whose home we would stay, I saw an open field with trees and a pretty sky above. "Hey, guys, let's get a picture in your summer clothes!" Grumbling from the back. "It's cold outside!" "I'm tired!" "Aw, come on, are you guys lazy?" The warm car did not compare to the ice and snow that rested on the trees and ground. The kids had prepared for fun in the sun. "Here, I'll park over by that car. You can stand by this tree." They all got out and posed. "Oh, you guys are so cute!" And so there they were, in their "Spring Break" clothes: tee shirts, shorts, flip-flops and, of course, sunglasses! Amid the cold, disappointing signs of an oppositional winter, there they stood, smiling! That picture made the trip.

So, my good intentions miscalculated the sun in Pennsylvania in March. We had hoped to escape from Indiana's cold by finding warmth along the way. Ohio had given little hope as the weather continued to be overcast and cold. The whole trip, we searched for the oasis of sun and 70s, never to be found. But here, on the sidewalk, we found enough sun and fun to make it worthwhile. Although our trip took place amid an ice storm followed by snow, we found humor in flip-flops and sunglasses! And we crunched forward.

Now, as a side note, Frank redeemed me. There in the middle of his living room sat a full-size pinball machine! I am not sure where he got it or why he kept it in his living room. But it delighted several young children I knew!

The next day, as we pulled up to the Pratt Street house, I felt strange. Here I was with my delightful present life in the car and before me stood an old photo that had aged and yellowed on the edges. It felt weird to be back and see it in the brick and concrete, the broken steps and the sagging windows. This had been the scene where it all happened: the adolescent urges, the flights of music, the high school drama, the anger and the death. In that house, hell had happened. Dark and dismal, gray in a gray suit sort of way, it waited for the wake to start. I had a feeling of nostalgia but other feelings, maybe a sense of shame or guilt in leaving and moving on. Maybe I tasted the old dark fear and anxiety. The front door spoke in a soft but menacing sort of way. It remembered!

The kids were happy to get out of the car. They probably didn't have a clue about my reaction to being back at my old house. But that was fine. My feelings didn't involve them. They would have their own issues about home, I am sure, as they got older. However, these visits were necessary. I had to share my young family.

The door opened, and the feelings evaporated. My mom seemed very excited to see everyone. She had aged as well. Of course, she made us a big dinner, even though she wasn't sure when we would arrive. She happily hugged the kids. "Hi, Yia Yia" they said. "Oh, children, you are so adorable. Pauly, you have grown. Thomas and Catherine, so cute. Steve come on in and sit down. Rochelle didn't come?" "Yeah, I told you." "You must be exhausted. Your parents are feeding you super food- you all have grown!" They were cute, and they were on good behavior. It had been a couple of years since our last visit. They made me proud. Catherine, being fairly young, took it all in. She was quiet and reserved, suggesting some uncomfortableness. My brother got a little loud and in your face. He went overboard. "These kids are so beautiful and Steve, they are smart!" He enjoyed having guests.

I am sorry that my father died so young and missed so much relationship. He would have liked my kids. My mother seemed preoccupied. She had a special son and other loyalties weighing her down. Her life seemed stretched and thin. The restaurant had closed. "Mom, how are you?" Direct, not looking for social niceties. "Oh, fine Steve, I'm fine." Forever guarded. But our visit allowed her to be the Yia Yia and helped her to know the kids. They were a part of her life, but only peripherally. I must admit, I didn't know the heavy load she carried, getting only a glimpse of it later on. She had a tough life. She never had much money. Her health declined having a bout of breast cancer and a serious car accident. She also cared for her grown son for years. While Nicky worked at the magazine place, he seemed to be relatively steady. However, after he lost the job, things seemed to unravel for him. Nicky would have volatile moods and actions as he got older. More about that later. But my wife and children were in such a different place than my family of origin.

Overall, the trip took in interesting and necessary places. We made it with the help of C.S. Lewis and a pinball machine! The kid escapade was one of the best trips we took.

Getting back to Waycross, home could be drudgery, but we tried to keep it interesting. Downstairs in the big finished basement was a large wooden structure on the wall, covered up by a white peg board. Opening it up, lay a figure 8 slot car track! This, of course, thrilled the boys and maybe the dad as well. Tied to this were the other basement games. Like Philly, we had a ping-pong table for a long while. We had a foosball table for a while at which Thomas excelled. The car track morphed into an HO train set and a standing HO car track. The basement would later see Thomas's basement band.

I must also note the exceptional Children's Museum in Indianapolis that just charmed our kids the many times we went there. From the liquid clock in the front foyer that stood 20 feet high to an Indy race car off the central circular ramp to the planetarium, trips to the Children's Museum were always a treat. We were good museum people.

My kids also developed a love for planes. Or was it genetic? We visited the Wright Patterson Air Force Museum in Dayton, Ohio, and the Smithsonian Air and Space Museum in Washington. The SR-71 was a big hit, as was the Spitfire. We have been regulars at airshows in Indianapolis, Leesburg, Virginia, Joint Base Andrews in DC, and the Blue Angels visiting Annapolis for the Naval Academy commencement. If we see and hear a British Spitfire and a growling Merlin engine at a show, we will give knowing looks to each other.

Rochelle and I enjoyed Bloomington and the IU Auditorium. Here we saw a Bob Dylan concert and over the years, Broadway plays and one-man shows. They always had top-notch acts. A local favorite folk singer named Carrie Newcomer played the auditorium and surrounding venues. She became Rochelle's favorite singer. She had a beautiful silky voice which, when combined with her evocative words, created a tapestry of emotional and personal images. Her songs presented a delightful narrative of being in love or caring for family or friends.

Of course, home ownership is an adventure! The house would produce unpredictable issues. For instance, we had a problem with the attic, for it drew bats. I spent hours putting up screening, trying to keep them from getting in. However, I also spent no little time chasing them around the house. "Paul, watch him. He's a big one and fast. He's coming at you" "I got him, Dad. I'll knock him down with my tennis racket." "Whoa, duck!" Of course, they had a foot long wing span and flew quickly. Certain members of the family would scream.

One time, as I dropped a dish in the sink, I thought I saw an odd movement. I moved a plate, a fork and spoon and looking up at me, were the eyes of an ugly bat with his wings by his side. Stunned momentarily and not sure what to do, I sprayed it with water. This only made it mad, and it started fluttering its wings. Expecting the bat to take off, I turned the bowl upside down and covered the bat with it. "Catherine, Paul, there's a bat in the sink. Quick, I need some help." Paul grabbed something and offered me a spatula. "A spatula? I'm not going to cook it!" "Here's a plastic bag. Will that help?" Catherine said. "Let's see if I can get…crap, it's going to fly!" It was really mad now. "I got it between dishes." I dropped them into the bag and took it outside like it was radioactive. There were several of these encounters. I found one bat in the window drapes, another in the cabinets. I am reminded of the scene in "The Big Chill" where bats come in to the room through an open hatch.

This brings up another battle with creatures that lasted for years. In our big backyard, we planted flowers and a couple of Forsythia bushes and trees. However, we had trouble with chipmunks. I know they are cute and have a wonderful reputation because of Disney films and Alvin and the Chipmunks songs, but in real life they are a pain in the butt. The word on the street suggested you had to take them across water or else they would find their way back. Because we were in corn country, a seed store in town sold traps of various sizes. I found that using a piece of bread with peanut butter attracted them as a wonderful bait. "Hey Thomas, check it out. I caught two at the same time. How does that happen?" I don't know how many of the critters I hauled away to the next county, the other side of the river. One time I caught an ugly possum. He went over to the river. I later found out that they are good for a garden.

Speaking of animals, Alex was a wonderful dog. However, I was not fond of all the cats we had. To be up front, I am sorry to offend the cat lovers, but I don't like cats. Catherine brought several home. They were just not good pets. They were unpredictable, a little psychotic. One cat, it may have been Murphy Gray (don't ask me), sat on the arm of the couch while our priest Fr.

Clem sat waiting for dinner. Clem liked cats, so he pet her nicely while we talked. Suddenly, the cat arches her back and stabs at his hand with her teeth. Totally uncalled for and antisocial. I might add embarrassing as well.

Paul had a guinea pig named Alf for a while. I went with him to get it. Alf's cage sat just under that of a monkey who kept shaking and slamming the cage. Ah, monkeys! Alf, the guinea pig, didn't last that long before he passed. The monkey traumatized him and he died of a nervous breakdown. Of course, that is my professional opinion. I almost ran a rat lab in my career, so I know!

The house had other surprises for us at probably the most inopportune times. We had a sewer line that often broke down. Of course, this got worse when use would be heavy, like at the super bowl party with Dennis and Debbie Stark and their kids or other parties we had.

As an owner of a house, I had maintenance like painting, that required attention. One significant job I did once but will never do again was to put on a new roof. I always felt that if I could do it myself, I could save money and learn things. Yes, putting on a roof taught me several things. One is that it is hot on a roof. And while it is hot, you are carrying 50 lbs. of shingles up a ladder. I had to use a lot of energy climbing up that ladder multiple times. My back also went on strike toward the end of the job and has not been the same since. I wanted to do a good job around the chimney to make it harder for bats to get in. I bought a book (my failing) which told me what I had to do.

Kiel, our nephew from Michigan, stayed with us for a couple of weeks. I couldn't do the job alone. "Hey, Thomas and Kiel, you guys want to help? I'll buy lunch?" They were about the same age. "Can you guys work on the back of the garage?" I explained and showed the process. "You are smart guys. I figure it'll be good." When I came back to look at the work they had done, I knew I had misjudged. They followed the process I showed them. However, the line of the shingles started low on the edge of the garage and rose as it got closer to the house portion of the roof, then went down again. They had created a work of art. They had a good time doing it, however.

This house had a lot of greenery. I will always remember the plants I kept. In my young and naïve drive to Michigan, I had a palm tree in the back seat that continues to grow to this day! Because I saw the Karate Kid, I bought my first Bonsai tree a couple of years later. The tree was a small Juniper evergreen in a small ceramic container. It lasted for only six months before it died. This didn't stop me. I got a book (of course) and bought another tree and kept this one alive for maybe a couple of years. The hobby grabbed my interest, and I started buying nursery trees and working on them. I bought tools and wire to train the branches into position. We had a fat Juniper bush by our house and I realized that there were small trees growing around it. I got small pots, dug them up, and planted them. Before I knew it, I had several trees on a table in the backyard. Although they were small and not well styled, they were alive. The pictures in the Bonsai books were beautiful. Mine left a little to be desired. The trees noted in the books were 50 years old or more, so I could wait. I have kept up with this for years. I now have trees that are 30 years old. For me, growing Bonsai trees is a meditative hobby. Sparks to that!

As part of my father's legacy, I made furniture. I have spoken about my large book shelf made in Tennessee. Columbus also saw me build furniture. I made tables, especially a mahogany table that Catherine still uses in her kitchen. For grandkids, I made a changing table and stools for them to stand on. It's a wonder, but I still have all my fingers. However, I carried on in a small way, the legacy of my father.

Water is another aspect of my father's legacy and holds a special significance for me. As my story suggests, since I was young, meaningful interactions have occurred on water. My skill at crabbing translated easily to fishing. I had a great Indiana buddy to engage in this pastime, Shane Teague. Shane's wonderful wife, Lisa, taught our kids as the youth minister at St. Columba Parish and as a babysitter. They liked her. We met them when they were boyfriend and girlfriend. We sponsored them in the church's marriage prep class.

Shane simply was a gifted angler. We did a lot of fishing together. Near Columbus, hidden down hard-to-find roads, existed a wonderful lake called Grouse Ridge. This magical little body of water brought me great comfort and a spot of commune and reflection. Paul and I fished and meditated there a lot.

I had on my refrigerator for the longest time a small cartoon. It had a guy with a fishing rod, sitting on the earth, fishing with the caption, "Little did he know that it really wasn't the fish he was fishing for." I fished for a sense of peace, an enjoyment of God's green and blue earth, a sense of my place in the grand scheme of things and to commune with the natural forces of nature. Probably another significant reason I fished was to recapture the sense of joy and belonging that I experienced when I went crabbing with my father. Fishing became a sacrament. It sounds strange, but to have a fish tug on your line was something mystical. This was a way of communing with God and seeking peace, validation, and belonging.

It wasn't always philosophical and deep. One fall, Shane and I drove the Civic down to the lake. We came down a hill and parked by the middle of the lake. This day, we were at it for several hours and caught several fish. After packing up to go home, however, we encountered an issue. Like Sisyphus, we couldn't get up the hill. Maybe the canoe on top added too much weight, or perhaps my old tires couldn't get traction in the soft and slippery mud. As we reached halfway, the car lost traction and went sideways. Like in a white-water raft, going sideways is a bad sign. "Crap, I can't get up this hill. We're going sideways. We gonna hit that tree?" "No, you're good. Will we stop at the bottom is my question?" "We will see…" I furiously tried to correct our direction, gyrating the steering wheel around. Luckily, we stopped at the base of the hill and didn't wind up in the lake. As the sky got dark, both of us tired, we made another attempt but slid back. After jettisoning all the weight, I drove alone and as fast as I could and finally got the car up the stupid hill. We loaded up the car at the top and drove to his house with little conversation. Embarrassed and angry, my once invincible Honda lost some respect.

Shane had the behaviors of a country boy. With his chewing tobacco in his back pocket and his overalls, he looked like a good old boy. For years, he invited me to his New Year's Day football bash with hot chili, beer, and college football. But he was a special education teacher. He wasn't a naïve and aw, shucks kind of guy, but a smart guy, refined under the big man's exterior. And Shane knew how to fish and taught me a lot.

Bloomington, the home of Indiana University, had a large reservoir called Lake Monroe. A couple of times, people from Quinco would rent a pontoon boat on the lake and party around all day. Our family did this several times. Rochelle did not like water. For her to agree with this made it a big deal. The kids got together with friends and we tooled around the lake, swimming and picnicking.

The lake had a fast side, without speed limits, and a slow side. Shane and I fished on the slow part of the lake during a weekend. The lake that day had many boats congregated in clusters. As we went around the edge trying to catch some bass, a couple of jet skis went rampaging through the crowd of boats. Soon after, a police boat appeared with his siren on and flashing lights. You could hear a cheer go up from the crowd. There were probably lots of kids in the water by the congregated boats and the crazy jet skiers were not safe for them.

Another special area of the lake had shallow water and on one end stood a restricted eagle nesting area. The scenery called me to just sit and reflect. As Paul and I sat in my boat, a bird started flying toward us. "Check it out Dad." "I wonder if it's a…" As it got closer and kept getting larger, we realized we were looking at an eagle. When overhead, it just opened its wings and glided by with the grace and beauty of a majestic creature. To be in the presence of one of God's magnificent creatures is truly astounding and takes one's breath away. It is why it isn't the fish that I am really fishing for but for that communal feeling, that sense of peace and belonging, that fills me with an awestruck wow resulting in anvil sparks.

An interesting fact was that the southernmost progress of the glaciers stopped around Bloomington. This brought geodes. Geodes would be half buried in the ground. Taking a hike, you could easily walk by many of them. These were roundish, light brown rocks that, when cracked open, would often yield a beautiful crystal panorama. I kept several of these.

I need to make sure that we include Catherine in the fishing stories I tell. One time at Lake Lemon, her brownie troop had a fish tournament. The boys and I went as well. While we were fishing, I heard her yell for me. "Dad, Dad, come here! I got one!" And, sure enough, she had a fish on. She brought it in and then ran with it to the scoutmaster. Her fish was the biggest caught, and she won a tackle box! Not bad for a girl known for her curly hair! Sparks!

Now, a couple of developments I have to speak to involved the role that technology played in our house in terms of computers and cars. Both my sons have jobs where computers play a significant role. The captivating power of technology touched us early in our family life. My kids began what would be the significant role that technology would play in their lives with a simple little device we bought, a Commodore 64 computer. Early on, it proved to be a computing wizard, mainly a platform for games. We still had a typewriter. But the Commodore held a mystique that far outshone the fancy calculators they used for school. There was a keyboard, discs and a TV screen. The games were simple like Pong or Donkey Kong. My first actual job involved running business computers, so I knew its importance. The home computer exposed our kids, and they never looked back. While I found it useful yet cumbersome, our kids grew up with it and were naturals at it.

The driveway at Waycross saw a parade of powerful and life changing technological wonders. These, of course, were the cars we owned, reflecting America's love of freedom and exploration. Maybe nothing will live up to the MG as far as character. But the humble Datsun was the first car my kids knew. As they learned the liberating and yet dangerous skill of driving, I taught them all how to drive a stick because the Datsun was a manual transmission. As I taught their mother, I would, one by one, teach the kids to drive a stick. This was a skill that my kids might need and should have in their bag of tricks. You know if you were robbing a bank and the getaway car had a stick! However, after teaching one to drive a stick, the car would need a new clutch! Maybe the car couldn't take the loud instructions to, "Put it in second, now!" Maybe the rolls of the eyes and the looks in the mirror that said, "Oh, my, why can't this kid figure this out?" affected the clutch bearing. It wasn't fair criticism for Paul. The car was halfway there to needing a new clutch because I taught his mom to drive a stick with it!

The trick to teaching a stick involved finding a place safe from crashing. One time with Thomas, we pulled up to the curb by a store to park. Well, we didn't pull up to the curb; we jumped the curb and made it a couple feet closer to the door. A nice open area by the airport offered itself to Catherine. A section of the mall lot, free of traffic, made a great place.

Now, with Catherine, the task was intellectual but also emotional. There were tears and there were tears. She swore she couldn't do it and that she never wanted to drive again. It was clear she hated cars with sticks. From her view, the devil invented the manual transmission. All the while, I gently and supportively reminded her she could do it. And of course, she learned.

The Datsun hit the milestone of 150,000 miles once. To show our respect, we drove around the block several times. "Here it comes, wait for it…Yeah, 150000!" We finally replaced the Datsun after many miles with a Honda Civic hatchback. This would be my car. It had a good pickup and room in the back for stuff. I loved that car. At one point, I had a hitch welded on to it so I could haul a boat trailer. I am sure the guy at the welding garage thought I was nuts or dangerous.

This car took me to Tennessee carrying a 15-foot canoe! Meeting my brothers, we went camping. I figured it would be nice for the brothers to get together. It didn't quite turn out that way. The weekend saw nice weather, but Nick had many complaints about the tent, his pillow, the food and fishing. He couldn't deal flexibly with the situation. This is how he had been for years. It was probably his first time in a canoe and I forgot about his terrible experience with water in Atlantic City. As we hiked, however, we enjoyed the beautiful scenery of the Smokies.

In a similar way, Thomas and I drove to Michigan after Paul left for college in the Civic. We took the fishing boat and trailer. After a warm visit with Rochelle's parents in Flint, we drove up to her brother's place on Lake Huron. We rode go carts, ate out and fished. While we caught little, we had a big one get away. From the shore, Thomas cast out, "Dad, I got a bite. Oh, it feels huge." "Keep it tight, Thomas. I wonder what it could be, maybe a lake trout?" The line went screaming into the deeper water. "Hold on, he's running out." He arched the rod back, but with a loud snap, the line broke. "Aw, crap. Sorry Thomas." The trip was wonderful. Opportunities like this probably didn't come enough. I enjoyed spending time with him. The hammer formed hot metal with this experience.

After the Datsun, we bought a dud, a blue Chrysler K car. With this car, we took the road trip from hell with the alternator going out on the car three times. Needing a reliable car, we got a Camry. To check out the new car, we took it for a Sunday ride to Bloomington. The kids were getting to where small skirmishes for autonomy and boundaries would erupt and we would hear who sat too close or looked at them in the wrong way. We had fewer skirmishes in the bigger Camry. "If you guys don't stop arguing, I am pulling this car over!" This would be a drastic intervention. I hadn't thought about what I would do after pulling over. Flashes of my mom threatening us with a belt came to mind. Rochelle loved her Camry. We bought several and drove them until they had thousands of miles. With relatives in Michigan and Philadelphia, this required trips. We drove to Michigan at least yearly for decades. These trips were pleasant and the family in Michigan always welcomed us. They all loved our kids. And our kids loved their many aunts and uncles. As Rochelle's family dispersed, we went visiting them where they were. We made innumerable trips around the Midwest!

As Paul came of age, he wanted his own vehicle. He saw a Ranger truck on a lot for a good and reasonable price. Paul worked at a local restaurant, and he had the money saved for the truck. However, I am not sure how it happened, but when he went off to Purdue, he took my Honda, and I drove the truck! I really liked it except for when it got smacked by the neighbor. Now I took this as a great opportunity to buy a paint sprayer and paint the truck! I hate to say that the finish did not look as good as I had expected. I held to my mantra that the right tools get the job done. But sometimes you need skill!

For his first car, Thomas bought an old BMW. Against my better judgment, the first weekend he had it, he took it out of state with a friend and got hit by another vehicle. But the car proved to be a decent one. It had a stick, of course. It fit Thomas well. Later, working on his clutch, I decided this would be the last major car work I did. Let me pay a mechanic to do it for me! An incident I had informed this decision. A hard plastic handled screw driver fell and rubbed against the fan belt of the running engine. This left a two-inch deep gouge in it. After just a few seconds against the fan belt, the screw driver catapulted up out of the engine compartment. I decided I didn't need that kind of danger in my life.

Catherine got the hand-me-down BMW when Thomas bought a Firebird! She later had a red Civic that had several near misses I will say nothing about!

After driving Paul's truck, having a truck won me over. So, I bought a newer Ranger. Not great gas mileage, but it could haul a boat trailer. With four-wheel drive, it felt almost invincible. I kept this truck for twenty years. It made the Midwest to the east coast trek several times.

Finally, I should mention a car we bought after the kids were gone, our empty nest car. We bought a Prius to join the hybrid movement. Rochelle just loved this car. We drove it till it died, but not before it took Rochelle and me on several memorable trips. I think you can identify periods in your life based upon the car you owned!

While cars played a necessary role in our modern family, and signaled a coming of age, another activity joined my sons and I. My dad taught me that men do things together. Boy Scouts helped to bond us. The Columbus scout troop brought about great development through significant experiences. In the garage, on the long shelf, rested all the boy scout equipment from backpacks to lanterns and water purifiers. The troop brought about a growth in leadership skills for the boys and helped form a great bond between us. Through this bond, we shared my love of the outdoors and forged many powerful memories.

Troop 555 was an active group of scouters sponsored by the church. During this time, Paul started as a Weblo with Thomas in cub scouts, following later. The troop had a proud history of earning badges and developing skills with several Eagle Scouts. One of the first men I met was Jerry Flodder. "Jerry, nice to meet you, Steve House." "Steve, do you know about our arrangement with Developmental Services? Every year, we arrange for an evening put on by the scouts for disabled adults in the area. The clients in the county look forward to it. But it gives our scouts exposure to special needs individuals. We bring prizes and have a lot of fun. They all love it!" Jerry would also show up on one of our rafting trips. He would fall out of the raft and live to tell the tale!

As Paul joined, the troop experienced a transition, as several of the older boys completed their Eagle ranks and left the troop. We had a new group of active parents, with Tom Rayburn as scoutmaster. One of the first trips we took was to Tennessee as we hiked the Appalachian trail. We then took a significant trip to South Dakota. Now that may seem boring, but the trip had many surprises. Greg Schershel, whose son Josh was in the troop, along with Tom, happily organized it. He urged us, "We have to stop at Wall Drug store in the middle of nowhere in South Dakota. It will amaze you. Believe me really, it is something! We gotta see the Corn Palace too!" Yes, Wall Drug was a phenomenon, a retailing oasis in the middle of nowhere. The Corn Palace also grabbed our attention, with its walls "painted" in corn husks and leaves.

Camping on a ranch owned by someone's relatives, our first unimpressive night saw us camp in the rain. In the day we found ourselves on a large hilly field by a small creek. It was that second evening that overwhelmed me. Looking over the rolling hills of "Big Sky" country, there before me shone the Milky Way. The immensity of the celestial sight took my breath away. Reflecting not an empty expanse, twinkles and lights arranged in a complex and numbing manner filled the sky. The silence allowed the mind to catch up to the eyes.

We visited the powerful Mount Rushmore. However, down the road lay the epic mountain carving of Crazy Horse, the Lakota Sioux warrior who fought against the United States at the Battle of Little Big Horn, Custer's Last Stand. Not nearly finished, this huge undertaking, started in 1948 by Sculpture Korczak Ziolkowski, put into form the anguish and anger of a proud but defeated and abused people.

Memorably, at Custer State Park, Paul and I took a walk on a free afternoon and we came upon a little stream. "Hey Paul, check out this stream." As we paused and watched and listened, some curls formed in the water, suggesting fish. "Did you see that?" "Yep," he said. "It's worth a shot, huh?" I took my rod and reel out of the backpack and threw the line in. I threw the plastic 10 feet down the creek, brought it back against the flow of the water, and pulled the jig out of the water. Nothing. After the third time, I got a little bite, I thought. "I felt something." The next cast, the line went straight and pulled back. I reeled it in quickly and a little brown trout, beautiful in color, looked up at me. "Hey, what do you think we walk up here a bit?" "Sounds like a plan to me!" We tossed in the reddish plastic and got another fish. This went on for a while as we walked over tree roots, rocks, and clumps of moss and dirt. Paul and I had a very successful walk in the park and we got back to camp just in time to start dinner.

Coming back, we made our way to the capital of Pierre, and got a couple of pictures with the governor! Here, we encountered a small herd of donkeys on the road. A youngster put his head in the car through the open window. That created quite a stir!

The trip home, however, got a little rocky. A kid rode in our car who had washed little the entire trip and he smelled rank. Someone in the car asked him, "Man, when was the last time you took a shower?" "Before we left home," he smugly remarked as we rolled down the windows! But the troop buzzed after the trip with stories.

When we returned, the parents got disenchanted by Tom's loud leadership style. After several difficult meetings, we asked him to step down. Over the next several years, we would do at least a yearly trip and a week at summer camp. We would also have several become Eagle scouts to continue the tradition.

I will always remember Camp Maumee, where we went for summer camp. One could work on badges, experience flag raising, troop competitions, and a daily camp fire with songs, singing and stories. As well, there was a shooting range, run for several years by an old Gunnery Sargent. One evening, shortly after lights out, a storm hit hard with heavy rain and wind gusts. Thomas and Gary Hunter, in a tent together, started yelling. I yelled through my tent, "What's going on over there?" "Our tent is falling down and we have skunks!" came the frantic reply! The skunks left without incident, with only a slight lingering smell. The next night, we were all called to the main building because a tornado went over head! Camp Maumee demanded a rugged, self-reliant lifestyle and, in return, offered a beautiful world in the woods. It opened us to adventure and usually left us with a desire for more.

We would later travel to the Adirondacks. We hiked and camped for a week in bear country. At several campsites, we found claw marks on the tree from which we hung our food bag. We climbed several small mountains in the area. "Look at that view, guys! Just magnificent!" We could see for miles. We traversed a lake by walking on a narrow wooden plank way fastened to the rock face. "Hey dad, I hope this wood holds you!" "Funny Thomas, real funny." The payment for our efforts was the spectacular scenery: the sight of sunset on the ridge; seeing peaks 20 miles away; hearing a gurgling stream; crossing a stream on a log; watching several deer cross the path in front of you.

One last story involves a trip to Isle Royale National Park on Lake Superior. This is a 50-mile-long island, rugged and undeveloped, close to the Canadian border. It required catching a ferryboat on the northern tip of Michigan at Copper Harbor. Unfortunately, as we woke up to get to the boat, we had a flat tire! But we were scouts and prepared to handle whatever came up.

Isle royale does not have cars or vehicles. Food and water, tents and sleeping bags are brought in your packs. "My backpack is so heavy," said Thomas. "Sorry, you'll just have to carry it. You want to eat, right? But this will be an adventure. Look, this place is beautiful." It tested us early. "Hey guys, I don't like those clouds over there." "Yeah, we should start looking for a place to shelter." The clouds brought rain, and it soaked us. We set up camp on a rock outcropping and made a small fire to warm us from the weather. The morning sun allowed us to dry our things. This began our 4-day trek across the island.

Our hike boasted of beautiful woodlands and rocky hills. Several packs of wolves and moose were on the island. The boys, at one point, chased a frightened young moose down a path and into the water. Luckily, they didn't encounter the mom moose. We stood in an unspoiled wilderness. The silence was beautiful. I could imagine the winter wind whipping through the tree stands and over the rocks, coming across Lake Superior with a vengeance. I heard the sure voice of God speaking in a quiet, yet unmistakable, voice. "Come, but walk gently and know that I am God and this is my gift!" At Isle Royale, we entered a church of sorts where the wind and the trees said the liturgy and sung the hymns. The sacrament of the land offered by God's hand manifested the hard but joyous life around us. I still believe you have to get a shot of the mountains and the ocean regularly. Gong.

The troop took several rafting trips to West Virginia, similar to what I have already written about. One brief incident, however. We took a trip in "duckies", which were single person kayaks. I flipped my kayak over and struggled to get right. However, when we stopped, someone noticed that my neck was red with blood. This stunned me. On closer examination, however, it turned out that the red was a stain from the Phillies hat I wore!

When they were older, my sons and I took a notable trip to Kentucky Lake for fishing and hiking. The crappie were biting during the spring, so we caught a lot of fish. Thomas got a bad sunburn on his face from our boating and fishing all day. Sorry Thomas, I apologize.

As often happened, we discovered a little gem on this trip, the National Boy Scout Museum at Murray State. "Do we have to go?" Thomas asked. The museum had a collection of Norman Rockwell paintings that were just magnificent. As we continued, the boys enjoyed hiking and camping out in the area between Lake Barkley and Kentucky Lake. I don't remember the conversations, but my time with my boys was precious to me. As with my father, this trip brought me a sense of close connection with these young men who were my sons. I don't know if they appreciated it, but for me, this resonated at several levels.

Waycross was a good anchor in our lives, from which we trustingly explored the world. Our best trips as a family were to Michigan for Christmas or Thanksgiving. They welcomed us with open arms to Rochelle's parent's home, which was always decorated. This was a place of acceptance and care. As I had, our kids learned deep lessons of love and respect by visiting. They taught family there. Christmas found us opening presents with a Christmas bell around our necks. Most gifts were "bell ringers"!

An important perk, Rochelle's sister Mary worked as a manager of a movie theater and so we could all get into the movies for FREE! For the kids, this meant free and good entertainment. On off years, we sometimes would stay home for Christmas. We would chop down a tree or else get one to plant after the holiday. As time went on, we had several tall evergreens on the fence line in the back!

We made one iconic trip to Disneyland in Florida. Rochelle's parents paid for it. Her enormous family all stayed together in a couple of apartments in Kissimmee, Florida. We have iconic pictures of the trip. The princesses impressed Catherine. However, she and I went on the Dumbo ride together, and to my dismay, Catherine didn't remember it. She was maybe 4. We went to Epcot Center and the part of Disney dedicated to many countries and cultures. We also visited Sea World and Cape Canaveral. The Space Shuttle was going up at the time and we toured the launch pad. This thrilled the boys.

On this trip, I went golfing in Florida with Rochelle's father, Jerome. The 8th hole was significant. We couldn't get to the green, for there by the hole sat an alligator sunning itself. We wanted birdies, not an alligator!

I think our kids realized the importance of family by our many visits. They certainly had a sense that they were part of a broader family. As Rochelle's siblings got married and had kids, our children developed relationships with cousins. Rochelle had a vast family, by my standards. As adults, our kids made their own trips and they would stop and see relatives along the way. This showed the power of forming those early bonds with family. As well, as our kids later got married, the parties were enormous with all the aunts and uncles, grandparents and cousins. We launched them not as a solitary practice but in a community, a community of love.

Our time in Columbus lasted many years. Our home saw significant changes in our lives as our kids grew up here. I can't think back on this time without a great deal of nostalgia and longing. The house tested and challenged us, but also kept us safe. It became our home, our fortress, our refuge, our safe base. The place did us well. I can understand the previous owner crying at the closing. That house loved families. It loved us and showered good upon us. It became a harbor, a safe place from storms.

At the top of the steps was a painting by Winslow Homer called "Breezing Up". It is a sailboat on a breezy day with an old dad and his three kids. The painting was the modern version of the blazing warship of Connecticut. It called to mind the significance of the sea for me. I came from families of sailors. This is my homage to them. It is still on the wall.

The story of our home, of course, included many mundane and repetitious things as well. But, hey, isn't that life? Long periods of pleasant tranquility punctuated by moments of sheer terror! Freud said that to be a mature human being, you had to be good at love and work. Columbus, Indiana, afforded us the chance to learn about both. Our kids have shown a mature level at both. This poem speaks to these times.

Today

In hope, I rise to greet the sun
With anticipation, I take on another day
I gently open my life to its unfocused opportunities
Aware of the greatness that can be achieved
And aware of the baseness that can be encountered
I stand perhaps shaky, perhaps smugly, perhaps saintly
And walk into the gust of my life, the heat of the raw and unpredictable encounter
The holy and tenacious ride that my steps will uncover
Something will happen today
Something will come about today
Something will transpire
And I will be different
So, hope and anticipation and gentleness and veracity and courage and foolishness and holiness:
Come with me
Let us discover what there is to be
Today

13 Columbus East High School

We had a nice big back yard at the house. Among Forsythia bushes and euonymus ground cover, I planted tulips and Black-Eyed Susans. Behind this island of sorts, I centrally planted a small cherry tree. As they all grew, it created a welcoming variety of colors and textures. Alex, however, had other ideas.

"Can you let the dog out?" I shouted as he sat patiently by the back door. It was Saturday, and I was in my pajamas and didn't want to mess with him. Catherine opened the door. "There you go, puppy!" Already dressed, she went out with him. He looked at her coming out and said to himself, "Wow, it is time to play!" This meant that he would get down on his front paws, wag his tail and expect to be chased. He had a nice circuit around my plants. Catherine stopped and looked at him. Then she made a sudden move toward him. Game on! He tore to his left and waited behind the tree for her next move. She followed, and a race ensued. "You are too fast, dog," she said to herself. Now Thomas came out as he finished breakfast. The two of them tried to corral Alex, but he deeked and moved, twisted and ran low. His tongue wagged in deep breathing. He paused, looking at them. Thomas and Catherine moved to opposite sides, but to no avail. The speed demon border collie moved too quickly. After several rounds, they gave up and called him over. He knew the sign and stood before them, wagging his tail. "Thanks for the exercise!" he said in his dog's smile.

I guess it is an understatement to say that our children had a great impact on our lives. We had almost a symbiotic relationship. As they grew, so did we. As they experienced new things, so did we. That is part of the beautiful dynamic of a family. Tension existed as we had grumpy kids in the morning. But spontaneous laughter and light-hearted interactions also sprang up. Such was the time that Thomas put straws up his nose. The dog acted as a catalyst for joy. He got in the middle of our life and wagged along as our sidekick. I do not know how I spent my time before these beautiful souls entered my life. Their presence seriously changed me.

As we entered this time of our lives, Paul had a good focus. He had better judgment now and didn't need the limits we set when younger. He and his mom, however, still had an old tension between them. Their beginning made it rough because of his early colic, which didn't help the child or mom. Rochelle liked order and Paul had his own order and could be the more stubborn one. By high school, these issues had receded, and he seemed more comfortable with himself.

Thomas, of course, easily cooperated with us and had a pleasant and positive nature. He had a calm smile. He also learned from the example of his older brother who showed him the way not to get along with your parents. Thomas, the middle kid, got along well with everyone, it seemed. He just seemed to fit in easily. His boundaries were more fluid. He was more accepting. His charm and his smile worked on you.

Raising Catherine made parenting easy and a delight. Cuteness can get you pretty far in life! Rochelle would say that Catherine had her dad wrapped around her finger. I found it hard to deny adorable! She didn't hide behind the cuteness, either. It fit who she was. She had a sensitivity and a bouncy, positive nature. The family structure made it hard for Catherine with her two brothers. They teased her often, probably because she was a good kid who didn't get into any trouble. I have heard from her she had dolls destroyed by her two older brothers. She never forgave them. Catherine won me over early in the game. She also had a good emotional connection with her mom. I figured the mom and daughter thing to be a natural bond. That connection has only gotten stronger as time has gone on.

These kids came in different temperaments and styles. They were all brilliant and fast learners. They were also eager to go places and do things. We didn't hear often that they would rather stay home. The little troupe intellectually challenged us and emotionally rewarded us. However, the enterprise was tiring. They loved their books and their favorite topics of the day, be it Sesame Street, or dinosaurs, soccer, fire crackers or space ships. We were zoo people, Children's Museum people, airshow people, sports people, music people, and scout people. They challenged us to keep up with them. They brought energy and focus. Part circus, part seminar, part platoon. I really did not know what it would be like raising these kids. It far exceeded my meager expectations, but I grew to love and cherish my role with these kids. I am glad this happened when I was young because I could not do it now! The anvil sings over those sparks!

I would have to say that Rochelle was a high achiever and our kids followed suit. With three kids and working full time, Rochelle worked on a Master's degree in counseling from IU. She added coursework so that she could also be certified in educational counseling. Being a strong woman, she held high-level positions with the Indiana Counseling Association, the Indiana School Counselor's Association, and the American School Counselor's Association. She did this over at least ten years, if not more. Through this, she met many wonderful people, had many great relationships and did a lot of travel. She worked hard as a school counselor at Franklin and then Greenwood Middle School. A testament to her patience, she enjoyed working with middle school-age kids. Finally, after several years, she got a job at the middle school in our county. As the kids were leaving home, she transferred to the high school and became a school counselor and then head of the department.

On top of this, she kept the family together; we didn't go naked or unfed. She could chew gum and walk and even walk fast. She took on challenging roles in her work. But I have to say I found joy in watching her confidence and her expertise grow. She is an amazing woman!

In part because of her model, our kids took on activities, got involved with organizations and didn't shy away from taking on difficult and big tasks. She had high octane energy, and they learned that from her.

Our kids prospered in high school, which went by quickly. This occurred in part because the kids were working as well as going to school and were not home often. Both Thomas and Paul worked at Arney's, a local restaurant.

In Columbus, we started our kids going to the Catholic school, but we didn't continue as issues developed. However, the kids did fine in public school. Hearing excellent reports at parent-teacher conferences was the norm. They made interesting friends. Their school projects and activities extended our lives with some amazing exploits.

Paul's grades were good, and he kept on top of it all. He grew tall quickly. We tried to get him involved with baseball as I had been, but it didn't interest him much. He played for a season as we felt if you signed up, you had to fulfill your commitment. But he didn't want to sign up again.

In Columbus, soccer was very popular, even at young ages. Paul and Thomas from early on enjoyed the game. They really liked to play in the rain when the field would be a muddy mess and they could make slide tackles. The quality of the game would go down in the rain, but the enjoyment of the players would rise! At one time, we may have had all the kids in soccer. This would mean spending Saturday at the fields for hours. We would take our lawn chairs and sit and have a pleasant conversation with another soccer parent. Punctuating the long moments would be shouts of "Good job!", "Stop that boy!" or "Ref you watching this game?" The level of play went from very simple and unskilled to a greater understanding and commitment to efficient soccer.

I wasn't one of those crazy, loud parents whose child had to be the star. It wasn't important to me and my kids didn't work that way. They liked to win, but losing wasn't the end of the world. They shed tears and voiced anger, for sure. But for me, I enjoyed watching them, cheering them on and being a part of it. We always approached our kids with a desire for their success, but with an awareness not to shield them from the hard stuff of life. There would be kids with egos or coaches who needed to win. I didn't expect that my kids would become professionals. My desire was for them to have normal experiences, gain skill and confidence, and have friends. Remember, Freud's dictate to love and to work, leading to balance and well-being.

When we arrived, Columbus had two high schools, Columbus North and Columbus East. North was in a more affluent side of town while East found itself in the workingman neighborhood. North had a larger population of kids. I hate to say, but rivalry existed between the two schools. Our kids went to East and Rochelle worked there. The competition between the two high schools would play out for the many years our kids were there. We had friends whose kids went to North, so we didn't feel forbidden to do things with North people. But, in the circumstance of a game between the two to determine who would go further in the state tournament, it could get a little heated and tense. The soccer games between the two schools were always hard.

Paul also played basketball from early on, probably because of my influence. We always had a basketball around. In Columbus, we had a half court in our driveway. We had several broken screen door windows because of it. He played in the parks and rec league, and in elementary and middle school as well. His height gave him an advantage, but unfortunately not near the 6-foot 5-inch variety!

Paul really took to soccer, however. He liked to run and soccer allowed him to do that. He played defense. In middle school, I coached a park and rec team that Paul was on. Paul had height, but he had a lanky frame as we grew them. He would be the guy who flanked the other team's forward, coming down the pitch on the right side. He would interfere in the simple movement of the ball and he did a good job at it. Thomas had speed and a lack of fear. Thomas liked to play forward and score. Being a forward fit him well. Catherine played a little soccer, but got involved in other things. Both Paul and Thomas both played soccer in high school. They liked Tom La Barbara, the soccer coach at East. A smart and effective coach, they both learned the intricacies of the game from Tom.

Because of the deep involvement in soccer and desire to improve, we engaged in indoor soccer and travel soccer. The boys would go to an indoor field a half hour away to focus on skills and practice. We also had travel soccer. More competitive, the guys would play against teams from far away counties. It would take away any hope of getting things done on Saturday.

During this time as a treat, we would go see the nationally ranked IU Soccer team. Much later, our nephew Joe played soccer for Michigan State, and Rochelle and I went to several games between IU and Michigan State.

I have said that soccer is not supposed to be a contact sport. A strong memory I have of travel soccer is watching Thomas play a game at a rural field far from home. During the game, a defender stopped a long kick from one of our players. The ball bounced off his chest and in front of Thomas, who was charging down the field. Thomas corralled the ball and dashed to the right of the center. "You got it Thomas! He's going to score." He paused for a brief second and was about to kick the ball for a certain goal. However, a defender charged upon him and kicking at the ball, cut Thomas' legs from under him and he fell hard to the ground. The spiteful play led to Thomas coming up in pain and breaking his tail bone. I found it difficult for Thomas to endure another broken bone. This also brings up the time that Paul broke his collarbone while playing. These guys strongly put themselves into it. They were selfless and paid the price for their abandon.

Paul also ran track and ran long-distances. His long legs and lanky body contributed to his speed. He ran a couple of years and at least his senior year. His stride was beautiful and smooth. He had a fluid movement that propelled him. One race, he ran against Jerry Flodder's son, who ran for North during Paul's junior year. They had a very close finish. He treasured his brown and orange letter jacket on which were sewn fleet foot embroideries and soccer balls. His grandparents came down several times to watch him and Thomas.

An incident with Paul gave Rochelle and me pause. Paul had a girlfriend who seemed rather controlling. She felt, I am sure, that we did not give Paul enough personal freedom. I don't think she liked us. We argued over them spending excessive time in Paul's room. Things were a little tense.

His senior year, he had a final track meet in the spring. However, he left a cryptic note at home and did not attend the track meet. The note said that he felt overwhelmed and had to get away. This was very unlike him, as he was typically conscientious. Well, his unusual behavior and the note concerned us, and we didn't know where he was. We made calls to friends and talked with people at school trying to find him. After a while, we were relieved to find out that he had gone to Grouse Ridge, the place we often fished. As he said in his note, he had to get away. He needed the peaceful quality of the lake. A couple of gongs in relief.

Paul had kicked around the idea of forestry or international studies, especially after shaking the hand of the Dalai Lama. He later contemplated ROTC. This became harder because he received ROTC scholarships to many schools. An interesting event took place. He had developed a view over high school that many kids didn't take things seriously. "Dad," he said, "these guys just mess around. They aren't serious. I don't like that. I want to do things that matter." Well, the time had come for him to decide upon his collegiate career. He had to choose among the several options he had.

One day, Rochelle and he spoke after he came home from work. This day he came home, coming halfway up the steps by the wrought-iron gate, and told his mom, "I have decided what I am going to do." She sat in the living room and this got her attention. She looked at him, pausing by the steps, and asked, "Great. What have you decided?" "Well," he said with a little Paul grin, "I joined the Marines!" Rochelle responded with abject silence, a wide-eyed look, and probably a sudden wisp of shock.

Let me pause the scene with the two of them sharing a powerful and life-changing moment. Several pieces of information may shed light on what just happened. For one, when Rochelle was in college, she had been a protester of the Vietnam War. She proudly talked about being at a protest in Ann Arbor and putting flowers in the barrels of the guns held by National Guard troops. Second, Paul saved his money well, and bought a paintball gun. He and his buddies would go paint balling. Well, this didn't sit well with his mother, who said frequently, "There will be no guns in my house. I will not tolerate it!" She took the gun and the receipt and got his money back and went to his work and laid the money before him. I don't think this sat well with him. I am sure that she felt angry and confused as she stood there and heard the news of his recruitment. Basically, Paul had traded in his paint ball gun for a .50 Cal!

Her first defense, "You can't join the military without my ok. I'm your mom!" However, Paul quickly said, "Being over 18, Mom, I can join without need of your signature. Now, the recruiter told me he would come and talk to you if you wanted him to." This added powerlessness to the array of emotions she experienced. Shortly afterward, the recruiter did just that.

Now this would not be the last time the military and Rochelle House would engage in a brief communication, you might say. The recruiter came and talked about what would happen. No active war going on, so her mind eased a little. He provided us with information, showed us a video, and reassured us they would take care of our son in San Diego. If we had questions, we could call the recruiter and he would have the answer. Paul would go to a Marine training base in San Diego, California. We soon took a trip to the airport to drop him off in the early morning hours to fly to California. He would be there for maybe 13 weeks of training and be physically and mentally tested.

The Marines were a family who trained the hardest, instilled pride and esprit de corps, and took care of their own. Boot camp was tough, and it strengthened Paul. It gave him the opportunity to prove himself and gain confidence and skill. Unfortunately, one of those skills would be in how to kill others.

While Paul was in California, we received several letters and maybe a phone call. One letter stated that he had been sick and didn't feel well. The rigorous training tired him out. Upon receiving this, Rochelle called the recruiter. She didn't like the tenor of the letter. She had to intervene. The recruiter said that he would get back to us. Apparently, he called the base in California to check on Paul, as requested by his mom. Well, we got a letter shortly afterward from Paul loudly proclaiming that mom shouldn't have done that! The drill instructor heard that Paul's mom called and the proverbial shit hit the fan! The DI took this as an opportunity to instill that esprit de corps! Whatever happened, the outfit got pushed harder than before. The DI dealt with this mamma's boy. Paul's sickness went away, and he pleaded for no more calls to the recruiter.

At the end of boot camp, we got invited to the graduation closing ceremonies. Paul's girlfriend insisted she go with us to California for the ceremony. Unfortunately, she added a burden to us on the trip. So, there was tension. However, the Marine Corps Recruitment Depot impressed us. We were very excited to be there and to see our son. Paul got a little time off the night before and we could visit with him. Thomas, Catherine, and Rochelle's parents were with us, along with his girlfriend. So, as dusk approached, they released the mass of young men and women who formed on the parade deck. Frankly, it took time and attention to identify Paul because many had the same black-framed glasses and a Marine haircut. "Hey Paul! Over here. It's hard to tell it's you." "Hi, dad, mom." Big hugs. Rochelle said, tearfully, "We missed you." His grandparents were all smiles. "You certainly look sharp in your uniform, young man!" grandma said. It seemed like Paul, but he felt different. The look in his eye just showed more maturity. He certainly stood up taller.

The graduation day found San Diego as beautiful as it could be. We sat by the large parade deck, upon which several hundred Marines would soon march in with obedience and precision. We watched in great anticipation as the men and women came precisely marching in. The choreographed and precise marching made for an impressive and powerful event. In the end, we found Paul in his smart uniform. He noted more of what he had been through and to him, the positive experience led to a final grand achievement, becoming a Marine. Standing most proud, he found a part of himself that he had searched for, a deep and personal strength forming him visibly. A fitting cliché, he left us a boy and came back a man. Some sparks.

Paul gave us a tour of the base. He introduced us to one of his drill instructors, who responded to us with "ma'am" and "sir". I am sure he had another vocabulary for his recruits! After some leave, he would go to Twentynine Palms in California for further training. He would then join a Marine reserve unit in Indianapolis that focused on communication capabilities. Paul also attended Purdue in West Lafayette, with a technology major. He was driven and we, it felt, were on for the ride!

Thomas had many high school adventures himself. In fact, Thomas' stories make up a big part of our repertoire of stories when someone asked about our kids! For instance, Rochelle attended a parent teacher conference with Thomas' math teacher. Thomas, perhaps with his orange hair, sat there in a state of confidence and a tinge of defiance. The teacher pointed out the homework that Thomas missed with frustration in her voice. Upon the review of the evidence, Thomas asked the teacher, "And what are my test scores? How did I do on the exam?" The teacher, with reluctance, pointed out that he got perfect scores. This showed a sign of his confidence but also a sign of his brilliance. Thomas' intuitive knowledge seemed fairly easy to access.

You recall the time Thomas took his old BMW out-of-state. He also borrowed a friend's Chevy Corvette, no less, and, yes, got into an accident with it. Thomas also drove the afore mentioned BMW into a farmer's cornfield, doing donuts with abandonment. After being identified, we required that he apologize to the farmer in person and pay for the lost crops, which he did. Thomas had an uncanny ability to land on his feet. Bright sparks.

Thomas as well had an unusual moment in high school. During his junior year, he dyed his hair turning orange. We have picture proof. He enjoyed himself and was a free soul. "Shaun and I are going to a big concert with several bands up in Indy this weekend." Shaun was his best friend. We didn't worry about them because they would take care of each other. I got a call from Thomas about three in the morning. "Dad, I have lost track of Shaun. I'm still at the concert. I think I need a ride home." Not happy, I drove the hour up to the concert and retrieved him. He was a little dazed. He lost his shoes. I don't want to think about what might have happened. Thomas didn't give me a very good explanation either! But we had a good idea. We put in motion some important consequences.

However, it came to us that our kids were doing things not necessarily criminal but perhaps outside the bounds of what their parents thought appropriate behavior. We hoped they would be honest with us, but knew we could not force them. However, we came up with the ten-year rule. This spared them the need to lie to us but also allowed them to tell us the truth at a later point. It went that in ten years after an event, as long as it didn't endanger one's life, the truth had to be told. This came in handy with an incident that had befuddled me.

Thomas borrowed my Honda Civic and after he returned, it didn't drive well at all. "Thomas, it is riding lousy and makes lots of noise. It feels broken. What did you do?" I took it in to our car guy to evaluate the situation. He came back with the astonishing information that the front axle had cracked on one side. Dismayed, I inquired of Thomas what had happened when he drove the car. "I just turned a corner, and it made a noise and something didn't feel right. I didn't hit anything." That explanation didn't add up, of course, but I couldn't get anything else about the situation.

The car had seen a lot of miles, so we totaled it because of this problem. It had been a splendid car but as cars age, you know when it is time! Katie Stallings soon would have her big youth retreat and asked to use the car as a fundraiser. People could smash it with a sledgehammer for a fee. This turned out to be a great sell, and she made money from it. We got tax money for donating the car. However, I felt sad to see the poor car hit and dented.

Well, anyway, the saga of the Civic eventually got revealed. Thomas did not simply turn the corner and break the car. Rather, he noted that he and several friends went for a country ride. They found a road that had a quick and large hill section. They figured out that if you went a certain speed when you hit the hill, you could get a couple of seconds of air before coming down. He obviously did that several times with the broken drive shaft the result!

Thomas also had drama in his decision about going to college. His grades were good, and he had several opportunities. He decided upon Kettering University in Flint, Michigan, importantly, Rochelle's home town. The school had a strong engineering department and a school/co-opt schedule. He would be in classes one semester and then have a placement at a business site using his newly learned skills for the next semester. It seemed a reasonable and useful model of education. The school had an excellent reputation and would put him close to family.

As he and mom were preparing to go to Michigan to begin the semester, Rochelle went to the bank to get money for the trip. As she returned home, Thomas casually lay on the couch in bare feet, not ready to go. She asked him, "Aren't you ready? Thomas, we have to leave." "I'm not going," he said. "What?! You and I are driving today to Flint!" "Nah, I don't think so!" Thomas said. She felt very perplexed and frustrated. "What are you talking about? We have to leave." She more urgently said. After a brief pause, with a little grin, Thomas said, "Ok, things have changed. The school called me. I'm going out to Milwaukee for my co-opt semester instead. It starts in a couple of days." After a deep breath, it became clear to Rochelle that things were still on track, just not the track her boxcar was on!

We drove Thomas' car out to Milwaukee. We went with Shaun, his good friend. The company was Rockwell International, and they set him up in a hotel until his apartment would be available. We delivered him and didn't stay that long. I have an image the last time we saw him there. He stood in his room. There were hugs and goodbyes. I trusted Thomas: he had smarts and a flexible and very capable attitude. But the last scene in Milwaukee hit me hard. He stood by his door. "Thomas, we love you. Have a good semester. We'll call." "Love you guys too," as we said goodbye for the third time. Big hug from Shaun. A look into his eyes to convey love and hope. And then the door closed and his new life started. Without us. Hopeful gongs.

To backtrack, it may have been in middle school that Rochelle and I made a huge mistake. We bought Thomas a set of drums! He was excited but most of all, there was the noise! Well, this opened up a tremendous opportunity for him. In high school, he played in the jazz band, the pep band and the Marching Band. He started a basement band! As time went on, he improved. Typically, you would hear him tapping away at the dinner table with his fingers, kicking out syncopation for thirty seconds! The basement band had a trumpet and other horns and a big sound while it lasted. However, he followed his drumming interest all the way to Marching Band and served as the Section leader his senior year. This opened us up to follow the marching band. It seemed to me to be a cheap date with live entertainment! Rochelle had to act as a school staff and so it wasn't even a date!

As I have noted, our kids offered many activities for us to attend. For years, we would spend our Friday nights at high school football games, not so much for the game as much as for the halftime show. While everyone else stood in line to get a hot dog and a candy bar, we would be by the fence, looking and listening to the newest iteration of the band. As we did this, we got better at discerning an outstanding performance. We went to enough band competitions, hearing the sound and movement of many bands, to discern what to look for. The wonderful shows had a strong and varied texture to their sound and got good scores because of it. Bigger bands found it easier to make a big sound. Columbus East had a smaller sound with fewer musicians on the field.

With the band, we went through two iterations, one with Thomas and the drum section and next with Catherine and the flute section and then as drum major. Thomas seemed to me to be a natural drummer. He had a rhythm in his soul that came out with drums. I so enjoyed hearing the drum line at football games. There is a feeling that is electric about that sequential tapping and rolling that delightfully grabs me. Thomas did the drum line for his tenure at school.

While Thomas led the drum line, Catherine took involvement with the band to a new level. At first, she played the flute and piccolo. For the last two years of high school, she served as the drum major. She led the band out onto the field and, standing on a platform, directed the group in keeping time with her broad arm movements. All eyes of the band were on her!

I have to share that Catherine also had leadership ability. She had held several positions of authority from the middle school days. She helped to organize the dance marathon, took part in the Youth Council for the Archdiocese and had taken several trips to Haiti. We allowed our kids to find their voice. We raised them to be their own persons and, within the constraints of our faith, to be good people. I think we succeeded and I would add, not simply by our efforts, but by the impact of a community of family and friends. To see her mount the platform and call everyone to attention did not surprise me. It left me a very proud father. Sparks.

During her senior year, the band had a good show. Many bands performed at the district finals. We were very pleased with their performance. This time waiting while the judges determined the order of the performances took forever. There were always several bands in East's category and so we were looking for a high finish, if not the highest. "Rochelle, you look nervous. It's only a band competition!" She gave me a shut up, it's my daughter look. We knew the quality of their performance.

As we heard announcements, we realized East had missed the cut by one position resulting in heart break! During the announcement, all the drum majors were at the center of the field and Catherine just bowed her head in obvious pain for the loss. We were not a little outraged that the judging felt so wrong. But nothing could be done. The competition ended; we endured the results. Seeing her all dressed up in her drum major finest with tears messing up her makeup devastated us. We stood by the bus and hugged and consoled her. You could feel the pain in the entire band family.

Although this became one of life's more difficult moments, another band activity made up for it, going to Disney World in Florida! This trip occurred at the end of the school year and I can only describe it as a hoot! The logistics of transporting the band and accessories were formidable. They were so formidable that we didn't leave until eight hours later than expected! This would get us all free airplane tickets we could use to take another trip.

Rochelle and I went as chaperones. While mostly enjoying the festivities, it meant spending a couple of late nights patrolling the sleeping area of band members. However, there would be several parents walking the perimeter of the rooms, and the conversations were pleasant.

We were excited about the trip, not simply because it was Disney World. Rather, while there, the band performed. There would be a 20-minute jazz band performance at a 50s style restaurant in the park. There would be an outdoor concert at an amphitheater on another day. And of course, the band was a part of the spectacular and colorful big parade down main street in the evening. The lights and the sounds made for a story book experience! The energy, the music, the sun, the camaraderie joined to create a great time, at least for this old man. Give a chang to the anvil for that.

I am torn whether the band trip outweighed the significance of the snow blizzard trip to Notre Dame Catherine and I took. In the early afternoon of a winter day, she and I traveled north to St. Mary's College, next to the campus of Notre Dame in South Bend, Indiana. It was her junior year. I expected the trip to take 3 ½ hours. It turned out to be much longer as it became more of a quest and you know, those things can last years! On leaving, the weather looked sunny with blue skies. I figured we would get something to eat and get there in plenty of time to find the concert. This was a special band that Catherine had seen at the National Catholic Youth Conference. Yes, that is right. Her father drove his daughter 200 miles in winter to see a band!

In her work on the board of the Indianapolis Archdiocese Youth Council, Catherine became acquainted with the National Catholic Youth Conference. This conference, several days long, brought together thousands of youth from around the country. There would be music, liturgies, adoration and talks by national speakers. Roaming groups of youth would assail downtown Indianapolis. Two groups of ten to twenty from different parts of the country would approach each other on the street. One group would start a chant, "N…C…" to be responded to with "Y…C…" by the other group, loudly with enthusiasm and applause. As well, most wore costumes that signified something about where they were from. One year, the youth director at our church had cow pants, cow print bandanas, and cow hats made for everyone. We wore them proudly!

At the conference, Catherine heard a musical group called "Ceili Rain", a rock band started by Bob Halligan, Jr., a veteran of rock and roll bands. Ceili Rain had an Irish leaning, Christian flavor; vastly different from his earlier iterations. They had a fiddle, various pipes and whistles, bagpipes, guitars, drums and Bob playing guitar and singing. An interesting assortment of sounds.

As we sat down to eat, the weather turned gray. "Catherine, what is the interest in this group? You haven't told me a lot about it." "Well, I saw them at NCYC. They were great. The leader is a guy named Bob Halligan. He has great energy. During a performance, he jumps up and down and dances around while they are playing. He is a superb guitar player. I know you like Bob Dylan and all, but I thought you might find these guys…interesting. My senior project has to get done, so I thought I would try to put on a concert and have the money go to Haiti." "So, we are here on a scouting mission? I mean this trip is for your education?" "Yep, and Haiti." "It sounds like a big undertaking." "Yeah, but I have organized things for church and for school, so I think it can be done. Kate can help me and if it helps Haiti, it's a good thing." "Yep, I know." "So, Catherine, what are we going to do? I mean, you can't just go up to the band and talk with them?" "That's the cool part. After their concert at NCYC, they had a booth, sold tee shirts and CDs, and signed autographs. They are friendly and care about their fans. I will have time to talk with them." "Well, ok. I hope you get a chance." "Don't worry Dad, it'll work out."

This pointed out how affected Catherine was by her trips to Haiti. Rochelle went as a chaperone with a group of maybe 8 kids to work on projects for the poor parish in Limonade, Haiti. Catherine encountered real poverty for the first time and it touched her deeply. "Dad, I went to Target with mom. I felt disgusted. I cried. In one aisle at the store, you could feed a whole town in Haiti! And we throw half of it away!" The Haitian parish provided them with a rich person's meals and accommodations. The people she said were so loving and yet lived in circumstances of abject poverty. This encounter opened her eyes to the world.

Catherine and I got back into the car and trudged on. We had a couple of hours maybe and were doing well with time. However, Mother Nature had other ideas. And what a mother she would be! We had lost the sun in an overcast sky as it became colder. As we drove up the interstate, it snowed, at first in light flakes. The sky got darker and you could see dark ridges in the clouds. I have lived in Michigan and in Indiana where snow is not an anomaly; you learn to drive in it. Except this got worse. In front of us, behind us, and above us, I guessed to be snow. It engulfed us.

We finally reached South Bend. We found our way to the college by Notre Dame. The quiet campus streets were brightly lit with newly fallen snow and plowed. They were obviously more prepared than we were. As we walked, we found the hall.

We got to our seats in the balcony with only a couple of minutes to spare. I felt relieved to sit and I could have taken a nap if I wasn't with a squirrelly anxious girl excited to see the show! She looked over, and I saw in her maturity a glimpse of the cute little girl I loved so much.

As the lights went down, there came a snare drum from downstairs. Tap, tap, tippity, tippity, tap. It resonated around the hall. He eventually became visible as he mounted the stage. Following his lead, the gathered band began a raucous and energetic song called Jigerous! The lead singer danced around the stage as promised. The rhythm bounced around in a congregation of instruments and melody, movement, and vocals. This perfect beginning grabbed my attention and surprised me. The lead singer's neon green shirt and flowing hair seemed a little dramatic and showy. But the musical skill and quality of the band felt entertaining and professional. The songs were a folky, Celtic pot-pourri of sounds and words. They carried a bright and articulate syncopation of joy and fun with an undertone of Christianity. The concert left me smiling. My kid had good taste!

After the concert, we made our way downstairs. A couple of people manned the merchandise table, taking orders and cash. As Catherine and I stood there, slowly making their way, was the band members coming toward us. Catherine boldly approached Bob and began a conversation that stopped him in the hall. I said hi to the guys who passed me, thanking them for a great evening of music. After their brief chat, Catherine gave Bob her information. As he approached, he said, "So here is the dad that drove across Indiana in the snow! Thanks for coming. See ya, Catherine!"

I didn't know what had just happened, but it sure felt like a good thing, and even a godly thing. Ceili Rain reflected a heavenly down-pouring of

God's love, as Bob would later say. I had to say, like Casablanca, this demarcated the start of a beautiful relationship! Gong!

Catherine contacted the group and began corresponding about a Ceili Rain benefit concert in Columbus. They planned for May 2000. They secured a middle school auditorium. Several other churches got involved. Catherine's goal of her senior project to make money for Haiti through a concert became a reality. For a 17-year-old kid to make this dream happen took no small investment in time and energy.

The band had a sound check in the afternoon at the junior high. We went to the auditorium to check things out. The stage was set. "Hey Catherine, how you doing?" "Hi. Bob. Great. You guys sound great!" "Hey Dad, you should be proud of your girl! She has put in the time!" He was a genuinely good guy.

Later that day, as we got to the auditorium, Rochelle and I could feel a tangible excitement. The concert began as the other did, with the drummer announcing in his sticks-on-skins-way that things were starting. I have to say that I was excited. The music had just started, and already, it got me moving in my seat! I so wanted this to be successful for my daughter.

The place just came alive with the music. Lights, sound and the movements of the band erupted on stage. These guys were entertaining and great performers. Soon after it started, the youth approached the stage. Before you knew it, they were ten people deep in front of the band. They would applaud, sing and definitely dance! The music had ignited their energy, and the place jumped with sound and movement. Between songs, Bob spoke about Catherine and Katy and that the concert had been Catherine's senior project for Haiti. This was a joyful and energetic group of musicians who shared their love with the crowd, who responded with a loud and affirmative thanks.

On one of the bouncier songs, out of the crowd came a couple of courageous souls, hands on the person in front, moving with the beat, forming a conga line. Unexpectedly, another person followed and another till a long line encircled the crowd in a moving and waving caterpillar of people!

As the concert came to a close, the group did their theme song called, appropriately, "Ceili Rain", reflecting the idea of God pouring out his love in a heavenly rain. At this point, we were all standing, probably close to tears, holding each other and in groups of three and four. It sounds overstated, but the band had played music that touched us and by the end we were in love!

While they made money (although probably not enough), they had brought an entertaining evening to the youth and parents. Truly, a movement started in the lives of so many. These concerts would occur yearly for the next 5 years. A child born of one couple who attended named their child Ceili! And to think that it all began on a small road trip in the snow up north to see the band my daughter liked! Sound the anvil!

As college choices had to be made, Catherine went to a school on Long Island for a week-long seminar in Marine Biology. Afterward, Catherine enthusiastically decided on Marine Biology. This set up a more profound trip as we later visited colleges with Catherine. Kate went with us as well. The back-drop of this spring break trip, and if you mention this to Catherine, you will see a visible shrug, concerned a thing called Word Smart. She faced the SAT and so Kate and her mother worked on improving her vocabulary score. Word Smart helped to improve her vocabulary through repetition and word definitions. After a while, Catherine came to loathe Word Smart, and all it represented.

However, the productive trip helped her and us get our heads around the fact that she would leave next year for college. This meant our children would abandon us and leave us home alone with no supervision!

We called it the Grand College Tour. The purpose of this trip helped Catherine clarify where she wanted to go. We visited several places that had excellent reputations in the marine biology field. We began by visiting the University of North Carolina at Wilmington. When the kids were younger, we had spent a summer stay there that included biking and the use of a small sailboat. This had been the trip where Paul found a blue crab shell and as we sailed around, the shell got washed away, making Paul inconsolable! As well, while swimming, Paul became surrounded by a pod of dolphins, scaring him because he at first thought they were sharks!

The college trip took us to a rainy University of South Carolina. Campus had a clean and beautiful look with green space areas contrasting the brick and concrete. The university nickname was the Gamecocks. As we walked around in the rain, we saw signs of the "cocks" prominent in hats and clothing. Am I a prude? I don't think so, but I would have to work up to wearing a hat with Carolina Gamecocks on it!

We then visited the College of Charleston. This had an excellent reputation in Marine Biology. Charleston is a quaint and historic place. The campus also had old and new buildings. One central, old building, Randolph

Hall, had been there since the Civil War, dominating the courtyard with its tall pillars. It would be the place of graduation, as men and women dressed in formal wear would process down the steps. The visit went well; it did not rain, and we had a nice tour with an enthusiastic tour guide. Catherine talked with people in the department and this became her favored choice.

For me, one interesting thing occurred as we toured Charleston. From the downtown streets, by a large fountain, one had a superb view of the ocean. While there, "Catherine, look, something is in the water, I think." As it got closer, "Oh cool. Look, it's some dolphins. See them?" We were here to look into marine biology and, so it seemed, this might be the right place. On the way home, Word Smart came out. While pleased with the college, she still disliked Word Smart!

Do you remember we had extra tickets after waiting in the airport for hours flying to Disney world? These tickets came in handy for a graduation trip out west with several of Catherine's best friends, Kelly and Emily. We first flew to Phoenix and visited with Rochelle's parents. We then rented a car and drove to San Diego, where we would meet Kate.

One of the best memories I have is of an ice cream shop in Yuma, Arizona. For whatever reason, "Mr. House, this ice cream is the best!" "I agree, girls. In the middle of nowhere!" It may have been that the drive had become monotonous, or the scenery grew mundane with brown dirt hills. Being in a car for hours with three giggling girls had drawn away my last reasonable breath. It may also have been the fact that they had automatic hand dryers and the girls were so impressed they spent about half an hour playing with them. But I swear, we had the best ice cream there in Arizona!

A big issue came up as we drove. Driving along the Mexican border, the girls voiced a desire to go to Mexico if just for an hour. It looked the same as the US side but for a sense of the foreign and mysterious. I had no desire, and Rochelle had no interest. "Can we stop in Mexico, just for a little while? That would be so cool!" "I don't know," I said. "We are so close to California. I want to keep driving." "Aw, dad!" As we drove, it came down to decision time. I got in a line of cars on a side road headed to a border crossing with Mexico. But as it got closer to the crossing with the Border police vehicles lined up and people out of their cars, my anxiety increased. Rochelle blurted out that she didn't feel good with this and we got out of line and turned around. Much to the great disappointment of the back seat occupants. We heard about it for several miles!

We eventually reached San Diego and met up with Kate. I have a picture of us all standing before the San Diego Harbor Cruise sign. I don't remember a thing about that cruise! The memorable trip gave our daughter a wonderful send off as she said goodbye to her high-school days. Gongs.

Before I leave high school, we had a couple of foreign guests who stayed with us. Martin and Melanie were both German exchange students who spent a year with us. Fr. Clem, who had studied in Germany for several years, knew Martin's parents. Martin needed a placement with a family. One Sunday before Mass, Fr. Clem came up to Catherine, Thomas and I. He said he would like to talk with us. The kids bugged him and he said that he wanted to ask if we could take in an exchange student. They both said yes before any discussion or even Mom's input.

We picked Martin up at the airport and you can imagine my surprise at the 6-feet 5-inch-tall teenager with spiked hair! Genial and bright, Martin and Thomas developed a quick relationship. Paul was gone. We enrolled Martin at East and he would take classes and take part in graduation. Thomas and he were in the same year in school. Martin had a sense of humor. "Mr. Steve," he would say, "your beds are too small!" "Back home I eat Brussels sprouts for dessert!" just to get a rise. He enjoyed having fun. While with us, we took a trip to Washington, DC, and to New York. We wanted to show him the "States" or at least interesting parts of the states. I have an image etched in my mind of Martin, Shaun and Thomas coming into the prom with their sunglasses on and with an exaggerated strut that must have come from an American gangster movie!

A couple of years after this, we had another exchange student from Germany named Melanie. Much different from Martin, she had a softer demur presence in Catherine's class. Her stay with us proved a little less provocative than Martin's stay.

Because we shared our home with both students, they invited our kids over to Germany for a visit. These generous gifts helped our kids to see the world, although Catherine had already experienced Haiti!

While our kids all graduated from East High School and had great tales to tell, our involvement with the school did not stop after their graduation. With a nice suit, a pretty dress, and an open evening, Rochelle and I became chronic chaperones to the Prom. Yes, I know that sounds too lucky an opportunity to have happened to me, but, alas; it is true. I have gone to many proms. The music, the transportation to the prom, and the style of dress vary from year to year. They have invested money and time in their clothes, their hair, and makeup. I truly know for a fact. One young woman, who shall remain nameless, convinced her father to buy her a shimmering dress found only out of state for an exorbitant amount of money. Sparks.

The unpredictable ways in which the kids arrived at the prom always drew a crowd of onlookers. For instance, there was the jacked-up truck, ten feet from the roof to the ground, illuminated with neon lights in the bed. Or a real-life firetruck, with lights flashing. Or the 6 couples arriving in a mini-bus, with music blaring so loud you could hear it inside the building on the second-floor. The entrance ride on a tractor seemed so Indiana! The means to the prom made it memorable. This made it a party, signifying a coming out, a conclusion to a long school career.

The energy would vary over the evening. A high point would be the crowning of the King and Queen. The loud music always received great reactions from the crowd. The best prom had a special needs young man voted as the King of the prom. His peers liked him and his reaction showed how thrilled he felt to be chosen and wear the crown.

One last story about East High School stands out for me and points to the giving culture of the school. Rochelle and Mr. Lewis, a history teacher who would dress up on President's Day like a particular president, founded a food pantry. Operating out of a small unused room of the school, there was room for a freezer, a refrigerator, and food shelves. There were students who used it regularly and found it sadly useful. Just another reason to admire Rochelle's good and gracious heart and the giving spirit of the school.

What can I say about the family I helped create and took part in for these so many years? Words cannot express the experience of participating in the lives of these others, flesh of my flesh, whom I knew from their birth. What of the dreams and the hopes that we carried in our hearts as three little beautiful children grew to a hard-earned maturity? This is the life of a family, its transitions and movements, interior changes and external manifestations. From going into their room often to make sure they were still breathing to deciding on what college to attend. How quickly it becomes time to have earrings, date, or learn to drive. How I wished to protect them even as we sent them into the world! They will always be a part of me. Serious sparks.

With this family, I hung on, by a thread and by a mile. The thing didn't explode or go into a death spiral. We spontaneously planned, endured, and survived! God blessed and carried us. Generous people touched us.

Goodness and opportunity supported us. I knew we did not control this life. But, ultimately, with the wonderful material we had to work with, we successfully got through to the next day and, with hope, awaited the new day sun.

We were a phenomenon. We had sweetness. Throw in sarcasm, laughter and anxiety. Add in a touch of anger. Don't neglect a cup of wit, nobility, and curiosity. Toss a helpful amount of caring and love, sacrifice and empathy. We had Connecticut clam chowder and Greek salad with our own delicious menu informed by the sea and the mountains, soccer and Alex, drums, band, and cars. Our family became a joyous and humorous band of spirits, held together by chemistry whose formula is a little too long to fit on the page. We cared for each other, although probably not all the time, and we stuck together and danced that hard dance of love. It penetrated our bones and flowed in a good, nurturing rhythm. This family became a place where we all could grow and prosper without fear of recrimination or put down. Our song of joy flourished under the belief that God had created it all in goodness and love.

We knew how we wanted to play the game in the face of our past. Our books and our intuitions, our religion and our philosophy led to a simple operating plan. Keep your cool, love when you can, show respect and patience, talk and listen and be present. We both realized that our kids were incomplete as they slowly fit into their shoes. It was our job to give space and direction as needed, and they responded. We expected them to be kids until they weren't and allowed their gradual maturity to show us when we could let go. People making is never easy. We focused on guiding our children to find their levels of joy and need, their place in the world and their need for community. Whatever the mix, it worked, and we grew into a family supportive of each other. They found their full-throated voices by the third act. This privilege, mystery, and grand experiment turned into a beautiful dance troupe! The music carried me away. It still sings in my heart!

Touching Souls

Touching souls quickly, a millionth part of eternity,
A flash in the eye of time,
Entering one's eternal conversation with life, we sit.
Time has quickly learned and quickly forgotten us
A blue drop of ocean, we are, for a second, glistening in the sun
For that second, that half second, let us glisten and rejoice

14 St. Bartholomew Parish

The couple came in by the side door at the front of the church. Mass was about to start, the priest and altar servers lined up in the back. The church, St. Bartholomew Catholic Church, filled with the parish's city congregation. They sang the opening song with familiarity and energy. The couple had their three children with them. They quickly sat in the empty pew at the very front. Most unusual, for Catholics avoided the front pew. Anyway, they sat in the pew designated for the readers. Fr. Mac, a beloved Irish priest, had presided over the church for several years. Getting to the front of the church, facing the congregation behind the altar, he declared, "In the name of the Father, the Son and the Holy Spirit", making a grand sign of the cross for all to see. "Let us begin with the sign of peace," he went on. "Let us offer each other a sign of peace." This part of the ritual called for the congregation to turn to each other and greet each other, normally occurring later in the service. As the sound of people speaking with each other gently started, Fr. Mac came down from the altar to greet the new family. "How are you this morning? How are you little guys doing? Nice to see you, welcome!" "Thank you, father". He then took his position again behind the altar and continued with Mass. This introduced us to the Catholic Church in Columbus, Indiana. The anvil smiled.

For some people, I guess, belonging to an association is important, like the National Rifle Association or the Saturday Bowling League. For us, the Catholic Church from early on became our home where we found community, friendships and meaning. Our work contained purpose and livelihood, but the Church became a comforting force early in both our childhoods, persisting into adulthood. We experienced periods of drifting through life and not being connected, of course. But after our marriage, the church was the anchor that held us upright in a sea of change. We didn't live near family mostly, so a place of community was important. We had connections to groups in other ways and had careers that tied us to facilities and organizations. But the spiritual benefit of our commitment and involvement with our church community paid off in powerful gifts.

Christianity and Catholicism for us were not just activities but a way of life. They made up a deeply rooted set of beliefs, actions, and institutions. Embedded within us, they brought power and truth. The intellectual and emotional value of the faith became a family thing, a cultural thing, and a psychological thing. The church focused on the life of Christ, and framed our identities, purposes, vocations, and our social commitments.

To my mind, the church stood as a counterweight to the culture. Promoting a theology of love and acceptance, a disciplined but giving life style, it offered an alternative voice. The church believed marriage was a vocation that required a discipline to one's sexuality, a safe place for children, and a virtuous living out love and work. As well, we were called to feed the hungry and give drink to the thirsty. We should treat the poor preferentially for the world doesn't. Christ radically advocated mercy. The world, in its selfish and survival-of-the-fittest approach, looked upon these tendencies as foolishness. The world's wisdom dictated to make as much money as you can and take care of yourself and what you have. God calls us to love as we believe God is love. An altogether different directive.

I saw that the world did not wholly accept these musings from a foolish man they thought justified to kill. The church embodied its special wisdom in the person of Christ. I saw authenticity in Christ in his realistic life acted out in scripture. His disciples didn't come across as intellectual giants or doers of great deeds. Peter, the main apostle, betrayed Christ three times, denying that he even knew him. I could identify with fallible human beings. The Bible portrayed the workings of God in an understandable human context. There were those like Fr. Mac who lived it out genuinely. This wisdom caught me off guard. It got into my heart. In the slow movement of grace, it opened me up to see with a heartfelt, spiritual vision. I have had too many occasions of the movement of the Spirit within me to say that there is no God. As well, the secular world is too brash and selfish to hold my attention for very long. I have long ago given up the shiny objects of the world. At least I hope that is the case.

I do not want to leave the impression that we were the best of Catholics and that every word that emanated from the Pope and the Vatican resounded in our hearts. No, we were good Catholics who tried to live according to the dictates of the church. We still struggled with the powerful economic urges to spend money. Not immune to the powers of fashion, we had our power suits and work clothes. The capitalistic notions of profit and the importance of money still affected us. Culture subjected us to the views of sexuality and avarice, gluttony, and pride that pervaded society. We didn't lead wholly consecrated lives filled with constant prayer and devout actions. But we believed in the presence of God. The Eucharist fed us. We prayed for peace and gentleness of spirit. Aware of the poor and the disadvantaged, we supported them with our meager donations. We acknowledged the blessings that were given to us. Certainly, we knew love and mercy and its power to heal and make whole. Our hearts were open to God. I saw pain and suffering that lifted me beyond the utopian view of capitalism and consumerism.

Upon moving to Columbus, I claimed to be a Christian, but an incomplete one. I knew the faith to an extent but did not live it out very well. I could be a giver, but now I would learn a true giving. Before, my spirit had awakened, but now the church would feed it with Eucharist, community and service. Perhaps my theology went from a mundane level to a more operative level. The trajectory of my faith took off in Columbus. It nurtured me. The foothold in my heart started as but a trickle of faith that then became a stream and then a river. The anvil smiles its power.

Because doing a thing pushes it to a different level than merely knowing it, doing ministry took my faith to a different level. I engaged in many ministerial activities directed by the church in Columbus. One early opportunity for me in Columbus dealt with a men's ministry group at church. Greg Schershel, a Scout dad, and Wally Glover visited a monastery in Southern Indiana called St. Meinrad. "Hey, Steve, we just back from Meinrad and want to share the experience with others in our church community. We want to form a men's ministry group. You interested?"

In the southern hills of Indiana is the beautiful Benedictine monastery of St. Meinrad. As one approaches it from the highway, there is a winding, humble road that carries no hint of the jewel it is leading you to. Then there is a turn and you can see the two high steeples of the main abbey in the distance. They emerge out of the morning fog like sentinels proclaiming the place where God's people have made their abode. This is where the monks live in a community, where prayer is always being said. The priests and monks follow St. Benedict of Nursia, who started several monasteries in the fifth and sixth centuries.

The archabbey of St. Meinrad, called "the Hill", occupies a beautiful land composed of rolling hills and green space. In the 1800s, a Swiss group of monks sought to replicate the land and scenery of their threatened home monastery. Amid fields of farmland, St. Meinrad appears as a magnificent two steepled arch abbey. It supplies the archdiocese of Indianapolis and others with priests through its seminary. St. Meinrad trains other religious staff such as Directors of Religious Education, Youth ministers and deacons. It also accommodates guests for retreats and spiritual programs.

Because of their trip, Greg and Wally recruited several guys in the parish and organized a retreat to St. Meinrad. The monastery had facilities and staff to provide retreats. "Well, Steve, Wally and I want to organize a group to go to St. Meinrad for a retreat. Would you be interested? It was powerful for us to be there." After some planning, we stayed on the grounds of the arch abbey for several days. They fed us, taught us and gave us drink (at the Unstable, a bar like place that used to hold the stables). The arch abbey inspired us. Its spiritual atmosphere took me in and moved me. At one point, they gave us a tour of the grounds and told of its history. Brother Maurice (not a priest) hosted us; He had lived, studied, and worked on the grounds of the arch abbey as a member of the Benedictines for 50 years or more. He would come around with a little cart of wine during dinner.

A high point of the stay involved praying with the monks. The monks follow what is called the Liturgy of the Hours. This series of psalms and readings are prayed and sung in morning, noon and evening prayer. They sing these psalms in the Gregorian chant which fills the heart with a gracious harmony. The Sunday Mass liturgy excelled our expectations, as there would be wonderful singing. Processing in two by two, the monks took up their positions on either side of the main aisle. The Abbot came in last with his crosier. Townspeople and those on retreat would be in the visitor section. The liturgy would follow the accepted form with a wonderful homily. There were scholars of homiletics who taught at the seminary, so the relevant message inspired and enlightened us.

You may think this is a very archaic place stuck in the fifth century. And there is truth to that in that this way of life has been going on for centuries. However, the monks of St. Meinrad were anything but "ancient and archaic". While they wore hooded habits, sandals, and rope belts, the message fit well with an audience with a modern knowledge and awareness. "Let me speak to you about the Gospel of John with its unique flavor and almost poetic style, unlike the other synoptic Gospels. I studied John while on sabbatical in Paris. Of course, this was between the wonderful meals I had on the Rue de Rome, close to where I was staying." These holy men had been in the world but were not of the world. Catholicism boasts of a great number of prestigious universities throughout the world. Such places educated these men.

For me, I encountered a religious way of life I hadn't seen or even understood. The monks had a lifestyle not like the secular world. Their slow and deliberate pace of life offered a welcome alternative to the aimless hustle and bustle of the modern world. But I have heard monks say that they have issues with each other that other people do. The Rule of St. Benedict sought to create an organized lifestyle where one could easily find peace and God's presence.

These retreats existed in rarefied air. They imparted unique knowledge. The offer of time for prayer and communion with God added up to a mini education in Catholicism and the faith. The presence of these devout and loving men showed me a deeper facet of my religion. Here, obedience and faithfulness were clear, in an unusual and uncompromising way. It offered a life of meaning. I have a framed calligraphy that Brother Maurice did that says, "The meaning of life is to live with meaning". That captures a part of the mystique and the attractiveness of the monastery. For me, I found it a formidable place of learning and spiritual maturity. I would find peace in the presence of God on retreat, a great privilege, and a gift. Greg fondly would point out, "Even in late winter, I could see a robin on the grounds and find a dandelion!" The retreat became a yearly event. I went to this retreat for a number of years.

After a couple of years, I started playing music on these men's retreats. I would take my guitar and bring along a couple of other musicians. We would play music during the Friday evening Mass and between the sessions. "You know real men sing real loud, right?" I would ask. "And you are real men, huh?" "Let's check out the song book we put together. Pg. 3, Loving and Forgiving." At one point, in the abbey, a religious brother wrote out a sign that told us we were singing too loudly!

Back home, we attended the Catholic Church on the north side of the city called St. Columba. They would later tear it down to make way for a new church. The pastor, Fr. Steve Banet, conveyed enthusiasm and taught us well with his homilies and talks. He spoke to me with his large view of God and his ideas of service. The retreats and the many opportunities for service to others helped me to understand the power of a giving spirit. My professional activities spoke to this as well. When I left the mental health center and joined a private practice, I asked God in prayer to guide me and to make it work, to allow me to serve others through my work.

While my faith gained energy and focus, Rochelle and I continued to do fulfilling marriage preparation work within the parish. "Jeremy and Debra, we're going to meet with you over the next 6 sessions. We will share what we think are important marital topics. Communication, family of origin issues, money, sex, kids, and the church's beautiful view of marriage. We hope to share the good stuff and the tough stuff." It excited us to share with them the reality of raising children and balancing the many facets of married life while partnered with God. Our kids would come in while we talked and would offer an authentic example of the dimensions of marriage.

Father Banet left in the late 90s and the role of pastor fell to a priest named Fr. Clem Davis. He would play a major role in my response to God's goodness in my life. Fr. Clem introduced a program called Christ Renews His Parish (CHRP). The retreat asked parishioners to share on various topics from the view of their experiences. I went on the first men's CHRP retreat. My wife went on the first women's CHRP retreat. For us, these were life-changing experiences.

The power of the retreat rested in telling your story and hearing that of others. Fr. Clem asked, "Steve, I think you would do well as the 'Spiritual Director' for our group. You've got the background for it. What do you think?" "Be happy to, father." It meant leading the prayers when needed and also presenting a talk. This pushed me to be more public about my faith and share that deep sense I had that God was with me. I spoke about my mother and father's acrimony and how God worked through it to bring me to his altar.

After receiving the retreat, we put on the next one. There were several heavy hitters in our CHRP group. These wonderful relationships would continue on in various capacities, in and out of church. After the experience, our group met for a while. Rochelle's CHRP group continues to meet many years after the retreat experience. They have become family and sisters to each other. As she would say, "Belonging and community, having a place, being known and knowing others deeply, is a powerful way to live out one's religious beliefs." We both see the need for a community as a necessary requirement of faith. Those who see religion as little more than a personal "spirituality" are missing out on a tremendous dimension of community. This call to love is at the heart of the Christian message. To give a retreat to others brings home the idea that we give ourselves to others.

A movement in the parish supported by Fr. Clem involved the creation of small church communities. "Let me share my belief that small groups of people meeting in each other's home can help parishioners comfortably share their lives with each other. I think it makes great sense and shows the wisdom and benefit of telling one's story. I have seen this have a positive impact on people." One of these groups lasted for at least ten years, if not more. We would meet and have a meal or dessert. We would catch up with each other's lives and children and then discuss the readings or the book chapter. The groups offered help, comfort, and support when needed. I loved how we all sought to find God in the common experiences of our lives. Community lessens the load of life but increases the joys of life shared. Gong!

After Mass, Fr. Clem spoke to us about another opportunity for service. "Let me say something about the diaconate formation program. From the time of Vatican II, the church re-instituted the deacon as a minister of charity, of service. This role carried the ability to baptize, marry, and bury the dead. Hatch, match and dispatch, they call it!" Laughter. "The deacon as well can preach at the Mass." The deacon, the priest and the bishop, he went on, are the levels of the clergy in the church hierarchy after Vatican II. Now a deacon could be married and have children. However, the position did not have a salary. The Archdiocese would soon begin the formation program. I made a mental note.

Fr. Clem came to the parish to complete the task of building a new church. Rochelle took part on the building committee. Building a new church and making all the many decisions seemed like a monumental job. As the church project neared completion, I served as head of the parish council. At one point, we had a tour of what would be the new church. A small crane sat on the giant slab of concrete that was to be the nave or where the pews would be. Standing by it, I offered a few words. "From this place, right here, imagine it, there will be an altar. From this place, there will be a coffin with the grieving family tearfully sitting in the first pew. The priest in his vestments will come down the aisle here, this concrete path you can see. He will begin the Mass with the sign of the cross. He will baptize an infant in this space, maybe over here where the baptism font will be located and the new parents will marvel at God's movement in their lives. Music will fill this large space and people will sing and fill it with the voice of God's love." I also pointed out that there would be weddings in that space. "Can you imagine a bride excited and tearful coming down the aisle, her fiancé waiting to see her for the first time at the altar? Maybe my kids would be married here," I suggested. Well, several years later, my son got married in that very church. Then my daughter and I, in fact, walked down that aisle as her fiancé waited for her with Fr. Clem as they began their married life together. I had predicted it! Sparks flew then, for sure!

The parish had great music groups. This connected me to the church through music. I played music with a group called "Giggin for God", led by Matt Sousa. Another member, Roger Banister, who played professionally, brought his mandolin and fiddle and gave the Giggin sound a country vibe. There were talented singers whose beautiful harmonies flowed. I had the privilege of playing guitar for a while with them. There were other groups as well, more traditional singers and organ music.

A big part of my music story at the church revolved around a group of teenage singers and musicians. The group called themselves, "Stained Glass". Katy Stallings started the group. She served as the youth minister and became a family friend over the course of the many years we were involved with the program. A single woman at the time, she had great energy and relatability. I thought her program offered the parish youth an excellent learning and spiritual experience. Katy developed a strong program. She also turned the youth house into a haunted house complete with zombies and chainsaws during Halloween! For many years, they teamed up with a farmer and had a haunted corn maze. "So, Catherine, how was the corn maze tonight?" "There were a lot of people! The chain saws were humming!" She was a part of Stained Glass and played the flute. I have mentioned that she and her mom went to Haiti several times with youth ministry. The youth program included Paul as well. He took part in Youth ministry and as he got older, got involved in Catholic Youth Organization (CYO) camp. That is where he met his later-to-be fiancé, Emily. Youth ministry started many things for us.

My experience with Katy and Stained Glass added to my understanding of ministry. She described her view, "Ministry has to be relational. The minister doesn't just lead others. The program requires a relationship between the minister and the participant. It has to contain qualities of caring, respect, openness, communication, community, and faith. That make sense?" I played music with Katy, but she taught me more than that. A joy existed in the youth program. Participants were treated with dignity and experienced the quality of being known. We were a force together, working for God's purpose. We made beautiful music together, the harmony of community, the melody of action focused on giving, the lyrics of love. My slow turning to God received ever higher levels of God's grace because of my involvement with youth ministry. Katy did that for many.

We played as a matter of tradition at the Christmas Midnight Mass. However, we played a song at the end of that Mass that the kids loved. "Children Go Where I send Thee", a raucous and speedy song contrasted the musicians and the singers and pitted who could do it the fastest. We also sang a set of Christmas songs prior to Mass that the kids and the congregation loved. Another song we played called "Seeds" really identified the group as a signature song. I can't hear that song without it bringing back many memories. The song provoked the image of seeds being nurtured by God's love. There were other favorites. I wrote songs at the time and we played several of my songs.

As I mentioned, Katy took several groups of kids down to Haiti. Catherine went, as did Rochelle several times. From there, we got several Haitian songs. We would do, "Father, I Adore You" in Creole and a version of "We are Marching", Siyahamba. These trips were powerful witnesses to how real poverty looks. They attested to the human ability to rise above those situational limits and discriminations. What they experienced in Haiti forever changed my wife and daughter. This attests to the great opportunity that came from the adoption of a parish in Haiti. Haiti opened up a reality not readily or easily comprehended by US citizens. Haiti taught my daughter troubling but life-changing lessons. These had a deep impact on Catherine and Rochelle.

Later on, we did a CD of Stained-Glass music with this group of high school musicians and singers. I recorded music with a friend of mine, Trent, and so with my Yamaha 16-channel digital recorder, we put together a CD of music. We had several recording sessions at the church. The new church built in 2001 had installed a large stained-glass window with bright blues and greens. I took pictures of it and this became the CD cover. It turned out pretty good.

We sang and prayed with a significant number of kids over the years. They were talented singers and musicians. They had the Holy Spirit's energy. It was a great honor to play and sing with them. I won't name them, but many were friends of my kids whom we have seen graduate, get jobs, get married and have kids of their own. I hope the legacy of Stained Glass remains in their hearts. After I left the group, Charlie took over. They gave me a farewell concert that touched me so much. I had written several songs that the parish seemed to enjoy. The concert allowed me time to play music with the group one last time and talk about what it all meant. Charlie had written a song for me they played. The evening met with sadness but also the joy at the accomplishments the group had achieved. And the hammer sings the anvil's delight in a beautiful harmony!

I have to mention Elijah's Whisper. While I played music for church, my friend Trent and I became a musical duo. He wasn't Catholic but had been thinking about converting and enjoyed the kid's music at church. Over time, we became friends. Trent and I started a little group called Elijah's Whisper. This referred to the great prophet Elijah and the whisper of God he heard. It seemed like a good name for a Christian group. I had been writing songs and with the birth of Elijah's Whisper, this sped up. Eventually Trent joined Stained Glass. He could play the lead guitar! Our styles fit well together and we had a lot of fun together. He would come over on a Friday night and we would head for the basement and play. The cool thing for me concerned improvising with Trent. I would keep the beat and rhythm going. As I improvised vocals, Trent would just take off on the leads. We engaged in the creative generation of fresh sounds, an activity that nurtured and fed me.

At the park in town, a large platform stands on a hill with a large canopy over the top. Organizers set up a Christian music festival there. Trent and I joined the parade. There were several acts. He and I got our turn, and we played several pleasant tunes. A small crowd attended. They seemed to enjoy the music. Well, the day's weather wasn't the best. As we reached the chorus of a song, "Have I done enough for you today?" a lightning bolt cracked several miles away. Yeah, we hear you! As we finished up, the announcer clarified that a severe thunderstorm headed our way. So, we were the end. As we took down our stuff, the heavens opened up.

While our band had further exploits, I was blessed to praise God in song. My music allowed me to articulate my growing sense of theology and capture the beautiful texture and feeling of God's love. We certainly tried with Elijah's Whisper. I am forever grateful to Trent for the inspiring music he helped to create.

Among the most interesting groups we joined, I would have to name the book club at St. Bartholomew. It included Steve Heimann, a judge, and his wife Ann and Fr. Clem, who proved to be quite the scholar. The Harpenaus and Pences also attended. Finally, as the cherry on top, Fr. Marty joined us. Marty had been a priest for many years, but had retired to the area. He would help from time to time in the parish. Surprisingly, he owned an apartment in Greece. He had strong ideas and was not shy about expressing controversial views. He loved the church, but showed himself to be a very articulate spokesperson for an expansive and large view of God. The books we read were powerful and enlightening. The discussions could be electric. Steve would come with his roll of index cards. "Now, on page 187, top of the page, I felt that the example of the priest's mercy toward the woman was just powerful. What did you all think?" Fr. Marty would have his take on things in unconventional terms. "I don't think the bishop would agree, but Chapter 5 shows the essence of Gospel for me." Fr. Clem would be the scholar and give us a deep analysis. The rest of us just sat and held on.

We also joined a card group through the parish. These folks would become dear friends. I can't believe that I would spend my time and effort playing cards. Rochelle loved cards. For me, they were a necessary nuisance.

Another big chapter in the parish's life opened up in 2005 when Hurricane Katrina ravaged Mississippi and Louisiana. Our church sent several groups of volunteers to help with the cleanup. A group of kids went on several trips with Katy. I went along with many Stained-Glass kids and Charlie Day, who played guitar with me. You can't forget visiting Waveland where the hurricane made landfall and devastated the town.

On one of those youth trips, groups of us went to people's houses in the community. We spent a couple of days doing what needed to be done, cleaning up, painting, and fixing things. My group went to an older woman's home. One thing that the hurricane took out was her magnificent magnolia tree. "Miss Barley, can we show you what we planted in the front?" This just thrilled her, and she broke down into tears. Those kinds of things were commonplace during these trips. We would process what we had seen or done at the end of the day. We were all affected. Here we were, important workers offering solace and support to others. It showed the kids a different way of relating to people and taught lessons of suffering and consolation.

By the church in Waveland, remained a statue of the Blessed Mother, unharmed even though the church behind it was destroyed. Driving around the community felt like going to a war zone. There would be a flight of concrete steps going up to nowhere, as the house would not be standing. The local parish had Mass on Sunday and we played the Mass music for them. There were lots of tears as our kids sang and played. They stood as a bright beacon of hope for a community brought to its knees. Charlie gave a Waveland kid a guitar. We saw miracles rooted in love and God's grace.

I also went several times to Waveland organized by Steve Heimann and Men's Ministry. We took a bus down and stayed in big tents. We went to a house where there were several teams of people working. "Hey Dennis, why don't we get working on this drywall here?" "Sure, we are here to work." As we were patching up the seams, a woman came over and looked at what we were doing. She told us in rather direct terms, "You two are not doing a very good job. My people can take over. Thanks." It turns out that she was a Mother Superior of a group of nuns who were there. Her sisters were talented at "muddin" so we lost our jobs! Who can argue with a group of sisters?

During these trips, we would begin the day with prayer. Steve asked me to do a reflection on the day's readings. This would further push the "slow movement of God" within me. I enjoyed getting up early with the sun, in a makeshift tent city, praying for God's healing touch on the people and the land blown away by the hurricane. We were in the war zone and we were the cavalry, not so much as saving the day but offering a helping hand where earlier none existed. We needed God's strength.

On one of those trips, Juan, a Cuban member of the parish, told us, "I have found a Cuban restaurant in town not badly damaged but open." They offered plantains. The trip, like an oasis, stood out as an engaging side bar to a trip filled with loss. Humor is always welcome when found alongside hard, sweaty work. Gongs.

These trips opened my eyes to see how easily things could be lost. There would be marks high on the walls of the homes and the homeowner would say, "See that line up there? That is how high the water got." One guy showed, "Had the water gotten a couple more inches, I would have drowned." Another person said, "After the hurricane, we found fish floating nearby that we had never seen before and couldn't identify. And we have lived here twenty years!"

We worked in a person's house who lived by the water. The flood waters inundated his house. However, through volunteer workers, the house was rebuilt. "I am so appreciative. Come back on Friday and we will have a seafood feast!" To hear the stories and see the hope alongside the trauma provided an amazing witness. I guess if it doesn't kill you, it strengthens you!

I have had many powerful religious experiences. The spiritual visitation on Howard Street that proved to be a blessing was one such encounter. I mentioned the supervisor at the railroad who suggested I consider college. I always thought he acted on God's behalf. Another significant experience left me convinced of the intervention of God in my life. I was on the leadership team of a retreat for youth ministry. I was sitting at a table in the back of the main room. One of the youth, Adam Anderson, made a presentation. His dad was a deacon. He presented a talk about Christ and focused on the idea that Christ's spirit lived in others, even those we may not like. As he presented and I sat there listening, I heard a voice that said, "Why don't you trust me?" The voice was a gentle young man's voice, spoken simply and clearly. I immediately looked around me, thinking someone near had spoken to me. But I sat alone at the table. I sat there, stunned. It was not Adam's voice. I quickly concluded that God had spoken to me. Trust was a significant issue for me for a good part of my life. This wasn't a hallucination, nor was I drunk, tired, or stressed. I knew I wasn't crazy; I was a licensed psychologist! It could not be explained away easily. Since then, when I have doubts or when a situation tests my trust or it falters, this encounter comes back to me. I don't understand it, but I believe it. I have tried as well to trust so that I can answer the question in the positive, if I am asked again!

Our encounter with the faith here had a tremendous impact on us. The church held an important place of community for us and a source of holiness. It gave us so many dear friends with whom we shared our lives. They let us in and shared their stories. We felt immersed in a wonderful community of holy friends. It created a fabric of meaning for us, a comforting blanket of safety, a warm quilt embracing us with stories and people. This church community fulfilled our lives. We walked in the gentle knowledge we were known, cared for, and embraced by God. We tried to return the affection. I think God had me just where he wanted me!

A Long Life Together

A long life together is no small thing, with its fickle tragedies and lonesome escapes
It is roundabout sensitivities, and days that lead to days, like a carousel, round and round
But a long life together contains cement whose strong attraction suffers not the ins and outs of love's fortune

We ride the wind above the din
We flow on a wave apart from the everyday conversations of strangers
We move about a space populated not by convenience but familiarity
Not by expedience but by trust, not by need but desire
Ours is a rare constancy
It is like the trees and the mountains, living in a place, changing slowly in concert, in a dance with the land
To live with another over decades, in that delicate ecosystem of human relationships, becomes a rare and beautiful jewel
Slowly its secret facets are revealed and slowly its priceless color fills our hearts

15 Archdiocese of Indianapolis

A man's reach should exceed his grasp. Thus read the magazine picture I had on my wall at Penn State. To reach for goals felt important and fundamental. To grasp what I reached for meant that the object was within my capability. I have been uneasy my whole life, seeking and searching. Yes, I have been restless, as Aquinas would describe. While I have reached success in many areas, some of my goals were difficult; I didn't always choose the simple or the low fruit. Maybe this is part of my problem, a sign of my foolishness. I sought the inspired. Why did I pursue these things? Is this God speaking to me, pushing me to heights I would not claim on my own? Or is it simply my foolishness for not discerning where my limits were? As Isaiah suggests (58:11), "And the Lord will guide you continually, and satisfy your desire with good things…" I do not deserve the gifts I have received in this life, but I will accept them as they are from God. This chapter particularly looks at how God has guided me and brought me to a greater identity.

This chapter speaks to a 15-year journey up a high mountain. Not that I am a slow mountaineer, but this trek represents a long quest for God. Thinking of blessings, this is the area of my life where I am most thankful. It is in my religious life that I am blessed beyond my dreams. I can think of only one other area with this blessing, and that is in my family, my companion Rochelle, and our children.

In the early 2000s, I applied to enter a program for spiritual direction at the Benedict Inn in Indianapolis. Benedictine and Franciscan sisters ran it. Spiritual direction, a contemplative activity, focuses on discerning the movement of God in your life. What is God's plan for you, where in your life is God speaking to you and how are you to respond to this urging by the Spirit? The program lasted a couple of years, but required a year of spiritual direction before entering instruction. I spoke with my friend Katy and she suggested I talk with a friend of hers, Julie.

Julie and I met once a month at the Benedict Inn. We discussed my ideas about God. She asked, "How can you more clearly discern what God wants of you?" This powerful question stumped me. "Julie, I am challenged by that. I pray and I know God has been present. But I'm not sure what he wants me to do." I took part actively in many church activities, but spiritual direction clarified the purpose of these actions.

An interesting image came up in spiritual direction. Julie and I met in a room at the center. There hung a painting on the wall of a boat in a large area of water. (Another boat painting!) "You know Steve," she would say, "I have thought about you and I believe you are in this boat in the painting." "Ok," I hesitatingly said. "Close your eyes and put yourself there. Sit in the boat. What is that like?" Surprised, I voiced my next thought. "I am sitting in the boat, but it doesn't have a rudder! I am in the ocean with no land in sight, but God is pushing the boat with the wind. He takes it where he wishes." Julie and I both concluded that this push seemed to point towards the spiritual direction program, to be a spiritual director. I had people skills, and I was being recruited by God in a helping capacity. It felt like a formidable task was before me.

Shortly afterward, the Spiritual Direction program required putting down several thousand dollars for the program. Rochelle and I discussed it and we let it sit for a while. When we came back to it, I had the painful realization that we could not afford it. I could not grasp the goal. We were in a deep hole of debt because of our misuse of credit cards and this amounted to tens of thousands of dollars. This hit me hard because I frankly tried to avoid dealing with money. I made money through my business and gave it to Rochelle; she would pay the bills. I never "liked" money, meaning it was a source of tension. Rochelle enjoyed doing the books, and I was happy to let her.

Well, I would not enter the program. Rather, we embarked on a path to clear up the debt issue. It would be a while before we were on better financial ground. But we got there after being frugal and soul searching. Several slow anvil syncopations!

However, I felt disappointed by not entering the Spiritual Direction program. As well, I felt embarrassed not to follow through with so important an opportunity. The next months were hard. I continued my work, but this kicked up guilt and grief, old friends of mine! While this may seem like a tough chapter of our lives, and I would not describe it as easy, it turned out to open up a great new opportunity.

Recall Fr. Clem's mention of deacons. These were an order of men dedicated to charity who helped provide for the women and children in the days of the apostles. St. Steven, the first martyr of the church, was a deacon. While the order had faded centuries ago, through Vatican II, in the 60s, the church opened up the ordination for men as deacons again. In Indianapolis, this process took time to be instituted where the push started in the 2000s. The first class of deacons began formation in 2003, going through a program administered by faculty at St. Meinrad.

From our parish, I knew a great guy chosen to be in the first class: Bill Jones. I could see why he made the cut. A strong Catholic, though not without his pain and suffering. He and I talked about the use of psychologists in the assessment of the candidates. He had questions about the testing and the process. Talking with Bill gave me insight into how the program worked. I enjoyed touching base and reconnecting with him from time to time to see how his formation developed.

When the possibility of entering the diaconate formation program initially came up, I thought about it. However, we still reeled from the financial discoveries and we weren't in a suitable position to take the step. However, when the inquiry presentations began in 2006, Rochelle and I discussed it. It seemed like something that I could do.

I had spent a lot of energy, and time involved in various ministries as a prelude. Being a deacon seemed to be a good retirement plan. I always thought that you can't just stop work and retire. You had to have a plan. Being a deacon would afford me good work without overwhelming me. As well, the diaconate program cost nothing, which counted as a big plus. Deacons did not receive a salary, but it required a significant sharing of time and energy.

Finally, I still had the memory of spiritual direction and God guiding my rudderless boat to a place of his choosing. Certainly, this entailed a serious life commitment of time and energy. The formation program would take five years and require a weekend of training 11 months out of the year. We would have instructors from around the country offering insights into all aspects of church and spiritual life. There would be books to read, discussions to take part in, papers to write. It appeared not just an intellectual exercise but a journey of discernment and discovery. We had to think about the church and serve others as an ordained minister. The formation program didn't equal a seminary, but was close. It sought to form men of God who could serve the needs of the people of God through the sacraments, the liturgy, and the theology of the church.

The church also desired a person who knew who they were, their gifts and their experiences. The deacon engaged in a charitable emptying of self. As I thought about it, I had to get through the usual anxiety and the voice that told me, "You can't do it, stupid." I saw that the clothing of the deacon might really fit. Maybe it was that to which God was calling me over the years.

Of course, I asked myself if I could make the commitment? Could I be a minister who gave himself to others, wholly and unselfishly? The instruction couldn't be any more strenuous than that of the doctorate program. Could I guarantee obedience to the bishop and church teachings? Could I seek holiness or was I simply a dumb sinner whom God couldn't use? My religion, my spirituality, my identity and my worthiness felt on the line. As James (1:6) suggests, he who doubts is like a wave of the sea that is driven and tossed by the wind." A rudderless boat, perhaps?

However, the process went both ways. The church decided as well how appropriate and suitable I was for the program. My answer to these questions and doubts loudly said I should let the program tell me I didn't fit in. Let God decide I didn't qualify. I felt I could succeed, and I was being called to it. God can make the dust come alive and I certainly had my thoughts about being dust! The anvil sang its passion, and I had to listen.

The process of inquiry lasted a year of meetings and paperwork. Baptismal certificates had to be found. Marriage licenses had to be found. Essays had to be written about one's spiritual journey. I completed a psychological evaluation to make sure I didn't have unwise tendencies. They carried out interviews. Frankly, I thought they would not consider me because I had too many flaws and I would seek to serve God in another way.

It turned out that from our parish there were three of us who applied. Tom Hill and Brad Anderson were guys I knew very well from parish activities, men's ministry, and youth ministry. They were both great guys and I could see them easily being deacons.

At a senior retreat with Katy, Tom and I were speakers and group leaders. At that point, we both had all our materials in and were waiting. After dinner, we were sitting on the floor, hanging out, chatting. The lights were low, music played. "Well, Steve, what do you think about the diaconate?" "Good question. I am in until they tell me otherwise!" I said. "This is exciting, but I am not sure they will choose me. For one, I am a little anxious about it. It is quite a commitment." "Yep, for sure." Tom agreed. "Tom, really, you want to know, I am unworthy of it. I am not a saint. I love God, but this calls for a holy attitude I am not sure I have." "I feel that same way." Pausing, "Are we looking at it wrong?" Tom asked. "I don't think so," I shook my head. "But if I am allowed to take part, I will. It is a great opportunity to serve." I said. "That is for sure," he said. "But there are three of us applying. Only one will get in, I bet." "Tom, that leaves two of us out in the cold. Could they choose two?" "Don't know." So, we tried to identify which one of us it would be. We concluded it would be Brad! This was like the three Christs of Michigan!

Tom said, "You know what?" looking at me wide eyed, "God, bring it on! Let the holy chips fall where they may! We will be your obedient servants no matter what the outcome of the decision!" I felt his enthusiasm! "Yeah, no matter. We will still be friends and support each other. I'll pray for you." "Same here. God's will be done." "Amen to that!"

We were not told much about the process for selection, but that they would notify us soon. We waited for the letter to come. Any day now. When judgment day finally arrived, I felt afraid to open the letter. I held it briefly and took a breath. I opened it and hurriedly read it, looking for certain words. It said that they had selected me to be in the deacon class of 2012! I had to read it again. Rochelle asked, "Well, tell me!"

I looked at her, handed it to her and said, "I'm in! I've been accepted!" Tears welled up in my eyes. We hugged. The words sank in. They accepted me! My doubts had been unfounded, my skepticism misplaced. A smile started from the inside and slowly crept up to my face, where it jumped around for a while. I knew that Tom and Brad had a good chance. My chances were low. But now I found myself accepted. I had to call Tom. "Tom, how are you? I heard from the archdiocese. Have you?" A brief pregnant pause. "Tom, I got in." "Steve, so did I! What about that? God is good!" "All the time! Have you heard from Brad?" "No, not yet. I will call him. I'll get back to you." However, if they accepted the two of us, that must mean that Brad didn't make it. I felt bad. We had to find out Brad's status.

Shortly afterward, Tom called and said that Brad was also accepted. "Oh my, Tom, how can that be? They took us all. Do they really know what they are doing?" I felt surprised but pleased that they had selected my ministry brothers as well as myself. During the program, we would come to be called the Columbus Mafia. Our own sons of thunder!

A big quest lay before us. A great journey of faith, filled with relationships and grace, a journey toward the church. The world had suddenly transformed, and my spirit renewed. I felt a new energy. New clothes were in the closet and the old clothes no longer fit. I looked at myself in the mirror to see a face that emanated a new brightness. A couple of loud swings on the anvil for that one!

News spread quickly, and people offered their congratulations. "So, Dad," Paul asked, "What does this mean? What about mom?" They were all out of the house and wondered how this could be my good retirement plan? Thomas asked, "If they don't pay, Dad, this isn't much of a retirement plan!" My secular friends thanked me, but they didn't have a clue what it meant. My Catholic friends didn't really understand either. For me, I wondered about the dimensions of it, felt a sense of challenge, but also a feeling of comfort. This would probably take me to a different parish. I had committed to not getting married again should my wife pass away. My time, I knew, would be in short supply.

The diaconate would become a part of my retirement plan. I knew that therapy took a lot out of me emotionally. It required quite a lot of mental work, attention, and alertness. The diaconate would allow me to work with others in a religious context. I could use my skills at relationship building but in a lighter, less driven manner. Our money situation had improved substantially. Social Security would kick in and investments could buffer us. This, above all, meant engaging in meaningful work. I felt I had been called to do it.

The venerable Fr. Bede, a St. Meinrad monk and priest, led our first year of training. A short man with a white beard and a quick and easy smile, he would teach us how to pray the Liturgy of the Hours, the prayer of the church. "We pray the hours slowly and deliberately. This is not a race. Take your time!" He would gently lead us in a wise, articulate, and caring manner. Not greatly self-disclosing, he would administer the program. Giving us a Bible study class just prior to the program beginning, he slowly molded our expectations. The study opened us up as a gentle introduction into the process that would shape us for the next 4 years.

As we went through the program, the focus rested on the men who would become deacons. The wives took part along the way, although we thought they weren't sure what to do with the wives! However, a saving grace came with a Benedictine sister named Sharon Kuhn, OSB. She helped the women by becoming the den mother to all of us. Sister also wasn't a big person, thin and short, with an ample smile and always a helpful attitude. She certainly served God and us as well. She brought heart to the place!

Another priest in the program was Fr. Larry Voelker. He proved to be an accomplished man, had held political office and had dealt with alcohol issues. He tamed that bear through AA, had the scars and the resilience. The program would see him as the Spiritual Director. Often, he would give the homily during Mass. He had a beautiful ceramic bowl that, when vibrated by a small tool, would make a haunting ringing sound. It would alert us to things starting up. Fr. Voelker served as pastor of an inner-city parish and the people loved him. We loved him as well. He acted as a wonderful pastor to us. Insightful, accepting, and kind, he showed us his open heart to God. He sadly passed away toward the end of the program. I spent time with him in Spiritual Direction and found him generous, gentle and the merciful presence of God.

We also had a couple from the first class who sat with us at every event, Deacon Pat and Lynn Bower. They served as guides who had been there and done that. Helpful, energetic and funny, they gave us hope. Pat said, "You will survive the ordeal and maybe even prosper! If I got through, your chances are high!" They gave us the sincere gift of their presence.

We sat in a big circle the first time we all came together. Many of the wives attended. There were 18 men. This would be the first of 45 weekends over the next 4 years. We went around the room and introduced ourselves. God chose these men and women to be in the program. It put its hope and its investment in these people. We were the modern version of the apostles, given a mission and a hope to right the world in a small way, that goodness would come from our actions. Joe Geiman dropped out shortly after we began.

When introduced, I spoke briefly about being a psychologist. "I want to apologize for my profession. Sorry, we devised those diabolical psychological tests that you endured. Let me apologize for the long MMPI assessment you all had to fill out. I will talk with anyone that it has seriously traumatized!" Some laughter and some grumbling.

Sitting around the circle were just common people. We had a banker, an IT guy, a state police officer, several business managers. Several worked for the church. One man had lost his wife. We were mostly older, but several had kids still at home. All of us were Caucasian. Several lived in Indy, but many were from far outside the capital. Looking around and listening to their stories, I wondered what God would do with us. What did he have in store for us and what would we bring to God's kingdom? He had transformed the world with only 12. And our powerful wives wouldn't be left untouched by the conversions their husbands were going through. Gongs.

We met often for class at Our Lady of Fatima retreat center. The conference center there would become a home for us. "Hey Tim, how are you? How's your month been?" "Good." He said. "And yours?" "Yes." "Are you ready for Canon Law?" "There's only ten of them, right?" "Ah, no, that's a different law!" Centrally located, the facilities housed us overnight and fed us while we were in class. A grotto outside had trails on the grounds. We developed the ritual of having Saturday evening social time after the last lecture. We would do evening prayer, have dinner and then begin a social gathering. "Hey folks, don't tell Fr. Bede, but somebody brought *wine*!" As time went on, I would bring my guitar and as before, we would have a folky sing along. The conversation would be stimulating. And of course, we always had chocolate!

Our gathering developed a sense of family over the course of our regular meetings. "Paula, I wanted to ask you, how's your mom?" "Did the newlyweds get off ok? Good." Our prayers went up for each other and for priests we knew. A few sessions were only for the men in the program. During these, as a way of connecting, the women in the group would have a separate meeting. We weren't really aware, but we were developing good, trusted relationships. We mixed and talked at every meal. Getting to know this ordinary group of men and women who had taken up a challenge to do something extraordinary created a close community.

At our first class, Sherry Brown introduced us to scripture. She had a Ph.D. in theology and loved the Gospel of John. Fairly young compared to us, she had a reputation for being a very hard instructor from those in the first class. She had us do role playing skits. Our group enacted an Old Testament verse. Frank Roberts played the king with a makeshift crown. We started off easy. She scaled down the intensity, and we enjoyed the class. One thing she said, however, stayed with the group from that time on. She spoke about what it meant to gird your loins. The typical clothing for the ancients comprised a long cloth loosely wrapped around their torso. To gird your loins meant you were facing battle or a stringent activity, so you tightened the cloth. We understood the need. From that point on, from time to time, there would be a call from the back row, "Gird your loins, gentlemen!" She would teach a later class about the Gospel of John. We were all inspired to have instructors who loved their subjects. It made it easier to learn the stuff.

We had a tough class on Canon Law. A professor from Washington State taught us. She loved the Oregon Ducks. On her weekend, the Ducks were playing USC. She took several breaks to check out her phone. The law is important. Christ came not to change the law but to perfect it. He made the law perfect according to her by seeking the salvation of souls. That always stayed with me.

A professor that stood out for me taught us several classes, Dr. Joe Raab. A theologian, he taught us Christology, Trinity, Mary, and Systematic Theology. His brother was a monk at St. Meinrad. He taught us heavy material. I discovered a profound theologian from Dr. Raab, Hans Urs Van Balthasar who wrote, Love Alone is Credible. He left us many handouts and much to think about. For this course in Systematic Theology, he required we read a book called, Method in Theology, by Fr. Bernard Lonergan. Lonergan, a brilliant Jesuit theologian, wrote about many topics, especially conscience and conversion. He saw religion, if I can offer anything about him, in psychological terms, as a process. I found God in a process of conversion as I slowly opened up to Him. I changed as I immersed myself in the Trinity. The book helped me to understand how I came to comprehend and believe in God. I was caught off guard by the book. It surprised and also intrigued me. It did not cheapen my view of God, but I felt clearer about how the experience of God comes about through the use of our mind. Even if we only first hear about God through Bible stories, these enter our awareness and further develop our experience. Lonergan struck a meaningful, excited chord in me. As the anvil sang.

So, you can understand my excitement as I went to class for the first time to talk about the book. I felt juiced! However, as I sat there ready to engage the rest of my fellow deacon candidates, to a man, "That was a terrible book. I do not know what it meant!" "It confused me more than helping me. Dr. Raab, what does it mean?" Not an ounce of energy arose when Lonergan's name came up. Their eyes went literally into the back of their heads! I felt so disappointed. Someone said, "Of course you, the psychologist, would like this stuff." "Guys, I loved it. It spoke my language!" "Steve, now we know you're crazy. Yep, you convinced us all!" I couldn't keep my enthusiasm in check and they knew I loved the guy and his book. "Maybe we will throw you off the same cliff we throw Lonergan!"

At another point in our instruction and discernment, as we learned about the Sacraments, we had a practicum doing the rites. We practiced the sacrament of Baptism while we were at St. Meinrad. One of us played the "mom", one the "dad", and others the God parents and the deacon. We had a baby doll for the child, a beautiful special doll with a painted ceramic head and ornate outfit that had been a gift given to the priest. We were by the baptismal font in the chapel going through the Baptism. As we came to the part, "I baptize you in the name of the Father, and of the Son and the Holy Spirit" the baby broke loose from the arms of its "mother" and fell to the concrete floor! Its poor little ceramic head split in two. "Oh, no, what have we done? We killed our practice infant! Father, we are so sorry!" What would we do with a real infant? The shocked priest could hardly speak. The wound appeared reparable, but still the wound and insult were there. We could only hang our heads in shame. We failed Baptism 101!

Now we had a class with which many of us had trouble. It wasn't so much the topic as the teacher. We had a young director of Religious Education. His approach had a strong conservative bend. His view was that no real theological developments occurred after the Council of Trent in the 1500s. He felt a devotion to St. Thomas Aquinas. This meant that he did not see the value of Vatican Council II. The Council introduced the Mass in the vernacular and brought many changes to the liturgy and ministry, including the return of the diaconate. The 2000 bishops who were present at the Council were, according to our instructor, not truly being led by the Spirit of God. Perhaps his age or maybe his message didn't impress me. While some were more sympathetic, the majority voiced disappointment with his instruction. I felt especially taken aback by his views of women. I don't think he said it, but perhaps implied that the women in the group didn't need the instruction they were receiving. This upset me to where I wrote him a letter showing my frustration and disagreement.

Our last year we did a weeklong class at St. Meinrad on homiletics, how to preach. We had Dr. Rick Stern, a noted authority. The facility videotaped our presentations, and we all critiqued them. I found it very useful and productive. However, toward the end of the week, I got sick with a fever. I had an infection and needed medical care. Staying in my room, I received antibiotics from the infirmary on the Archabbey grounds. I felt awful, but they took good care of me. However, I missed doing a funeral homily, although I felt I may need one!

A couple of years into our study, it was time to be assigned to a parish we would be at for the next several years. I went to Holy Trinity parish, a small rural parish, 15 minutes up the road. I had been there several times. The beautiful old wooden church on a hill built in the 1800s had a high steeple on which stood a tall golden cross. The people were friendly, open, and happy to have me as their first deacon. As well, they shared a priest with a parish up the road.

Our program had a schedule to increase our responsibility before ordination. We were first to be a reader and then an acolyte helping the priest set up for Mass. At ordination, we could step right into the role of deacon at a parish we already knew. Going to Holy Trinity afforded me several opportunities. Musicians I knew from my home parish played at Holy Trinity. Victoria, a trumpet player, led the group. I brought my guitar when I wasn't busy serving the Mass. I also conducted a book study reading Henri Nouwen's the Return of the Prodigal Son. The book concerns his meditations on a painting, the Return of the Prodigal Son by Rembrandt. One of Nouwen's best books, it gave our group a lot to think about. In his beautiful, semi-poetic style of prose, it conveyed beautifully the love of God for all of us sinners who stray from the faith. We had informative discussions.

Near Holy Trinity church is an old military base called Camp Atterbury. A training ground for soldiers going off to WWII, it now served as a joint force training base. But it also had a minimum-security state prison on the grounds. When I began at Holy Trinity, a man went to the prison to provide religious services. He shortly became ill and gave it up. I took it over. The church expected us to be engaged in an area of service, and the Archdiocese wanted ministers to go to prisons. I loved this ministry and did it for several years. I would do a bible study on the Sunday readings and have a communion service. Many who came were not Catholic but were looking for spiritual nourishment.

In prison, one has time to think about things. You can contemplate your life and the decisions you have made. The prison population had many African Americans with fewer Caucasians. All the inmates had large plastic cups for water and they were all decorated. Some decorated their cups with family, others had crosses and Bible verses, and others had porn.

The older residents I spoke with were there to do their time and get out. People stayed there for less than 3 years. Others, the young guys, were there to make it known how tough they were. They got shipped to other prisons after incidents of violence. The guys that came to our religious services were seeking God and looking for mercy. "Hey, Reverend, can I join you tonight? I come to as many of these as I can. I want to check out the new Catholic guy." "Sure, join us." He told me that the prison had been his seminary. What a beautiful way to look at it. He knew more about the Bible than most pastors and could recite chapter and verse from memory. He came a couple of times and then was released. Some residents came out of boredom and didn't really have any interest. A man in our group came several times. He took part in a small way. We heard after his release that they had found him dead in Indianapolis of a drug overdose.

Spending time, I got to know the regular guys fairly well. "Larry, last time you talked about your daughter. Have you heard from her?" "No, and I'm not sure why she isn't responding to my letters." "Well, I am sure there is a reasonable explanation. Can we pray for her and for you?" "Sure, I hope there's a reason. I'm not sleeping well. She used to do drugs. I'm worried she's back doing 'em again." He turned away and looked sad and concerned. My job was to bring them to God and help them work their issues out with him. I would often say that if Christ could come through the locked door of the Upper room, he could make his way to them in this locked place. Genuine gongs echo around the room.

I learned something about the guards while I did this ministry. They have a tough job. They pay them to keep order in a place that seems often to be on the verge of losing it. Because this was a minimum-security prison, violence didn't occur often. However, it didn't prevent the guards from throwing their weight around. For instance, we met for a while in the building where visitors came to be checked in. This meant that we were always within earshot of the guard at the front desk. This put limits on our discussion, as people were hesitant to be very open about issues. Some people didn't trust the guards.

The suspicious guards could be hard. In the front area, we met at a nice table with comfortable chairs. The guard insisted that the residents go back to their dorm area and get their plastic chairs. The nice chairs were for visitors and not for them. As I continued to volunteer at the prison, I gained the trust of the guards and I got a separate room that offered us a little more privacy. I can understand the need for control, but the guys that came to my prayer group were not the ones that would cause trouble.

Another incident showed the lack of trust the guards had. I had a resident in our group whose behavior bordered on manic. While we were talking, he gave me a piece of paper with a Greek prayer that he wrote out. He had access to an English-Greek dictionary. Well, the guard saw that he had given me a piece of paper. This broke the rules, as we were not to accept gifts or convey messages to others on the outside. The guard approached me and asked about the piece of paper. I showed it to him and, of course, the letters were Greek and thus odd and not English. He took it as a gang code. So, I had to explain to him and the shift supervisor what it meant. I eventually got the paper back and had a priest I knew translate it. Such was my interesting time in prison.

Because of the shortage in priests, the Archdiocese began a process to merge parishes. I took part on the local committee to determine the fate of Holy Trinity. Many believed the church would be closed. However, the parish remained open and joined with St. Bartholomew in Columbus, sharing resources. A positive and welcome outcome! The anvil sings a verse!

I cannot adequately describe the gift of the relationships we developed over the course of the diaconate program. As well, I can't demonstrate the changes that I experienced in myself. Studying to be a deacon offered me knowledge and truth, joy and love. It exposed me to a history of the church that I didn't know. Surely, I better understood Christ, the meaning of his life, his times, and the church he started. This education, immersion and conversion took me to a beautiful place of resonance and holiness. Of course, I didn't make this happen, but received a gift from God that brought me these insights and this discovery. Maybe I still feel like Tom and I did, that we were unworthy. Only now I understand I must seek to be worthy. Sparks.

Our ordination took place at the Cathedral of Saints Peter and Paul, an imposing structure in downtown Indianapolis. It has a front facade of Greek columns listed as Classical Revival style, built in 1907, constructed out of limestone. Upstairs is a spacious and reverent nave with statues, stations of the cross and stained-glass windows adorning the interior. The tall cross in front had two statues at its foot, Mary and Joseph. We gathered in the rectory building next door, quietly chatting, thick with anticipation.

The day in June was beautiful, warm, and breezy. We had worked for 5 years for this day. Our families and parishioners would witness the culmination of that work. The ceremony would transform us from secular workers to clergy, appointed to work in God's fields of suffering, mercy, faith, and joy. We were excited and pumped up. We came in wearing our albs and would be vested during the ceremony in new dalmatics and stoles. There would be a change, but really, the change had already begun.

As time neared, they gave us instructions. You could hear the music from outside as the large doors opened wide. It echoed through the walls. The statues sang. Someone in the back of the line yelled, "Gird your loins, men!" And we did. The anvil sang its passion in red heat and sparks, signifying the forging of a new identity in charity, faith and love.

Our wives followed us in the procession, carrying our vestments. In a solemn and poignant procession, guided by swirling organ music, we came in. The accessories of the liturgy, incense and candles, along with the clergy, made for a long procession. The bishop with miter and crosier was last. Archbishop Beuchelin could not attend the ceremony because of his health. The Assistant Bishop, Christopher Coyne, would preside.

We stood at the end of the pew and later came forward to form a row at the front of the Cathedral facing the bishop. The music became thunderous and beautiful. The incense filled space spoke of the reverence of God. For only the second time, the Archdiocese ordained a group of men as deacons. Our trip had been long but, like climbing a mountain, we reached the summit. We entered a luminal space, a transcendental space. The music, the incense, the words spoken and read, and the actions demarcated the boundary of another world.

The ceremony answered the fundamental question as we faced the bishop. Fr. Bede stated it clearly to the bishop. Those charged with training us judged us worthy of ordination to the diaconate. We then made promises to conform ourselves to Christ. As I kneeled before the bishop, he held my hands and asked if I would be obedient, respect and honor him and his successors. Later, we all laid prostrate on the hard marble before him while all in the church spoke to the saints in heaven to have mercy.

The bishop then prayed silently over each of us, holding his hands on our heads. From ages past, this is a sign of the passing on of God's care and love. The laying on of hands has blessed priests, bishops, and deacons for centuries. That sign changed us. It was a sign of love and obedience to a new way of life. I felt lucky that Brad's son Adam caught the moment for me in a picture. A priest we selected then helped us put on our new vestments. Fr. Clem helped me put on my new work clothes.

Finally, another powerful thing happened. When my turn arrived, I approached the bishop, kneeling again, as he and I held between us the Book of the Gospels. He said, "Receive the Gospel of Christ, whose herald you have become. Believe what you read, teach what you believe, and practice what you teach." Those are words have stayed with me and continue to give me spiritual blessings. Glowing sparks light the air.

We then received hugs from the bishop and all the priests and deacons. The Mass then went on to the Eucharistic celebration. We were all then given the privilege of giving communion to those present.

At the end, we walked out new men. It felt like the road rose up to meet us, the sun shone on us, and God smiled. I felt overwhelmed. I filled to bursting with pride and grace. What came to mind was Philippians (1:6) "And I am sure that he who began a good work in you will bring it to completion at the day of Jesus Christ." After the ceremony, the Columbus Mafia got pictures together with our pastor and our wives.

Silence and Sparks
Do not speak, but listen
And feel.
God's light has passed
Through us.
We need only to collect
The silence
And the sparks.

16 Men's Group

There we were, four old guys in a flat bottom fishing boat. Luckily, there were no waterfalls because I bet we would have gone over them, screaming and flailing. The crowded boat sat heavy, rocking slowly on the large lake. The shore stood half a mile away. Of the group, two claimed to be anglers, comfortable and knowledgeable in these surroundings. Two were not, a little awkward, hoping to witness a big catch. I could see little sections of blue sky among low clouds. The wind pushed the choppy water. My depth finder showed fish. They were below, but seventy-five feet below. This early September morning brought crispness to the morning air. Cool weather would soon occur. Summer was on the outs.

It took determined convincing to get the two non-fishermen into the boat. The unfamiliar experience made them uncomfortable. It felt like a pay to fish scheme. They were tourists who wanted a fishing experience. They were fine on the large houseboat with its chairs and food, its access to a toilet and books. It took persuasion to get them out here in close touch with the water and now that they had paid their fees; we had to deliver fish.

Although we had been on many men's group vacations, on houseboats, in condos and cabins, this new experience brought them to quarters snug and intimate. "It's a little more confining than I expected." One of them said. We already had experienced a disaster. The other angler, Ray, had set up his line for deep water with several hooks and plastic baits. This thing looked awesome; fish were going to go crazy over it. However, he had neglected one thing. He forgot to tie the hooked contraption onto his line. Thus, when he threw the untied bait over the side, it disappeared into the deep. So much for years of experience!

Our little boat slowly putted along, brightened by the playful sun. Several lines were in the water. The bait needed care and calculation so that it would drift into the range of deep water where the finder showed the fish to be. As we moved, a slight tension and little conversation occurred. As I had a hopeful anticipation, the depth finder assured me with several beeps. There were big fish in the lake and just below us. They met these beeps with skepticism. "What's that sound?" one asked. "It shows when it identifies a fish. See the screen here." "Really?" was the doubting response. "I'll believe it when I see the fish!"

For me, I wanted to get the bait to the fish and entice them to bite. This is the essence of fishing: finding the fish for one and then getting them to put energy into eating what you offer. Each of these steps entailed a major mystery and required needed hypothesizing. The others in the boat were skeptical. As we drifted along, nothing indicated a bite or any interest from the deep. "This is why I don't enjoy fishing. It gets boring. No offense, but this is ...slow". He pointed out unceremonially, "I don't remember you catching many fish on our trips all these years, Steve!" We had rented the smaller fishing boat to go on brief excursions. Fishing off the big boat was usually unsuccessful.

Kim brought his jet ski on this trip, and this attracted more attention than our attempts to catch dinner. Riding down the middle of the lake at full bore on the sleek and fast water motorcycle outweighed the current outing by many folds.

Well, our time dragged on. We had difficulty keeping the lines straight and deep. A couple of times they tangled up. The atmosphere in the boat grew more despondent. "Time to go back, you think? Not much happening out here." As we prepared to disengage, pull in the lines, and head back, I felt a slight tug on the line. I figured I had hit wood or rock structure. I retrieved the line and as I did so, it became clear that I had a fish! "Fish on, gentlemen!" I said brightly. Everyone paused, looking into the water for a sign. "Oh, man, this is strong." We could clearly see the rod bend in its jerking reaction to the fish. "Hey, Bob, looks like I got one!" He watched expectedly. "Keep reeling him in," said Ray. As it got closer to the surface, it probably sensed it and took a run from the boat. The line zinged off away, and I feared the fish would throw the hook and all would be lost. "What's he doing?" They asked. "He's making a run." I kept a steady pressure on the line. As it approached, maybe 15 feet away, the fish surfaced in a 3 foot jump out of the water! "Whoa!" exclaimed one of the non-fishermen. "That was cool!" Eventually, I brought the fish to the side of the boat and it showed itself to be an 18-inch striped bass. I brought it in the boat and showed it off. We took pictures and soon the jet ski appeared, looking for the big and only catch. While not enough for dinner, it would supplement the meat course. Such illustrated one of the few times that we caught a fish on a Men's Group trip. It had the markings of a legend from that point on.

In the comings and goings of life, certain occasions bring real meaning to the journey. These moments come around the corner and catch you when you aren't looking. You remember the details of the encounter, the sequence of events, and the things said and done. It arouses feelings. The experience of Men's Group has provided many such experiences for me.

We were a group of men who regularly met to discuss our issues. It acted as part support group, part awareness expanding, part confessional and part drinking buddies' group. I joined in the mid-80s. I worked for Bob Siegmann, a wonderful Jewish social worker at Quinco. He asked me if I might be interested in joining a men's group and if I could use a place to talk about issues? Why he spoke with me about this group of guys, I don't know. I guess I must have looked like I had issues. Well, I had a family and a marriage, a job, a childhood, and a mortgage. So, you could say, I had issues.

Starting around 1977, and continuing until today, this group has been meeting on a weekly basis to share their stories. Men's Group, a not so creative but straightly pragmatic title, has been the place where group members share the many incidents in their lives. We bring up, kick around, share, and dissect the good, the bad, and the neutral of our lives. As a result, we find a greater life balance. We gain feedback from others we trust and we grow comfortable sharing deeper and deeper aspects of ourselves. And of course, this comes with the chance to drink beer, not that beer drinking is necessary, but it goes with the territory of men's interior explorations. Beer is the social lubricant that perhaps loosens the tight rein we have on our vulnerability. The hammer kisses the anvil and there are manly sparks about.

Our unpredictable group has been the place where tragedy, regret, curiosity, humor and the mundane occurrences that fill everyone's lives are uncovered and shared. My grandmother's wall masks would fit right in. In group, our lives are on display more or less directly during these occasions of encounter. "Can I talk about my son again? Something happened over the weekend." "You remember last week? I was so confident in our relationship? Well, over the weekend, my girlfriend showed her true colors." "It has been hard for me. I'm glad I can talk with you guys about this." "Can I call in from my office? I am not comfortable talking from home."

Meeting together in person, except over the troubling months of Covid, has been our signature for a surprising number of decades. As several members have moved away, they have joined the group via computer and taken part remotely. Only a couple members have consistently taken part in the near entire history of the group. Several were there close to the beginning and can tell the tale.

The group started, as the legend goes, in Bloomington, created by the director of the mental health center, Dr. Carver. In the 70s, mental health centers were a fairly recent phenomenon. A new and vivid time of exploration of one's issues begun. He founded the group, if not a direct result of the tumultuous 60s, then at least an echo of the upheaval and its repercussions. In a progressive way, a group of therapists, social workers, and psychologists got together and began meeting and talking. The group focused on putting words to masculine inner experience. At first, plenty of drinking and drugging went on, complementing the open and deep sharing. While Freud opened up the inner psychological geography, the early iteration of Men's Group took the map and started walking around the place. Relationships, feelings, expression and community! All this occurred in a gathering of men, sharing, commenting, and giving narration to their stories. Could you call it courageous or did it simply allow the release from the John Wayne caricature of power in silence? Group manifested a talky enterprise, with the idea that what we discovered became grist for the communal mill. Honesty and openness prevailed. Asked to join after an interview with a couple of members, one had several sessions to decide if it fit for you. Probably because life wounds us all, most who came, stayed. And those who stayed, stayed for a long time.

After its earlier iteration in Bloomington, Indiana, the group settled in Columbus. The mental health center in Columbus brought many members to the group. That is how I joined in 1987. I found it easy to do things with men. Yes, I felt stressed at times from the kids, marriage, and work. I could use a place to talk. My many group experiences made it an easy sell.

It is always interesting to explore why a man joined the group and what kept him coming. I am a psychologist who enjoyed the camaraderie of the group. I don't think that they could identify me as a mental basket case (who really knows!). My issues were enough to bring my presence to the group and to share. This followed a lifelong habit of introspection. My skills were such as well that I enjoyed hearing stories and asking questions that furthered self-exploration. Advice was always handy.

Psychologists and social workers, engineers, business people, and entrepreneurs, we were all skilled with advanced degrees and vital work and social experiences. Probably on the political left side of center. Most members started in the 80s, though some have joined later. Several, a beloved African American member among them, have passed away.

We brought the wounds, the will and the wonder of our lives to bear on each other. In that meeting space, with our sharp intellects, our lives were open for evaluation. We also wanted to keep the ball of conversation rolling each week. We could go through minor silences, but not for long. Each of us brought our bag of stuff and had enough laundry to sort out, that infrequently did the conversation lapse into gibberish. If that happened, there were too many other needy voices that grabbed the mic. Certainly, sometimes I sat back and asked, "What the hell did I just hear?" in astonishment, sadness or just shaking my head. Rarely did anyone throw direct insults, even under the accumulated influences of mind-altering substances. No one bled to death but our collective prowess set aright any ship of folly. "I'm sorry, but that doesn't compute for me. There is something deeper going on!" The crowd had a critical eye and voiced it. I found that to be part of the allure. We were honest, intelligent, exceedingly knowledgeable and direct, but also patient and giving. "You know, I think this infatuation, if I can call it that, is going to burn you. Is she really interested? So, just be careful not to invest too much emotional capital in this relationship." This allowed one to find the voice, to gain an adequate vision of the issue, and to put the thing into a meaningful perspective. Often, one session did not solve the issue. But, if you asked for time, you got it. Gong.

As these things go, by the time I got involved, they had honed the process. A group norm had developed, and there were clear expectations. We all had a desire more or less to apply a talking cure to life's difficulties. Inherently, we mined the mental ground with our college degrees and wits. Fearlessly, we went into the dark caves of the psyche to find and eradicate the point of irritation, the conflict, or the irrational. No elephants remained in that room.

The question, "Does anyone have any work to do?" became a mantra that signified the seriousness of the undertaking. It signaled the time to share. However, varied topics came up. From your latest surgical procedure, what your daughter said to you on the phone, the status of your romantic life, or an excellent wine to have with ribs. It could be the last joke you heard, the latest and greatest yard tool (such as a flame-throwing weed killer, yes!) to the news about Covid in Indiana. Those words ushered in stories of work, children, houses, wives, and girlfriends. They allowed for the emotional spilling of a dad whose son went to war. There were stories of romantic exploits and the crash and burn that resulted when she said she was leaving. There were reports from disgruntled employees and the struggles of bosses. The significant deaths of parents, children, and colleagues came up from time to time. Sharing encompassed trips around the world, to the next state, and the many restaurants in between. We heard of a yearly sailing trip this time around Iceland or a submarine ride under the ice. The building of a miniature railroad track in the basement would impress us. Someone would share the ongoing dealings with a disabled brother. The mental health of a child or divorce might come up. It could be the internet's best short video about marble races. Probably, if a topic came up, someone had done it, been there, lived there, or flew over it last week!

One member shared, "I have to say that we are all one day closer to death. Just so you know." He shared this in a smug but real way. There was truth in it as death hovered over us guys, who were all getting old before our eyes. The youngest member was no longer young! A few old sparks!

A never-ending supply of talk centered on the relationship issues of participating men. We shared the many relationships we had with joy and angst. Differing degrees of detail and disclosure came forth given who did the reporting. The voyeuristic captivation of the sharing could leave the group spellbound. We could dedicate many months to the ongoing saga of a single relationship. The abundant wisdom of the group would apply to the problems and, over time, and the expression of many a feeling, we would find a level of resolution. The emotional intensity of the group would abate until the next ongoing issue surfaced. Then the diamond sharp wit and wisdom of the group came out. We developed a treatment plan and wrestled the life struggle to the ground.

Being men, the level of competence with tools proved great. We were experts in a variety of areas of mechanical skills. From making an expert and delicious cup of coffee, understanding the mechanics of flight, expertly using the best grills and routers, designing the ceramic parts of a diesel engine. We knew about things, how they worked and how they broke down.

A quasi-expert opinion always stood ready to be given, if not a real professional commentary, in the group. Legal issues, culinary, psychological, political, social and medical issues were all heavily debated and analyzed. Although at first, we avoided religion and politics, these too came to be accepted and explored.

Musical talent was in no short supply. Entertaining occurred on group trips where guitars and spontaneous concerts occurred. Ralph, a long-term member, and I played music on most trips and would meet and play before the group. "Hey guys, care for music? Steve and I will play ya some good old tunes." This led us to record a couple of CDs together. I had a basic recording studio in my basement in Columbus and had produced several music CD's, one for Stained Glass for instance, as well as other recordings. Ralph and I spent several months in the "studio" rehearsing and recording our favorite songs. The resultant CDs were lively and captured our skills (or lack thereof), our voices and our enthusiasm. Harmonious gongs.

As I mentioned, one simple truth faced us all. We were all getting older. As we aged, it became more frequent that medical topics came up. The prostate became probably the high organ of the body that got the most attention with secondary participation awards to knees and teeth. "Can I tell you my catheter story?" "Again?" There have been occasional scary cancer diagnoses. Other issues such as back problems, nasal issues, skin issues called for second opinions and expert medication analysis. We avoided talking seriously about dementia, for fear we may spook it and wake it up! We have shared about knee surgery and back surgery, gallbladder surgery and that bloody form of surgery having to do with the prostate. Fighting with the fact that old men trickle, we are no longer embarrassed! This latter topic has also been present on boat trips where peeing off the edge of the boat became a sport and night time pastime. Of course, Covid occupied us at length. A member once employed at Eli Lilly was greatly helpful.

Perhaps a frequent and heartwarming topic has to do with our dogs. Our dogs are significant members of our family and, of course, come up in conversation. "Hey, turn the camera on Beau so I can see him tonight." As I regularly offered my house for the group, Alex would be present and greet everyone and get lavish attention. The downside is the loss of our favorite pets. Especially here, the moral question becomes when do the medical issues and suffering outweigh the continued benefits of our furry friend's companionship and his or her quality of life? These are tough issues, especially for guys who can speak about the affection and depth of the relationship with an animal.

On animals, we have also discussed the best way to get rid of chipmunks and bats. With chipmunks, how far to take them away and is water needed to be between you and them? We have also discussed moles as the headache of any good gardener.

My son Paul, who fought as a Marine in Iraq, came up for a while in group. I talked about the fears but also voiced the pride that his military sacrifice brought. Another member's father had been a Marine during World War II, and this brought me comfort and camaraderie. Because he garnered so much attention, Paul importantly came to visit the group after he got home. That memorable session brought tears to my eyes as he brought memorabilia from the war and willingly entertained questions. "Gentlemen, here are pictures of me and my outfit at one palace in Baghdad." Silence and attention from all in attendance. "I also brought this Iraqi flag I took from one room" showing a large, dirty and torn flag. "That's cool Paul."

To counteract a prevalent stereotype of the disengaged father, issues with our children have often come up and gotten serious and heartfelt attention. We love our kids and are quick to show pictures or tell stories, both the good and the bad. Some of the greatest ongoing issues have to do with our children and our relationships with them. There are a couple of men in group who carry great pain over disengaged children. There have always been stories about my son, Thomas. Men's Group lore had Thomas doing donuts with his car in a cornfield and the time the axle on my Honda Civic broke because Thomas said he made a turn!

At one point, we shared our biographies. Here we heard of the adoption of a member as an infant. Another had lost his brother at a young age. Another had an alcoholic father. One guy's father was a medic on Iwo Jima. These presentations took up the whole evening and included maps or paraphernalia to support the narrative. The histories were told with great angst and, of course, biting humor. "Here is my wedding picture. I am the long-haired one in the brown 70s suit. I could probably get maybe one arm in the thing today!" Our stories showed the large fund of experience in the group: familial, marital, job related and educational. With pictures of self as a young person, we could see each other in a different light. This gave us a lens through which to see a person and to share early personal stories. These sessions were well worth the cost of admission.

Let me share for me a difficult episode. For the longest time, there would come a call for a book to be written. The title would be like, Two Thousand Thursdays. This call would surface when a significant occasion happened or after we engaged in a memorable exchange. A powerful memory could surface of past group exploits and lead to the call for a book. After hearing this over several years, I suggested I would like to undertake to write such a book. Discussion ensued, but the conversation went elsewhere. So, I put together an outline that structured several chapters covering what the group meant to me. I brought this to the group with an introductory chapter to show my serious and capable intent.

I didn't realize how vulnerable this made me. It hit me especially hard. Several members pointed out that the group had rested on principles of confidentiality. That trust pointed to respect for each other and our stories. To make these public violated that trust. Some consulted their wives, who voiced opposition. A couple members voiced discomfort with what I would share and the general editorial policy of the writing. The upshot of the discussion was a decision that no book should be written, as we could not broadcast the details of the group experience. There were some more positive suggestions, but this all left me hurt by the comments and rebuff. I took some time off, didn't attend for a while, and didn't think I would continue.

The response of the group brought up for me an array of feelings. One thing I saw was the high importance of the confidentiality of the group. While many of us focused on others in our jobs, the group norm felt awfully self-focused and protective. While we questioned and supported in the group, a strong boundary kept any of that from reaching the outside. As well, it seemed we did not generously deal with each other outside of the group. Occasionally, we helped each other move, got together for an occasional significant birthday, played golf, or we went on a trip together. Otherwise, these caring men had little interaction between groups. Perhaps the group didn't see outreach as relevant to the group or as a value. The group felt biased, like therapy, to avoid outside entanglements.

A larger area of resentment arose in my disappointment. For the longest time, the group shunned topics of religion and politics. We eventually relaxed these restrictions, despite the danger. The group, however, is more uniform politically and much less so religiously. Talking about my religious journey became important for me because my spiritual path had brought me to a powerful sense of my religious identity, informed by my diaconal experiences. But I have felt a clear inhibition to talk about my religious journey. Group has allowed little of this religious sort of discussion. Common responses are, "I am uncomfortable talking about religion!" or "Religion doesn't matter to me, so I have little interest." I realized I felt oddly out of balance with the group. This brought me to a conflict that I continue to sit with. The group was a valuable experience, but it had limitations for me. A part of me felt closed off and definitely not fed by the group. Eventually, I attended again, but really with lower expectations. My experience took me beyond the accepted norm of the group. Slow sparks.

Let me share an outside gathering that has regularly taken place over the years- Christmas dinner in Bloomington. It starts at the Irish Lion with a yard of beer, then moves to the Uptown Café in Bloomington. There would be the perfunctory picture of smiling faces holding up a beer or glass of wine. "Hey waitress, could you take our picture? Thanks" "Guys, lean in here!" Long-lost members would cavalierly show up. It had a feeling of good will and sense of a family reunion. The Christmas lights of the Courthouse circle were always beautiful. The small shops around the circle lit up the night, and a joyous time of light and warmth would ensue. During the Christmas season, they string lights from the courthouse to the buildings across the street. Going to a Men's Group dinner at night when the lights were on created a beautiful canopy of light. Sometimes falling snow would leave little noisy shoe prints on the sidewalks. There would be a whiteness of color on the sidewalk, a little chill in the air, but a warm heart full of Christmas camaraderie.

Until Covid hit, we did a group trip in early fall. Several of the most pleasurable ones were when we rented a houseboat and spent a week tooling around Patoka Lake. The fishing could be lousy because we went in September, but being on the water always made it a treat. The man in the group with sailing experience would captain the boat and tie us down in a cove for the evening. "I'm going to bring us about settling us in that cove over there. I need someone to get the ropes ready and jump ashore to connect us to that tree over there. See that rock? Maybe we can tie a rope around it." Others would bring great food. "We are having steaks for tonight, then my pulled pork. It has been cooking in my oven for quite a while. You will like the sauce, a little tart but spicey!" Of course, we had beer and wine, with the latter paired to the food by our personal sommelier. "I have brought several good bottles and a supply of everyday wines. This Sauvignon will do well with the steaks." The trip down to the lake would be fun as a group. The boat story at the beginning of this chapter came from one of those houseboat trips. It may have also been the trip where a lightning storm caught two members on the other side of the lake. We couldn't decide who would tell their spouses of their sudden deaths?

Another wonderful trip brought us to a Chautauqua village near Cleveland, Ohio, that a member had been to as a child, I believe. We rented a house. The community had a diversity of activities that made the week interesting and varied. A guest religious lecturer spoke for the week (who didn't like Catholics). In the large theater in the town, we saw Carrie Newcomer, a wonderful folksinger from Indiana one night. We all learned how to play shuffleboard, which we practiced as an adjunct to our getting old. The fishing off the dock in Lake Erie yielded several fish. We even caught a fairly large Walleye that we cooked up for dinner! Another high point of the trip occurred when we rented Laser sailboats we took out on the lake.

Not everyone, however, has stuck with the group. Several have dropped out due to work changes or moves. Some have come back after a hiatus. We have had a person taste and test the group and just stay away, probably thinking us crazy and dangerous. Some have left for political reasons.

Probably all of those who have been with us for a while have left their mark on the corpus of group lore. Mention of a certain log by a lake in Indiana will bring a chuckle to group members. A defrocked therapist will also bring an agreeable head nod. The story of an exploding house also brings to mind a tragic story that touched the group.

However, a fair list of the membership has carried on week after week, maintaining a long running legacy of care, intimacy, and humor. We have heard jokes and stories that clothe the inherent openings and closings in our lives. The tales that we tell are all true and feature a chorus of ideas and feelings, some relevant or not. These tales are told through male social expectations and trappings, with expert political commentary, well-intentioned cultural bias, honed and professional psychological technique, and all kinds of attempts to make sense of baffling situations. Knowledgeable sparks!

This chapter represents my attempt to acknowledge the profound effect the group has had on me. But also, I have sought to write in such a way as to respect the privacy and boundaries of the group. The full story of the group lives in the hearts and minds of those in attendance, and I can only describe it as an authentic response to the unspoken life most men pursue.

This group of men makes up a circus of many acts, lion taming and plate balancing. There are moments of boredom and moments of awe-struck revelation. We have boring stories of which we can predict the ending before it starts. I can only hint at the shared lore of the group here. The stories, like wonderful wine, have been dark, bright, heavy and significantly intoxicating as to allow a great sigh of relief that the police or undertakers were not called!

During Covid and with long distance group members, we resorted to meeting via teleconference. This form cut down on the drinking and the pizza. But it allowed us to see each other clearly. Especially since several people have moved from Indiana and also live away from Columbus, the remote process of the group is attractive. It helped as well that we had an expert in the group who answered our Covid questions.

For me, when I joined in my late thirties, I felt moderately skilled at "adulting". Exploring my role as "man" and what it cost was useful to me. I also felt the group's acceptance and a lack of judgment. Over these many weekly meetings, Christmas dinners, and houseboat trips, I have grown close to these guys. For me, opening up doesn't happen quickly. Because we would meet in the intimacy of someone's home, it is hard to be hidden and under the radar. Eventually, someone will ask pointed questions, "How are you really doing?" and we will not take a socially skilled rebuff as truth, but dig further. Socrates would have liked the process and the questions. But maybe the range of areas touched on not quite up to his comfort.

While our lives continue, the group narrates them with its presence, stories, and lively discussions. Individuals come and are greeted as friends, not unlike that of "Cheers", where everybody knows your name. Group offers a place at the table and a comfortable chair to let down and recall the battle wounds of the week. At least we can have a beer or a glass of wine and practice the lost art of listening to friends we have shared with and sometimes even care about!

The group really has longevity. The glue that holds it together defies clear understanding. Maybe the familiarity we have for each other holds the fabric together. Once you hear a person's life story and they listen to yours, it is hard to walk away, especially with the presence of beer, chocolate, chips and pizza. Members of the group mysteriously come together with an openness and eagerness to be present to each other. The conversations are civil and show respect and interest. We are like a stew, with marinating chunks of slide rule and psychological theory, group process, financial acumen and legal commentary. We bring tech skills and international awareness. Group can fix almost anything, or at least offer a running start. We get you into second gear! The understanding of life's problems, from moms and children to roofs and prostates, emerges through our direct testimony and experience. The motivation focuses on helping, clarifying, and supporting. No one leaves without a goody bag of ideas and comments with which to engage the next day.

The secret medicine is that, over the years, we have been present to each other. We each attentively give a part of ourselves to the others during the group. I see this as a powerful process of becoming a real person with a genuine presence. Maybe that is my takeaway from the group. I have become more genuine by finding my place in the large, airy three dimensions of the group.

There have been tensions, conflicts and drama, like the time our beloved African-American member felt affronted by another member, the time on a group trip where tension over workloads surfaced, or my book drama. These did not interrupt the general feeling of respect that we have for each other. We disagree, but in the end, we try to understand and work out a benevolent resolution. Maybe we realize we are only a sounding board, a place to talk, a space to share and practice. We are in the Greek chorus, voicing the principal theme and shadowing the main character. We bring an education in therapy and for those who did not do it professionally, we offer an honorary degree. Group gives us a place to talk, listen, and to hear ourselves try on solutions that we may later employ in the real world.

Group has been successful because we are bright, diverse, interesting, and generally caring people. In God's wisdom, we all unexpectedly shared the area of southern Indiana as home and came together in this unique meeting of men. Men's Group has allowed us to supportively interact with each other and to take in the wisdom of friends whom we trust. Our story tells of a group of men who, over the years, unusually, honestly, and deeply have shared themselves. Life has done its thing and moved through our relationships, bodies and minds and given us the opportunity to discover each other. We are a celebration of men, developing bonds of affection and meaning in the long course of years. Group is a small monument to a group of men who have long been present to each other's pain, joy, humor, and issues. This has been an important part of my life. Let me leave you with my poem about the group.

A Band of Brothers, to Men's Group

A band of brothers are we, a chosen family, an easy company
We tend together, now comfortable with each other, feeling open, for as 30 years go, so go trust in friendship and union
But we can also be misguided and wayward, soft and hard, loving and not
Not one of us is the better and all the worse at times
Our dreams and pains, our complicated geography of relationships which are not to be sorted out without blood and Scotch, we bring to group
We meet, and over time, hardships, beer, and frustrations, we open our lives
We give an opening to others whom we trust with our secrets and our expedient liabilities
We do not know nor do we strive to understand completely our soul's needs
It is enough to show up and be counted in this week's lottery of issues
We are but there to see what can come from a group of men brilliant and fragile, seeking what no one knows and fewer can articulate
Our stories resonate with our common bearing on this life of love and work and the manly intensity that has to do with our hand's decisions
Sharing soul may meet with a tear or a joke and not one of us can predict with any degree of collegiate accuracy which way the zeitgeist will sway
We have been in both spheres of discussion
One says that this is a life work solidified by our friends' reactions
The other speaks to the need for a hook to oust the faking perpetrator, wasting our time and freedom
To be a man is no clear trip these days
There are many roads and many flights to catch whose destinations are not reported until on board and with bags in the overhead
Blind leading the blind, mice in charge of mice, will not suffice to answer the heated questions
But we have shot our darts close to the target and at least have made it stick in the wall
We have taken our collective wisdom, earned by our trips across the ocean and down the Mississippi, across the street and across the table
Our intuition is not a woman's prerogative

We have found the truth in ways that Sherlock Holmes would bargain and in ways that a politician would commit grand larceny to achieve
We acknowledge this life is better when shared and talked about
It is made less costly by meeting in the context of sharp minds remembering their dull moments
We attach weight to another's troubles in the hopes of finding a solution if one is asked for or at least visible
We do offer more than nothing for hard earned testimony
We do not take lightly membership in our troupe of would-be actors who except for luck, have been gainfully employed and gainfully loved
We accept that these are our peers, these are our equals, these are men who have been in the fight, in the movement, in the wars, and in the corner office
They have seen the world and have the scars to prove it, at least that is what they say
They have lived the scene, and they have read the script they were given and it fits most of the time
They offer their gut compasses and their childhood impressions and their ideas deeply rooted in their revealed angst
I cannot envision myself without my men and their counsel and challenge
Love is probably not the right thing to call it, nor is it a malevolence of will
In group, there is an edge upon which we stand, like on an overhang twenty stories up
You are on your own until there is blood, at which point there are more than enough medicinal ointments brought out of our bags to kill a horse in stride
We mean only to maim but not make it fatal
This comes on the back of respect like a bronco: jump on or get out the way
We are not insensitive nor overly committed
We walk a tightrope line, the life allowed to men, to be present and capable of the most heroic acts
But then as well, in the same breath, we allow to face dispassionately the crisis knell of a person we dare to call in our better moments, our friend
We will not allow one to fall too far without a net but we also will not say who brought the net or in what drawer it is hidden
And this dance of options, that is group, this carousel of arguments, that is group, this agreement to give up your first born, that is group, this is what has led me to this point
I have found myself reflected in the musings of group more than I care to note

I have heard my name; I have seen my body shadow; I have lived out the boundaries that bind my soul in this group and I do not regret its impact on my life
It is in my bones as I now live and the strength of my bones is only the harder because of it
I shall the worse at some point be
But that will be my doing
For the lessons of group, this band of brothers, shall persist and follow me, even beyond this life.

17 Philadelphia, Adieu

I looked at them. "Come on, you punks! You can't get me. You guys are sooo weak. Wusses, you guys are wusses." The 12-year-olds were getting tall. Tony had a hint of facial hair on his lip. The main event took place on the rug over the living room floor. Along the walls, the builders had inserted a lighter, decorative plank of wood. It spoke to beautiful floors years ago, before the house had aged with children. Arched columns separated the living room and dining room. Being older, I sat on my knees, almost as tall as the two younger ones. This comprised the annual "try to beat Stevie" wrestling match. "We're gonna knock you down. You are nothing but a skinny wimp." Tony said. "Oh, yeah? Big talk, little man, big talk!" I grabbed him by the arm and pushed him away. Nicky came at me full on and I swiped him with my forearm. He grabbed it and held on. He pushed himself against me while standing, his shoulder on my chin. Tony circled around and got on my back. He grabbed my neck so I could hardly breathe. I moved my torso, which usually shook them off. But not today. They were stronger today. "Pull Nicky!" Tony said. I broke my right arm free, and I grabbed his shirt from behind and pulled him off me. He tumbled onto the couch. "Hey," he said, "that wasn't fair." "Too bad, loser!" He got up and approached again. Looking a little angry, he went for my arm and bent it back. I turned to keep it from bending too far. Then I lost my balance. Like in slow motion, I tried to catch myself. I tried to move my knee to hold myself up. But the force of Nicky on my arm was too much. There were several hard-earned grunts. Eventually, after watching the ceiling pass over my eyes, I fell on my back. Tony escaped being pinned under me and moved to the side. Nicky laid on top of me. On the rug, all our heads were close together and I could feel hot breath on my cheek. "Yeah, yeah, we won. Stevie is a loser; Stevie is a loser!" I moved and let Tony get up, who then triumphantly pounded his fist in the air. Nicky got up and said he hurt his back, but he smiled about it. It didn't hurt that much. I got back up and said, "You guys are too much for me. You won." I hung my head in mock failure. "We won, we won!' They said it together as mom came out of the kitchen with a plate of food. "Time for dinner, you boys."

In this chapter, I would like to share some of the memorable stories of my brothers. They are a big part of my story, for they have been present for many of the earlier experiences that I went through. We were brothers and shared that special bond accorded to male siblings. They were younger than me. But as we have spoken over the years, growing up wasn't a simple task for either of them. Tony has said that he didn't know our father very well. He died when they were 15. They missed out on the 4 years I had as the only child while we lived in Connecticut. They also lived in Philly with our mom for years longer than I did.

My earliest recollection is being in the same toddler bed with them. This must have been in Bridgeport. I must have been small because I could stand up in the bed and hold on to the rails.

I don't have any cute stories about how I reacted when they were born. No memories or pictures exist of my mom being pregnant. Frankly, I felt good with them joining the family. Maybe being an only child for 4 years left me with an openness to others to join the party.

Being twins, they were small when they were born. Nicky was first, 4 minutes ahead of Tony. The doctors thought that Nicky may have had the umbilical cord around his neck, which starved him for oxygen. This explained some of his peculiarities. Nicky had a mole on his wrist, the only identifying mark between them. They were identical twins. To make it worst, for a number of years, mom dressed them the same. They had these pretty white sweaters they wore in Connecticut in an iconic pose. Another early memory concerned them playing in the dirt in Fairfield, maybe next to each other with identical shovels and clothes. It wasn't until several years later that Nicky got glasses.

Because they were five years younger, we had different friends and were into different things. Being older put me as the pioneer but the actual difference concerned the fact, they had each other, and I played more on my own. Now don't get me wrong, we lived in the same house and we played together. I have already pointed out several common incidents we experienced. They were always around and underfoot. Maybe I felt close to them because we were survivors of the same crap. We were comrades in arms. Maybe we rooted for the same losing teams. (Ah, Philadelphia!) Perhaps, we were all males in a world that had a lot of women that dominated it. I'm not sure. They were my brothers and over the course of many years, they have been in the same scenes. We have shared dialogue and taken big roles. When it comes down to it, they are part of my family of origin and hold a close place in my heart. If not directly, they have been aware of all that has happened to me.

At my grandmother's house, my brothers and I did things together. We didn't share school experiences, but at dinner and watching TV, going places in the car, they were present. For instance, a glorious memory I have is of the abundant Halloweens at the Howard Street house!

I thought of them as a unit, probably until they became teenagers. Certainly, since that time, they are different because Tony ventured out while Nick stayed and lived with mom. This seemed to be ok, for it wasn't until the latter years, the 2000s, that problems really began. More about that in a moment.

According to Tony, he didn't enjoy being at grand mom's house. "They didn't tell us anything and Dad wasn't around. I felt ignored. I also had a feeling that they did not welcome men." Tony confided in me. He said he had sleepless nights there. From his view, Aunt Joyce had a kind attitude, while Aunt Renee could be volatile and violent. He didn't think that Aunt Tonia liked us living with them. She could be hard on Nick from Tony's view.

Because of my age, I attended a different school than they did. Tony recalls, "One time in elementary school, they accused me of stealing a pencil. Aunt Joyce said that she would come to my school and paddle me in front of the class. On a frightening day, I remember seeing her through the door window of his classroom." He didn't get spanked in public, but he still felt the anxiety.

I knew little about Nick's educational experiences. I always thought it strange that he didn't get tested or placed in remedial classes. It is perfectly possible that it happened and I didn't know. Perhaps his level of difficulty did not warrant a school intervention. However, even at an older age, with the issues becoming more volatile and pronounced, my mother did not seek any kind of professional help.

Nicky grew up as a part of the neighborhood crowd on Dyre Street, although again, he had weird idiosyncrasies. He would be the one who made a comment out of place or hard to interpret. I recall one such comment and I am not sure why this stands out in my mind. There were several of us together on the porch at Dyre Street engaged in a fantasy play. Several of us were police detectives and others were witnesses to a crime. We were strategizing about how to go about the crime scene. I played one inspector and asked the group to check out this or that. Nick made the comment that he would "Spectate the house." The statement makes a certain sense, but his phrasing seemed a little out of the normal. He made many such comments. His physical awkwardness also seemed to be an issue. He had less speed and agility than Tony, even though they were twins. While not an issue, it put him behind in the culture of the kids on the block.

A great memory growing up, we discovered a comedy troupe called Firesign Theater. They had several records of absurd stories and skits. A man, for instance, goes in a time machine and visits ancient Greece. Coming back as proof, he says, "Look, I brought back this grape!" We would all recall portions of their narratives. Nick liked especially the one about Nick Danger, private eye. He would often close his letters with "Love, peace and Rocky Rococo," a Firesign character and Nick Danger's nemesis.

While I am on the subject, Tony talked to me about high school. "I went to a technical high school and developed skills, like drafting. I also played as the star quarterback. After a wonderful season in 10th grade, the gym teacher bought us all a Kentucky Fried Chicken lunch! I also set the school record for making baskets at basketball. I made 16 baskets in 30 seconds! Now, the Boy scouts were also important for me. My scoutmaster was a hero. We did a lot of camping. Dad was gone. You left for college." He also worked at Mom's restaurant. However, like me, Tony went to the Community College of Philadelphia, at first for drafting. He then moved to a program preparing for architectural school. He stopped after a couple of years, as he sadly felt he didn't have the discipline to succeed.

Nick graduated high school, but he didn't pursue anything further. I don't think that he liked to read books. He had a "lazy eye" growing up and had to have a patch over one eye for a while. Nick wore glasses since I could remember. He didn't like them.

I am not sure when, but after working at Mom's restaurant, he took a job at a magazine distributor. He worked there for 20 years. This would be the most stable period in his life. He had season tickets to the Eagles. He hung out with good friends from school. During this time, he developed a love for music, jazz included. He knew a lot about jazz. However, one day, he had an accident at the job. Big conveyors sorted and bound the magazines. He lost an inch long tip of his thumb, reaching for a bundle. This trauma added to his already nervous disposition. He went to the hospital, had surgery. Afterward, the stub of a nail on the thumb continued to grow weirdly. Interestingly, he got a nice settlement that he used in part to have plastic surgery on his nose. He got a Michael Jackson like nose. I never talked with him about it, but he gave up on his Greek heritage by getting rid of his rather large Greek nose. I don't think it changed his social life!

Nick also got assigned after the accident to a lower job in the maintenance department. This made it easier for him. He relished the opportunity to go around and converse with everyone in the building. This became something loved to do. He would talk to anyone about anything and had a friendly disposition. Nick had strong opinions, however, that were not exactly grounded in facts. He didn't like Nixon and complained often about "that bum!" He knew what he knew and believed what he believed. However, he was quick to say hello. He had an innocence about him. It could be embarrassing for me when he greeted a stranger on the street. "This is my brother, Steve. He's a psychologist." The company eventually moved out of the city and he didn't work again. This began his deterioration, I think.

Another story about Nicky and work showed that he applied for a job in New Jersey. He got the job and prepared to move. He had a license, but he didn't own a car. The plan fell apart, however, when our mom called up the employer and told them that her son could not take the job because of his disability. She protected him but did not empower him. This would not be good in the long run.

In our neighborhood on Bridge Street, my father frequented a bar down the street. In that block, however, lived a disabled man who would walk the block and wave and talk to you. He would walk awkwardly down the block with a large jaunting gait and wave and say hello. My brother Nicky had that role for our block. The city can tolerate a lot of that eccentric behavior.

My interaction with Nick over time involved the yearly or biyearly visits we made to Philly. My kids knew my brothers and my mother. Tony had a great sense of humor and had good relationships with my kids. "Woah, Paul. You are getting tall. You can probably dunk over your dad. I want to see that-he deserves it!" Nicky awkwardly tried too hard. Our kids also knew my aunts and Yia Yia from these visits. They did not visit us. None came to our wedding, but we visited the east on several occasions. We visited Renee down on the shore. Our kids remember she had a stable of dogs that she bred. We would visit Aunt Joyce. At one time, Thomas tried to pet her dog under the couch and got bit. We would visit Tonia. I wanted my kids to know my family.

We had a significant visit with my family in Philly after Paul was born. Tony, Nick and my mom drove back with us for a long weekend. My mom drove her big Chevy. We had the green Datsun. There was a harrowing part of the trip. In the mountains of Virginia, at night in the rain, I let my brother Nick drive the car. "It's a four speed, Nick, a stick. Can you drive one?" "Sure, a friend of mine has one." Little Paul was asleep in the back seat. We had stopped to find gas, which was a difficulty as there was a gas crisis going on. After getting gas, Nick drove. His shifting was not good. I should have done something right then and there. I recall coming down a hillside. The road had many turns. "Nick, watch what you're doing!" "I'm ok, Steve." We were on the white line several times. "Nick, I need to drive. Woah!" as he over corrected. He downshifted for no reason. The engine whined. "Put it in 4th Nick!" We got to flat ground, and I convinced him to pull over. Paul slept through it all.

After arriving in Tennessee in one piece, we showed them around Nashville. Toward the end of the visit, Tony said, "Steve, I can't go back. It is a bad place for me. Mom is working a lot. Nick the Greek is around and sometimes they don't get along, just like with dad. It's a depressing place. Can I stay here?" "What about Nick? You ok leaving him?" "He's got his friends. He drives for the restaurant. I need a break from there." We said yes. Nick and Mom drove back to Philly without him. I think mom wasn't happy about it. Tony seemed depressed and not in good spirits. So, he stayed with us. It worked out because we had a job as house parents and Tony stayed in our apartment. Eventually, Rochelle told him he needed to find a job, and he started looking.

Because of his technical background, he got a job with a land developer in Nashville. The town was growing tremendously, and Tony's surveying and drafting skills usefully paid off. He eventually got an apartment near us and met a woman in the complex named Ruth. They hit it off and later married. They continue to live in Nashville. He adopted Ruth's kids and they are now grown up and have kids of their own. He is the proud and well-loved grandfather of the clan.

After we moved to Indiana, we would travel to Kentucky to a place called Mammoth Cave. We would meet Tony and Ruth, who would drive up. Amber and Erik and our kids would play at the park and we would visit. We would have lunch together. I always enjoyed seeing them. We went to the cave at least once.

Not living in Philly, I was at a disadvantage. Mom didn't share much. Aunt Tonia, one time, called me with terrible news. Mom tried to cross Frankford, and a woman hit her, claiming that she couldn't see because of the sun. The woman did not have any insurance. They took Mom to the hospital via ambulance. She had broken several ribs and bones. One side of her took the brunt of the injury. We visited the hospital to see her and made a couple of visits to her rehab center, where she stayed for several weeks before coming back home. I installed a porta-potty in the dining room so she didn't have to go upstairs all the time, but she refused to use it. She could be stubborn, but also strong and independent.

While in the hospital and on pain medication, we visited with her, where she talked candidly about her past. I learned about the wrestlers who would come to Bogota. She spoke that day in a positive, smiling, and dreamy manner. She spoke about her giddiness with them, sounding infatuated with them. I had not seen that side of her before.

The hassle of her recuperation involved Nicky being home by himself. Calling frequently, "Hey mom, when are you coming home? How long are they gonna keep you?" "Nicky, I am in rehab because of the accident." "I know that." "It will be a while longer, dear. I will send you some money, ok?" He didn't live well by himself. "Nicky, I will get out when the doctors say I can leave. Maybe soon." "Steve," she told me, "he annoys me. He can't do anything by himself!" They had a codependent relationship, probably not good for either of them.

After he stopped working, Nick became more emotionally unstable as time went on. He would be almost echolalic. For instance, I might say, "Mom, how are you doing with the house?" He would say from another room, "How are you doing, mom, with the house?" "Nicky be quiet, stop talking." From the other room, sarcastically "Nicky be quiet, stop talking." He might not repeat the entire sentence, but a part of it. He also showed signs of being aggressive toward others. Tony mentioned that he and Nicky had a fight during a visit. Mom took a more passive role with him and did not challenge him. This did not look like her response to our father, whom she readily engaged in loud yelling matches. She probably lived in a bind with Nicky. "Steve, I don't know what to do with Nicky. He can't live on his own. But he gets so angry. He yells and scares me." "I am sorry to hear that, mom." I would call him on it when I visited, as he made me angry with how he treated her. "Nick, you have to be more respectful. She is your mom and provides for you." He would loudly retort, "Oh yeah? What do you know? You don't even live here. You don't know, you don't know what it's like!" He would storm off, leave the house, and not come back for hours. He had a rigidity and did not flexibly deal with conflict or tension. "See Steve." Mom would say, "This is what I have to put with."

A different side of him came out regarding the cats in the neighborhood. Nick took it as his mission and his duty to feed all the cats he could. This, of course, brought more cats around. The cost of food and milk must have been high. They lived on a fixed income. As well, stray cats would bite them. This happened several times. He and mom went to the ER because of serious cat bites and the prospect of being infected by Rabies.

As another sign of his unusualness, Nick would sit around the front stoop. He would often just sit or sweep up. He took pride in sweeping the sidewalk in front of the little block of houses. Sadly, he noted people would come by and hit him or try to trip him. However, also around the steps, one would find many crosses made of twigs crossed at the midpoints. It showed an interesting spirituality.

The Phillies won the World Series in 2008. Nick sent me pictures of the event. However, he took them the day after the parade and showed an empty street. He also went to the ballpark and sent me a picture of the empty field!

In a more serious vein, at one point, he talked about killing himself. This seemed serious, and I took him to a mental health center. I made the appointment. After I spoke with an intake person, Nicky went in. He denied any suicidal ideation or even saying anything about it. Rather, he noted he came to the interview because he needed a job! They did, however, set him up with a therapist. This went on for several years. He would tell me what his therapist told him. He had a female therapist for a while, but he came on to her and she felt uncomfortable and transferred him to a male. I spoke with the therapist from time to time, hoping he might wind up in a group home, or at least on anti-depressant medication. Our aging mom couldn't be expected to take care of him forever. He received individual therapy in a hit-or-miss style. He would miss an appointment, then randomly stop in for an appointment.

I took him to several places to fill out job applications. He had difficulty if the questions were on a computer screen. Katy, our friend from Columbus, came with us once and took him around for several interviews. But to no avail.

The next big event that happened would upend all our lives. I got a call from Tony one day. "Hey, Steve, you got to call Mom. She has something to tell you." "Like what?" "You gotta call her," he insisted. "Tony, alright, what is it about?" "No, she has to tell you. Call her up and ask her about her news." "Well, ok. But should I be worried? Is something wrong?" "Just call her up!"

So, I did. "Hey, mom how are you?" "Oh, Steve, I'm fine. How are you? How's Rochelle and the kids?" "They're fine, Mom. Everybody is fine. Tony called me and told me to call you. He didn't say what. Are you ok?" "Yes, dear, I'm fine." A pause. "Everything is fine." "Well, ok, glad to hear it. But he said there was something." "We are all fine, Steve."

"Hey, Tony, she didn't say anything! What's the deal? She said that she is fine." "Well," a long pause, "I heard from a relative today. When they were in South America, a bad thing happened to Mom. She was raped." "Shit!" "And she had a child." Whoa, I couldn't believe it. "That child was Aunt Tonia!" "Huh? Wait a minute. You are going too fast. Mom was sexually abused and had a child." "Yeah." "And what now?" "The child she had was Aunt Tonia." I had to think for a second. This seriously upset the world I knew. I calculated the changes. "So, she isn't our aunt, but she is our... half-sister?" "Correct!" "Woah, how did you find this out?" "Not going to say. A family person. Call mom up. I already talked to her." "Is Tonia aware of all this?" "She is now." A wave of pressure overcame me. I felt thrown into an emotional state, sudden and shaking, a sad realization that moves the cogs of history a couple of degrees to the north. "All right. That's unbelievable! Thanks. I'll call her again." I hung up.

Sitting for a brief period, I let the thing roll over me. It bounced around the room a little. I concluded this news was unbelievable. This weird family got several notches weirder. But I had to talk with my mom. So, I called again.

"Mom, I talked with Tony and he told me what happened to you in South America." I felt very uncomfortable. She hesitated and vaguely said,

"Yes, Steve, well..." This opened a space where she could say what happened. But she had kept this secret her whole life, so avoiding it now became automatic. I felt sorrow and maybe a little anger. "Mom, I'm... sorry, really sorry." "It's ok, Steve, it's ok." "Alright." I succumbed to the silence and let it reign over us. Our relationship hadn't been that close. I could formally describe it as "nice". I had moved on from the family to an extent. But this instigated my empathy. I lived 500 miles away, and she felt unreachable. More silence. "I'll talk to you later, mom. See ya." "Bye dear." Sad sparks.

And so began a midlife correction. Adjustments had to be made. Realizations had to be thought through and understood. New relationships had to be forged apart from the old ones. I felt awkward and uneasy. The anti-masculine sense we had from grandmom's made sense, however, with this information.

Tonia, now my half-sister, took it hard. She said she was angry and sad. She and mom didn't talk for a while. It must have been a difficult thing to even think about, let alone to deal with emotionally. What you thought was the reality of your life proved to be a lie and a significant one. Your relationships were not based on fact. A lifelong cover up had occurred. Had mom died after being hit by that car, she would have taken the truth to her grave and Tonia would not be aware of it.

Things got worse after this. Mom could not keep up with the house. The place needed lots of repair. At one point, my kids went over to Philly and worked on the steps as well as did several inside repairs. The floors were in awful shape. The ceiling plaster in Nick's room and Mom's room had come down in large patches. On the outside, the front façade had serious water damage, the window sills were rotting. The front door didn't shut completely. In the back, the big basement door badly leaked and water often collecting in the basement. The old house barely functioned. I had gone several times along with Tony to fix things. This made it difficult living in Indiana. And although we got things done, a never-ending list of things needed to be fixed. My mother lived on a fixed income and Nick didn't help much. The money from my father's death evaporated quickly and there were even bills after she closed the restaurant. Nick had money after his accident at work, but it dwindled quickly. This became a source of tension, as he believed Tonia took his money. He didn't pay for everyday expenses, and certainly not regularly. Their system of living seemed dysfunctional. His relationship with mom deteriorated after the revelations of the past. He felt angry and did not believe that Tonia was his half-sister. This created more animosity towards her.

I would receive rambling letters where he complained about Tonia. He treated Tonia with contempt and laid on her any problem he had. I bought him several cell phones. He would lose the charger or the phone or forget how to hook it up. He blamed these problems on Tonia. If he misplaced a jacket, he thought, Tonia came and stole it. Their relationship was tense as she didn't like Nick for how he treated mom and for his dependence. She attributed to him greater skill and more manipulative scheming than, in fact, was probably the case. Also, after the revelations came to light, she took a renewed and deeper interest in mom's life. Her relationship went from a sister to a daughter.

We had been talking for a while about getting mom out of the house. She could come to live with us in Indiana, live with Tony or Tonia. After hesitating for a long time, she seemed to soften as Nick became more aggressive and emotionally unstable. She stayed with Tony for a while.

We finally convinced her to come out to stay with us. We talked about coming out for a couple of weeks just to see how it would be and to get away from Nick for a little while. All my kids were gone to college and beyond. We painted Catherine's old room in what we thought would be attractive colors for mom. She came and stayed briefly. It proved difficult for her because Nick called her every day with complaints and made her feel guilty. He cried on the phone. "Mom, I can't do this by myself! You need to come home! You need to come home." We hoped she would feel more relaxed and comfortable. However, she insisted on going back home. With our schedules we couldn't drive back, so we got her a plane ticket, and I drove her to the airport.

I have to say that the trip to the airport became strange and disquieting. The airport in Indianapolis entailed a 40-minute drive. I felt disappointed at her leaving but had resigned myself to it. However, while we drove, she became almost paranoid. "Where are you taking me? You're not going to the airport." "Mom, we are going to the Indianapolis International Airport." I tried my best to reassure her. Around this time, signs for the airport appeared, so she calmed down. I had not seen this agitated reaction from her before. Perhaps it reflected old trauma.

Well, after her trip back home, Tonia finally convinced her she should move in with her. And she accepted. At first, this felt like welcome news for all of us, as this meant she didn't need to continue to maintain a house. However, this opened up another problem. What would happen to Nick? I thought Nick could stay in the house and, with support, make it work. He might get aid for food and have enough support to pay the minimal taxes and costs to keep up the house. But this would not be the plan.

After mom moved to Tonia's, Tonia decided they would sell the house. Tonia knew a person who bought and sold houses and she planned for him to buy the house for probably a very reasonable amount. She did not put it on the market, but sold privately. I realized Tonia felt in charge and would communicate or consult after the fact. This strained the relationship between her, Tony, and I. For the next several months, in reaction, I admit, I said things that were ugly and insensitive. I saw her as selfish and controlling. I soon got labeled as "evil".

For me, a tough point occurred when Tonia thought Nick could live on the street. She knew a minister who ran a homeless shelter in North Philly. She apparently supported his ministry. The shelter took in many homeless each night. She reasoned Nick could go there and find shelter. Basically, to my ears, she said that my brother could be homeless and fend for himself on the streets of Philadelphia. This simply outraged me. The resulting concession allowed Nick to stay in the house for a month before the sale went through.

I felt surprisingly sad as well that they would sell the house. It had been a home to our family. This brought up old feelings for me. I felt bad for Nick as well. The house was what he knew.

I asked about the things that were still in the house, such as a Greek doll I got as a kid, my old film developing equipment, or the crabbing net my father and I had used. Tonia said that if I wanted it, I could come and get it before the house sold. I quickly arranged a trip to Philly and recovered several things that had value to me, including my father's wooden tool box. In the meantime, Nick somehow lost all the important writings he had accumulated over the years.

While Nick was in the house for a brief amount of remaining time, "Nick, you have to find a place around here. There are apartments and probably rooms to rent." I started looking in the Inquirer for places. The costs, however, were high. He called me up and told me he saw a room for rent. The land lord's name was Larry, a middle-aged black guy who owned a house with several rooms he let out. Nick talked with Larry and put me on the line as well. After sending him money for a month's rent and a security deposit via

Western Union, Nick had a place to stay. However, we had to get his bed from the house. We retrieved the clothes he needed, which were in awful shape. Our kids had a college refrigerator he could use. We got him a TV and an antenna. We had averted a major crisis. Relieved gongs from the anvil.

Tonia and Kim, her daughter, had explored getting Nick on state support. They filled out paperwork and he got on a small amount of monthly support. He had very little savings at this point. As well, they filed paperwork for him to be on Social Security Disability, another program that turned out to be very helpful. A program in Philly ran homes that took in homeless people. They began the process for Nick to enter the program. Because of the tension that developed between us or because mom lived with Tonia, Nick became just a difficult afterthought. While started, they did not complete the paperwork for these programs. I made several trips to Philly to take Nick to appointments and to complete what was necessary. On one trip, I drove to Philly to take him to an appointment, but he didn't meet me at Larry's as we had planned. His phone worked only half the time, so I encountered difficulty in setting up another appointment and in making sure that Nick made it. It aggravated me he lacked concern for what were important meetings.

To get on disability, Nick needed an evaluation and to go before a judge to determine his appropriateness. He complicated this because he went to the courthouse on the wrong day and became belligerent with the staff who threatened to arrest him when he went. He clearly misunderstood what the proceedings were about. This really proved the case that he needed to be on disability. I spoke to the lawyer several times who conducted the case, appraising her of what I saw in Nick. She had a good idea from what she saw for herself. Her persistence and sensitivity were very gratifying. Getting him through the process constituted a miracle. As well, getting him into the housing program was a trial but one that worked out. Tonia said she was tired of messing with these issues. I became his power of attorney and representative payee.

We set up a month-by-month agreement with the landlord, so that Nick would pay a weekly rent. Nick had a key to the front door, which opened up to his room upstairs. We moved him in and it felt that he would survive only with a song and a prayer. The prayer felt the greatest need.

Nick's life there became very loose. We set up a bank account for the little money he had coming in. Talking with him about a budget resulted in a hollow "yes". He quickly spent whatever money he had in his pocket. We initially set it up so that he could take out money when he needed it. I quickly discovered this to be wrong as he spent his entire monthly check in but a few days. He didn't like it, but I put limits on him. This led to several yelling matches at the bank when he didn't have access to the money he expected. Getting a hold of him by phone felt impossible because his phone was out of juice or lost. "Hey Larry, this is Steve, Nick's brother. Is he home? I have been trying to get a hold of him." "Wait, let me check…no he isn't home. I haven't seen him for a while. I will have him call you when I see him." His relationship with Larry turned negative when Nick left the front door unlocked several times. He lost the key at least twice. Larry also would lock the door before he went to bed, as he had to get up and go to work. Nick would get in late and bang on the door and yell to get him to open it up.

On one particular occasion, Nick created a situation that almost resulted in serious consequences. He had befriended a lesbian couple across the street. They were supportive of him and liked him. He spent time over there. Well, as was Nick's style, he would complain to them about how badly Larry treated him, probably after losing the key or coming in late. This aroused their ire and convinced them of Larry's unjust and significant abuse of Nick. This reached a crescendo, and they all went across the street and confronted Larry "the abuser". To make matters worse, their "cousin" came along who brought a gun. The altercation occurred in the street with the gun shown threateningly. Eventually, the police were called. The gun owner ran off when the police showed up. I heard this first hand as Nick called me in the middle of it to complain about Larry's mistreatment and that I had to fix the situation. The police threatened to arrest people, and the thing died down. But the damage was done and Larry said, "I'm over this. Steve, sorry. He has to go." So, we started planning for a different place for Nick to live.

I am not sure of the timing, but the disability and the housing programs came through about the same time and not too soon. However, I must describe what became for me a traumatic occasion in moving Nick from Larry's room to his new place. After being thankfully accepted into the housing program, Nick had to move from the room to the caregiver's home. We would move his clothing and decide on the bed and his other things.

I went up to his room. I followed him up the steps and he opened the door. Before me stood a scene I cannot get out of my head. There on his floor, about a foot deep, lay trashed McDonald's bags, French fry containers and Big Mac cartons. He had a bureau with several drawers. On top of it were strewn old food containers with half eaten or rotting food. There were clothes everywhere, a white bag or two, and a foot wide hole in the wall by the door. He had two windows that had broken shades and an old sheet covering one. The walls were grayish colored. It amazed me at the utter dirtiness and foul smell of the place.

But what added to the shock, and this still gives me chills, was the other presence in his room. Crawling upon trash on the floor, upon the clothes on the chair and the bed, all over the desk, over the TV screen, the speakers, the refrigerator, the walls, the curtains and the sheets, were a thousand, no, a million, brown, two inch long, cockroaches! They were all in movement. We apparently disturbed them by our presence. They flew, yes, literally flew and jumped, walked, ran and hid, moved and stopped, jumped again and flew. There was no inch of space not occupied by one of those darkish, devilish, moving sticks. One could almost hear an uproar from them, complaining at being disturbed. The rotten hamburgers, fries, ketchup drippings, pickles, onions and the partly eaten buns were their domain. The highway they used to get from other parts of the house to the throne room of refuse was the hole in the wall. I bet the cockroaches from this small 8 by 10-foot room propagated the entire section of Philadelphia! I have heard it said that cockroaches could withstand a nuclear attack. This room alone would survive a direct hit.

I stayed only briefly. I couldn't handle the mass infestation. Everywhere, I saw their nasty antenna wiggling, communicating, and planning their assault. I had to leave and exit to the street where I could again breathe! It utterly amazed and dismayed me that my brother could live in such squalor! Did he not have any dignity? I could only shake my head at the low level his life had fallen. Indeed, there were mental health issues here.

We promptly went to a hardware store and bought insecticide, insect bombs, trash bags, cleaner, and thick gloves. We used all our ammunition in our cockroach war. It took a while, but the room cleared moderately. We bagged up trash. I dared to look into his fridge. The fridge was black with mold. Whatever had been in there had transmuted into a black and gooey substance. On the shelf by the TV, I found a cup with an Eagles logo on it. Inside the cup rested a dead mouse.

The guy from the other room knocked on the door and asked if he could help. I noticed that his room looked neat, his bed made, and things put away. I felt sad, but my brother had a responsibility to bear in this debacle. He helped us clean up for the right to keep the fridge. He said he would take it out back and hose it down.

The debacle of his room and his inability to keep up with the tasks of living convinced me he needed supervision. His mental health issues limited his ability to live independently. His life style appeared primitive and irresponsible. It left me shaking my head at the incomprehensive reality of his situation. The anvil speaks intensely in long gongs.

On a brighter note, they accepted him into the caregiver program. I drove again to Philly to take Nick to visit several care giver's homes. We talked about the several options he had. One existed on the other side of Philly and he didn't like this because he didn't know that part of the city. Another elderly woman seemed nice, but I had the feeling it wasn't a good fit. Finally, we went to a house of a woman who lived with her husband and this seemed intuitively like a good fit. The woman agreed to take him in and we began a new chapter in Nick's life. This was successful for maybe a year. Here, Nick walked around in his underwear or was callous in taking care of the caregiver's things or taxed their patience in what he wanted to eat. He had particular likes he strongly desired and rejected other choices. I spoke with the caregiver and tried to listen to her issues with Nick. She gave him several chances, but he continued in his difficult demeanor and she called the administrators and asked that they move him elsewhere.

We tried another caregiver whose home was closer to Nick's old neighborhood. Placement there seemed promising. Indeed, it worked out for several years, for which I am grateful. They liked Nick. However, after a while, the same issues appeared. He would act like the oppositional teenager, selfish in his desires and lacking in an ability to work with others. As well, Nick would go out and not return until the next day. Several times, they found him in the local ER. He would go there complaining about having pain in his knees or in his groin area. He had medical issues, but to an extent used them to gain attention. At other times, he stayed out all night downtown and just walked around. He talked about the saxophone player on Spruce Street or the park he liked or a friendly store owner.

One story I heard, "Yeah, I was out most of the night. Oh, it was cold that night. I didn't know where I was. These guys talked to me. They took me to this place. I don't know what it was. There were a lot of people there. Geez, a lot of people. I spent the night. They took me to the El in the morning." It sounded like a homeless shelter. They probably saved his life from exposure or from violence. He didn't have a clue to what extent he had been in danger. His memory was poor, and you had to put together the details that came sparsely from him.

Several nights, the caregiver called, "Steve? Nick is missing again. We went to the ER and talked with the police. No one has seen him. Can you talk to him? This is getting old." This taxed the caregiver, and she decided she couldn't keep going after him. They warned him not to stay out all night and to be home at a reasonable hour. It, in fact, broke the rules of the program. But he ignored it and even flaunted it, as if to say, "You can't tell me what to do."

It had come to Nick being released from the program with no other homes available. The supportive social worker said the agency had a group home like facility to which, perhaps, he could live. There were limited beds. It got tense for a while as this was the last reasonable possibility. He needed supervision. He had money from his disability, but it wouldn't go very far. After a few days, they called me and said that they had a bed for him. I felt relieved. As well, the facility in an old detention center did not allow the residents to leave. After visiting, I felt good about it. The facility was called Riverview. Sparks.

Nick spent several years at Riverview until the city closed the facility. He then transferred after an evaluation to a nursing home with a surprising diagnosis of dementia.

With Nick, I have put in my time. I have had enough sleepless nights wondering if the morning would bring news of his untimely death. I earned my social worker degree through dealing with him. As well, Clarence, maybe my wings!

I love my brothers. They hold a part of my heart. We have seen a lot together. But in a slow, sad way, our lives drifted apart. I guess this just happens. We are different people whose lives have taken different turns in the road. It is disappointing to me it has turned out as it did. I was my brother's caretaker, regarding his Social Security Disability. I am aware of the tragedy of his life and the pain he has endured. But even with all that has happened, he tried to be free. Maybe that's what the walking around was about. He felt free in his choice to turn left or right. He needed freedom. His personality was such that he spoke readily to people he met, but they probably went little beyond acquaintances. Nick had old buddies, Tom and Pete, whom he spent time with, but this became less frequent as time went on. He kept in touch with these guys who had seen him go from a decent lifestyle with season tickets to Philadelphia Eagles games to one much more limited. He often said he wrote letters but didn't get replies. I don't think he wrote the letters as he thought. He could call people, but didn't seem to have their numbers. He made volumes of notes that would be his book. I heard the same stories over and over. Wherever we would go, he would note that he had walked there before. He also would say, "There is a doctor's office around the corner I had to walk to. They made me wait hours." In later years, he walked with a pronounced limp and said his groin hurt. He had trouble with steps and almost fell over getting out of the car. Also, he said he was always between doctor's appointments. He seemed like an alcoholic, perseverating and making things up. But at every church we passed, he crossed himself. He would always have a hug and a "I love ya Steve, thanks for your help." We had moments of genuine care and goodness. Moments of simple innocence.

Tony and I share many memories. He struggled because of Nick. Twins have an unusual affinity for each other. But I can still see them in their cute white sweaters or playing in the dirt with their shovels. They had a tough life. They endured, and they stood together as best they could. I think of them as trees, thick and old, standing tall. Their connection, the deep loving soil that rooted them, held them in place and kept the wind from knocking them over. There is sadness and angst in their suffering, like occasional storms passing through. But there is also joy in the accomplishment of relationships that have endured and withstood the flings of undeserved shadow and fire. It has been a trip, gentlemen, a trip and a blessing!

As a sad postscript, Nick passed away in December 2022, after a year in the nursing home. He grew more scattered and eventually his body gave out. He carried diagnoses of depression and dementia. After a while, he stopped eating and went down quickly. Losing structure and routine made it hard for him to function. I conducted his funeral, and we filled the room with people who loved him. Many of his old friends came and wore their old Philadelphia Eagles jackets. Goodbye Nick, my brother!

Shortly afterward, mom passed away in January, 2023, on her birthday. She had lived with Tonia for a number of years. Those were good years of peace in the presence of her daughter. She finally moved to a nursing home and seemed to enjoy it. Visiting found her jovial and bright. She deserved it, as her life contained a large share of pain and loss. I had the feeling she had resolved her life's conflicts. But she aged and her body became weaker. She died peacefully with Tonia by her side. I conducted her funeral as well, which was my gift to her. I believe the following took place. God summoned Nick to the throne room to talk. "What do I hear about you complaining Nick?"

"Well, God, I need to have apple sauce when I eat. I have always had it and I want it here. And, I could use a new pillow. I'm not sleeping well! The harp choir makes too much noise." God looks over at Christ sitting on his right. "Dad, I have tried to talk with him." And shrugs. God calls one of his trusted angels. "How old is his mom?" "96 today sir." "Well, call her up here. Her son needs her loving care!"

<u>Gritty Days</u>

The sun can burn and torch my garden
And parched and burnt can be my fate
The sea can drown and deeply cover
My dreams and aspirations of the day
The words and deeds of righteous men
Tear and pain my fool's goodwill
The windows break the shaking walls
Hatred's metal twists and fills
The tortured day may beg for night
While some may fear a baby's cry
While I but stay through sweat and fear
Continue on through tears and sigh
I hold my head, listening for love
and sing my song without regret
I paid the price and danced the tune
I've seen the shadow of cursed death
I've touched the dark and lesser side
and carried the pail through tortured air
I've felt the goal to slip away
I've smelled the scent where loss was there
I've been ignored, I've lost my faith
I've traveled desperation's path
And only the stronger have I become
I laugh and stand before life's wrath
I know that death shall one day knock
And little can I deny or rest
But hold my head in upward sight
Be glad in love I did persist

18 Growing Up and Out

During Paul's last semester at Purdue, President George Bush invaded Iraq, and Paul's outfit was called up to active duty. In 2003, they would send him to Kuwait and prepare for the impending war. While they sent others in the group to artillery duty, Paul and a buddy were charged with communication duties in a rear battalion. "Shock and Awe" were the operative words.

I had never thought much about those whose sons and daughters, fathers and mothers were actively in harm's way. But we found ourselves thrust into this unsought situation. I am not sure how you prepare for it. There were sleepless nights and tears. A saving grace we experienced involved a little white building in Indianapolis that housed naval operations and offices. Held there were family readiness meetings that provided support, comfort and helpful information. We attended several of the programs, along with Paul's girlfriend, Emily. It allowed us to get to know her. By the way, she is a gracious and caring individual.

We had a Ceili Rain concert that year in Columbus. God smiled at me in several ways at this concert. Paul was at war with little communication and lots of prayers. I got to know Bob Halligan and the band. Because my little musical group Elijah's Whisper had a repertoire of music, I asked Bob to let us be the opening act. He agreed, and we practiced with a good mission in mind. We played several songs that I wrote at the concert. The crowd seemed to enjoy the music. At least we didn't get booed or had rotten tomatoes thrown at us. We sang a song I had written about Christ's peace. It had a line, "My peace be with you" among other allusions to Christ speaking to the disciples in the upper room after the Resurrection. Stained Glass had played the song at Mass. It almost didn't come off, however. I introduced it as a prayer for my son, who was at war along with the many other soldiers, sailors, airmen and Marines. The opening bars perhaps lasted a little longer than usual, as I had to gain my composure in order to sing. The tears were not far away then as they are now!

In an active war, information about your relative is lacking. We knew he was stationed in Iraq, but we had no further information. To endure the absence of information is one of the most difficult things for a family to do during a war. I came to be aware of the little banners in people's doors and car windows showing an active military family member. We followed the news religiously while the conflict went on. The news shared was typically general and often the worst. "Rochelle, the news says a Marine died last night. God make it so it isn't our son!" They stated no further information. This could apply to any of several thousand Marines in combat. Thus, after this report, we waited for the Marines to show up at the door with their condolences. Luckily, it never happened.

Paul's war experience went as well as expected. He spent time in a Baghdad palace and was there when they toppled the Hussein statue. He came home after a number of months, but was not part of the contingent that stayed. The war would go on for quite a while longer with an insurgency that proved formidable and deadly. As they exited the country in a convoy, Paul noted that one of their vehicles broke down. It took precious time to hitch it to another Humvee and get going again. This time spent stalled was probably unnerving because an ambush could have occurred easily. He said that as they were going through Iraq to return, an Iraqi grabbed the sunglasses off the face of a Marine through an open window. That could have been a grenade just as easily.

What I am amazed about is what happened after he got back. Paul was in his last semester at Purdue when his unit was called up to active duty. When he returned, he went directly back to school, finished up his classes and got his degree. For me, this is unreal.

He shared stories when he returned. He was not wounded, and he didn't kill anyone. But he was on the lines and in the conflict. Worse yet, he had access due to maintaining the communication apparatus to sensitive information. He knew a lot about what was going on. And yet, to jump back into civilian life quickly and seamlessly seems like quite a feat of adjustment.

No doubt there were effects of the war on his psyche. He noted he had plans to go to officer training school, but decided that he did not wish to go to war again.

The day that he returned was a powerful day. We went up to Indianapolis, to the naval station. The family made a big sign welcoming him back. We sat along the road outside the building, waiting. "Oh, look, there down the road! Here they come!" It was something to see the busses escorted by the police, sirens and lights on. After waving at the buses, we quickly retreated inside to the gym area. Shortly, the unit marched in and formed before us. When they released them, it filled me with the greatest feeling to see him and hug him. It had been quite an ordeal, and for us, it concluded well. That day found us with tears and appreciation for our son returning whole. Smiling sparks.

He and I went golfing after he returned. We went to a nice and expensive course in town. "Paul, I am so happy you are back. I can't tell you!" "Dad, I'm happy to be back!" He shared some stories, and I felt renewed to be with him. It felt that he had changed inexplicably. He had seen the world in perhaps its most tragic and ugly way. "I tell you, dad, I don't want to go to war again!" His look underlined his words.

Two other things happened I should mention. One was that the church had their annual golf tournament. They invited Paul, and he started part of the first group, that included Tom LaBarbera and Fr. Clem. They invited me to join them. Tom LaBarbera had been Paul's soccer coach. Paul and I weren't very good golfers, certainly not at the level of scratch golf Tom played. But we had a wonderful time, and they treated Paul as the honored guest.

The second occasion was the 50th anniversary of Rochelle's parents' marriage. They rented several cottages on Mackinac Island for several days for the whole family. They planned a lot of activities. We had a big dinner to honor the significant achievement of Rochelle's parents and Paul attended in his Marine uniform. I felt very proud of him.

After the war, Paul and I went to the Marine Museum in Washington. It illustrated the colorful history of the Marines in pictures, paintings, artifacts, and stories. On the front wall stood a picture of the long line of vehicles on the road to Baghdad as the war began. Paul noted, "Dad, I was on that road!" He also showed us a picture of him and his buddies in a large room with tall ceilings, their guns at their sides. I have seen lots of such pictures, probably from every war. There were white lines drawn in the corners and I asked what they were. Paul responded, "That is where the unexploded cluster bombs were. We tried to stay away from them." There would be stories of sand crabs the size of pies, sand storms and pulling down the statue of Hussein in Baghdad. His war experience also had tension, long 12-hour shifts, and death.

One last item about Paul, as this is about going east. What made Paul go east had to do with his last semester at Purdue. Going back to school, one of his professors invited him to attend a conference in Washington. Paul called me up. "Hey Dad, I have this professor who wants me to go to a conference in Washington, DC. I'm not sure. I can't say I want to go. What do you think?" "Paul, what's it about?" "Facial recognition work." "Are you interested?" "Kind of." "When you have an opportunity, open up, go through the door and see what is on the other side. You should go. I went to conferences looking for work. It may be useful; it may be nothing. God offers things in a roundabout sort of way, one door opens to another, etc." So, he went. Because of his high security clearance and his Purdue pedigree, they offered him a job. Soon enough, he moved out east to the DC area. That is how Paul found himself out east! Gong.

Now it would be a couple of years before Paul and Emily married. She joined the Teach for America program for a couple of years. However, as we expected, they became engaged. I must share about Paul's memorable wedding with Emily. The night before, the uncles and I, Paul and Thomas, went drinking in town. I guess to say drinking is a misstatement. A lot of drinking went on. It rained. They notified us that someone from our party sat in a car passed out, with the door open, being rained on. The night included shots and cigars. I have said enough. The wives, girlfriends and fiancé of the aforementioned men were not happy. We could describe this night of celebration and family as, yes, excessive and flagrant!

We held the beautiful wedding in St. Bartholomew Church. You recall, I spoke of such an occasion when the place was just a roof and concrete floors. Emily looked beautiful and Paul played the handsome groom. My mother, Tonia and brothers attended. I believe I played the wedding song by Paul Stookey, which I had played at several weddings.

We held the reception at the Fairgrounds. Setting up the room festively, we had borrowed pole lights from the church to create a pleasant mood. While dancing and singing along with the DJ, the chicken dance came to be played. Thomas took on an important role in this entertaining exercise. While the crowd danced and sang, Thomas ran around the crowd in an enormous and utterly distasteful chicken hat. He did it with such relish and joy as to think that he missed his calling as a wedding singer and entertainer!

The final little job for the heartwarming evening concerned returning the lights to church after the reception ended. We packed them into my truck and Uncle Tom brought them back to church. However, along the way, a man drove up beside him and asked if he had lights in his truck. Tom said yes, and the man informed him they were no longer in the truck but strewn across the street. A bump had propelled them out!

Now, to tell how Thomas ended up east, we must begin in Flint. He finally got to go to Kettering in Flint. Of course, he did well. His classes were challenging, but he met the challenge. It was probably a God thing that he went to a school around family.

As his time went on, he pledged a fraternity at the university. He told us about the dumb stuff he had to do. This probably involved drinking. But one incident stands out in significance. Part of the activities for getting into the fraternity involved a trust fall. We weren't aware of this until we got the phone call. "Hello, yes, this is she. Who is this? Oh, what has hap…oh no, my God, yes, yes." Rochelle looked at me in a panic. Her face went white. Thomas had fallen and was in the ER with significant injuries. The hospital needed insurance information, etc. The next call went out to Mary, Rochelle's sister in Flint, asking if she could get to the ER. Her husband Tom, a police officer, said he would go. Mary would get there as soon as she could. The trust fall had gone badly. Thomas fell backward and others caught him as expected. However, he then fell forward. No one caught him and he slammed into the concrete face first. This broke his jaw among other injuries! Tom went to the ER and met with the fraternity brothers who accompanied Thomas. Tom had been a cop in Los Angeles and had been a Marine. "You guys may be liable for all that has happened to Thomas. You may be negligible!" He probably scared the crap out of them, as they were already stunned by the events of the day. We got to Michigan as soon as we could. They wired Thomas' jaw shut. He had lost several teeth. His injuries were serious but not life threatening at this point. His face contorted and swollen. The presence of the family proved so important. The family came together, circled the wagons, and took care of him.

For the next several months, Thomas would be in a tough way. However, he took things in stride. He could flow. When his leg broke in

Madison, Indiana, there were no complaints. He endured. In Michigan, the same result occurred. He had obvious pain and difficulty, but he endured. He got the treatment he needed, and he survived to tell the tale. Although we talked about suing the fraternity, Thomas decided not to pursue any legal repercussions. Actually, he eventually became the president of the fraternity.

Thomas graduated and continued on with the company he co-opted in Milwaukee. At graduation, he took us around the small Kettering campus. He introduced us to several of his professors, who spoke highly of Thomas. He had a way with people and an easygoing approach to life, a life which wasn't so nice to him.

Thomas started working for the sales team of the company. One of his first duties took him on a country-wide tour of the company offices. The tour focused on sales and it had an interesting twist. He and the several guys he went with did so in a new and bright yellow Hummer! Of course, it would not be an ordinary ride for Thomas! Paul had a brown Hummer, Thomas had a yellow one!

Thomas had an interesting job. His company made machines for manufacturing. He visited electric companies, a brewery, and the factory that makes a popular licorice. He brought several bags home and my how a fresh bag tastes! Early in his career, Thomas had the job of creating an exhibit at the Hershey facility in Pennsylvania. The same place we had visited years earlier. He designed and built a conveyor that made and packaged a candy bar. There were several stations to it and you could decide what flavors, what toppings, what packaging and finally print your name on the thing. We visited and bought candy bars and ran his working display!

One last quick story about Thomas. He attended the 50th Anniversary on Mackinac Island. He brought his girlfriend he had met in Michigan. She had a lively spirit, and they had a good time. "Hey everybody, let's line up here for a picture of the family at Mackinac Island!" asked Uncle Matt, Laura's husband. He worked in real estate and had a bubbly and effusive personality. "Mom, look up here." "Oh, Matt." Anyway, the picture captured the fun moment. Shortly after the occasion, Thomas and the girlfriend had a falling out and broke up under nasty circumstances. Upon hearing that, Uncle Matt deleted her from the grand picture through the mystery and power of Photo Shop! I could only shake my head! My mother-in-law did not approve!

A little later, Thomas told us of a new love in his life. He met Lisa, a psychologist, online. She was of African American descent. This wasn't an issue for us. No one felt surprised as we had befriended a colleague of mine, Grace, who had married an African American. Their son, J. Chris, was a steady fixture at our household for many years. He stood in as the little brother that Catherine never had. Although six years apart, she and J. Chris were good buddies.

Thomas had gone out east to work at his company's Pennsylvania office. Lisa had graduated from Princeton and gone on to Rutgers for a Ph.D. in psychology. Lisa seemed a wonderful match for Thomas. She countered his enthusiasm with a thoughtful, planful, slow-to-react approach to things. We first met her and Thomas for a very pleasant dinner at a restaurant near where Thomas worked. I wondered what Lisa thought, however, perhaps a shock of sorts to see folks from Indiana. She was the Ivy Leaguer and here we were Midwest friendlies.

Well, we didn't scare her away. Several years later, they were married. They had a beautiful wedding around Trenton, N.J. I gave the blessing and Bob, her father, told me to keep it short and not give a lengthy prayer like one of religious relatives! Bob made the best comment at the reception. He thanked everyone from the bottom of his wallet! Lisa came from a strong family and they came to love Thomas. How could you not? That is how Thomas found himself out east. Smiling sparks and many gongs!

After Paul and Thomas completed college and were out east, we had an iconic fishing trip. In my mind, it had equivalent significance to the boat trip I took with my father and grandfather in Atlantic City. It reached that level of a religious experience akin to Christ telling Peter to cast his nets out in the deep water. Paul decided we should rent a boat and go fishing for striped bass in the Chesapeake Bay. Paul lived in Virginia and Thomas drove in from Pennsylvania. I drove from Indiana and met them. We drove to a marina where the captain of a large boat met us. The 40-foot boat had a large area with spaces for several rods. They provided all the tackle. We had to help the captain and the first mate to bring in the fish that were caught on their deep swimming and highly sophisticated tackle. The hooks were huge and connected to foot long plastic yellow and white fish like lures. Cast from the back of the boat, the sides and from outriggers going out for maybe 30 feet to the sides, we had the fish surrounded. The captain had a sonar screen that would show a large patch of underwater red, showing a group of fish chasing after bait fish. "Get ready gentlemen, fish are on the screen!" Soon after there would be a yell, "Fish on!". The line would zing out of the reel and the rod would bend and vibrate and you knew that the deep was about to yield one of its magnificent secrets. "Here, take this," said the first mate to Thomas, "and keep it tight."

The air would grow hot as the boat responded to the momentous awareness of a fish on. "You're doing well." As the first mate drew in the other lines. "You go Thomas. Show us how to do it!" The first mate gave Thomas a thick belt to hold the end of the rod. "Reel it in quickly on the downswing. Keep up the pressure." Eyes would go out searching for signs of the fish. The boat would rock with the waves. All would feel anticipation as he reeled it in. "We will bring him up the back of the boat," as a large net appeared. This beautiful and ancient dance, a sequence of nautical ballet, came knowing that the sea only reluctantly gave up one of her own. The fish might jump out of the water a way off the boat, as if to register its disagreement. "Whoa!" from the crowd. Then it would come closer and all could see the size. "What a beauty!" The net would cradle the fish. It flashed about, angry at its predicament, angry it wasn't fed by actual food and bewildered at its out-of-body experience. The proud fisherman held it up and smiled. You kissed the fish if you could. And placed it in the box on ice.

We each caught a couple of fish. We could only keep one. While we were fishing, the captain asked if we wanted to enter our fish in a contest for the day at the marina. It would cost extra. However, we were having a good time and said, "What the heck, let's do it." These fish were big, 4 feet long and 30 pounds. Paul caught a huge one. We figured for sure it would win the tournament. But no. Other fish were monsters! We got a picture at the end with the three of us holding up our fish. After that, the first mate turned our cold and dead fish at the end of the dock into bass steaks and we were done. I had a most enjoyable day, to be on the water, to catch huge fish and to do it with my sons. We have a picture from the back of the boat, the three men with their catches! It doesn't get much better than that. Gong!

This began a trend as we took this trip half a dozen more times on different boats. We invited people to go with us. We had scout friends and relatives. One time we took Shane and his dad Fred with us. Given all the fishing experience Shane had, he never did this kind of fishing before. His dad was a hoot. He talked a lot and had interesting stories. "Did Shane ever tell you about the time we went to the cabin and it poured rain, but we caught a slew of fish?" He enjoyed the fishing. He enjoyed talking to the captain as well. Shane's dad worked for Cummins Engine Company in Columbus, and the boat just happened to have a Cummins marine diesel engine.

The curious part of the trip occurred coming home. We got into a discussion about the woman in the news who had been in a coma for quite a while. Fred said, "It is immoral that the husband should decide to take her off the machines. That's just evil!" I stupidly said, "But Fred, the woman is brain dead and he is her husband. Do you think they should keep her in that state forever?" He insisted that allowing her to die made up an evil act and railed against the husband's decision. We went around for quite a while. "I can understand where you're coming from, but Fred, I'm thinking more practically." "You don't know what you're talking about." Shane told me afterward that once his dad decides about an issue, no one can change it. Thanks for the late advice!

Several years later, his father passed away. Being recently ordained a deacon, Shane asked if I would do his dad's funeral. I said yes, of course. His mom wanted me to sing an old country song that had been their song early in the relationship. That meant a lot to her. I found the music and the chords; I sang and played it to her directly at the funeral. This brought her to tears.

But secondarily, a cousin asked to speak at the funeral. His testimony brought smiles to all who were there. He told a story about Shane's dad from when they were growing up, how the kids in the neighborhood were at war with a neighbor. "Us kids would get in his yard and mess with his tool shed and if he saw us, he would yell and, if really aggravated, take shots at us with his 22. I know it sounds just baffling. Well, anyway, we came up with a scheme. The young Fred put on a coat of armor, the metal sleeves from duct work and other sources we found around the farm and challenged the old guy. Fred went into the yard, running as fast as he could, carrying an open gallon of paint. All the while, the guy is shooting at him. You hear and see where bullets were bouncing off the armor. He got to the shed and tossed the ugly color of paint on the shed door and ran back just as crooked and fast as he could." The crowd applauded. The unbelievable story amazed me. But so funny. That was the most unique funeral I had done up to that point, but it befitted his extraordinary dad.

Catherine got a taste of the east and the south by being admitted to the College of Charleston with a major in Marine Biology. The school was in the middle of the city on an old stately campus. During orientation, the school threw us a feast that included wonderful oysters. We ate oysters on large tables with a hole in the middle for the shells, garnished with a tangy red sauce. Welcome to the south!

Catherine shared her room with a young woman art student. She seemed to be a free spirit. Catherine complained she would come back home from classes and her roommate would lounge on the floor with art materials around her stark naked!

Catherine had another roommate. "Christina," introducing herself, "I'm an English major. And you?" "Catherine House, marine biology." They shared an apartment in town as they finished up their studies. Christina matched Catherine's personal style as an intelligent and soft-spoken person. We moved them a couple of times. I remember they had the biggest couch I have ever seen that weighed a ton. As well, why they lived in upstairs apartments that had narrow and long stairs befuddles me. What is most clear in my mind is the fact that they had cats, not one but several. The issue became what to do with the cats? I have blocked out of consciousness what happened. She always brought them home from early on, even as a kid!

I felt sad that she eventually graduated. We met the caring sponsor family, the Irby's, who spent time with her. Charleston is a great town to visit with its Civil War history and beaches. The carriage ride around town exposed the secrets of the place. The ghost walk also gave us insights into the old harbor town. Maybe even some of it was true! We rented a nearby beach house for graduation. That weekend, we truly enjoyed ourselves. In the ceremony, the women graduates walk down the steps at Randolph Hall in beautiful white dresses holding red roses.

For her graduation gift, she went to the Galapagos Islands to walk in the footsteps of Charles Darwin. A group from the College of Charleston went. She was thrilled. The pictures show a beautiful place. Yes, there were tortoises! She also toured Ecuador, which was in the frenzy of World Cup soccer. I'm sure the visit was fascinating for her. "It was another world there," she said. "I was just amazed!" She brought back large framed copies of photos she took for us and the boys. Ours was especially powerful. It is from the front of a boat on a foggy Amazon River. A subtle yet powerful boat picture!

Catherine followed through with her degree from the College with a job at the University of Delaware. She worked on a grant project counting fish populations. She held that for a couple of years. Then, she took a job at the National Institute of Health running million-dollar machines that analyzed pediatric cancer tissue. This necessitated that she stay with Paul and Emily for a while near Washington until she got situated.

One evening, "Catherine, you want to go out to a club a friend of mine likes? Paul, you want to go?" "No thanks, have fun." On this evening, Catherine met a guy, "Hi, I'm Chris, I like this group. You like their music?" "Yeah, reminds me of a group from Indiana." "You're from Indiana? I'm from Kansas! Let's go Midwest!" He was an engineer from Kansas. This chance meeting went well, and the couple started dating. As it went, they returned to the bar in which they met, and he set it up that he would go to the stage and, with the band playing, get down on his knee and propose. Of course, she accepted, and that is really how Catherine made her way to the east coast. The anvil sings its approval!

Catherine's wedding took place at St. Bartholomew and Fr. Clem witnessed her marriage to Chris. They married on a freezing winter day. The date was 1-1-10. They set this deliberately so that Chris would easily remember his wedding date! The day was just beautiful. The church remained dressed for Christmas and the weather was cold and bright. Catherine insisted that on the altar would be a picture of her late grandfather, Jerry. This beautiful gesture for her family showed that somehow, we brought these kids up right! Bringing up flowers in a red wagon were Chris' nieces and nephew, who were small. I walked her up the aisle. My goal was to keep her from crying. She was on the verge of crying. "OK, so we have to figure this out before you say yes." "What?" "How many kids do you want?" "Dad, I don't know!" "The bigger question is, what names do you like? Now before you answer, just know that Sebastian should not be on the list, no." "Dad, you are impossible!" She laughed. "Yes, I am. But if you choose Sebastian, I will love him anyway!"

The only other thing that I am reminded of from year to year is that we bought several tall cylinders covered in red sequence that looked very Christmas like. They were in the reception room at the hotel and served the party well. However, we brought them home with us and now every year we must decide if we bring them out and decorate our space with them. They leak sequins whenever we move them!

Rochelle and I at this point were empty nesters. Our kids came home from time to time, but they lived elsewhere. Isn't it interesting that after living with somebody for 30 years, you naturally need to reframe the relationship? We had to find ourselves again, without children. It became easy to lose oneself at work or play. The church work we did, especially our work with engaged couples, kept us grounded in part. This kept us young to an extent in that we watched our lives from their view!

At my work, there was another psychologist named Dr. Grace Long. She was an Alaskan who had gone to school in Ohio and had been an intern at Quinco. Her late husband, Bruce, was an African American who had worked for the railroad. She lived in the neighborhood, and she and Rochelle became friends after the tragic death of Bruce. I have seen it where Rochelle consoles a grieving person in a deep and healing manner. Rochelle and Grace resonated beautifully. A few years later, Grace moved back to Alaska. Rochelle kept in contact and their relationship continued to prosper. We had talked about visiting Alaska for quite a while. Catherine made the trek out there with us. For me the trip was stunning because wherever you looked in Alaska, the mountains were present. Like sentinels watching over the mortals, they stood in the distance, tall, majestic, and silent. We visited several areas near Palmer outside of Anchorage and beyond. We found a glacier and rushing rivers, long vistas bordered by the mountains and marshy wetlands. Alaska amazed us and one night I saw the bright sky at 3:30 am!

A fond memory I have is combat fishing, of course! In Anchorage, a small stream gorges itself over the course of a couple of hours. It becomes a major road for salmon to travel to spawning grounds. This becomes the site of combat fishing. Standing 3 or 4 feet apart along its edge, anglers cast their red laced hooks into the water with a downward thrust. One would hear the cry, "Fish on" from time to time, yielding a large red-faced salmon. The subtle skill was lost on me, for I did not get a bite. I was good with that outcome. The fishing left me tired, but with a wonderful sense of extreme fishing I had never done in pastoral Indiana!

We also visited Seward by train, allowing us to traverse beautiful mountain valleys, purple grasslands and rivers. Connecting with a boat, we went out into the waters around Alaska. We witnessed puffins in great numbers and varieties of sea life such as whales and harbor seals. Renewing our friendship with Grace filled us both. We vowed to return some day.

A couple of years later, to show our comfort and confidence, a spontaneous road trip took us out west. "Ok, so let's plan enough to stay out of the rain, but not so much as to miss random and surreptitious encounters with people and scenery that come our way!". A Prius took us in its hybrid arms and, while not a mountain slaying monster, got us comfortably and cheaply around. We tested our comfort with unplanned adventures by riding off the beaten path to the Field of Dreams in the middle of Nowhere, Iowa. I cannot watch the ending scene with Ray playing catch with his younger father without tears in remembrance of ball with my father.

From Wall Drug (again!) to Yellowstone and the Tetons, we drove and stopped as we needed. In Cody, Wyoming, we had a great surprise. As we got into our car after visiting the dam, we heard someone call out, "Steve and Rochelle!" We looked and in a car near us were the parents of Chris Tolman, Catherine's husband. We had lunch and spent time with our spontaneous guests, who were on a road trip from Kansas. The Tolmans came up again later as they gave us lodging in a condo the family owned in Breckenridge, Colorado, for a couple of days. We visited Colorado for a few days and after the mountains, we drove downhill, attaining 70 miles to the gallon! As we traveled further, we finally stopped to see our old friends from Hanover, Margie, and Ron in Kansas. They are champions of the prairie. The adventure fulfilled our need for scenery but also fed us with memories, conversation, and renewal. We returned with our spirits filled to overflowing.

My life at this point experienced a steady period of work, church, and relationships. Our kids were gone, married, working, doing life for themselves. It took a little while, but Paul predicted children would come in a batch. And indeed, that happened. Rather quickly, they each had two. Paul and Emily, Allison and Ainsley. Thomas and Lisa, Ella and Ava. Catherine and Chris, Amelia and Natalie. I will not say much about these beautiful, energetic and wonderful grandkids. I need to finish this book. But I will leave it up to their parents to write the stories of their lives, including the many significant stories about their children. Catherine and Paul now have three and they are all girls! I have baptized all of them! We would come out east for baby showers and birthdays. And what a joy this has given us. It is heartwarming to see your kids take on life in its fullness and become parents and say and do things you did and spoke. We watch and mentally note that they are pretty wonderful parents who love their kids. Catherine and Chris have a tough road to travel. Their second child, Natalie, because of her needs and limits, is not self-sufficient or independent. Her eyes and smile inform you that there is a kind soul in there. That leads us to the next chapter.

<u>On Leaving</u>

Leave not in sorrow, for sorrow points to loss and regret
Rather, leave in gladness and triumph
Opportunity and relationship have touched you generously
Their words make love's receipt strong and whole
Rejoice in the past, for it has carried you well to this day

19 Annapolis

We got an email from Catherine and Chris asking if they could do a video conference with us. It seemed kind of strange, as we really didn't know what to expect. But we agreed to meet with them. The video opened up, and they were sitting down in front of the camera with glasses of wine in their hands. They seemed relaxed and curiously focused. They looked at each other several times and smiled at us. We engaged in small talk about how the kids were and, of course, the weather and work. This didn't last too long. Catherine said, "We have been talking, and we have a question for you." "Sure." We both said. "We know you are considering retiring and coming out this way," she said in a matter-of-fact way.

Rochelle and I had, in fact, been thinking strongly about it. When the move would happen or where we would move were open questions. But we had The Map. We marked up the paper road map of the PA-Washington-Virginia-Maryland-Delaware area with red and green dots over various towns. Traveling the area, we would ask ourselves if we could see ourselves living in this or that town. Based on really just a gut kind of reaction, we would go green, "yes, I could live here" or red, "nope, let's move on." We wanted to get within an hour or two of all the kids. Our target was a big 150-mile circle.

"We understand you are thinking about moving within a couple of hours from here. How about moving a couple of minutes away? We are thinking about buying a house so that Chris can be closer to his work. His trip to work takes a while from Damascus." Chris chimed in, "We are looking to move further east." Catherine paused. She then said more seriously,

"Natalie's needs overwhelm us and we could use your help." "So," they both looked at us, "we think we want to find a place with a basement apartment. If we found one," a long breath, "would you guys consider moving in with us?"

I felt stunned. Rochelle had a similar reaction. The question came out of the blue and I couldn't answer it. I took a deep breath and with my best therapist technique, nodded an aware, "Hmm." It worked as expected: it bought me a small amount of time. Rochelle made a reflective comment as well. "Well, that is a big question! Things have been tough on you guys, huh?"

They went into a little more detail about the difficulty they faced with Natalie. You could hear their courage but their fear. I imagined it must have been very hard to talk about. Probably the biggest moment for a young adult is to move out of their parent's home. They were asking us to move in! Surprised sparks.

We knew what they were talking about. We had come to Maryland when young Natalie got hospitalized at Children's Hospital in Washington. She was admitted because of the condition of failure to thrive. This meant that she hadn't gained weight as expected and her bodily signs were not good. "Catherine, dear, she looks blotchy and discolored. Her eyes are vacant, and she verbalized sounds of distress. Her body seems almost limp. She looks so sick and small. What can we do for the two of you?" Poor sleeping and eating exhausted the two of them in the hospital. They took care of the business at hand by one of them staying with Natalie and the other staying with Amelia. They later told us that the doctors at the hospital had prepared them for her probable death.

The video call showed a couple who were serious, communicated directly, felt emotionally guarded and hanging on to their sanity by a thread. They were obviously living on fumes. Catherine and Chris were stoic, but scared. They had learned a lot about her condition during that stay and it traumatized them.

We came to visit when Natalie was in the hospital to help with Amelia, who was maybe three. She knew us, so we were familiar and safe. We took her a couple of times to daycare. This felt so difficult as she screamed at being separated from us as she had when we left her parents. The staff knew the story, and they were helpful. Amelia did well once the initial separation occurred. We struggled because we knew she didn't understand why things were as they were. The nice weather outside allowed us to go to parks and get ice cream. But she wanted to be, understandably, with her parents.

On the video call with them, we knew things were in a serious place. We ended the conversation with a promise that we would talk about it and get back to them. We did this not in an avoidant way but with a respectful, "Give us time to process this, OK?" We didn't know it then but the anvil spoke loud with weeping.

That we had The Map showed we knew we would move, but not just yet. We expected the move out east would happen in a couple of years. We just weren't aware of how near the time was. Moving out east to help our kids, solidified, in my mind, our role as parents. The video call made it clear the urgency and the direction that would take.

Rochelle and I spoke after the Skype call. Rochelle said, "You know, there really isn't anything to discuss. They convinced me they are struggling and they need help. Our kids need us." "Yeah, my view exactly. It's really a simple decision. We have to say goodbye to all the people we love. Quit our jobs and fully retire. Sell our house. Prepare to move to a future that we were not sure of, in a place we do not know, for a yet to be identified basement apartment. Piece of cake!" "Oh, Steve!" But really, the choice came quickly. Our hearts told us the answer. We said yes. And that is how Rochelle and I made it our east. Sparks.

We did another Skype meeting. "Well, guys, you asked us a heavy question," I said. "But Catherine and Chris," Rochelle went on, "we know how you are struggling and the tension you face. We have talked and yes," a noticeable exhale, "we accept the offer." They were relieved, but they probably knew that we would say yes. There were tears. It isn't every day that you outwardly and publicly voice your love and willingness to change your life because of another's needs. But that is what we were doing.

This put our plans to move in motion. My colleagues, with whom I shared my practice, knew I was thinking about closing my practice. My other jobs as supervisor of therapists could stop fairly easily. I saw several weekly treatment teams at the Adult and Child mental health center in Greenwood and Indianapolis. They had hired a new psychologist, a friend of mine from Columbus. I figured I was now expendable. At the Family Service office in Columbus, I had supervised their clinical staff for several years and it would be harder to say goodbye. I did psychological testing for a local private adolescent hospital for a number of years and this would not be a difficult resignation. I had taught at least one psychology class a semester at the IUPUC campus in Columbus for over 15 years. It would mean they had to find another professor to teach the Learning or the Cognition class.

My work as a deacon would be more problematic. This required time to make plans. I had been at Holy Trinity Catholic Church in Edinburg for a number of years. I did weekly ministry at the minimum-security prison at Camp Atterbury and the jail in Franklin. Leaving the community there would be difficult. If we moved, I would have to receive faculties as a deacon from the local Diocese in order to continue to do deacon work. I wasn't sure what this entailed.

As we were driving, "This begs the question that we haven't really faced, saying goodbye to all the people we know." "Oh my, Steve, as you say it, that's huge!" "We have been a part of this parish community for over 30 years. Do you believe it, Rochelle?" She pointed out, "We could go to any Mass at St. Bartholomew and we know people. This is our spiritual community. So," Rochelle started in her calculating voice, "our friends, this community, includes the book club that has met for years on a monthly basis." I thought about it. "Wow, so many wonderful meals and discussions. We could not replace the inquisitive minds and sharp wits of that group. Marty, Clem, Steve?" "And the card club, but will you miss taking home the pennies?" (For the poorest score.) "Funny you. I will miss the conversation and community!" "What about the Bible study group? I think we are all friends." "Yes, it will be hard to say goodbye to the Small Church folks."

The task before us was to leave these precious relationships. "Steve, this means we won't be a part of the ins and outs of the lives of our friends. We will lose those connections. I think with all these changes, there will be a loss." "I know, Rochelle. Our social fabric is about to tear. It won't be a whole cloth." The reality of this sank in.

"I'm thinking that I will lose Men's Group! This will be a significant change. No Group meetings every week. What will that be like? Now Kim has already moved away, but he keeps up through Skype. Rochelle, I don't know what it would be like to not meet, eat and drink with my bros?" She just shook her head. "What's worse, what about the music recording that Ralph and I do?" "You should keep meeting with them on video. You can do it that way." "You're right." A little relieved.

Finally, I said out loud to Rochelle, "The fact is that we will move away from the deacon community. There are, of course, ordained deacons serving out east. But they aren't the class we went with through formation and ordination. They aren't the guys I share all the memories with, you know, the laughs and the tears, the tests and the joys." I shrugged my shoulders. God had made us a community and we would leave that group of peers who mean so much. To think of it, we would leave St. Meinrad as well. There will be some mourning.

After our decision, we found a lot to do. Moving out east was premature for Rochelle's plans. It could be done, but in order to receive her pension, a must financial situation for us, she had to work till later in the summer. God opens doors for you and nudges you a little and you move along a direction that you later see as good and necessary. At other times, God tells you outright what he has in mind. There is choice, but when you come to that moment, it really isn't a choice but a necessary decision. Ours was the latter. Like the colored signs on a tree next to the path, the goal and our direction were clearly marked. Our heart decided this is an imperative. No more questions.

We had lived at our Waycross house for years. As every homeowner is aware, there are things you want to do to the house, but you put them off. We had done what we knew was necessary. There was a terrible hailstorm, for instance, that damaged the roof and siding. That got repaired. We also did what we felt to be attractive. I had planted shrubs in the front and painted parts of the house as accents. The cherry tree I planted in the back had grown tall and noble. In the house proper, the garage had gotten re-wired with a separate electric circuit for my table saw. We painted Catherine's old room when my mom thought she might want to move in with us.

Now, to prepare for the move, we remodeled the dull and old kitchen, by putting up a backsplash to give a taste of newness and color. Also, we painted the cabinets and put in a new faucet and sink. The wrought-iron railings by the steps got painted. Downstairs, we had an old bathroom. Its age made it terrible, old and ugly. The plastic shower looked like it came from an army barracks! They had manufactured the sink in the 1800s! We knew it needed a redo. I could see a prospective buyer walking through and liking the rest of the house but coming downstairs and walking away, very disappointed.

We knew a guy from church, Andy, an excellent remodeler. "How about I ask Andy about the bathroom? He has that small thriving business. I like him." "You were with him on Haiti trips, huh? I know he went with us to

Waveland after Katrina." One powerful image I have of Andy is carrying two 4-feet by 8-foot pieces of drywall at a time. I could describe Andy not only as a competent and hard worker, but he was also a warm and kind man. I had spoken with him in my capacity as a deacon after his dear wife had died.

We talked with him about the plans to move east and why. We asked if he could help us with our bathroom. He agreed but couldn't guarantee when he could do it. He also wasn't sure how much it would cost. It drained us trying to get the house in good shape to sell. We agreed we would buy the materials and he would do the work. I would help as I could. We had a window of only several months to get a lot done. However, it happened, and the work got done. I helped as I could, although Andy, the master craftsman, needed little help. The bathroom looked wonderful, better than the main one upstairs!

Throughout the project, I bugged him about the cost. He would vaguely say he would get back to me. After the project ended, he still did not give us the expected bill. The cajoling continued when I saw him at church, as he did his "oh shucks, I'll get to it" response. Maybe I finally convinced him I wasn't sleeping well, thinking about what I owed him. He came through and handed me an envelope. I was eager to see what the cost would be. I opened up the envelope and read a brief letter. It said that there was no cost. He knew we were sacrificing to move out east for our kids, and he wanted this to be a gift. We were doing the right thing. He asked us to pay it forward. I read the letter and gave it to Rochelle with tears in my eyes. Cue the anvil!

Andy's generosity overwhelmed me. I felt totally surprised, and yet it fit with what I knew about Andy. It made us incredibly humbled as his action was perhaps the most generous thing anyone has done for us. Our hugs and thank you didn't quite seem to fit his generosity.

Now, the saga of selling the house got interesting for us. We had lived there for a long time. I contacted the wife of a social worker I knew and had worked with in the past. She was a very successful real estate agent. We sat down with her. "Yes, I can list your house. How long have you lived here?" "Probably 29 or 30 years." "I think it would make a nice starter home. It could use updating. But it's a nice house with adequate grounds. I have looked at houses that have recently sold in the neighborhood. Here is what I think it could sell for." Showing us her computer. The price she asked for felt somewhat low. Maybe I'm overvaluing my home because it's mine. We were also concerned how long it would take. "Houses are selling within a month."

"That fits our needs." Shortly after we listed it, to our great surprise, we had several offers rather quickly and for more than the asking price. The outcome gratified us. We sold it to a nice young couple. The race track embedded in the wall downstairs, we were told, impressed the dad!

While this solved a significant issue wonderfully, it also created another issue. We had left several months to sell the house. You can't predict how this process will go, nor do you completely understand the whims of the market and buyers. While the outcome was wonderful, we had to find a place to stay before we could move east. We faced a thorny problem.

I have a firm belief that when God wants something for you, doors will open and he will make the path straight. This occurred with the five years of deacon formation. It happened, and it became part of our normal activity. God had opened doors. The anvil worked hard.

As we prepared to leave, we got a video from Catherine and Chris. They found a house with a basement apartment in Annapolis, MD. With his phone, Chris took us downstairs and played a wonderful tour guide. "Let me go through the place. It's a small space but with great possibilities. Here's the bathroom. You can easily update the fixtures. Next is the small old kitchen. I think new cabinets would do wonders here. It's a decent size with all these cabinets. We have the washer and dryer on top of each other. Old, but they work well. Over here, a couple of rooms, and a big closet. I don't know if you would want this exercise bike sitting alone in the middle of the room? I think the place has a lot of potential!" Frankly, it seemed tiny. A couple of small windows let in light, but not enough to overcome the sense that the space was a basement! "Oh my gosh, this is the direction my life will take!" I said forlornly. "The rest of my life will now be spent in a dungeon basement. I will die and no one will search for me for 5 years!" However, it excited Chris in a cute sort of way. They were excited and so were we. This would be where the retirement part of life would begin. Or something like that!

Contacting Deacon Mike East, I let him know where our process stood. I wasn't sure how to go about getting faculties in the Archdiocese of Baltimore. I needed a letter of suitability, saying that I was a deacon in good standing. He thought I should talk with the archbishop. The fairly new archbishop was Joseph Tobin, a Redemptorist priest. Pope Benedict XVI had sent him to Indianapolis. I called his office and asked them if I could meet with him. I soon found myself in his office. "Deacon House, it is a pleasure to meet you. I serve the people of the Archdiocese, but also the priests and deacons. I understand you are moving? Here, please sit." "Archbishop, our kids have said that they can't continue on with their special needs daughter without help. They asked us to come out to Annapolis, MD. and live with them to make it easier." He nodded, "I see. They are young and overwhelmed and they need you two to help. What do you and your wife think?" He asked. "They are our kids, we can't say no." "Yes, true." He interjected. "It sounds like a big undertaking." I nodded. "But I also want to continue as a deacon. I love my work as a deacon." "Ah…well we can send you off with a letter of suitability." He looked for my response. "Thank you. A lot has changed. I will probably fully retire. But I love serving people as a deacon." Annapolis came up. The archbishop told me, "Once, I visited Annapolis for Redemptorist meetings. I jogged every day, and I noticed people paused and saluted me as I ran by. The feeling was strange. But I wore dark blue pants with white stripes and so I figured they must have thought I was an admiral!" He was a tall and large man, having played football. As well, he had an aura of leadership about him. After a gracious thirty minutes, he offered me his blessing. Pope Francis would later elevate him to the office of cardinal and send him to govern the Newark Archdiocese. This would open my service to the Archdiocese of Baltimore.

Let me not get ahead of myself. I have mentioned a dear friend of ours, Katy. As we mulled over our next move given the quick selling of our house, Katy called and said she had an offer. Because she recently bought a new home, she had a vacant house in Columbus. She wanted to work on it before she put it up for sale. She suggested we could move in to her old house while preparing to go to Maryland. God again opened the hearts of those around us. Katy's generosity was so timely and beautiful. Things were falling into place. So, we had to move twice, pack up our Waycross house and then pack up again and move to Maryland. We put boxes and items in Katy's garage and all around her house. The mess wasn't pretty, but it worked and we were thankful for the house.

You are not aware of how much stuff you have until you try to move it! Then things come out of the woodwork, it seems, and boxes and boxes of things become visible. As well, they are heavier than they look. The attic and the closets had mysterious boxes of things that had been useful and put away with the idea that they may become useful again.

Many mysterious boxes of books sat dusting away in the attic. It is a wonder the ceiling didn't collapse! I took 15 to 20 boxes of psychology books to a used bookstore. The guy was tired of seeing me. I had one book that got me $150 on the internet. I have to admit I enjoyed the nostalgia going through them. The used bookstore guy had little understanding of the importance of these books. But like old clothes, they no longer fit and were out of fashion.

I found my old Grundig reel-to-reel tape recorder. One speaker didn't work, and a tube had blown out. It didn't feel worth it to fix it. It had become a big and heavy door stop. To let it go meant a loss of an era, but necessary. A couple of clinks of metal on metal as the anvil commented.

We had to take down my tall bookcase. It held many mementos and books that have traversed the years with us. Taking it down has always been a challenge and a hassle, but almost a ritual. As well, it weighs a ton. But there in Katy's garage, the wood took up a large section of garage.

Next, I had many bonsai trees. These I kept on Katy's back deck and inside. They had to be tended to regularly. It turns out that a friend of ours from church was going out to Washington, DC, to visit his daughter. He had a van and was happy to bring the trees to our new house on his way out east! I should never doubt that things will turn out well.

Ralph and I drove out to Maryland with a packed trailer behind my truck. The old Ranger, still reliable and strong, got us there! Katy's garage contained the used vestiges of our modern life. Our trip dented the house stuff that had to be moved.

Selling our house for a nice profit gave us money to put into remodeling the apartment we moved to in Annapolis. We wanted to make the dark and old basement more livable. With cheap home designer software and the dimensions of the space, we worked on a floor plan. We went to Lowes and bought cabinets for the kitchen, a stove and refrigerator.

I need to describe the wonderful and gracious goodbye party we had at church. Several parishioners were there, as were several deacons and wives. We began with evening prayer and ended with a wonderful blessing. In between, there were stories. We were treated to a warm and loving embrace from people who mattered to us. We told the group, "Any of you would do what we are doing if asked by your children to help. The hard part is acknowledging the pain of it and the sense of loss we are feeling." Rochelle was tearful. She said, "We also want to thank all of you for your goodness to us over the years in the many ways we felt loved. You are all special to us." She had to stop for the tears. In the end, they all gathered around us and with a laying on of hands, they blessed us and asked God to protect us and be with us on this new adventure. Our experience was an evening of pure goodness.

Eventually, the moving day arrived and with the help of friends, Paul and Thomas, the truck quickly filled up, as did the other vehicles, and we got on the road. We rented a big U-Haul truck and luckily all things fit in it, complemented as well by the car and truck. They all crossed the state lines and made it intact to the new future that awaited us in Annapolis. Paul and Thomas helped, as did Catherine and Chris. It was only right that it should be a family affair. Ralph helped as well. He got to meet Natalie during the move.

I am not sure how I felt about leaving Columbus. Living in Katy's house had made it feel alien from our typical experience, so even at that point, we were in a different space, physically and mentally. Columbus had been a place of significance. Our time there had seen substantial changes and developments for all of us. Parts of our hearts remain there. Sparks!

To end here with the sun blazing on our backs as we wave goodbye and head east to fame and fortune would not be the total story. Arriving in Annapolis and moving into our space should have been an easy and straightforward undertaking. We hired a firm to do the remodeling work. As they completed the work, we lived upstairs in the guest bedroom. It really worked out nicely except, of course, for the hidden beam that held up the entire house! "Rochelle, they took out the wall like we planned. But they found a metal post holding up an I beam that runs the length of the house. We have to change our plans for the space on the fly. The kitchen space has to move over a couple of feet and the bathroom space has to change. We have to decide what to do with the ugly metal post in the middle of the bedroom holding up the floor above it! We shouldn't have bought the stuff for the house before we opened up the space!" Well, necessity is the mother of invention and a tough mother she can be! We lost a window, yes, we literally lost a window. There was to be a window in the kitchen. The placement of the kitchen cabinets, stove and refrigerator already purchased closed off the window. Behind one cabinet is a window that no longer allows God's sunlight to come in. We had the contractor put a hole in the wall and make a new window. Really! The most time-consuming part, however, concerned the flooring. It took the floor guys forever to do the work. All the while, we lived out of a 12 by 10 room with all the belongings we could fit and the rest in the garage or in a storage room. It felt like we were on a long vacation trip visiting an unknown place, not our home, except without all the romance, mystery, and good food!

There were perks to the move. We were now both retired and so we had time. The time felt nice, as we had to adjust to a new life. Rochelle took up things she had been putting off. "Steve, I have decided I want to learn how to quilt and to knit. I have mended clothes before, but this is a serious new move. There are several knitting and quilt stores around. What do you think?" "I think it's great!" She decided early on that she needed a nice sewing machine. This didn't mean a nice Singer. She bought a recommended brand that was expensive. But, hey, it is retirement time and if you don't go big here, when will you? I was all for it. I felt proud of her enthusiasm and effort. There were several projects to do, material to be bought, and time to spend sewing, quilting, learning and creating. I built her a little desk for her machine and the little corner became her quilting corner. The anvil sings but no sparks, you know, all the material and stuff!

For me, I hadn't thought about what I would do. The head of the psych department at IUPUC asked me if I would teach a learning class online. They really didn't have anyone to teach it and if I could adjust it to an online class, it would help them out. I did, and it turned out fine, although different. The class was the same course I had taught for several years with Sniffy the Rat, but put into a video format. My technological limitations showed badly. But it all worked out, although teaching without direct student contact felt unusual.

Another interesting turn occurred when Fr. Bede visited us in Washington, DC. He spent time at the Catholic University of America on sabbatical. He asked me if I would be interested in running a seminar at the university for seminarians. A friend of his was looking for a clergy with a psychology background to teach an applied ministry course. I told him yes and thus began a teaching stint at the wonderful Catholic University of America.

After contacting a deacon I met at a Mass while visiting, I sent my letter to the Baltimore archdiocese, where they accepted my credentials. They would assign me to a parish 30 minutes away, named St. Frances Chantal. The pastor, Fr. Carl Cummings, was a retired Navy chaplain. I would serve the wonderful people of the parish for the next five years. Service at a local soup kitchen would await me. The anvil smiled with sparks. A new spiritual life began.

In Indiana, I had carved small things with a set of carving knives I bought. I made a little flower out of cherry wood. Here, I bought more tools and, over the first couple of months, used time in the garage to carve several scenes on wood. I can't say that I am good at it, but it is an enjoyable pastime. I carved a relief of a tall lighthouse off a rocky shore. It stood guiding ships that may appear on the horizon.

A surprise I hadn't expected was that Annapolis reminded me very much of Atlantic City during my youth. There were bridges and waterways and many sailboats. The carved lighthouse found reality in a decision to buy a sailboat. Recall my sailboat in Philly. I decided to get another one. I always had a canoe, a fishing boat, or a kayak. So having a boat would not be new. The cost was greater and the dock fees higher than my fiberglass plaything in the 60s. But I researched it. I looked at reasonable boats that I could afford and that would be seaworthy. I also took sailing lessons at the Annapolis Sailing School. The course, over several days, took us out on the water in 20-foot boats with an instructor going over sailing basics. There were supposed to be other students but a woman who attended one day didn't come back, so just the instructor and I went out. He took it as, "Let's go sailing for the afternoon!" I excitedly agreed, and we spent a great afternoon learning and sailing. I decided I had to get a boat similar to what we had sailed. After several months of research, I bought a Cape Dory Typhoon. These are old boats but well built, maneuverable and solid. I found a slip at a marina just down the street. I was in business.

The first time I went out, Catherine and I sailed. She had college experience with sailing. We went only with the headsail. As we tooled around the bay, I couldn't believe it. At one point, I looked at her and said, "Catherine, we are sailing around the Chesapeake Bay! Who would have thought this years ago?" "It's something, isn't it? This is nice." I used an old trolling motor, but this proved to be a mistake. The battery quickly drained. We were almost back to the marina but got caught without wind and battery in the harbor. I called the marina and asked embarrassingly for a tow. Well, I bought a new battery and hooked up the small engine I got with the boat. That boat carried my sons and I a number of times. We sailed the Bay, and they enjoyed it.

That is the beginning of life in Annapolis and life in retirement. We help with Natalie and it is good that we are here. Life goes on and not unlike before. Rochelle and I enjoyed a significant and solid relationship built on trust and mutual care. This continues, although a little tested by the new circumstances. As she often told, she started her career as a special ed teacher and roundabout; she came back to a similar situation with Natalie.

We settled into our little basement apartment and, looking forward, supported by our belief and faith in God, awaited the openings of life. Close to water and family and supported by meaningful work, we didn't see this as an ending, but a new beginning. The great winds of life prepared and brought us here. As always, we were open and looked forward to what would happen as the story of our lives continued.

Rochelle bought me access to a genealogy website. As my desire to write my story strengthened, thinking about past events, beginning to fill in the gaps of my past, I felt the urge to visit my grandfather's grave in Cape May. In my hands, I felt the weight on my heart of people and places calling out to me. It brought an awe that, like lightning, traversed the many places I had been. I felt connected to all of those moments by this streak of goodness, of identity, of will, and of grace. Urged by past voices, I gathered up memories. How do I take in all the conversations, opportunities, decisions, and reactions that brought me here? Would all have been the same had one word changed, had one moment been missed, had one scarlet sunset lasted less? Did we know where this journey would take us? Did we know the turns in the road, the detours, the passages and the side trails? Could we have predicted the adventures our marriage offered? Could we imagine that our children would become a source of such joy and meaning? Did we know where education would take us, what music would bring, or how the church would affect us? This was really a leap of faith. Life does not ask permission, but treats you with its gentleness and the raw power of its own accord. For me, for us, our journey has left us upright, open and loved, gifted in a most immense way. To look back with tears and smiles, and with gratitude, calls forth a deep thankfulness. It brings us to the realization that God had our back to which the anvil sings loudly and correctly, "Remember it all, remember and rejoice."

<u>I Sing the Celebration of Life</u>
I will carry my song to the peaks of the mountains
And into the deepest of valleys
I will sing to the places unknown and unseen
And sing to the heavens alive

I will sing with the joy of a songbird in spring
And let my voice rise like the sunlight
I will be like soft wind brushing your soul

And seeking the most tender light

I will sing the day in the clearest of winter
The song that captures the summer
The song that brings forth the newness of spring
Brown leaves in the fall I will murmur

I will be heard round the cities and sung round the table
I am song and dance to the tune and its rhythm
At work and in play, you shall find me aloud
In the hearts of the lover and eyes of the children

I will sing truth in the morning and truth of the noon
And call out to the moon in the night
I will open the closed and courage shall be
The echo of my delicate might

And in my prevailing, the coming of faith
The raising of hope is my power
I am lifeblood to all who breathe of this life
Of joy and delight, I am seeds and the sower

My goal to bring forth a witness of love
My joy has none other than this
That to be at the center and core of his love
To seek his perfection and taste of his grace
For God is my song and my song is in God
I sing the celebration of life

20 Epilogue

My father built things when I was young. He was a machinist who made helicopters, and as a hobby, furniture. I still have a small bookcase he made. As I look back on my life, similarly, I see I was a builder. The voice of the anvil, signaling the guiding sound of God, urged me to create and build. It opened the world around me, pushing me to sing its praises with my hands. I learned to crab and gently to catch butterflies. Early on, I learned to throw a ball and to fly toy airplanes. Useful hands inspired by my father have blessed me. But moreover, these hands have taken on gentler tasks of welcoming and support. As I look at their wrinkled countenance, oh, the many things these aged hands have accomplished! How the anvil has spoken through them in love and mercy!

God has also guided my eyes to see the wonders of creation in the natural world. In Connecticut, I saw the snowfall's identity and the sublime beauty of smoke rising from a chimney in winter. Brought to the sea by my father and my heritage, I fell in love and saw in its misty company a sign of God's presence. Later, the mountains would join in the soul dance that captivated my spirit. When in their embrace, I felt stable and good. The sea and the mountains were places I shared with others. Family and friends became partners in this love affair. Despairing I was without them.

But my eyes were wearied as they were awed. Besides my love of God's creation, long ago, the anvil called me to relationships with eyes of compassion and to respond with the voice of support. I saw despair and suffering, weakness and affliction, the hard truths of life. I sensed my mother's distance, saw subtle human criticism and rejection, and later, witnessed my parent's tumultuous interactions. My brother Nick taught me lessons on compassion. Little did I know the psychological and religious mission fomenting in me. Frankly, I didn't need a license given by the board of psychology. My experience wrote the certificate of a caring heart on my soul from long ago. Over time, this manifested in a quiet, supportive presence I used to walk with others. I believe I would have used this facet of my being regardless of profession. It is clear how my heart destined me to minister to others.

The anvil molded and formed my understanding. Little did I know the power and fruit of its use. Filled at first, more with anxiety than insight, I had to realize the gift my mind offered. But as I focused, it sharpened with curiosity and purpose. The humble halls of the Community College of Philadelphia validated my judgment. Tested by the EEG machine of Eastern, I stretched my reason. It brought me to Sniffy the Rat. It offered me a backpack full of ideas to share in classrooms, churches and therapy rooms. As my toolbox, I used it on the problems my clients faced. I came to regard my curiosity and awareness as a substantial gift, an understanding guide, and a trusted reservoir of ideas and information.

As my intellect strengthened, I also discovered my voice. What called me to sing at the Venice Park church at that young age but the anvil? While illness tried to inhibit me, and family messages urged me to be silent and nice, it did not stop me from singing. What moved me to join in that marvelous high school choir but the anvil striking its tones on my heart? I sang, and a voice came from deep within, releasing my passion and truth. My, how music has brought me to community! It has inspired me all of my life.

A deep question I have long contemplated. Why did I not succumb to despair and depression? I can only say that the anvil worked to counter my loud negativity. From Philly, I have lived in a hard place. I saw hard things, difficulty and conflict as a kid. The anvil worked on me and spoke with its insistent, hopeful voice that this world was a place of goodness to marvel and enjoy, a place of awe and honor. It lifted me up and I now see that God used it to rescue me. The anvil taught me to listen and follow, slowly pull up the line, and engage gently with its tension. I learned the crazy skill of catching a butterfly by its wings! The anvil sang its faith and hope in my ears.

In addition, I believe that others have acted like angels and directed me. When I faced the forked road, a messenger guided me. I listened and benefitted. This got me to college, sent me to Michigan, and opened me up to the diaconate. Eventually, God spoke directly and gently. I truly believe I have not been in charge of my winding life. Rather, I am the anvil's handiwork. The beauty I have seen, the intercessions of my mind and heart, have been gifts I did not deserve or earn. As well, the anvil has put many things in my path as lessons of its goodness.

For instance, the anvil's wisdom led me to many tables, offering me places of community. Catherine's family gathers each night around a mahogany one I made. But even more, the anvil has brought me to tables where I have sat with friends and family, conversing and exploring the world in each other's words. What lessons I learned around a certain family's table in Michigan. Where would I be but for a table at Eastern Michigan University where sat an auburn-haired young woman?

The meals at those tables, wow, what a generous sharing! Philadelphia housed wonderful dinner tables, lovingly worked with Greek hands from Howard to Pratt Street. What of my grandfather's counter where I found his gentleness? The random tables of university cafeterias, like a spring in the desert, sustained me. The many tables around which we gathered to share a community meal, cards, books, or Marriage Encounter's love letters are too many to mention. Of course, I recall the powerful Waycross table of our growing family. That alone wiped out the tragic table of Nick's abuse. Now, the wine drunk at these tables alone would fill a small lake! The bread broken would startle any good baker! The meals, filling those plates with a cuisine that fed my life, I could not easily catalogue. And, whatever the menu, it is of no significance. The laughter supported, the tears wiped away, the connections deepened, and the problems solved! Lives grew around those tables.

What of those many chairs the anvil offered? They witnessed to all manner of conversation, listening, and laughter. I have sat in chairs with those I loved and strangers on their way to friendship. A chair held my father as I kissed his forehead, going to bed while he sat and drank his beer. That long couch made by the anvil's hard labors was where I rested while preparing to go off to the midnight shift. What of those 3rd grade chairs or Penn State chairs or heavy Vanderbilt chairs? Let me not forget Catherine's recalcitrant couch in Charleston! In my older days, I may take a nap in the afternoon on one of those chairs. They propped me up to read a good book, to contemplate a homily or to hold a granddaughter. Importantly, there were therapy chairs, made with love and a listening heart. They facilitated conversations with those suffering and in pain, traumatized by injustice, wounded by scars of mental illness. Those chairs faced each other to convey words of healing and respect. Had my mother but sat in one of those chairs!

I have built many bookshelves. But far fewer than those libraries the anvil has offered. They have held the uncounted pages of books so important to my journey. I stand, a well-trained psychologist and a caring and knowledgeable deacon, instructed and formed by books, new and old. They offered psychological theory and religious truths that added layers of meaning to my understanding. Those wide and long book shelves have held a lifetime of wisdom, knowledge and imagination. They form a rich community of ideas. In gratitude, I must acknowledge the wisdom, understanding, and insight shared at the feet of wonderful teachers, Miss Pigeon, Mrs. Ulrich, Steve Greenstein and Fr. Clem. They taught from the book of life! I am thankful for their cherished words. My livelihood owes those words!

I am thankful to the anvil, whose loud power made doors that opened to so many adventures. They became guardians of the passageway and withstood the flash flood of arguments. But they joyously flew open to Marriage Encounter meetings, card playing and book clubs, sharing love and laughter. Those college doors, work doors, hospital doors, and therapy doors welcomed and invited me to walk through! They have opened and closed eras, chapters, ages and passages, taking me from one day to the next, one year to the next, one conversation to the next.

How many windows have I looked out on beautiful days of promise or sat frustrated by the rain and cold? Those windows produced by the anvil opened to the vast world outside. The power of those windows kept me connected to the horizon that rested past the electric plant in Atlantic City and down the street in Venice Park. A window showed me a butterfly in Connecticut. A special half-moon window opened up the campus of Hanover. Another window sought to engage me with my Waycross cherry tree and the garden, where Alex raced. What Alaskan vistas those windows allowed.

Where would my life be without machines coming from the anvil's hard sparks and steel? Those sparks manifested into helicopters that supported my father's work and our family. It made complicated and comfortable cars, driving me from yesterday to today. The Hudson, the Chevys, my Volvo and, of course, the beloved MG. Later, the Datsun, the Honda, the rugged Rangers and the Camrys. Those wondrous moving machines took us places. We crossed bridges, like the Ben Franklin, so many bridges, built with muscle and steel. We drove through the vastness of the mountains and meandering streams on unnamed roads. Cars drove me to tranquil dawn locations. They conveyed me down Kensington, Frankford, and Columbus streets bustling with commerce and lively energy. I drove to work and to play, with golf clubs and fishing rods in the back. They carried my canoe, my kayak, and pulled my boat to Michigan, Tennessee, and Grouse Ridge. How about the impact of their manual drives on my wife and kids? These cars whistled the heat of broken hoses and saw flat tires. Humming and racing over county and state lines, they sped, and they died. Their metal gleamed and rusted. But what trips they spurred! In their friendship, they tolerated poor driving and lousy roads. They protected me through winter storms (remember Notre Dame?) and rains engulfing the windshield in vague and shadowed color. Those cars took me from here to there and back again and the anvil's joy propelled me across the years through their loved and restive momentum.

I would lead half a life, but for the tools that the anvil forged and afforded me. My Dad's circular saw, the table saw, the hammers, the chipped screwdriver, the wood carving chisels, the old hand drill, and the "CCHouse" toolbox. Tools activated my imagination, instigated my understanding and carried my purposes. They gifted my life with creations and carvings. The anvil's demands were loud and clear. I felt called to build and create. Not for fame or fortune, but for an occupation of will and mind, to share rich gifts of love and purpose, to carry on a legacy of building. The tools it gave me forged a life.

The anvil fashioned me several guitars. My first guitar, hard to tune, instigated by the Beatles, opened me up. Later, what do I owe my big Guild, or the Taylor that brought to life Elijah's Whisper and Stained Glass? My late edition ukulele brought delight. There were music stands and my early Grundig recorder. The Yamaha recorded Stained Glass and Steve and Ralph music CD's. Several amps and microphones joined along the way. I fondly recall one amp that joined me to my Uncle Don. These released that inherent harmony held in my bones, resting in my heart and so willing to manifest my voice. This gift of sound narrated the darkness and the light, the solitude and community. The melodies took me to South America and to friendships bound by the musician's oath to carry one's burdens with courage and harmony. Johnny, Trent, Joe, and Ralph joined the chorus. These joy-filled occasions of rhythm and tone, syncopation and harmony enlivened my life and that of others. The songs of my life produced such light and energetic moments as to convince me that even God sang along!

What of the houses built by the anvil's handiwork that sheltered me? I can only imagine the many houses I have entered. This book compiles the stories of the significant ones. I have here immortalized them, Howard Street, Dyre Street, Waycross Drive, and Windwhisper. They all hold glimpses of my story. They had addresses and character, presence and atmosphere. I have forgotten so much about their faces, but I remember their voices and the feeling they left me, the way the sun fell on the bed or the moonlight on the wall. What life spent in those rooms? The anvil smiled at me in those rooms.

Perhaps, finally, its greatest gift. Little did I know, but God forged a boat with his anvil. It carried me above the water line of tumultuous circumstances and wonderful sunlit evenings. Memorialized in boat paintings throughout my life, the anvil reminded me of my sailor's heritage and my heart's nautical identity. Even as my life changed, the sea remained. Over class five rapids and down the quiet streams of my life, I floated in the sure direction of goodly purposes.

This boat saw so many people come across its threshold. Some stayed for a while, others left quickly. But all wrote their names on the bulkhead, left souvenirs of their lives in the cubbyholes on deck. We played cards, sang songs, talked and drank beer. Together we opened our souls, learned, cried, prayed, and mourned. Their conversations have molded me. The voyage has been wondrous, made perfect by their presence on deck. But this boat, this ark, has chartered me over my life's waters. It knew the sun and the sea, charting a course not without danger but with the assured purpose of seeking calm and gentle water. On bright days with both sun and moon present in the blue sky above, it has galloped the waves with passion. With moonlight as a guide, it has focused on a path straight and clear. We dipped our fingers over the edge and felt the warm water and the bright sun. It carried us and protected us. It brought us to our harbors, tolerated our mistakes and opened our vistas to the horizon's unexpected joy.

My trip is not unusual or uncommon. I have seen success and tasted failure. But this thankful path leaves me on my knees, giving praise to the anvil's genius. Its wisdom exceeded my own. The anvil's insight saw further than my own. Its great gift of love held stronger and deeper than my own.

God spoke to me of the anvil's power. It rose in action to resolve and heal my many broken moments. It knew its presence and the power of its sparks. The clamor it made resonated deep in my gut and coursed through my heart in waves of mercy and goodness. I needed its presence to counter my shame, my guilt, and the weight of prideful judgment. For instance, it got me through my poor failure of high school, the Penn State trial, the psych board rejection, and my other dark moments. Somehow, it made me ready to take on the Community College and Vanderbilt challenges of my life. It rode with me to Michigan. The anvil proved to be my friend and confidant, protector and guardian angel. Marking the times and places, it brought the awareness of truth and surety to the endless questions and doubts that were my failings. The anvil spoke with a strong and sure voice in my toppling moments, when my broken humanity engulfed me. It was my wind chime and sounding board, my witness and comforting ally as I strove to be a son, brother, student, friend, husband and father.

Truly, the anvil deeply forged my hope and my ability to love. It directed my vision and my passion, and the loud resonance of my sure living. Addressing my fears and confusion, it consoled me when my father died and held me when I grieved the loss of Michelle. It comforted me when I spoke angry words. The sparks of the anvil were tolerant when my many doubts surfaced and rejoiced when my smile regained my humor. Knowingly, it smiled amid resolution and beauty, such as the day I met Rochelle or when our babies were born. The anvil knew my plans and didn't laugh, but gave a kindly and confident word, even as I wove an orange engagement ring. Chancing the day, it sang deeply my need for courage. It knew, it knew with a wisdom cosmic and reverent, the goodness of the world and lit my heart with that goodness. Bringing hope to my weary being, it led me to engage my life. With a gentle purpose, it reflected the light shining from God. Illuminating me with God's love, it rippled silently across the sea. Forgiveness and thanksgiving resulted. Insistently, it asserted God's love even when all evidence looked ambiguous. It brought me to the threshold of faith and knew that God would fill me.

My life has been long and meandering, variously focused. With poor attention and holding on to superficial desire, I have wasted days. But God's anvil, calling me to virtue, has always held me up. From my Panamanian heritage to the shores of Annapolis, I have been carried in its arms. My friend, confessor and guide, it has stood by my side. Only now do I recognize its airy presence. The anvil with its sparks and forging love has guided me, supported me, illuminated me, and shown me its unselfish wisdom. It has been my spiritual friend, the voice of God, reading me the scriptures that I could not read between the tears. Speaking to me in a calm and clear voice, it protected me from the fiery moments of unguided energy, need, and desire. It is the manuscript of a life accompanied by harmonies from heaven, angels speaking love and wisdom. I am here because of its purity and duty. Humbly, I thank you, O passion and guide.

The Anvil's Passion

There comes a point in sorrow and thought
In crisis, tense with confusion
When waiting ceases and action begins
It is when the clock chimes the moment of decision
No longer is sitting allowed
No longer is passivity accepted
Action is called forth and comes with a loud retort
In restraints, it is quiet
But unleashed, it gushes like an over ripe river with no respect for the banks of old
There comes a point in the caged silence of unsuccessful breathing
That a gasp for new air bounds out of the lungs
And raw heat reddens the moment
Bones rattle like sabers, long dusting away in forgotten sleep
A pleasure abounding in its cart wheeled movement
Nothing commands power as much as direction found on the tip of expression
We ride action into the furor of pent-up dreams and awakened desires
A sunset is pretty and night demands silence
But the charged daylight of motivated muscle with its clarion call for action
Is power awakened
Is power ignited
Is power struck like the hammer on red hot iron
Singing the anvil's passion
The sparks abound
It is no longer time for sleep

Acknowledgments

This project has been in the making for some time. I desired to write something years ago but never found the spark. The trip to Cape May provided it. Several friends and acquaintances have supported me in this endeavor, and I owe them a great round of gratitude. I owe a significant thank you to Bob Seigmann, who laboriously read through the manuscript and offered a good critique with notes. As well, Ann Marie Drew, coming from her English professor's perspective, offered many useful suggestions along with her gentle disposition. Thanks as well to Eric Smith and John Gianetti for plowing into the text and helping me to focus and tune it. My brother Tony and my daughter Catherine have been helpful in their critiques during the numerous occasions I asked them to read a section. I value Tony's input, for he was there for much of my earlier experiences and added his perspective and detail. My wife offered me useful comments after reading the completed manuscript. On several occasions, we disagreed on the where or when something happened. I'll help her when she writes her memoir! While I benefitted from the generous help of these and others, all the failings in the telling of my story are mine alone. It has been a project, however, I will miss.

Annapolis, December, 2023.

Author's Bio

Born in Hartford, Connecticut, the author grew up in Philadelphia to parents who met in Panama during World War II. The eldest of three sons, he somehow graduated college and went on to a doctorate in psychology. He met a wonderful woman in grad school. They married and had three beautiful children. Building a sturdy structure of a marriage, family, and career, they spent several decades in Indiana. The years have seen strong family bonds and a commitment to the Catholic church. The author is a retired psychologist and an ordained Catholic deacon. He worked at a State Hospital, mental health center and in private practice for over thirty years. He was ordained a deacon in 2012. Now living in Annapolis, Maryland with his wife of 48 years, they have eight grandchildren. He is an avid angler, a musician, a bonsai enthusiast, a spiritual director, and a seeker of God in all things. The couple live in the basement of their daughter and son-in-law's home, helping to care for their special needs granddaughter.

www.ingramcontent.com/pod-product-compliance
Lightning Source LLC
Chambersburg PA
CBHW032050020426
42335CB00011B/263

* 9 7 9 8 9 8 9 7 9 4 4 0 9 *